THE FUTURE OF
PEACE

THE FUTURE OF
PEACE

ON THE FRONT LINES WITH THE
WORLD'S GREAT PEACEMAKERS

SCOTT A. HUNT

HarperSanFrancisco
A Division of HarperCollins*Publishers*

HarperCollins books may be purchased for educational, business, or sales promotional use. For information please write: Special Markets Department, HarperCollins Publishers, Inc., 10 East 53rd Street, New York, NY 10022.

HarperCollins Web site: http://www.harpercollins.com
HarperCollins®, 🏠®, and HarperSanFrancisco™ are trademarks of HarperCollins Publishers, Inc.

FIRST EDITION
Designed by Joseph Rutt

Library of Congress Cataloging-in-Publication Data
Hunt, Scott A.
The future of peace : on the front lines with the world's great peacemakers /
Scott A. Hunt — 1st ed.
p. cm.
Contents : Aung San Suu Kyi : triumph of the spirit — The Dalai Lama and the power of compassion — The peacemakers of Israel and Palestine — Thich Quang Do : Vietnam's Champion of Hope — Oscar Arias : Central America's ambassador of peace — Maha Ghosananda : the Ghandi of Cambodia — Jane Goodall and the fight for the planet.
ISBN 0–06–251741–4 (cloth : alk. paper)
1. Pacifists—Biography.   2. Political activists—Biography.   I. Title: On the front lines with the world's great peacemakers.   II. Title.

JZ5540.H86   2002
303.6'6—dc21
[B]   2002068509

02 03 04 05 06 RRD(H) 10 9 8 7 6 5 4 3 2 1

To William Foote, Winona Gifford,
Mindrolling Trichen Rinpoche, and
all the peacemakers of the world

CONTENTS

FOREWORD

by The Honorable Ela Gandhi

Today, when we think about peace, we inevitably think of Mahatma Gandhi ("Gandhiji") and his epic struggle to demonstrate that nonviolence can overcome even the most entrenched hostility. If recent events have told us anything, it is that there is undoubtedly a need for a force greater than military power, a force greater than material wealth—a force driven by all that is good and humane in our society. The Gandhian ideals loom up again as being the most relevant and practical principles that can save us from further harm.

Not only has Gandhiji been a great inspiration to me in my social and political work (opposing apartheid in South Africa and helping to build a just society after the transition to democratic rule), but I also feel a special connection with him, for he was my grandfather. As he inspired me in my life, I know that he continues to inspire millions of other people around the world.

Above all else, Gandhiji's struggles affirmed the importance of peace, for without it there is neither happiness nor justice nor any meaning to our political or social unions. He taught us the very clear lesson that it is easy to postulate principles but very difficult to put them into practice.

Believing in peace and a good life for all is very well, but the final step is putting into practice what we have learned or begun to believe in. This final step is what eventually determines the quality of our lives. The great living peacemakers profiled in this book believe, as Gandhiji did, that peace requires action, not merely expressing its importance and hoping it will happen.

When Gandhiji came to South Africa he saw that the people had acquiesced in the harsh treatment to which they were subjected. Some chose to run away from the unbearable conditions of indenture; others chose to commit suicide. But a large majority succumbed to the harsh conditions and continued to work. In India the poor farmworkers suffered similar treatment and had also given in to these conditions. One of Gandhiji's greatest achievements was to instill in them dignity and a sense of direction. He raised their consciousness about their rights and aroused in them a will to resist the oppression they suffered.

The recent, fleeting millennium spirit, as well as recent tragedies, caused us all to stop and reflect on our lives—the conditions of our neighborhoods, villages, towns, and cities, and our world as a whole. While there are many meaningful achievements to be thankful for, some of the key issues that arose out of our reflections should cause us more agony than joy. What we see is a disharmony between the rapid advances and luxuries made by science and the suffering of those who still linger in poverty, hunger, deadly disease, crime of the most vicious proportions (often against the most vulnerable in our society), violent wars, terrorism, and strife. This violence and injustice is a scourge that destroys thousands of lives on a daily basis.

There is yet reason for hope, as this book well affirms. As Scott A. Hunt points out, set against the savagery of the past century are people of great stature and courage who have stood up to declare a war against violence and strife, injustice and exploitation. These are people with extraordinary talents and commitments who have been able to advance their goals through nonviolent means. These lives reflect a divine power that far surpasses the transitory, worldly power of the mighty and the rich. These are lives worth getting to know, and worth emulating.

We all have to accept the responsibility to change the world by cultivating some of the principles by which Gandhiji lived and by which a new generation of peacemakers continues to work. We have to begin to look at sharing and ensuring that resources are distributed equitably, and we must ensure that people can see and feel the change and be able to identify a niche for themselves in the world.

In addition to political oppression, we have economic, intellectual, religious, environmental, and gender oppression in the world. When we talk about peace, we cannot view indiscriminate killings and destruction of property in isolation from the poverty, illiteracy, religious intolerance, environmental threats, and gender oppression faced by people who have been left out, who are unable to see their niche, who may have lost their sense of dignity and direction.

Gandhiji, who has inspired so many people around the world, had three powerful concepts that embraced his nonviolent action. These are *satyagraha, sarvodaya,* and *swadeshi. Satyagraha* was a word coined by him to describe his nonviolent struggle, as he wanted it to be seen as being different from the other nonviolent movements. He maintained that *satyagraha* was more than the absence of war or violence—it was a way of life, a discipline, that required training. *Sarvodaya* was aimed at an approach to political theory, which was different from existent utilitarian theory. It advocated a dedication and commitment to all the members of a community as a prerequisite to community work. His third concept was *swadeshi,* which was based on an approach to economics aiming at self-reliance at the local level. In this way every person can be guaranteed an employment and livelihood. The actual sustenance of such a venture would be driven through the purchasing power of the people, retained within the local area. Dependency on cities would be reduced, and people would be able to coexist on a plane of material equality. Support of local products, even if more expensive, is key to this concept. For me these three concepts woven together form the tapestry of Gandhian ideals. They are a recipe for peace, as a contented people will not want to go to war.

Having identified problems, it is also always necessary to look for solutions. It is clear that change of political power in itself will not be able to achieve peace. As you read this book, it may be helpful to recall the things that Gandhiji would consider as essential conditions for peace, each embracing his concepts of *satyagraha, sar-vodaya,* and *swadeshi:*

- People in power, whether political, economic, religious, civic, or administrative power, need to develop a holistic view of peace. If we want a better country for our grandchildren and great-grandchildren then we need to act and ensure that such a holistic view is adopted and that a comprehensive approach is used in addressing the issue of peace. We also have a responsibility to ensure that the community understands and approves of this approach. We must be willing to share expertise and funds, and at the same time develop the community's capacity to meet the challenges of the future.

- We cannot expect government to change things on its own. We have to take responsibility for bringing about changes. We need to develop a climate of love, caring, sharing, and communal consciousness as we begin the process of building an equitable society through community programs.

- We need to build a culture of nonviolence among our children and youth, through actively ensuring that we (and they) do not support war toys or violent games and other negative influences, but instead promote a culture of resistance to injustice. We need to inculcate a communal responsibility among all our people.

- We need to create a culture of work, and recognize the dignity of work, so that we can learn to meet not only our own needs but also those of the whole community.

- We need to develop a new identity so that we can be rid of the racism and sexism embedded in us through life under violence and begin to love our people and our world.

- We should be vigilant to the needs of the community and begin to lay the foundation for a more equitable society where everyone may have access to opportunities. The present unemployment situation needs to be seriously challenged and work opportunities created for all people.

These are the goals Gandhiji set for development work in India, and they continue to apply equally to people everywhere in the world. Only when these goals have been achieved will we be able to say to ourselves that we have achieved peace in our world, a peace for which Gandhiji lived, worked, and died.

I hope this book, through Scott A. Hunt's journeys and his conversations with great peacemakers, helps you discover your role in the future of peace. I know Gandhiji would have welcomed this book. It is a call to action, and hopefully it will inspire you to do something of your own that contributes positively to the advancement of humanity.

Perhaps the sum total of the work done by luminaries who have worked for peace, those who have gained recognition and those who have been working quietly in the many corners of the world, can help us and guide us in our search for a better life. Some of the lives illustrated in this book will undoubtedly not only serve as an inspiration for future generations but will contain valuable lessons in peacemaking and peacekeeping for all of us today.

Ela Gandhi
Capetown, South Africa
May 2002

EDITOR'S NOTE: *Ela Gandhi, a Member of Parliament of South Africa, is a longtime member of the African National Congress. During the apartheid regime in South Africa, she was under house arrest for her advocacy of democracy. Among her many achievements, Ela Gandhi formed and served on The World Conference on Religion and Peace.*

THE FUTURE OF
PEACE

INTRODUCTION

Never doubt that a small group of thoughtful, committed citizens can change the world. Indeed, it is the only thing that ever has.

Margaret Mead

Kindness is alive and well, and we have good reason to be hopeful about the future. Despite the horrors that we see unfolding daily on our television screens, every day around the world there are countless acts of restraint, decency, and goodness. As we shall see from the very front lines of the struggles for freedom and justice, the good far outweighs the bad. That is why we can be confident in our capacity to overcome anger, hatred, and obsession, which fuel the fire of violence.

It is true that one can scarcely look at the history of humankind without noting how frequently we have hurt one another. The century just past was the bloodiest ever recorded, and we have begun a new century with new fears and animosities that threaten to tear peace apart. Yet nowhere is it written—either in our genes or in the stars—that we are fated to repeat our mistakes. Our world, like our own mind, becomes exactly and only what we make it.

As we grow in awareness of one another—whether two people beginning a romance or two disparate and far-removed strangers taking an interest in the other's culture—a wonderful thing begins to happen: we begin to care for the other as if the other is part of us. This is the magic of life that our ancient teachers have bid us to see: the invisible filaments of interconnectedness that bind us together in love and appreciation.

We see also, when we look past nationalism, racism, and all the other artificial divisions that pry us apart, that people everywhere, no matter how they look, dress, speak, or act, want to be happy. This desire for happiness is universal, fundamental, and irrepressible. And it is the starting point for cooperation, decency, and justice. Our obligation is to find out how we can fulfill our desire for happiness while we allow others to fulfill theirs as well.

The happiness I speak of does not come exclusively, or even primarily, from acquiring material goods. If it did, then nearly everyone in the West would feel content while everyone in poorer regions would feel despondent. Yet I have seen depressed celebrities in Hollywood mansions and laughing orphans in squalid refugee camps. It is a common mistake around the globe, of course, to confuse material attainment with happiness. As the world population increases and the desire for bigger, better, and faster consumer goods spreads, this mistaken formula for happiness poses serious challenges to our planet.

True happiness cannot exist without hope. True happiness requires the hope that our own actions can bring us joy, that we can do something productive for ourselves, and that those around us will do us no harm. We must be able to use our creative energy and be free from fear. And true happiness requires a further hope—that people will help us when we need help, that they will be sympathetic to our feelings, and that they will cooperate in a system in which we can succeed both spiritually and materially. Without such expectations, the future looks bleak and we cannot help but succumb to anxiety, fear, and inaction.

There is yet a greater hope still: that everyone everywhere can join us in our attainment of a happy life. It is not a requirement that everyone be equal in what they attain. Yet it is reasonable to expect that freedom, basic living standards, and access to medical care be afforded to all. Unfortunately, the political and economic frameworks that exist today have not created this shared experience of a good life. This is not the only reason for wars, of course, but it is certainly a predominant reason. In my experience, happy people don't start fights, much less wars. If not for justice itself, then simply for harmony, we must create a more equitable framework affording opportunities to everyone. And we can do it if we can only, finally, muster the will and make the required sacrifices.

This vision of a world without conflict in which each individual has opportunities and enjoys the freedom to pursue his or her own sacred journey is a powerful impetus to change. Without the vision, it is doubtful that we will alter the way things are. Yet we need only encounter the right individuals and have the right experiences in order to invigorate our vision of a better world. It is such an appealing and alluring prospect, so consistent with our innate sense of right and wrong, and so affirmed by centuries of our spiritual practices, that should we embrace it wholeheartedly and pragmatically, we could transform, in rather short order, the very character of the world.

Unfortunately, for most of us hope atrophies in the face of persistent negative images and experiences. That is why it is so important for us to focus on the goodness of humanity, even in times of peril when the world seems awash with violence. We have to remind ourselves to look past the nonstop stream of news reports, understanding that the very reason for the news broadcasts is to gain our attention, to gather ratings, and so to enthrall us in tales of despicable acts of aggression and inhumanity. It is up to us to moderate our intake of such news and to use the information wisely; to analyze and demand solutions to the troubles, not to wallow in the problems, thinking them unintelligible, inevitable, or unsolvable.

Even in the darkest times in our history, people of extraordinary character have lived among us, showing us a way out of the deplorable cycle of hatred and aggression. They exist this very day. It is to these people that we can turn in order to replenish our encouragement, hope, and inspiration. Martin Luther King Jr. called such people the "creatively maladjusted," for they live outside the standard view, unwilling to accept the predictions of continual tragedies, incessant warfare, and racial and religious avarice. They are the heirs of our great spiritual masters from centuries past, continuing now to challenge us to think and act differently, to live more productively and harmoniously.

These people are gifted with an irrational faith. Their faith is irrational in the face of seemingly insurmountable obstacles. They maintain their vigil for peace, day in and day out, no matter how dismal their situation becomes. These are the people who look into the gloom and see the foundations of light, who fail to be dissuaded from doing what is morally correct despite years of setbacks or minute gains, who show us in their words and deeds how we can turn our torments into triumphs.

This book contains powerful messages of hope and inspiration from some of the most fascinating people of our time. They are all great peacemakers who rose out of the ashes of conflict. From some of the most horrendous chapters in human history, these great leaders have emerged to show us a different path, proving not only that cessation of war is possible, but that the removal of hatred and violence from our hearts is possible as well. We can have peace not merely between nations, but also in our streets and in our homes. They rebuke the pundits not simply with academic theories but also with hard-fought actions waged on the front lines of the world's most troubled regions. In short, they show us that the promise of peace remains intact, and so does our enormous potential to achieve it.

Aung San Suu Kyi is sometimes called the world's leading dissident. Thrust into the political arena by her sense of duty to the people of her country, Suu Kyi won the most stunning democratic election in history, overcoming the brute force of the military dictators who used all means at their disposal to thwart the will of the people. Suu Kyi was never permitted to take office. She was kept under house arrest for years in near-starvation conditions, and today her freedom—if she can be said to have any at all—is still severely restricted. Speaking from her house in Rangoon, she tells of her continuing struggle to bring freedom to her people.

The Dalai Lama escaped Tibet before the Chinese Communists could place him under house arrest or silence him outright in more barbaric ways. Though he tried to reach accommodation with Mao and the Communist leadership, His Holiness could not prevent the brutal military invasion of Tibet and the ensuing destruction of most of his country's monasteries, cultural sites, and even its way of life. Though China claims it will never give up its control over Tibet, the Dalai Lama continues to meet China's hostility with compassion. Now on the world stage, he has become one of the world's moral authorities. During several meetings at his home in India, this holy man talks about the healing and creative powers of compassion.

In Israel and Palestine, three poignant voices who denounce violence and intolerance on all sides help me sort out what is truly fueling the continuing conflict in that region. Dr. Hanan Ashrawi is a Christian Palestinian who condemns abuse of power, whether it stems from the Palestinian Authority or from the state of Israel. She talks with me in the West Bank while violence rages around us. Two other well-known figures in Israel also speak with me, Uri Avnery and Shulamit Aloni. Both are war heroes and political leaders who call for peace through the end of contentious settlements in the Occupied Territories and the establishment of two truly independent and equal states of Israel and Palestine. Together, these three voices clarify the history of the conflict, piercing through widely held misperceptions and providing the blueprint for lasting peace in the region.

The kind old monk, scholar, and religious leader Thich Quang Do has spent many years in a prison cell for advocating freedom of worship in Vietnam and for trying to organize humanitarian relief for starving and sickly flood victims in the south of his country. Thich Quang Do's Buddhist order was the country's most prominent, oldest, and largest, and it was responsible for building and maintaining many of Vietnam's hospitals, orphanages, and public works projects. Yet the government outlawed membership in the church and confiscated all the church's property. Worse, it began to twist the words of the Buddha and refused to allow anyone, especially the recognized scholar Thich Quang Do, to correct the false teachings. His captors removed him from the squalid conditions of his solitary confinement only for interrogations, through which they hoped to break his spirit. Yet they never did. Neither did they manage, to their frustration and dismay, to extinguish his ever-present laughter. He has been nominated several times for a Nobel Peace Prize. Still under house arrest, he talks, and laughs, with me at a small temple in Saigon.

Oscar Arias presided over a country without an army and helped forge peace in Central America at a time when hawks in the United States opposed and tried to thwart his efforts. Arias not only had to contend with the parties to the dispute in Central America, he also had to face the full force of the covert and illegal operations directed by the Reagan White House, the State Department, and the Central Intelligence Agency. Arias was awarded a Nobel Peace Prize for his successful peace plan. He has helped since to create the world's first border with no standing army on either side and has been one of the leading advocates of arms control and economic fairness as methods of curbing warfare around the world. At his home in Costa Rica, and on the move in San José, he speaks to me about his vision for international cooperation and what he is doing to help create it.

Maha Ghosananda has often been called the "Gandhi of Cambodia," for he is perhaps the one person in all the world closest in demeanor and achievement to the Mahatma himself. Maha Ghosananda is a monk (the Supreme Patriarch of Cambodia, actually) who brought spiritual practice back to a country devastated by one of the most horrendous episodes of genocide in history, administering his healing words and actions even to those who were responsible for the murder of his entire family. He has led courageous peace marches through heavily mined war zones and has embraced all parties with his trademark smile and gentle gaze. He has been nominated several times for the Nobel Peace Prize. From his monastery in Phnom Penh, he shows me his great intelligence and kindness and fascinates me with his amazing capacity for forgiveness.

Finally, the internationally renowned scientist and humanitarian Dr. Jane Goodall speaks with me about her quest to promote harmonious living around the globe. Many years ago, as a gutsy young woman, she entered the remote jungles of Africa at the behest of the famed anthropologist Louis Leakey. Leakey suggested that Goodall could help further our understanding of human evolution by observing the natural behavior of our closest animal relative, the chimpanzee. In the process Goodall made groundbreaking discoveries and gained enormous wisdom. Surprising to many, she also enhanced her belief in God and grew in the conviction that each of us is a precious and indispensable part of the whole of life. Though even her beloved forests of Gombe are threatened by the environmental degradation taking place all over the world, in our every meeting she spoke with the utmost faith in humanity's vast creative potential to overcome environmental destruction, inequality, materialism, and violence.

In the Epilogue, three peacemakers from Northern Ireland—Nobel Peace laureates John Hume, Betty Williams, and Máiread Corrigan Maguire—provide a final reminder about the causes of conflict and our ability to overcome animosity.

As you will see in the coming pages, all of these peacemakers share the belief that the quest for a peaceful world is essentially the quest to awaken the compassionate spirit in each of us—to invigorate hope, to reconnect with the universal kindness that our great teachers have tried to cultivate for thousands of years. They recognize that peace is not something we can wait on a divine power to establish. It rests in our hands to learn virtue and respect for one another and to practice tolerance and forbearance.

Yet this book is not simply a retelling of conversations. It is also about observations and my personal journeys beyond the limits of my own horizon, past the humanly constructed barriers of states into the heart of conflict and human potential. During each journey I tried to better my understanding of antidotes to violence and to gain a new confidence in our ability to establish lasting peace. My journeys were often long and tiring, sometimes quite dangerous but always meaningful and rewarding. Along the way, I met countless individuals, and I listened to their stories over cups of tea and coffee, in the heat of the tropics and the cold of the high mountains, in cities and in remote villages. As I researched and investigated and listened, I did my best to keep my mind and heart open, to set aside my preconceptions, and to hear their concerns with genuine empathy.

To tell the tales of my encounters with the world's greatest living peacemakers, it became necessary to write about the origins of

many conflicts. It is important for us not only to understand where
we have gone wrong in the past (in order to avoid doing so again, as
best we can), but also to bridge the gap between ideas considered
spiritual and those regarded as intellectual.

Two of the greatest minds who ever lived walked among us in
this past war-filled century. Albert Einstein was a man of science,
but one who saw a spiritual duty to promote and protect peace. He
viewed it as his "solemn and transcendent duty" to do all in his
power to prevent warfare. Without needing to profess any religious
doctrine, he saw peace as a moral imperative—a universal obligation that can best be described as spiritual. "Unless the cause of
peace based on law gathers behind it the force and zeal of religion,"
he wrote, "it hardly can hope to succeed." Not by logic alone, he
said, can peace be achieved. "There must be added that deep power
of emotion which is a basic ingredient of religion."[1]

Mohandas Gandhi came from a different discipline. Trained as a
lawyer who fought for justice, Gandhi embarked on a spiritual path
that would transform him into one of the most extraordinary people
of all time. While he became known as a *mahatma,* or "great soul"
of incredible wisdom and skill, he never lost sight of practical considerations. "I could not be leading a religious life unless I identified
myself with the whole of mankind," he said, "and that I could not
do unless I took part in politics. The whole gamut of man's activities
today constitutes an indivisible whole. You cannot divide social,
economic, political and purely religious work into watertight compartments."[2]

These two remarkable people provide important examples for us
all. They both saw peace as a deeply moral obligation that required
faith, vision, and courage. Yet they also knew that people cannot
simply pray for peace and praise its name; they must undertake the
hard work necessary to make it happen. As Einstein said at the end
of World War II, "The war is won, but the peace is not."

And today peace still is not won. Yet that doesn't mean it is
impossible. We must create it. Like Einstein and Gandhi, we must
work on both the spiritual and conventional fronts. Intellectuals
may find it challenging to work with the lexicon of spirituality, and
the spiritually minded may find it difficult to bear the world of

intellectuality. It is imperative for us to do both, however, if lasting peace is to have any real chance.

I emerged from these journeys optimistic that the human sense of right, the sense of justice, and the spiritual yearning for deeper meaning and expression will ensure our eventual liberation from violence. We may continue to suffer needlessly and to cause suffering for generations to come. Yet I am certain that violence will diminish and that eventually the wisdom of our compassionate nature will win out. What makes me so certain of this fact is my incredible encounters with the living peacemakers you will meet in the pages to come.

One

AUNG SAN SUU KYI: TRIUMPH OF THE SPIRIT

I vividly recall the scene in the film *Beyond Rangoon* in which a dignified woman walks confidently through a large crowd. The woman is small in physical stature yet enormous in prestige. Her supporters are cheering, waving flags, and hoisting her portrait. Her slight build, colorful dress, and gracious smile stand in marked contrast to the heavily armed, drably uniformed soldiers lurking in the shadows. Without warning, the soldiers burst from the darkness, storm into the crowd, and form a line to keep the woman from reaching a nearby stage.

The standoff is fraught with danger. The woman and her compatriots are well aware that the soldiers have a history of firing on peaceful demonstrators, and they would not hesitate to do so again in the name of public order. Yet the woman shows no hint of fear. She steps forward, waving off those who try to stop her. She advances slowly, resolutely, staring deeply into the eyes of the soldier who is pointing his rifle directly at her. The woman stands there as the symbol of freedom, face-to-face with the soldier, a symbol of violence and subjugation. Her determination and confidence begin to unsettle the soldier. He starts to tremble in confusion and fear and finally relents. The woman steps gingerly, even graciously, through the line, followed by a flood of her supporters. It is a small victory of peaceful means over aggression.

Though the scene might be Hollywood fiction, the event was quite real. It happened in the Southeast Asian nation of Burma[1] in the late 1980s. The woman depicted is named Aung San Suu Kyi (pronounced Ong Sahn Soo Chee). Suu Kyi has become perhaps the leading political dissident in the world. Her struggle to bring freedom and justice to her country garnered her the Nobel Peace Prize in 1991 and many other awards, including the Presidential Medal of Freedom from the United States.

When I sat down to plan my journeys, Burma was one of the places I put at the top of my list. I definitely wanted to meet Suu Kyi, but I knew that would be no easy matter. In fact, it was nearly impossible in recent years for a writer to speak with her. Journalists were rarely permitted to enter Burma. Those who were discovered inside the country were promptly detained and unceremoniously deported. The government has been terrified that Suu Kyi and her pro-democracy colleagues would gather further international support and incite a popular uprising. They have good reason to be fearful.

In March 1988 groups of university students took to the streets of Rangoon, Burma's capital, peacefully demonstrating against the totalitarian regime founded by General Ne Win in July 1962. Responding to this perceived threat, the police shot to death two hundred demonstrators. Halfway around the world, Aung San Suu Kyi, a woman of slight build with delicate features, long black hair, and extremely elegant manners, was living a normal life in Oxford, England, with her husband (an Oxford University professor) and her two sons when she received word that her mother had suffered a severe stroke. Suu Kyi immediately flew to Rangoon to be by her mother's side. She had no idea at that time that she would eventually wind up in the heart of a brewing social storm.

Burma is a country of approximately fifty million people in a land area just slightly smaller than the state of Texas. It borders the Andaman Sea in the south, Tibet in the north, Bangladesh and India in the north and northwest, Thailand in the east and southeast, and Laos and China in the east and northeast. The people are chiefly Burman (68 percent) with minority populations of Shan (9 percent), Karen (7 percent), Rakhine (4 percent), Chinese (3 percent), Mon (2 percent), Indian (2 percent), and other ethnicities (5 percent). Though the official language is Burmese, over one hundred languages are spoken in the country.

Eighty-five percent of the people are Buddhist, 4 percent are Muslim, 4 percent are Christian (mostly Baptist), and the remaining are of other faiths. The country has abundant natural resources, including petroleum, natural gas, timber, tin, coal, and precious gems.

In the sixth century the Mon settled in the Irrawaddy River delta in Lower Burma, as well as in Thailand and Cambodia. Several centuries later, when the indigenous Pyus had been vanquished by the Yunnans (from China), the Burmans descended into central Burma from the eastern Himalayan region, bringing the Burmans into direct contact with the Mon. For hundreds of years the two races fought many wars with each other, carting off captives to be used as slaves in the construction of Buddhist temples and in cultivating rice.

In 1044 the Burman king Anawratha established control over much of the country and vanquished the Mon. Anawratha established his capital at Pagan, the "city of a thousand temples," which was the seat of his dynasty until the invasion of Kublai Khan in 1287. Thereafter the country vacillated between chaos and the kingdoms of the Shan in the north (who were closely related to the Siamese) and the Mon in the south until the sixteenth century, when the Taongoo dynasty firmly reestablished Burman control over the Shan and Mon.

The Mon rose up again in the eighteenth century but were crushed by the armies of Alaungpaya in 1758. Alaungpaya expanded his kingdom to include the present-day Indian territories of Assam and Manipur and areas in present-day Thailand as well. His son, Hsinbyushin, completely destroyed the ancient Thai capital of Ayuthaya and drove the Thai to Krung Thep (present-day Bangkok). Hsinbyushin also conquered Rakhine, the border region between Burma and India.

In 1824 the Burmese and the British began to spar over the borders of Assam, Rakhine, and other areas. Two years later the British forced the Burmese to cede Rakhine (cutting off Burma's coastline along the Bay of Bengal) and the coastal region of Taninthayi along the Thai border.

Fearing French influence in the region, and desiring control over Burma, especially the valuable port of Rangoon, the British used a pretext to launch a second war against the Burmese. In 1852 the British captured the rich population center of Lower Burma. In 1885 the British used another petty dispute to justify a third war against Burma. The central Burmese city of Mandalay was captured within two weeks, and the British then conducted a ruthless and bloody campaign to consolidate power over Upper Burma. Many innocent civilians were murdered and villages destroyed, resulting in Britain's control over the entire country.

Burma was initially governed under the British Raj in India, but in response to growing nationalism among the Burmans, the country was separated from India in 1937 and governed as a sister colony. British exploitation of the country's resources and people continued, however, and opposition to British rule was substantial. Yet Winston Churchill remained flatly opposed to any erosion of British authority over its duly conquered colonies.

The Burmese pro-independence forces turned to the Japanese for support. Japan assisted them in forming the Burmese Independence Army (BIA) headed by General Aung San. Burma was also frequently occupied in the east by Chinese Nationalist troops, who were fighting against the Japanese imperial forces in China. Within weeks of the Japanese attack on Pearl Harbor, the Japanese Imperial Army, aided by the BIA, attacked the British-Indian and Chinese Nationalist forces in Burma. For the Japanese, the attack was a way to destroy the U.S.-backed supply lines keeping the Chinese forces alive, as well as to capture the airfields that supplied the defenses of Singapore. For the BIA, the attack was a means to finally gain its independence from British repression.

Japan, which had long argued that its military actions throughout Asia were counterimperialist, declared that Burma was now a free nation. Aung San and thirty colleagues were permitted by the Japanese to create the independent Burma National Army (BNA). General Aung San became the defense minister of the BNA, and a man named General Ne Win (to whom we will return momentarily) became its chief of staff. The Japanese, however, did not come into the country as mere liberators. Their military advance was brutal, needlessly taking lives in repeated atrocities and destroying village after village without mercy.

In 1944 the Japanese invasion of India failed, and the Allied forces of the British, Americans, and Chinese Nationalists counterattacked Japanese-occupied Burma. General Aung San convinced the Japanese to let him lead the BNA against the invading Allies, but when he reached the front lines, he turned his forces around and joined the Allied invasion to liberate his country of the Japanese. During the ensuing military campaign, Aung San remained steadfast that Burma should be free from foreign rule, and he resisted the British desire to reestablish control over the country as a colony. Aung San's personal charm and charisma made him both a formidable military ally who could command the loyalty of the various peoples of Burma and an eventual hindrance to the British desire to recolonize the country.

At the end of World War II General Aung San demanded and obtained Britain's pledge to grant Burma its independence. Aung San, like America's George Washington, quickly transitioned from a military to a political leader and became the leading voice for democracy and civilian rule. Yet six months before the nation's independence was proclaimed on January 4, 1948, Aung San was assassinated. It is widely believed that the assassination was the work of his colleague General Ne Win, who was bitterly opposed to civilian rule.

Aung San was thirty-two years old when he died. His daughter was only two years old. Little did anyone know that tiny Aung San Suu Kyi, daughter of the "father of Burmese independence," would play a crucial role one day in the country's difficult march toward democracy.

Suu Kyi was raised believing in her father's sense of duty to his people and in democratic ideals. But during much of her childhood the political landscape in Burma was chaotic. After independence the country plunged into turmoil as various ethnic groups revolted against the new government of Prime Minister U Nu. Order was restored in much of the country by 1951, but then the U.S.-backed

Chinese Nationalist forces seeking safe bases from which to fight the Chinese Communists effectively annexed territories from Burma. The United States regularly flew in military supplies to these bases and purposely turned a blind eye to the fact that the Nationalist forces raised a great deal of their funds from the sale of opium on the world market. (Former Chinese Nationalist military officers continue to this day to control much of the production of opium and its derivative heroin in the Golden Triangle of Burma, Thailand, and Laos, thanks in part to U.S. support years ago.)[2]

In 1958 the economy was in shambles, the Chinese Nationalist forces still occupying parts of the country and various groups in armed rebellion against the government. Prime Minister U Nu temporarily gave power to General Ne Win, who formed a military government. Ne Win successfully brought stability to the country and permitted free elections in 1960. U Nu and his coalition government won a clear majority.

At that time Aung San Suu Kyi's mother, Khin Kyi, was appointed ambassador to Burma's large, democratic neighbor, India. Suu Kyi, then fifteen years old, accompanied her mother to New Delhi. Within two years, however, U Nu's coalition government began to splinter and General Ne Win staged a coup, abolishing the parliament and announcing that Burma would become a socialist country under the Burmese Socialist Programme Party. Virtually all of the country's industry, including retail pricing, was nationalized and heavily controlled.

Suu Kyi left the country in 1964 to pursue an education and graduated in 1967 from Oxford University with a degree in philosophy, politics, and economics. Suu Kyi then moved to the United States to work as an assistant secretary to the Advisory Committee on Administrative and Budgetary Questions in the United Nations Secretariat. During nearly three years in New York, Suu Kyi closely followed and empathized with the demonstrations against the Vietnam War.

Suu Kyi's sense of duty to Burma was not diminished by her time abroad or by her decision in 1972 to marry Oxford Tibetan studies scholar Michael Aris and live with him in England. Before they wed, Suu Kyi wrote to him, "I only ask one thing. That should my people need me, you would help me do my duty by them."[3] Suu Kyi also wrote, "Sometimes I am beset with fears that circumstance might tear us apart, just when we are so happy in each other." Those fears were realized in 1988.

In 1987 and 1988 there was growing unrest among the Burmese people as staggering inflation, corruption, and failed policies caused the standard of living to plummet. In July 1988, after twenty-six years in power, General Ne Win, the dictator, stunned the nation by announcing his resignation and calling for an open referendum on the future form of government. For a brief time it seemed that freedom was just around the corner. After all, Ne Win had voluntarily given up power and permitted free elections in 1960, so there was good reason to believe that he would do so again.

Unfortunately, Ne Win's colleagues were not eager to move from a dictatorship in which they held all the power to a democracy in which they would be accountable to the people they had repressed for nearly three decades. Top party officials promptly denied Ne Win's request for a referendum. The expression of anger among the Burmese people was swift and massive. Millions of people took to the streets to protest peacefully in nearly every city and town in the country, demanding that the authoritarian regime step aside and hand power over to a civilian government, which would restore civil rights and arrange free and fair elections as expeditiously as possible.

The military now had a crucial decision to make: whether to bow to the popular will and avoid bloodshed or launch a campaign against the pro-democracy movement. Unfortunately, they chose the latter. Government troops were dispatched with orders to shoot to kill. On August 8, 1988, the shooting began. Thousands of peaceful protesters were shot and killed over the next few days, and hundreds more were injured. The killings, which came to be known as the "Massacre of 8-8-88," were rivaled in recent times in Asia only by the atrocities in Beijing in June 1989 and Jakarta in May 1998. We did not see the events in Burma on our evening news or in pictures in our morning newspapers in large part because the soldiers had standing orders to shoot on sight anyone with a camera.

Suu Kyi was horrified by what she saw. Hundreds of pro-democracy demonstrators were rounded up and put in jail. Many of those who had demonstrated peacefully had carried posters of her father, Aung San. The time had come from her to act.

With her strong sense of duty, her deep faith in the power of the popular will, and her disgust for the ruthlessness of the military crackdown, Suu Kyi addressed half a million people who gathered in Rangoon at the base of the famed Shwedagon Pagoda on August 26, 1988. Suu Kyi declared, "I could not, as my father's daughter, remain indifferent to all that was going on. This national crisis could in fact be called the second struggle for national independence." Then and there, the daughter of Burma's greatest hero became the leader of the pro-democracy movement.

Suu Kyi joined with other opposition leaders to form the National League for Democracy (NLD). She pursued a tireless schedule, giving over a hundred speeches around the country, advocating a peaceful transition to a democratic state. She was received with great enthusiasm wherever she went. Suu Kyi's mother died in December 1988. Thousands of people attended her funeral and later formed a rally for democracy.

Knowing that events were getting out of their control, the military, still loyal to General Ne Win, joined in an elaborate plot to seize power from the ruling Burmese Socialist Programme Party. In September 1988 they declared martial law, killed at least another one thousand demonstrators, and consolidated power in the hands of a small group of military officers known as the State Law and Order Restoration Council, or SLORC.

Hoping to quiet dissent, SLORC promised that free and fair elections would take place in the spring of 1990. SLORC offered up its National Unity Party against some two hundred challenging parties. Far from acting in a "free and fair" manner, SLORC used its troops to arrest, intimidate, and disenfranchise many voters that it knew would support the NLD. Suu Kyi herself was nearly killed by soldiers in April 1989 when an officer ordered his troops to gun her down, an event that served as the basis for the scene in *Beyond Rangoon* mentioned at the start of this chapter. At the last possible moment, a higher-ranking officer countermanded the order to shoot.

Despite its heavy-handed tactics, SLORC must have known that public support for the NLD was steadfast. Suu Kyi was berated as a "housewife," which in fact she had been, but SLORC knew that she was much more. Her family, her education, her beliefs, and her personal charisma made her a formidable leader. Fearing her popularity, SLORC placed Suu Kyi under house arrest in July 1989. Amnesty International and other human rights groups protested the detention, declaring that Suu Kyi was being held as a prisoner of conscience, but the government ignored all international criticism.

With Suu Kyi unable to campaign, and firmly holding the reins of power, the government permitted the elections to go forward as planned on May 27, 1990. When all the ballots were counted, the NLD had won a stunning, landslide victory over the military's National Unity Party, capturing 82 percent of the parliamentary seats.

Instead of honoring the elections, SLORC disqualified, detained, arrested, or drove into exile the successful candidates.[4] Suu Kyi was offered the "right" to leave the country "on humanitarian grounds," but she refused to abandon either her people or her new role as opposition leader. She would remain incarcerated in her house, often suffering from severe malnutrition and other sickness, from 1989 until her release in July 1995. She was placed under house arrest again in September 2000 and released in May 2002.

SLORC's actions were widely denounced by human rights organizations and in governmental reports, yet that did not translate into an international movement among governments to oppose the council, as there had been against apartheid in South Africa. To its credit, the United States took steps to back its human rights rhetoric, unilaterally cutting off its assistance programs, opposing international lending, and initiating an informal arms embargo against the regime. When President Bill Clinton came to office, his administration also declared its support for unilateral sanctions against new investments in Burma, and the United States later became the only major Western country to put them into effect.

Meanwhile, European countries took little tangible action against SLORC, and Asian nations, as well as Australia, flatly refused to do anything at all. In fact, Japan and Singapore poured tens of millions of dollars into the country, Thailand and China both continued normal trade relations, and China continued to supply arms to SLORC.

Suu Kyi continued to oppose SLORC even while under house arrest, meeting whenever she could with NLD party members to plan their opposition activities. Her letters, tapes, and statements were smuggled out of Burma and delivered to international conferences and news outlets. Suu Kyi was awarded a number of prestigious prizes in absentia while under house arrest, including the 1990 Sakharov Prize (the human rights prize of the European Parliament) and the 1991 Nobel Peace Prize.

When she was released from house arrest in 1995, little changed for Suu Kyi. She remained under close surveillance and subject to restrictions on her freedom of movement. For example, in March 1996 Suu Kyi's train to Mandalay was disabled by SLORC's all-pervasive military intelligence officers, and she was forced to cancel her appearance there; in April 1996 she was prevented from performing a traditional New Year's celebration at a Rangoon lake; in July 1998 her car was blocked by troops when she tried to meet with NLD members, and Suu Kyi was forcibly returned to her house; in August 1998 she was blocked in her car and forced to return home; in August 2000 two hundred police forced her to return from the suburbs to her home; in September 2000 she was prevented from boarding a train and forced to return to her home. Also in September 2000 Suu Kyi was placed in "temporary detention" in her home, where she remained, as noted above, until May 2002.

The state-controlled press in Burma has called Suu Kyi and other NLD leaders "poisonous snakes," "traitors," and a host of other slurs. She shrugs these off, knowing that desperate people do desperate things. Yet the one incident that seriously struck at Suu Kyi's heart was the government's refusal to grant her husband, Michael Aris, who was dying of prostate cancer, a visa to enter the country to see Suu Kyi one last time before his death. Aris died in March 1999 in London. As foretold in her letter years earlier, circumstances would irreparably rip their happy lives apart. Not even this cruelty, however, could deter Suu Kyi; she overcomes any impulse toward self-pity by thinking about the worse fate of her people, especially those who have been enslaved, tortured, or murdered.

In December 2000 Suu Kyi was awarded the Presidential Medal of Freedom by President Clinton. Her son Alexis received the award on his mother's behalf. Both of her sons have been unable to enter Burma to see their mother.

The military junta continues to use all available means to suppress freedom and perpetuate its corrupt rule. Its instruments of governance seem to be lifted straight from George Orwell's *1984*. As the U.S. State Department noted in its report on human rights released in February 2001, "Burma continues to be ruled by a highly authoritarian military regime," which "reinforces its firm military rule with a pervasive apparatus led by the military intelligence organization." "Control is buttressed," the report continues, "by arbitrary restrictions on citizens' contacts with foreigners, surveillance of government employees and private citizens, harassment of political activists, intimidation, arrest, detention, and physical abuse." Further, the report stated, basic rights of free speech, press, assembly, and association were restricted by the government. "The military forces routinely confiscated property, cash, and food, and used coercive and abusive recruitment methods to procure porters. Those forced into porterage or other duties faced extremely difficult conditions and beatings and mistreatment that sometimes resulted in death. . . ."[5]

Amnesty International's "Report 2001" places the number of political prisoners arrested and sentenced after unfair trials at more than seventeen hundred. "Prison conditions constituted cruel, inhuman or degrading treatment, and torture of political prisoners was reported. The military continued to seize ethnic minority civilians for forced labour duties and to kill members of ethnic minorities during counter-insurgency operations in the Shan, Kayah, and Kayin states," the report continued.[6]

While the junta continues to cling to power, the country continues its slide into crisis. It is rightfully deemed a pariah state by much of the world, and its economy is crumbling. The situation is exacerbated by rampant corruption, mismanagement, and vacillating policies. Though the country is rich in natural resources, hunger is widespread, disease goes untreated, and tens of thousands of refugees flee ever-present fighting between the government and insurgent ethnic minorities. While the average citizen makes only three hundred dollars per year, the regime continues to spend massive amounts to build one of the largest armies in the region, having increased its troops from 175,000 in 1988 to more than 400,000 today.

Trying to arrange an appointment with Suu Kyi involves careful planning, secret communications with underground operatives, and an unnerving amount of scheming. I've never been drawn to such intrigue, much less to the precautions I would have to take once I entered Burma. My contact in the West had informed me that I was about to take a frightening journey that would pit my nerve against military thugs who were quite capable of barbarous acts against foreign "intruders." I tried to joke about the danger, only to receive a stern warning not to belittle the risk I would face. "It will take several years off your life," she cautioned.

In Bangkok I obtained a Burmese visa and arranged my flight to Rangoon. A contact that had been arranged from abroad informed me how to reach a safe house in Rangoon, where final arrangements would be made for my meeting with "the Lady." I was also instructed how to evade the military intelligence officers who would monitor my movements. If they discovered where I was staying, I was told, they would certainly search my room and take anything they found to be threatening. My final instruction was to establish a code word with a friend outside of Burma who, if I happened to say the word during a phone call, would know that I was in need of assistance from the U.S. State Department.

Just before I left Thailand I reread an account of Leo Nichols, honorary counsel to Burma for Denmark, Norway, Finland, and Switzerland, who was imprisoned in Burma for possessing a fax machine. According to a law decreed by the military government, all inhabitants of Burma, including foreigners, are prohibited from owning computers, faxes, and modems without approval. Nichols was tortured in prison and later died. While he languished in his cell, international protests went unheeded, and the American oil companies ARCO and Unocal continued economic ties with the dictatorship, as did Japan, each sinking tens of millions of dollars into the military's coffers. As my laptop was equipped with a fax modem, I would leave it in Bangkok.

Even with all the advance arrangements, a meeting with Aung San Suu Kyi was by no means assured. The government might figure out what I was up to and expel me, or they might simply forbid all foreign visitors from seeing Suu Kyi. In the worst case, they might imprison and beat me, as happened to another Westerner that I had spoken with. (He still has scars and hearing loss from his beatings.)

The flight from Bangkok was a short one, although Rangoon felt a million miles from freedom. Upon landing, I instantly felt a tension in the air. It was a tension born of suspicion and servitude. People could not trust me, and I could not trust them—two facts disheartening to my nature.

Though the official requirement calls for all foreign visitors to change three hundred dollars into Foreign Exchange Certificates, a bribe of ten dollars at the exchange counter enabled me to change less money. Should I leave the country within a few days, I didn't want to be left holding on to FECs, which are completely worthless outside of Burma. Besides, it was possible to exchange dollars into Burmese *kyat* on the thriving black market. This would increase my buying power immensely and at the same time deprive the military government of hard currency.

I was picked up by a driver sent from my hotel. The hotel was quite posh, a mixture of Burmese traditional and Western architectures, with few guests. I arrived in the late afternoon and relaxed until nightfall, when I could begin my activities.

When it was finally dark I put a black shirt, a black jacket, and black hat into a bag and left the hotel. I caught a taxi and had the driver drop me off in a business area. I ducked into a darkened doorway and quickly put on my dark shirt before flagging down a second taxi. I had the driver drop me off in another business area. I then put on my jacket and caught a third cab.

Unfortunately, the third driver claimed not to know the street where I was going. He drove up and down a number of roads, some of them very dark and isolated. At one point he drove very slowly past a military compound and yelled to one of the guards. My heart raced. I had been warned that most drivers in Rangoon are informants for military intelligence, and I was afraid that he was telling the soldier where I was going. I was worried that my journey might be over and my attempt to see Suu Kyi foiled.

The guard began approaching the vehicle. "It's okay," I said to my driver nervously. "I'll show you how to get there. Let's just go." I could just imagine the soldier asking me why I, a tourist, was going to that quiet neighborhood late at night; as reinforcements came out to join in the questioning, someone would surely know that I was going to meet with a head of the NLD. My driver didn't listen to me, so I tapped him on the shoulder. "Go now!" I commanded. He finally complied, and we sputtered off, leaving the soldier looking confused and angry.

It was a full hour later when I spotted the convergence of two streets that matched the map I had been given. I told the driver to let me out, and I purposely walked in the wrong direction until his car disappeared from sight. I then put on my dark baseball hat and began looking for the safe house.

Down a dark side street I heard a barking dog rapidly approaching. Again my heart pounded. No one was near to help me should this dog attack. I stopped and peered into the darkness. The dog continued its advance. When it was two yards away I could see the snarling mouth, teeth gleaming in the dark. I held very still, not daring to breathe for fear of agitating the beast. It seemed like an eternity, but perhaps a minute or so later the dog's growling lessened, it barked several more times, then slowly turned and disappeared into the night.

"Screw this James Bond shit!" I said aloud.

I now had to decide whether to walk down the road and risk facing the dog again—not to mention the military intelligence compound that may have sprung to life at the dog's barking—or to scrap the attempt to reach the safe house that night. I slowly turned to my left, then to my right. No one was in sight—no cars, no taxis, and for the moment, no dogs.

"I didn't come all this way and go to all this trouble for nothing," I said to myself. Like Suu Kyi's character in the movie, I needed to gather myself and move forward.

It might bring hardships on certain dissidents if I discussed the safe house in any detail. But I can say that the house was not the type of "safe" that one might imagine. It was not a secret refuge. The military intelligence compound keeps the house under constant surveillance and is only a dozen or so yards away, in the direct path of those approaching the house. I had been instructed to arrive at this time of night for two reasons. First, there was a good chance that intelligence officers would be drunk or asleep. Second, the darkness might prevent them from getting a good description of me and from taking a clear photo of my face. On this last point, I was told to pull my hat down over my eyes as much as I could.

I managed to locate the house. It was behind a high rod fence and locked gate. I grabbed the latch and tried to open it, but it just clanked loudly. It was locked. Unfortunately, a dog inside the yard heard the clank and began barking. I could do nothing but stand there and wait while an occupant of the house peeped out at me, trying to see who I was in the dark. I waved, trying to show that I'm a foreigner and therefore probably had business with the NLD. Meanwhile, I heard voices in the military intelligence compound. I lowered my hat and tried to keep my face from view. I was finally let through the gate and shown through the house, but under the porch lights the intelligence officers surely were able to snap photos of me.

Once inside, I delivered a small parcel and a pack of letters addressed to Suu Kyi. A letter introducing me had preceded my arrival thanks to another poor soul who had mustered the courage to deliver it in the same manner.

I was told that Suu Kyi would be informed that I had arrived, and I was asked to come again in a few nights to find out when the meeting could take place.

"Come *again?*" I questioned unhappily.

"Yes. In a few days," the man said.

I hated the idea, but there was little I could do but comply. "Okay," I sighed, "I'll come back the day after tomorrow."

He smiled and asked someone to escort me to the gate.

I had to walk down the road quite a bit before I found a taxi. There should have been no taxis whatever in the area, but I suspected that the military intelligence had called one to pick me up and report where I was staying. To prevent this, I took two different taxis to get back to my hotel, and then I went straight into the tourist bar. After having a much-deserved drink, and when I felt assured that no one was tailing me, I went into the hotel lobby. I sat briefly in the lobby then took the elevator to the wrong floor, taking the stairs to my floor just for added measure. "I can't imagine living like this all the time," I said to myself as I latched the door to my room behind me.

On my second visit to the safe house, I was more confident in my movements. No dogs hindered me this time, and I marched quickly into the house. Unfortunately, I was told that Suu Kyi was ill and under instructions from her doctor not to receive visitors for some time. I would have to lie low for about a week and then return to the safe house to see if Suu Kyi could see me at all. Things weren't looking good, but I was more determined than ever not to leave without seeing Suu Kyi.

I spent the week touring the city and some parts of the countryside. I noticed bulletin boards around the capital reading, "Anyone who is riotous, destructive, and unruly is our enemy," and "The Tatmadaw [as the army is called] shall never betray the national cause"—slogans reminiscent of the prominently displayed signs in *1984*: "War Is Peace. Freedom Is Slavery. Ignorance Is Strength." Wanting to project an image of just rule, the government changed its name to the State Peace and Development Council. But no amount of newspeak can change the fact that the military regime is brutally repressive and maintains power against the express wishes of the people.

On one of my outings outside Rangoon, I decided to wear the traditional *longyi,* a colorful sarong that is folded and wrapped tightly to stay around one's waist. All the men wear them, often with a Western button-down shirt. I found the *longyi* cool and comfortable, although I felt a bit self-conscious wearing it. I set out to visit a temple that rests on a small island in a river. As I stepped from a boat onto the shore of the island, the hem of my *longyi* got caught under my foot and the whole thing ripped from my body. Amid a burst of laughter, and some applause, I tripped onto the shore completely exposed to the crowd of Burmese who were visiting the temple. It was the first good laugh I had enjoyed in Burma, and I'm sure the villagers had something to joke about for months to come.

I saw enough on my short journeys to know that Burma is one of the most beautiful regions in all of Asia. The countryside is green and lush and dotted with ancient villages and pagodas. I hoped one day to visit a free Burma and to explore the vastness of this land. (For now, the NLD strongly discourages tourism, which would put dollars into the hands of the military government.)

In one small village, consisting of half a dozen thatched homes, I sat for a time and watched the people go about their lives. A young boy chopped bamboo with a machete twice the size of his arms, while his little sister swatted at bugs with a stick. At another house two mothers washed their children and rubbed a white paste on their faces to prevent sunburns. Everyone who saw me greeted me with surprise, then with a huge smile. I feared interacting with them, as the nature of my visit to the country was not welcomed by the government.

Along one of the roads we came close to Insein prison. Yes, it is pronounced "insane," and that is exactly what the living conditions are like in the facility. Many NLD members and other political prisoners have been carted off there to face isolation, torture, and even death.

Returning to my hotel room one day, I saw from the other end of the hallway that three men were leaving my room. They were burly men, well dressed in Western shirts and *longyi*—obviously not part of the housekeeping staff. It appeared that military intelligence was curious why I was traveling alone. Since I had hidden my sensitive documents and recording devices in the bathroom ceiling by removing and replacing one of the hanging tiles, I was not too worried about them searching through my belongings. They would find a guidebook but not much else. Yet it was now certain that I was being watched.

In the late afternoons, as the saffron-colored sun turned everything a golden orange, I would venture down to Kandawgyi Lake and sit in contemplation. I often thought of Suu Kyi's writings. I had been particularly impressed by her *Letters from Burma,* in which she writes eloquently about gentle Burmese traditions and the valiant struggle of her pro-democracy colleagues.[7] As the sun went down, I would say a prayer for all the people in the city who had lived through another day of tyranny. I recalled what Suu Kyi had written in one of her letters:

> How simple it would be if a mere turn of light could make everything that was ugly beautiful. How wonderful it would be if twilight were a time when we could all lay down the cares of the day and look forward to a tranquil night of well earned rest. But in Fascist Disneyland the velvety night is too often night in the worst sense of the word, a time deprived of light in more ways than one. [8]

I hoped each evening that there would be no political arrests. I also felt a sense of powerlessness that annoyed me. I wanted to be able to change the regime, to protect those who were being repressed and brutalized. Yet I knew the best I could do at that moment was to continue to pray for peace to take hold.

Praying for peace, I had to remind myself, is not an unimportant or insignificant contribution. Whether one believes that prayers are answered by God or by deities of some sort, it is certain that the mere act of praying establishes the right vision, the right motivation within oneself. It is the beginning of taking positive action, and it sets up an irrepressible faith that cannot be defeated by external circumstances.

I recalled an episode that started me on the adventure of writing this book. High in the Himalayan mountains of northern India, I emerged from the cold, damp air of a dark cave into the warm afternoon sun and stretched my arms out wide. After four days of meditating in the cave, I felt an overwhelming sense of freedom under the open sky. A few minutes later a Buddhist nun appeared, carefully carrying a cup of hot tea over the rocky path. She must have been waiting a number of hours for me to emerge from the belly of the mountain, keeping the teapot heated over a bed of coals in her nearby hut. She bowed slightly, smiled, and extended the cup toward me. I grasped it between my hands and watched the steam swirl into the air, smiling in appreciation as she slowly withdrew from view.

After finishing the last sip of my tea, I hiked up to the highest point on the mountain and sat on a large rock. Around me were strings of prayer flags, bleached white and tattered by the elements, flapping raucously in the wind. It is said that as the prayer flags flutter the wind carries the prayers for peace and happiness to all beings who are touched by that current of air. I looked out across the lake-filled plateau far below me. In the distance, the snow-covered mountains rose up like never-ending steps. Just the sight of them inspired a religious awe in me. As the wind whisked my hair gently around my head, I too felt that I was free to rise and spin and tease in the air. It was as if, had I wished to, I could have risen of my own accord high above the mountains, high above the world and all its problems.

My feelings poured from my body, like a container overfilled with water. A strong desire welled up in me to share this sense of peace with everyone in every corner of the globe, and I imagined this peace streaming from my body, flowing down the mountains and across the plains like a river and further still across the oceans and distant continents, rippling in the currents like the prayers from the flags around me, healing all that it touched, relieving the suffering of millions of beings throughout the world. It was in that moment, in that dazzling flight of the imagination, with the most profound and sincere desire to help spread peace, that the idea for this book was born. And no danger or hardship, in Burma or elsewhere, was going to dissuade me from fulfilling the prayer that came from the depths of my heart.

The evening before my scheduled departure from Rangoon I received a telephone call from former general U Tin Oo. I had met with him (the details of which I must withhold) and enjoyed several engaging conversations about the situation in Burma, about Suu Kyi's keen intelligence and leadership abilities, and about his own imprisonment for being a senior member of the opposition party.

U Tin Oo never showed any fear of the military regime. He had refuted all the trumped-up charges against him and repeatedly stated that the military courts did not have the authority to imprison him. He showed his courage again by calling my hotel room, for he could be imprisoned again on any mere appearance of impropriety.

"Suu Kyi will meet with you tomorrow at three in the afternoon," he advised me. "You have the directions to her house already."

"But . . ." I paused. "Isn't this conversation being overheard?"

"Yes, yes. It is. But why should it matter? I told them that you are writing a paper and you wanted to talk with Suu Kyi about peace. Why should they care?"

"Okay," I answered with a small, skeptical laugh.

After checking out of my hotel, I told my driver that I was heading to the airport. He told his fellow drivers of our destination. When we had gone a mile or so down the road, however, I told him that I had a stop to make before the airport. "I am going to see Aung San Suu Kyi," I said. "I have an appointment with her."

"Okay," he said without surprise. A brief time later he inquired more about my visit. "You have an appointment with *the Lady?*" he questioned.

"I do. It's all set up. It's approved. Do you know where her house is?"

"Of course," he replied. "Everyone knows. It is the most famous house in Burma. It was her father's house before."

"Is it any problem for you to go there? Will you be in any trouble?" I inquired.

"Oh, no. No problem for me," he responded.

I had no idea what would await me at Suu Kyi's house. Foreign visitors were often turned away or escorted under armed guard to the airport. Even if this happened, I consoled myself, I would write about Suu Kyi and the conditions in Burma. But it wouldn't be complete without a direct conversation with her.

We reached a checkpoint, and several soldiers with automatic weapons stood on either side of the car while one of them told my driver to turn around. I thought at first that I was being denied access, and I wanted to protest. I began to open my door but was forced back inside by an advancing soldier, who was agitated that we were not following orders. My driver finally told me that we would have to leave immediately.

"But I have an appointment!" I exclaimed.

He looked at me in the rearview mirror and shrugged his shoulders. "Well, what can you do?" he said.

"Isn't there another way to get to the house?" I persisted.

"Oh. Yes, there is," he replied.

I was annoyed that he hadn't suggested it. It seemed he didn't want me to keep my appointment with the Lady. "Well, let's go," I said. "And let's hurry. I'm going to be late."

"We'll be there in just a few minutes," he said calmly.

As we turned onto Suu Kyi's street and headed toward 54 University Avenue, I could see a group of men standing by a table under an umbrella. As soon as I stepped from the car several men flanked me and directed me to the table. Meanwhile, half a dozen yards away several other men were busy taking photographs of me. I was asked to surrender my passport. The officers carefully inspected all the pages and copied information into a log. I also had to fill out a log entry with my name, nationality, home address, passport number, local hotel, and so forth.

During this process I glanced briefly toward my driver. He was shaking hands with several of the military intelligence officers. Once logged in and photographed, I was told to proceed down the blocked-off street.

Another photographer squatted down in the street before me. His assistant held up his hand, motioning for me to stop. When he had clicked a few photos, the assistant nodded his head and I continued on my way. As I walked unescorted down the street, I saw a group of children playing in the middle of the road. It was such a contrast: children behaving like children, while adults were behaving like goons. I waved to the kids and was comforted by their smiles.

Just before I reached the house, a lone soldier in fatigues stepped forward and pointed his rifle at me. I couldn't help but notice that his finger was already on the trigger. It was quite unnecessary and hard to imagine why he needed to be so aggressive. Simply waving his hand at me would have gotten my attention, but he was waving his rifle instead. He spoke loudly in Burmese, apparently telling me that I had to leave. I found this puzzling. How in the world could he think that I just managed to go past a dozen military intelligence officers without their approval? I stood my ground and remained calm.

"I already signed in, my friend," I told him, pantomiming the sign-in process and pointing back at the agents under the umbrella. He continued to point his rifle at me until one of the agents at the gate yelled that it was okay to let me pass.

I'm not sure whether the men who opened the gate to Suu Kyi's yard were military intelligence or NLD members. They smiled politely and waved me toward the house. It was a small, white, rectangular, two-story house with a covered porch extending over the circular driveway. The walled yard was dotted with palm trees and shrubs, and a garden led down to Lake Inay, which, incidentally, is shared by General Ne Win's residence on an opposite shore.

A middle-aged woman let me in the front door and showed me to a receiving room. The room was fairly dark and sparsely furnished: a few chairs and a barren, low table in front of a couch. On one of the walls hung a large portrait of Aung San painted in a colorful Andy Warhol style. I took a seat on the couch and wiped the sweat from my brow with a handkerchief. I pulled my microcassette recorder from my bag and checked to see that it was working. And then I waited.

The house was very quiet. Five minutes went by before I heard the sound of a door opening and light footsteps approaching. Suu Kyi came into the room, her hands interlaced in front of her. I rose to my feet to greet her. She wore a beautiful orange Burmese dress. Her hair was pulled back immaculately into a bun. Though her frame was thin and short, I immediately felt her commanding presence.

"You are late," she announced sternly. "I expected you ten minutes ago," she said, looking down at her wristwatch and shaking her head in displeasure.

"I'm . . . sorry . . . ," I stuttered, surprised by the scolding. "I had trouble getting here. You see, we first went to the other road and . . ."

"Well, that was your mistake," she interrupted. "You should have come to this gate. I'm absolutely certain that U Tin would have instructed you to go to this gate," she admonished. The Lady did not like to be kept waiting, and I had offended her even before meeting her.

Suu Kyi sat on the couch next to me, smoothed out her dress, then folded her hands in her lap. She was very elegant and graceful, and at the risk of sounding reverential, she looked a bit like Kwan Yin, goddess of compassion. Kindness showed in her eyes, even if she was angry with me for being late.

I told her how much I appreciated her work and her devotion to peaceful social change. I then tried to hand her an envelope containing several hundred dollars to be used by the NLD.

She didn't extend her hands to receive the gift. "I'm afraid I can't accept that," she said in a proper British accent, looking down at the envelope. "One of the charges made by the government is that the NLD has ties to foreign interests. We don't want any appearance that their charge is true. We simply cannot accept any donations from foreigners."

My long-awaited meeting with Suu Kyi did not appear to be going well. It certainly wasn't as I imagined it would be. I wondered if she would turn down the next gift that I offered: a silk scarf, called a *kata,* that the Dalai Lama had given to me as a blessing. Normally one would never give away a *kata* from the Dalai Lama, and though I had no idea what she thought of him, I felt strongly that she should have it.

"This was given to me by His Holiness the Dalai Lama," I said a bit nervously. "I would like you to have it."

Her face suddenly softened, and a delicate smile appeared as she gently took up the gift. "Thank you," she said lightly. "Thank you very much. I am very happy to receive this. I love His Holiness very much."

"We have that in common," I said, returning her smile. "I love him and the example he sets."

We paused and looked at each other for a few moments. I wanted to chat and ease into our conversation, but I had a lot of questions to ask in a short amount of time. Accordingly, I said that we had better address some of the questions that I had jotted down for our meeting. She nodded in agreement.

"You are considered one of the greatest living peacemakers," I observed. "So, I must ask you, what is your definition of peace? Is peace simply the absence of violence?"

"No, I think, for me, it is something more positive than that," she replied. "The mere absence of violence, that is a good enough start, but I think of peace as inner calm and serenity. If you're haunted by any kind of fears, then certainly you cannot say you're at peace, even if your surroundings are peaceful. If you're at peace, then you are not haunted by fears. So, peace is not just a negative state of affairs; it's not just an absence of violence. It means you can enjoy inner serenity because there's an absence not just of violence but of fear— freedom from fear."

"With that definition," I pointed out, "in many places in the United States people would say that there is no peace, because of crime and fear of gangs and so forth."

"Complete peace, I think, is very, very difficult to find in any part of the world," she replied. "But I think there are degrees of peace. I think there must be parts of the United States where you can say there's no peace if you can't go out into your own street without fear of being mugged. But on the other hand, wherever you go to work there may be nothing threatening in the work environment, so you enjoy eight hours of peace, and then come back to a neighborhood where there is in fact no peace. But there must be very, very few places in the world where there is complete peace."

"I'm very interested in knowing how your thoughts on peace-making developed, where your philosophies came from," I said. "Were there particular texts, particular people, particular religious training that informed your opinions?"

"Well," she laughed, "I didn't really start out with the intention of making peace, as it were. So I didn't do any research on peace in that way. But of course one comes across the word very often, and one reads about it just in the course of one's lifetime. But since getting into politics we [the NLD] have very much exercised nonviolence. And we have concentrated on the aspect of democracy which we feel is conducive to peace. We think that you cannot have peace and justice without a democratic system because, fundamentally, unless the people's basic rights are protected you cannot give them a sense of security. And without security there's no peace, because what I said earlier, one needs freedom from fear. So security, peace, fear—all these I think are linked. And I suppose my thoughts on peace developed as a result of my experiences during the last ten years since I entered politics." She paused and smiled. "I don't think before that time I had any particularly developed ideas on peace. One talks about peace in the world—everybody wants peace—but I don't think that everybody goes into this concept in great detail."

It is important to note that Suu Kyi is a devout practitioner of Buddhism. Unlike many of her fellow Asians, she regards Buddhism not just as an inherited religion, but as a living faith that must be carefully cultivated and mastered through study and practice. It was perhaps her faith, more than anything else, that saw her through the years of confinement, near starvation, and illness.

Unfortunately, the military regime has little generosity toward Buddhism and battles continuously with Buddhists in order to quash dissent. Monks have been forcibly disrobed, detained in prison, and prohibited from leaving the confines of their monastery. Meetings called by monks to discuss the harsh treatment by the military have been obstructed by the government.

Suu Kyi spoke to me briefly about her practice. "Meditation is a form of cultivating inner strength," she told me. "And inner strength means inner peace. If you acquire inner strength that means that you are in a position to be able to face the troubles of the external world. And in that way, you can create your own sense of security, which comes from your inner strength. So, therefore, you are creating your own peace, as it were."

In speaking of meditation, Suu Kyi did not mean to imply that anything in the external world is permissible as long as one has inner peace. "I do not think that very many people achieve that kind of spiritual status where they have acquired such inner strength that they are totally at peace in whatever may be going on around them. Certainly, I am nowhere near that stage," she said with a small laugh. "And the great majority of the world's people are nowhere near that stage, which is why it is so important for us to create an environment where people will be able to enjoy a certain degree of peace."

"As you participate in politics," I asked, "working for peace, stressing the importance of nonviolence, do you read particular texts that are inspiring to you? Do you study the activities of other peacemakers?"

"I don't go out of my way to do that," she replied. "If I have a speech to prepare, or if I have an article to write, of course I do refer to books. But I don't sit down and say that I'm going to study peace or nonviolence as a subject. Of course I read books that I'm given, and in that sense I do study the idea of peace, but not in a systematic way. Not like you," she said, laughing. "I'm not sitting down to write a book on peace!"

"When members of the Tibetan community want to turn to violence," I noted, "the Dalai Lama uses arguments much like those of Mahatma Gandhi to promote the power of nonviolent means. What are the arguments you use for nonviolence as a means to achieve your goal?"

"The power of nonviolence is not easy to develop," she replied. "And I think that Mahatma Gandhi would be the first person to have admitted that. He didn't say that nonviolence was easy. I think he made the point that nonviolence is not for cowards. Nonviolence requires strength, requires courage. The power of nonviolence, if it is disciplined and systematic and if it can be organized as a mass movement, of course can be extremely powerful. But even Mahatma Gandhi didn't succeed 100 percent in organizing such a movement. He himself had difficulty, you know, disciplining his followers to follow strictly the norms of nonviolence.

"At the moment in Burma, we don't have the kind of *satyagraha* movement going on that they had in India. So nonviolence for us, apart from my philosophical acceptance of the idea of nonviolence, is also a practical matter. Because I feel very strongly that we have to break through this vicious cycle of violent politics. In the last few decades, the changes in governments in Burma have come about through violence. The first military coup was in 1958, and the second one was in 1962. And of course there were all these uprisings in 1988. Political change instituted through violence has become a bad tradition in Burma. We want to put an end to this vicious cycle of violence and change, violence and change. We want a fresh start where political change—genuine, fundamental political change—can be brought about through nonviolent means. It is much more difficult than through violent means, but I think in the long run it's worth it."

"Well," I pressed, "what is the chief way to accomplish nonviolent political change in the face of violent repression?"

"It is, of course, through education of the people. And it is through perseverance," she said.

"But is it the people who need to be educated?" I argued. "Do they have violent tendencies, or is it the military that is predisposed to violence?"

"I think it is both," she retorted. "Not necessarily because the people have violent tendencies, but because we need to instill confidence in the people, to make them realize that the 'powerless' do have power and that power can be manipulated though nonviolent means to get to the goal. This is what Václev Havel calls 'the power of the powerless.' And of course, one wants the military to look at it from the other side, that violence may work for some time but it will not work forever. There is a lot of power in nonviolent means. This is shown by the fact that we, the opposition, the dissidents here, have managed to win a lot of support internationally and nationally. Nationally, there's proof in the elections in 1990 that the people preferred to have the NLD to the armed forces as a form of government. So we want them to understand that there is a lot of power in nonviolence."

"There are for me three vivid images of nonviolence," I said. "The first comes from Gandhi's movement. During a protest people lined up shoulder to shoulder, row after row, and peacefully marched up to the guards, who beat them over the heads with batons. One after the other, they just kept coming, without resisting the violence with any violence of their own. And the women carted off the dazed, bloodied, injured men. The next powerful image comes from the antiwar movement in America in the 1960s, where young activists placed flowers in the barrels of the soldiers' rifles. Perhaps it seems a bit childish, but the contrast is very striking to me, turning weapons into vases, if you will. The final image is that of you walking through the row of soldiers who had their weapons pointed at you. That image is so powerful to me."

"Well, the first two are rather difficult to achieve in Burma," she replied. "In India, they used the police, not the army. Yes, they beat them down, but that is a very different matter from shooting people down with guns. I think it would be much more difficult to get wave after wave of people going up to face guns and getting shot down. And then also, by the same argument, I don't know how far the military in Burma would tolerate people coming up and putting flowers into the barrels of their guns. Now, as for my walking toward the guns . . ." She paused. "It's . . . it's . . . I sometimes think that the whole thing has been exaggerated a bit," she said. "They were sitting there pointing their guns, and one didn't really have much choice." She laughed. "You either kept walking or you retreated. And if you're not prepared to retreat, you just keep walking. That's all."

From what I had read and heard about Suu Kyi, she is quite humble about her leadership, and she often minimizes her accomplishments. "I wonder, Daw Suu Kyi, do you feel sometimes that you've woken up and found yourself cast in the role of 'extraordinary champion of democracy,' while you think of yourself differently?"

A bright smile swept across her face. "Oh, yes. I never think that it is really me!" she replied with a laugh. "You know," she said, shaking her head slightly, "I'm just me! I mean, I'm not trying to be modest or anything like that. I think everybody is unique in his or her own way. But this great, big label Champion of Democracy . . . I always find this very strange when people refer to me as a heroine and so on and so forth." She laughed. "I sometimes think it's a bit of a giggle. You know, it's got nothing to do with me. I just do what I have to do."

"And yet, you realize, of course, that many people need a leader to put faith and trust in, and they need to build up that leader," I observed.

"Yes, very much so. But also I'm very much aware of the Buddhist teachings about the eight human conditions, you know. [Though we may for a time enjoy gain, status, praise, and pleasure, we eventually experience loss, disgrace, censure, and pain as well; all human conditions are inconstant in life.] And whenever, in the early days, I went out to campaign across the country, and there were huge crowds wishing me good health and all the like, an awareness would always come to me that this does not necessarily last forever. Because the same people wishing me good health and long life might one day turn against me. This is politics. This is life. This is the human condition. I've always been aware of that. And I think leaders are particularly vulnerable to such changes in people's attitudes."

"Speaking of leaders, what do you think your strengths are as a leader?" I asked.

She paused for some time. Looking almost bashful, she finally replied slowly, "I'm not sure that I have any particular strengths."

"Well, that's very disappointing!" I joked, pretending to pack up my things and rise from my seat. "It's been a very difficult trip just to find out that you have no particular strengths! Now what can I write about you in my book?"

She laughed. "I don't know! What do you think? What do *you* think my strengths are?"

"Courage!" I replied instantly.

"Courage?" she questioned. "Well, yes, I suppose so. I've always fought against people succumbing to fear. I've talked a lot about that. But that does not mean that I'm trying to say that people should never feel fear. Of course, you cannot help but feel fear from time to time. And as somebody said, it's not a question not of whether you feel frightened, but of how you cope with your fear when you feel frightened. And so, I suppose courage is an ability to cope with your fears in a sensible way. But I've never thought of myself as particularly courageous."

"I guess you have to leave that to others to judge," I proffered.

"I don't know. What is courage, after all? As I say, courage to me is just a matter of coping competently with your fears."

"What about patience?" I added, thinking about how long she has maintained hope in the face of little noticeable change.

"Patience, I think, has to go together with perseverance and hard work. I don't believe in sitting like Patience on a monument smiling at Grief. You know, that's a big waste of time in my opinion. When people say that we are very patient, I'm not sure I quite like the way they say it. It is not as though we are just sitting and waiting patiently for the military to suddenly decide that they might as well after all give the people democracy. Patience for me is acceptable only if it means perseverance, sometimes a dogged perseverance!"

"But patience also has a connotation of wisdom," I offered, "and not being stirred by mere passion."

"Well, true. That's right. Self-control comes into it. You've got to control your impatience. Patience in terms of controlling your impatience is a good thing!" she said, smiling at her playful choice of words. "Anyway, don't they say that impatience is a sign of immaturity?"

"What is the flip side of the coin? What are some of your weaknesses?" I asked.

She laughed. "Of course, there are so many I don't know where to start!" She paused, looked down, then raised her eyes to me. "I suppose in that sense, I am very Buddhist. I do believe that you can never have enough of mindfulness. That I try to cultivate. And then, of course, wisdom. Well ...," she paused again. "What springs to mind is the idea of *bodhicitta* [enlightened mind, or altruism], compassion and wisdom. I suppose this is what I'd like to cultivate, more compassion, more wisdom. I still lack both. And I think the way to raise them is through mindfulness."

"Tell me, if you will, about compassion in the peacemaking process. You've been through a great deal of suffering at the hands of the military. How important is forgiveness?"

"When you talk about forgiveness, you really have to talk in terms of 'forgiving' and 'forgetting.' This is something that people have discussed very often. Can you forgive without forgetting? Is it possible to forgive without forgetting? I'm inclined to believe that true forgiveness means not forgetting. If it is because you've forgotten it, it is not really forgiveness, it's simply because you've *forgotten*. But to remember and yet be able to forgive, I think that's real forgiveness. Some things should never be forgotten for the sake of the future. You don't want to repeat the same mistakes. You don't want to go through the same kind of suffering, and you don't want other people to go through the same kind of suffering over and over again. Therefore, I'm not one who would recommend forgetfulness. Besides, forgetfulness is not quite in line with mindfulness, is it? Forgiveness, again, would be connected to compassion and wisdom, wouldn't it? I mean, if you have true wisdom you will understand why someone did something against you. And if you have compassion, you will be able to forgive them."

I offered an observation. "Maha Ghosananda [Supreme Patriarch of Cambodia, and the subject of chapter 6] in his teachings is very clear on the fact that with mindfulness, being in the present moment, there is no room for negative emotions—hatred, anger, revenge, and so on."

"Oh, yes!" she responded immediately. "Actually, I had my first lesson in mindfulness in New York, in Coney Island. I never realized then that it was my first lesson," she said with a smile. "I went with a family of friends to Coney Island, and they took me to this thing called Wildcat, a kind of helter-skelter, what you call a rollercoaster. They had all been there before, and they said they were never going to go on this thing again. But of course I had heard so much about it, I wanted to find out *why* it was that they would not dare go on it again," she laughed. "What was so awful about it, what was so dreadful about it? I wondered. So I went up alone. You know, the seats are double seats. I was alone because none of my friends would come with me. The other people were mostly two together. And we went up and down almost at ninety-degree angles, and that's pretty frightening! And what I found very disconcerting was the fact that they didn't have any seat belt or anything to hold you back. They only had this very low bar," she pantomimed in the air while I burst into laughter. "Have you been on this?" she asked.

"No, but on similar ones," I replied.

"They had this very low, little bar, but it was quite low so that one could pitch over it and go toppling down. I was petrified. It was really quite frightening." She sat up very straight. "I thought, I'm not going to scream. Everyone else was screaming and clinging to each other, but since I was alone I had no one to cling to. I clung to that little bar. And at some point I thought to myself, 'So, this is fear! This is what fear is.' And I calmed down. I realized years later that in a sense I was meditating on that ride. This is a form of meditation, this is *mindfulness*. This is watching your emotions. And by watching them you do control them. So I think what Maha Ghosananda said is right. If you have developed perfect mindfulness then you are perfectly free from all the negative emotions." She stopped and took a deep breath. "But of course very few of us are able to cultivate perfect mindfulness!"

"Many magazine articles say that you are free after years of house arrest. But coming here this afternoon, I don't have the sense that you are truly free."

"No, I'm not free," she replied. "I'm not free in the sense that you are free to come and go. But, well, I'm not under house arrest. You can say that. And then, of course, I can't go everywhere that I like. So I can't say they have freed me completely. And yet, that sort of thing doesn't worry me. It didn't worry me when they kept me under house arrest. Physical freedom doesn't mean that much to me."

"Why?" I asked her. "Are you content as long as you have the freedom to communicate?"

"Well, when I was under house arrest I didn't have the freedom to communicate, either. But I don't know how to explain it. Each individual is different, and the degree to which each individual can tolerate being alone is probably different from one person to the other. I can tolerate being alone to quite some degree."

"I take it that the government enjoys having you in solitude," I said, referring to the fact that the military has refused to allow Suu Kyi to participate in negotiations. "I understand that you are not invited in government initiatives to talk about their proposals. Is that true?" I asked.

"But they haven't invited anyone!" she said emphatically. "The so-called invitations are not invitations at all. They staged two or three meetings last year where our people were summoned to come. And then they were given a lecture or a scolding and sent back. I think probably the authorities want the ASEAN [Association of

South East Asian Nations] countries and other potential allies to think that this is some sort of step toward negotiation, and that I am just being a fly in the ointment."

Disinformation (which can be plainly referred to as lies) abounds in the news media throughout Asia. Burma is, after all, a member of ASEAN, and strong economic ties exist with powerful business groups and government officials. Some reporters simply pick up the misinformation and then repeat it as rumor from "informed sources." I pulled a magazine out of my bag to discuss this with Suu Kyi.

"In an issue of *Asiaweek* magazine," I noted, "they have an interview with David Abel [a government minister], and he says that you are not invited to talks. But in the same magazine, another article says, 'Privately, the government and the National League for Democracy are showing some flexibility. Informed sources say this has led to recent clandestine meetings between the NLD head Aung San Suu Kyi and [Lieutenant General] Khin Nyunt [the regime's chief of intelligence] that could lead to a breakthrough this year. Partly at the behest of ASEAN leaders, the notion of power sharing is being considered.'"

Suu Kyi shook her head slowly from side to side. "I have always said that if you want to talk about power sharing, let's have a dialogue and you can put forward your proposals. Whoever wants to put forward a proposal can do so, and we'll discuss it. But I have not had any clandestine meetings with Khin Nyunt."

"Or his representatives?" I asked.

"No. And as for flexibility, we have always been flexible. This is a great, big propaganda effort by the authorities that we are inflexible and stubborn and all that. We have bent over backward to show that we are flexible." We both laughed at her choice of words. "To stretch the metaphor!" she added, causing us both to laugh even harder.

"An issue of critical importance to the situation in Burma is whether international sanctions are needed," I observed. "This comes up all over the world. Some people argue that sanctions do nothing to hurt a repressive government; instead they inflict harm on the people. Apparently, there is a human rights lawsuit in California against

Unocal in which the defendants claim that you are unclear as to whether sanctions against Burma are good or bad."

"I think sanctions are good," she said pointedly.

"David Abel recently said, and I quote, 'Sanctions don't work. Besides, we virtually sanctioned ourselves for twenty-six years and we survived. We are self-sufficient.... And now, once we've opened up, they've sanctioned us again. What's the use?' How do you respond to his argument?" I asked.

"Well, I think the situation is much worse now than it was during the twenty-six years of the [previous regime], because the standards of both health care and education have fallen. And inflation is absolutely rampant. So I would say that the economic situation and the social situation are much worse than they were under the previous regime. I read something brought out by ARCO recently saying that *unilateral* sanctions don't work. So, my response would be, "Okay. So let's go for *multilateral* sanctions! Let's get the Europeans to join, and let's have multilateral sanctions!"

"Do you think the current sanctions against Burma are tough enough?"

"No," she said with a smile, signaling that her wit was about to erupt again. "ARCO says they are not tough enough, and ARCO should know! It's time that we had multilateral sanctions!"

"Internally, Burma has a long-standing problem with ethnic tensions," I observed.[9] "Burma is an ethnically diverse country, and the different groups often have conflicting agendas. But I am told by U Tin Oo that you are the one person that all the ethnic minorities trust. How have you established that trust, and in a free Burma how would you keep all the ethnic groups working together?"

"Well, first of all, I'm not sure that I am the *one* person who is most trusted by the ethnic minorities. But to the extent that I am trusted, I think that comes from my father, the fact that I am his daughter. And also we were brought up in my family by my mother to respect and to love the ethnic nationalities. Because of this I grew up with very warm feelings toward the ethnic nationalities. I have very positive feelings toward them. I have a lot of goodwill toward them. I'm confident of that. And I don't go around making facile promises. We have got to struggle together."

"In fact," I noted, "I think you've been honest in saying that democracy will be very messy when it comes."

"Yes. Democracy will be messy, because this is the way of democracy."

"As your large neighbor, India, has shown."

"Yes," she replied with a smile. "But when you look at India, you feel it's quite a nice mess."

While I was in Thailand, I had read daily accounts about the plight of the eighty thousand Karen refugees on Thai soil. The Karens have struggled for autonomy from Rangoon, and many support the Karen National Union (KNU), which is waging a battle to gain freedom from the Burmese military regime. In retaliation, the Rangoon-backed Democratic Karen Buddhist Army (DKBA) was crossing the border into Thailand to carry out attacks against the unarmed refugees. They would fire automatic weapons and launch grenades into the housing structures, setting fire to huts while the refugees were sleeping. In this way they hope to terrorize the refugees into withholding support for the KNU. I asked Suu Kyi to address this situation.

"This government says it's not involved," she said, slapping her lap and shaking her head in disbelief. "The first comment I want to make is that this is a very sad state of affairs. I think it is absolutely tragic that there should have appeared this division amongst the Karen peoples, that there should be this division between Buddhist Karens [the DKBA] and Christian Karens [the KNU]. The Karens are an extremely nice people. They are one of the nicest ethnic groups in Burma. I really feel so sad that this has happened to them. Nobody should encourage such divisions. This is so terrible!"

"Under a democratic form of government," I asked, "what would you do if the Karens still want complete autonomy? Would it create a situation like we have seen in the Balkans or other parts of the world? Would there be a civil war?"

"I think what happened in the Balkans happened because there was no freedom of speech or freedom of discussion," she observed, "and no tendency toward dialogue. Because the Serbs, everybody knows, are a very militant people, and they put a lot of importance on military prowess and military solutions. I think if we concentrate on political solutions—and there of course you have to cultivate patience, hard but patient negotiation—we can come to the kind of settlement that would be acceptable to all the people of Burma. It's not going to be easy."

"But do you think that Burma, once democratic, can keep its boundaries intact?" I wondered.

"I think only a democratic Burma can keep its boundaries intact in the long run," she said.

"And that requires a constitution that adequately protects the minorities, does it not?" I asked.

"It requires a constitution that is *acceptable* to all our nationalities," she stated vigorously.

"Regarding the 'democratic' constitution that the military government is purportedly coming out with in the near future, has the NLD had any input into its provisions?"

"No. No," she said shaking her head. "We don't agree with this constitution."

"Is it like Chilean former dictator Augusto Pinochet did, giving protection to military leaders in the constitution?" I asked.

"Well, roughly speaking, it gives the military the power to take over whenever they think it is necessary in the interest of the country. It is they who will decide whether or not it is in the interest of the country. And the head of state must be a former military man. And also all elected assemblies, from the central level right to the local level, will have 20 percent of the seats reserved for military personnel. So it's not much of a democratic scheme," she declared.

"One need only look at Cambodia in recent history to see how power sharing with a strongman works—that is, not very well," I noted. "But can something work here, whereby the current leaders are given some kind of post, some kind of significant say, and some kind of significant pension perhaps?"

"This is the sort of thing that can only be discussed across the negotiation table," she responded. "I think it would be premature to discuss such matters now when we haven't even seen any signs of . . . ," she paused and laughed, "the *initial* stages of dialogue."

"Reviewing the military regime's record in recent years," I said,

"I see no progress toward basic freedoms, much less a power-sharing arrangement. I wonder whether you are optimistic about the future. Do you have any idea or any feeling in your heart when true democratic changes will happen here?"

"No," she said flatly. "Of course, we always hope that it will happen as soon as possible. Tomorrow is not a bad idea." She smiled broadly. "Put up a few prayers for us, will you?"

"I will *certainly* remember you in my prayers," I responded, reaching out and taking up her hand.

She smiled warmly. "There are so many people that have been very kind to us and are helping us simply out of sheer goodwill, not because they hope to get anything out of it—except, perhaps the satisfaction of having helped us. And we really appreciate that very much, very much indeed. We won't forget our friends."

We stood up and walked outside together, strolling through her garden. We chatted as friends do, about little things that reveal a vast array of feelings and beliefs. We talked also about our common Buddhist faith and our mutual reverence for the Dalai Lama. She told me that she prays to him daily for strength and compassion, something Tibetans term "calling the lama from afar." I too, I told her, call for help from the distance.

"Be sure to put the *kata* on your altar," I told her, "and His Holiness will be here with you in spirit."

I didn't know then how important it would be for her to continue to focus on being with people in spirit rather than in the flesh. Not long after, her husband Michael Aris was denied entry by the military government in Burma, and Suu Kyi would never see him alive again. The pain of his death and the self-sacrifice of not being able to see him seem almost unbearable.

After a few more minutes I had to leave if I was going to make my flight and have any hope of getting the interview tape out of the country. Suu Kyi and I said a quiet good-bye. "I'll be back to see you one day," I declared.

"I do hope so," she replied, smiling sweetly.

As I left Suu Kyi's house, the military intelligence agents stared at me. I was still smiling from my conversation with Suu Kyi. My driver saw me and jumped in the car. When I had closed my door, I said to him wryly, "You won't get in trouble for bringing me here, will you?"

"No. That guy there," he said pointing to one of the men in a white car that pulled up alongside us, "he's a friend of mine."

"Oh, well, I suppose it's good to have connections," I said.

A white car from the checkpoint tailed us for a while but then disappeared. Perhaps they simply wanted to ensure that I was headed to the airport (which my driver undoubtedly told them) and was not going to rendezvous with anyone to pass along any tapes.

When we got to the airport, I shook my driver's hand and thanked him for taking me around the city this past week. I had no hard feelings toward him, even if he was working for the military regime.

While I was waiting in the long and slow check-in line, I thought things had gone a bit too easily. I had entered the country, met with the two most senior members of the democratic opposition, and discussed the government in critical terms. Could it be, I wondered, that there really was a new openness beginning in Burma? But I also thought I saw a man point at me and the airline agent look at me frequently.

I checked in without any difficulty then proceeded to the customs counter. I handed my passport to the customs agent. He flipped it open and rose to his feet. Two other uniformed customs agents appeared and stood beside me. They were soon joined by three large men in white button-down shirts and *longyi*. Behind me was another man ensuring that I couldn't retreat, even if I had wanted to do so.

"Are you Scott Hunt?" the customs agent asked me.

"Yes. Yes, of course I am. You have my passport," I said politely.

"And what hotel did you stay at?" he asked.

I found this an odd question. They surely knew the answer already. "I was at the Kandawaggi," I replied.

He nodded his head to a group of at least six men standing by a table across from the customs area. "Come with us," he said, pulling at my arm.

My carry-on bags were taken from me and meticulously emptied onto a table. Meanwhile, I could see that they had collected my checked bags and were running them through an X-ray machine. As I watched them, I observed my reactions, as Suu Kyi had done on her terrifying roller-coaster ride. I remained surprisingly unattached to any fear. But I was concerned about preserving the tape of my interview with Suu Kyi, not simply because I wanted to recall her words with accuracy, but also because I didn't want it used as possible evidence against her or the NLD.

I recalled what U Tin Oo had told me. "If they try to search you, complain. Complain loudly. Tell them, 'Why are you doing this? You're supposed to be a civilized nation. I thought you wanted tourists to come here.'" According to U Tin Oo, this morality play might make them less severe in their treatment.

I heard several men say that I should be taken out of the terminal. One man started to lead me away, and another was going to collect my belongings, but they decided to do their search on the spot. I demanded to know who was in charge, but everyone played dumb.

When I saw a group of Westerners passing by, I shouted out to them. "See what they are doing here in Burma?" I said. "I have done nothing wrong, but they are detaining me. In case they take me away, please remember my face."

"Please, quiet down," one of the agents told me. One of the larger thugs looked as if he wanted to break my neck. Half of them were on cell phones. When I again demanded to know who was in charge, they simply said their commanders were on the phone.

They removed every item from my bag and searched it thoroughly. They opened my shampoo and lotion to make sure nothing was hidden in the liquid. They did the same to my toothpaste by squeezing the tube. They checked my shaving cream to make sure it had no false bottom. They confiscated all my notes, took my music cassettes and blank microcassettes, and took the tape of my conversation with U Tin Oo. They also took all other documents I had, while checking my bags for hidden compartments.

I noticed that the louder and more vehemently I complained, the more they turned away from me, annoyed by my antics. I quickly decided to use this to my advantage. I unleashed a barrage of protests, and the agents looked away. I quickly took the microcassette tape from my pocket and threw it into my open, empty bag. I looked up and caught the eye of one of the agents. I didn't know if he had seen what I had done. It was a tense moment. But he looked away and continued to search my items. The tape sat there at the bottom of the open bag. Then I demanded to repack my empty bag with the items they had already searched.

"You've already looked through these things," I said hotly. "I'm going to put them back where they belong—in my bag!"

One of the agents received approval and nodded for me to repack the searched items. That allowed me to cover up the tape. When I was patted down and my pockets were searched, they found nothing. After about an hour, they let me go to the departure gate. I was anxious to get on the plane, knowing that they could certainly grab me at any time and search me again.

Even when I was finally on the plane and the doors had shut I didn't feel secure. It wasn't until we were in Thai airspace that I felt more relieved. But what if, I thought, the tape had not recorded properly? What if they had erased it with a magnetic field? I fished the tape out of my bag and popped it into my recorder. When I pushed the play button I heard the comforting sound of Suu Kyi's laughter: "I sometimes think it's a bit of a giggle. You know, it's got nothing to do with me. I just do what I have to do." I looked around the plane, thinking any one of those people could be the next housewife or businessperson who just does what they have to do and changes the world in the process.

I switched off the tape, let out a huge sigh, and sank back in my seat.

Several weeks after my trip to Burma, journalists from several leading U.S. periodicals made it as far as the roadblock by Suu Kyi's house. I understand that out from the bushes ran a dozen soldiers, and the journalists were unceremoniously ejected from the country at gunpoint. I had managed to slip through their net, but it wouldn't happen again. I knew that I wouldn't be able to return to Burma until the dictatorship ends.

Suu Kyi has not yet managed to oust the generals who use every available means to suppress the people of Burma. Yet her endless determination and courage, despite years of mistreatment, show that she has found her life's purpose. She has already triumphed in spirit, and nothing will dissuade her from continuing her efforts to bring peace and democracy to her country. "There has to be a united determination to persevere in the struggle," she has written, "to make sacrifices in the name of enduring truths, to resist the corrupting influences of desire, ill will, ignorance, and fear."

When the regime finally ends its unjust and immoral reign, the nation will turn to its rightfully elected leader. And Suu Kyi, by all hopes and prayers, will be there to help rebuild, reconcile, and reinvigorate that wonderful country. We can only hope that she will turn her attention and skills to other parts of the world as well, helping to shape the future of peace around the globe.

In the meantime, I continued my journey, hoping that I too was instilling in my heart the deep determination and courage exhibited by Aung San Suu Kyi. My next stop would take me into the mountains of northern India to meet one of the world's most respected figures, the man of peace to whom Aung San Suu Kyi prays for guidance every day—the Precious Protector of Tibet, His Holiness the Dalai Lama.

Two

THE DALAI LAMA AND
THE POWER OF COMPASSION

My first visit to India nearly a decade ago was quite shocking. In the cities my senses were assaulted from every direction at once, and I could do little more than take in bits and pieces of it all: the smell of spent petrol and smoldering dung; the hot, sticky air, which clung to my skin and burned my eyes; the incessant clamor of the streets teeming with cars and trucks, buses, motorcycles, scooters and auto rickshaws, carts and bicycles; the endless crowds walking, running, squatting, lying down, hoisting bundles, dodging traffic; the thin white cows nosing through heaps of rotting garbage or standing idle in the roads, unconcerned with human actions.

In *A Passage to India* E. M. Forster asked, "How can the mind take hold of such a country?" Standing in the whirlwind of activity in India, I could not help but ask the same question. All around me were confounding disparities. Material poverty and spiritual richness, corruption and kindness, commotion and calm existed side by side. It was not unusual for me to see a woman nursing her newborn next to an old woman who lay diseased and dying, a man preparing his meal a few steps from where another man defecated, a family in a Mercedes overtaking a family in an ox-drawn cart.

It is important for people from prosperous nations to visit places like India. It gives them a much better understanding of how most of the world's inhabitants live. In fact, in a place like India, we can easily recognize that we in the West possess and use more resources than necessary. We collect incredible amounts of unnecessary items and spend small fortunes on our amusement, while in developing nations people suffer for want of what we take for granted. No matter how you look at it, this is a moral issue. Yet it is also a pragmatic one: How can the Earth cope with endless consumerism, and what conflicts will arise from scarce and unequally distributed resources? (We will address this throughout this book but most comprehensively in the concluding chapter.)

I first ventured to India to meet His Holiness the Dalai Lama in 1993. I had longed to meet the Dalai Lama, a man of incredible optimism and inner peace, ever since my childhood, when I first heard about the religious king of Tibet—a reincarnated saint whose purpose in life was to spread compassion to all sentient beings. I was always curious what it might feel like to be in his presence and how it might change a person's life afterward.

Stepping from his home into the stifling Indian heat in 1993, I had the answer to my curiosities. I felt no sense of magic, no mystical sense of floating or piercing the dimensions of time or space. Yet I found something much more straightforward and useful. I found that my heart was bursting with hope. It was not a fleeting sense of giddiness or exuberance but rather a profound recognition that true peace—the ultimate goal for all religious and spiritually minded people—can in fact be achieved. And here was proof positive in this unassuming, jovial man, this refugee from the rooftop of the world.

I returned now to Dharamsala without any indication that the Dalai Lama would receive me. I had sent faxes and letters and e-mail but had received no response. I determined that I had better just get there and pray that he was in residence and would carve out some time from his extremely busy schedule to talk with me about peacemaking.

Dharamsala, where the Dalai Lama's residence is located, offers more relaxed, yet still somewhat trying, surroundings than one finds in the cities of India. Situated in northern India in the state of Himachal Pradesh, Dharamsala is nestled in the Dhauladhar range of the Pir Panjal region of the Outer Himalayas. Above

Dharamsala, the jagged white peaks of the Dhauladhar rise seventeen thousand feet into the sky. Below, the wide and fertile Kangra Valley supports crops of rice, wheat, and tea.

Dharamsala is an unlikely place for a person of the Dalai Lama's stature to reside. At more than a day's journey from the capital of New Delhi, the area has the second highest rainfall in all of the Indian subcontinent. Consequently, the roads are often filled with potholes or washed out altogether, and phone and power lines are frequently downed by mountain winds. The Indians were probably trying to tuck the Dalai Lama out of view when they moved him here many years ago. But the Dalai Lama doesn't object to the clean air, majestic views, and relaxed conditions of the remote village he now calls home.

The Dalai Lama's residence (which used to be called Highcroft House when it was occupied by the divisional commissioner during the days of the British Raj) sits at the end of a narrow road, in a fenced compound across from Namgyal Monastery, surrounded by pine, oak, rhododendron, and deodar trees. Namgyal is the chief monastery of the Gelugpa tradition, one of the four major schools of Tibetan Buddhism, of which the Dalai Lama is the supreme head. Though the original monastery in Tibet is said to be quite beautiful, this utilitarian re-creation is not. The temple is very plain, of pale yellow painted cement, and would not hold any beauty at all if not for the interior paintings, the large gold statues of Guru Rinpoche and Chenrezig, and the magnificent view of the Kangra Valley below.

At one time the Dalai Lama was one of the most secluded leaders in the world, sequestered most of the year in his cavernous, thousand-room, 350-year-old Potala Palace. Perched atop Marpori Mountain in the capital city of Lhasa high on the remote Tibetan plateau, the Great Ocean of Wisdom spent his days studying ancient Buddhist texts and learning how to govern the religious and secular affairs of his far-flung kingdom. The theocratic country, separated from India to the south and China to the west by some of the highest mountain ranges on earth, was isolationist in the extreme. For the most part, Tibetans were not interested in the technological or scientific advances of the modern world, and only a small number of foreigners either ventured into or were welcomed in this land.

Yet today, far from his former obscurity, the Dalai Lama is one of the most well known, well traveled, and beloved leaders in the world. He was selected as one of *Time* magazine's top twenty Asians of the Century,[1] and is widely considered to be the greatest living exemplar of compassion. His teachings on kindness and universal responsibility, which are filled with sensible and practical concepts, draw tens of thousands of people at a time. Several of his three dozen books are international best-sellers, and he is regularly received by heads of state, from the president of Poland to the president of the United States.

His Holiness achieved tremendous international notoriety after receiving the Nobel Peace Prize in 1989. The Nobel Committee stated that the award was being given to the Dalai Lama for his consistent opposition to violence in his campaign to free Tibet, for his "concept of universal responsibility embracing all mankind as well as nature," and for his "forward-looking proposals for the solution of international conflicts, human rights issues, and global environmental problems." The committee further noted that "his reputation as a scholar and man of peace has grown steadily," and many institutions had conferred peace awards and honorary doctorates upon him in recognition of "his distinguished leadership in the service of freedom and peace."[2]

The Dalai Lama readily acknowledges that achieving world peace is an enormous goal and one that many people say is impossible. Human nature is violent, so-called realists argue, and nations will never refrain from attacking each other. Many people even argue that violence is a necessary evil in successful statecraft.

"Some people will say that while the Dalai Lama's devotion to non-violence is praiseworthy," he observes in a recent book, "it is not really practical. Actually, it is far more naive to suppose that the human-created problems which lead to violence can ever be solved through conflict."[3] He says, "I am convinced that the main reason so many people say the path of non-violence is impractical is because engaging in it seems daunting: we become discouraged." Arguing

that we must overcome this pessimism and discouragement, the
Dalai Lama notes,

> Peace is not something which exists independently of us, nor is
> war. It is true that certain individuals—political leaders, poli-
> cymakers, army generals—do have particularly grave respon-
> sibilities in respect to peace. However, these people do not
> come from nowhere. They are not born and brought up in
> outer space. Like us, they were nourished by their mother's
> milk and affection. They are members of our own human
> family and have been nurtured within the society which we as
> individuals have helped to create. Peace in the world thus
> depends on peace in the hearts of individuals.[4]

Some people will still argue, the Dalai Lama adds, that peace is
not workable in the "real world." "But while people are often content just to criticize and blame others for what goes wrong, surely
we should at least attempt to put forward constructive ideas. One
thing is for certain," he adds. "Given human beings' love of truth,
justice, peace, and freedom, creating a better, more compassionate
world is a genuine possibility. The potential is there."[5] His Holiness's greatest contribution lies in helping people of all countries,
religions, and races tap into and cultivate this potential.

Many political observers note that there is perhaps no more
important figure in Sino-Western relations than the Dalai Lama.
"The bespectacled figure in maroon robes," *Newsweek* stated, "has
become the focal point for the world's anxiety about Chinese
authoritarianism."[6] Always reminding the world of China's unjust
suppression of the Tibetan people, the Dalai Lama, reminiscent of
Gandhi's peaceful crusade to free India, has won friends on all sides
of the political spectrum.

Nearly every human rights organization and major Western state
agrees that China's human rights record in Tibet is appalling. The
U.S. State Department noted in a report released in March 2002,
"Chinese government authorities continued to commit serious
human rights abuses in Tibet, including instances of torture, arbitrary
arrest, detention without public trial, and lengthy detention of

Tibetan nationalists for peacefully expressing their political or religious views."[7] Great Britain's latest human rights report concluded that "the situation in Tibet remains particularly bleak,"[8] and Human Rights Watch declared that "the Chinese leadership's preoccupation with stability in the face of continued economic and social upheaval fueled an increase in human rights violations," especially in Tibet.[9] Alexander Solzhenitsyn described China's actions in Tibet as "more brutal and inhuman than any other communist regime in the world."

Over 1.2 million Tibetans (or one-fifth of the population) have died as a result of China's harsh occupation of Tibet, and tens of thousands have been arrested for their political views and tortured in the most horrendous ways conceivable. The Chinese are also pressing ahead with their goal of rendering an independent Tibet impossible by transferring millions of ethnic Chinese to Tibet and systematically destroying Tibetan culture. To date, over six thousand monasteries—the backbone of Tibetan culture—have been razed, ancient texts burned, and followers prevented from becoming monks or nuns. The once peaceful nation is now host to 300,000 to 500,000 Chinese troops and nearly a hundred nuclear missiles. The toll on the natural resources and wildlife has also been devastating.

Despite the terrible abuse against his people, his country, and his religion, the Dalai Lama steadfastly refuses to feel hatred toward the Chinese. "I have no hatred toward them," the Dalai Lama told me when I first met him in 1993 at his home in northern India. "The Chinese people have suffered too. Even the ones who are doing these terrible things to Tibet are suffering."

"I pray for Tibet every day. But, also, I pray for China," he told a reporter a few years later.[10]

The Chinese people, too, have a rich culture and long history. For thousands of years the Tibetans and the Chinese have lived side by side. Sometimes there were very happy moments. Sometimes there were very difficult moments. But one day they will see that my middle approach will bring us all genuine stability and unity. I am sure that a day will come when there will be good things, full of friendship, mutual respect and helping each other.[11]

"To me, feeling no hatred toward the Chinese didn't seem possible," the Dalai Lama's private secretary, Tenzin Geyche Tethong, told me frankly. "For decades now His Holiness has told people that *we* don't feel hatred toward the Chinese. I respectfully asked His Holiness to stop saying *we,* and instead say *I,* because it was not the reality that the rest of us didn't feel hatred. There wasn't a Tibetan family who had not been terribly affected by the Chinese occupation of Tibet, and we did feel hatred toward them. How can you expect people to have love, to have good feelings toward the Chinese? But then, years later," Tenzin continued, "when His Holiness began to meet with Chinese groups around the world, I noticed that these Chinese would express their support for His Holiness and his nonviolent struggle. They demonstrated their deep regret for what the Chinese government had done in Tibet. This opened my mind. It was deeply moving, and I knew that His Holiness was right. I became convinced that His Holiness was correct to tell us to develop good feelings toward the Chinese. And now, after many years, His Holiness has softened the hearts of Tibetans toward those who suppress them."

Though the Dalai Lama is well aware of his importance on the international stage, and the significance of his religious position to Buddhists, he is not a person who seeks out or even welcomes fame. "Dalai Lama means different things to different people," he writes in his autobiography, *Freedom in Exile.* "To some," he continues,

> it means that I am a living Buddha, the earthly manifestation of Avolikiteshvara, Bodhisattva of Compassion. To others it means that I am a "god-king." During the late 1950s it meant that I was a Vice-President of the Steering Committee of the People's Republic of China. Then when I escaped into exile, I was called a counter-revolutionary and a parasite. But none of these are my ideas. To me "Dalai Lama" is a title that signifies the office I hold. I myself am just a human being, and incidentally a Tibetan, who chooses to be a monk. It is as a simple monk that I offer this story of my life. . . .[12]

In fact, the Dalai Lama summarily dismisses the notion that he is a god-king. "Some consider me a living Buddha," he said in an interview. "That's nonsense. That's silly. That's wrong."[13] At every turn he tries to dispel the notion that he is a mystic, Eastern holy man with all the answers to life. "Individuals from all walks of life come to see me," he writes.

> Among these are people who have suffered greatly: some have lost parents and children; some have friends or family who have committed suicide; are sick with cancer or AIDS-related illness. Then, of course, there are fellow Tibetans with their own tales of hardship and suffering. Unfortunately, many have unrealistic expectations, supposing that I have healing powers or that I can give some sort of blessing. I am only an ordinary human being. The best I can do is try to help them by sharing in their suffering.[14]

"I must have heard a hundred times," I said to his private secretary, Tenzin Geyche, "that His Holiness appears to people, flies through the night into people's homes, purposely enters their dreams, and other such supernatural occurrences. What does His Holiness say about this?" I asked.

Tenzin furled his brow. "Oh, he totally disregards it!" he said firmly. "Even in public talks he often speaks about this. He says it is not true. He doesn't accept this at all. He tells people, 'I don't have any of these powers.' Some people come to him in very advanced stages of disease, and His Holiness says this is very stupid. 'You have to take care of yourself,' he tells them. He is very practical about this. But people will believe what they want to believe," he added with a laugh.

Yet no one who knows the Dalai Lama's story can legitimately see him solely as a simple monk or an ordinary man. His great fame, I believe, comes from his great abilities: an intelligence, compassion, and wisdom far beyond normal.

The Great Fourteenth Dalai Lama was born in a small stone and mud house in Takster, a tiny village in the northeastern Tibetan province of Amdo. He was named Lhamo Dhundrup, and he lived his first few years as a typical farm boy. His father was a modest, hardworking man with a quick temper. His mother was a kind and patient woman who, in the Dalai Lama's words, "was loved by all who knew her."[15] His mother would carry him on her back as she went to work tending their fields of barley, buckwheat, and potatoes. She would also take him to milk the *dzomos* (a cross between a yak and a cow) and to look after the chickens. The Dalai Lama still recalls how he enjoyed sitting on the hen's nests and making clucking noises.

The young Lhamo Dhundrup was said to be very strong willed, obstinate, and mischievous and would lose his temper if he was denied anything. He was possessive and would not allow his siblings (of which he had seven) to call *his* mom "Mother." Only his mother was permitted to touch his bowl, and he demanded to sit at the head of the table. He was completely intolerant of fighting and would intercede on behalf of the underdog, brandishing a stick if need be.[16]

In 1937 the young boy's life would change forever. A party of monks, led to Takster by visions and auspicious signs, arrived at his front door disguised as merchants. They had been dispatched secretly by the central government in Lhasa to find the reincarnation of the deceased Thirteenth Dalai Lama. The monks had reason to believe that Lhamo Dhundrup might be the child for whom they had been searching. The precocious young boy showed no fear of the strangers. To everyone's surprise, he called out to one of the men posing as a servant. "Sera Lama, Sera Lama!" he declared. Indeed, the man was a lama (a teacher) from Sera monastery. The boy was then given an array of difficult tests. When presented with various objects, he would choose those that had belonged to the Thirteenth Dalai Lama, proclaiming, "It's mine. It's mine." As he passed each test with ease, it soon became apparent to the monks that the boy, who was barely two and a half years old, was indeed the reincarnated Holder of the White Lotus, the ruler of Tibet.

Amid a huge procession, the young boy was taken on the three-month journey to Lhasa and eventually installed on the Lion Throne in Potala Palace in the winter of 1940. A regent governed the country while the Dalai Lama completed his rigorous religious education.

Ten years after the Dalai Lama's ascent to the throne, the newly created People's Republic of China launched a massive invasion of Tibet across the Drichu River east of the province of Chamdo. Eighty-four thousand troops of the People's Liberation Army (PLA) launched the initial assault. Most of Tibet's ragtag and ill-equipped army of eighty-five hundred men were quickly vanquished. Radio Peking announced that the invasion was part of the PLA's mission to liberate the country from "imperialist oppression" and to "secure China's western borders." In a blatant perversion of history, the Chinese also declared that Tibet was and always had been an integral part of the Chinese motherland.

China's primary aims were twofold. First, China wished to create a buffer zone against invasion from the west, either by a European power (particularly Britain, which had set itself up as a broker between China and Tibet through a 1904 military incursion), or by India or the Soviet Union. The Chinese also seemed never to have forgotten that, roughly fifteen hundred years before, pre-Buddhist Tibet had invaded China and sacked its capital. In addition, China wished to capture Tibet's vast natural resources. The Chinese had long called Tibet *Xizang,* or "the Western Treasure House," and coveted the enormous tracts of unpopulated land, the huge quantities of timber, mineral deposits, and animals, all of which China lacked.[17]

Though His Holiness was only fifteen years old at the time, many officials called for him to assume full control over the government in the face of the crisis. They had faith that their Precious Protector could save them from enslavement at the hands of the Chinese. Others, however, argued that he was much too young and inexperienced to handle the complicated affairs of state, especially during a time of national emergency. "I agreed with the latter group," the Dalai Lama later wrote, "but, unfortunately, I was not consulted." The government decided that the matter should be put to an oracle, who would serve as a medium (or *kuten*) to confer with Dorje Drakden, a deity said to protect Tibet from harm. As the Dalai Lama recalls, "It was a very tense occasion, at the end of which the kuten, tottering under the weight of his huge, ceremonial head-dress, came over to where I sat and laid a kata, a white silk offering scarf, on my lap with the words '*Thu-la bap,*' 'His time has come.'"[18]

Though the young leader proved effective among his own people, he could do little to expel the Chinese invaders. The international community ignored Tibet's pleas for help, leaving this previously isolated and peaceful country of 6 million people alone in its confrontation with the most populous nation on earth.

China's welcoming of its Tibetan "brothers" "back to the motherland" was anything but warm. The PLA simply took whatever it needed from the Tibetan people without regard to consequences. Food, houses, animals, machinery, and natural resources of all kinds were commandeered. Within nine months of the invasion, the PLA had devastated the economy of the capital city, Lhasa, and the Tibetans faced the first famine that they had ever known.

The Dalai Lama hoped to alleviate the crisis by going to China to meet with Mao Tse-tung and Chou En-lai in July 1954. He was received with great fanfare and warm welcomes by the Chinese and was soon given access to Mao. The two engaged in long conversations. Mao impressed the Dalai Lama as a man sincerely dedicated to the plight of the peasants. "Chairman Mao did not look too intelligent," the Dalai Lama noted. Instead, he looked "something like an old farmer from the countryside. Yet his bearing indicated a real leader. His self-confidence was firm, he had a sincere feeling for the nation and people, and also, I believe, he demonstrated great concern for myself."[19]

That is not to say that His Holiness failed to perceive that Mao was a dictator and was bitterly opposed to the "poison" of religion. The Dalai Lama was deeply disturbed by Mao's diatribe against religion, but the Dalai Lama did believe that Mao would keep his promises that Tibet would be treated with respect and would be able to govern itself as an autonomous region of China. "I thought my visit to China had helped in two ways," the Dalai Lama declared. "It had certainly showed me exactly what we were up against, and, which was more important, it seemed to have persuaded the Chinese not to go ahead with the original plan, which Mao had admitted, of governing us directly from Peking through a military and political committee. Instead, we seemed to have been left with some authority over our own internal affairs, and we seemed to have a firm promise of autonomy."[20] The Dalai Lama hoped that if Tibet was unable to get rid of the Chinese invaders, at least the two countries could live together peacefully.

But Mao's promises were worthless. By 1959 the situation in Tibet had grown desperate. The Chinese army was brutalizing the Tibetan people, killing tens of thousands of resisters, imprisoning dissenters, and committing many crimes against civilians.[21] His Holiness was treated with disrespect and was forced to live virtually under house arrest. Finally, he was directly threatened by the Chinese army; indeed, several mortar shells were fired at his residence. The Dalai Lama knew that if anything happened to him, it would lead to a violent rebellion that would ensure the annihilation of many of his people. Faced with these circumstances, he and his advisers concluded that he should flee Tibet and try to rally international support for the enslaved country. Dorje Drakden was again consulted and, communicating through the Nechung Kuten (the medium of the state oracle of Tibet), revealed the safest time and route for a daring escape through the lines of the Chinese army.

On March 10, 1959, after a harrowing trek through the high mountains of southern Tibet, exhausted and extremely ill, the Dalai Lama finally crossed the Indian border into exile. It is said that when he learned of the escape, Mao exclaimed, "In that case, we have lost the battle."

For the Dalai Lama, however, an enormous battle was just beginning. The first twelve months of his exile were, in his words, a "desperate year." While he tried unsuccessfully to enlist India, the United States, Britain, and a number of other countries to intercede in the Chinese invasion of Tibet, tens of thousands of refugees streamed across the Tibetan border into India. Destitute and ill from the treacherous journey over the high Himalayas, thousands of Tibetans gathered at Missamari and the former British prisoner-of-war camp of Buxa Duar, both next to the Bhutanese border. Unequipped for and unaccustomed to the heat and the diseases in India, many refugees died. The Dalai Lama had to take immediate action to save his people.

One of the most immediate changes the Dalai Lama made was to insist that the people around him dispense with some of the formalities and courtesies shown to his office. For instance, he stipulated that visitors would sit on a chair of equal height to his, and most visitors were dissuaded from prostrating before him. This sounds like a small change now, but to Tibetans at the time it was a radical departure from their old ways. The Dalai Lama was trying to get people to modernize their thinking and wished to foster more candid and direct discourse. "I was determined," he has written, "to be entirely open, to show everything and not hide behind etiquette. In this way I hoped that people would relate to me as one human to another."[22]

The Dalai Lama proved to be an extremely progressive and astute administrator. He successfully lobbied Prime Minister Nehru for suitable settlements for his people and established governmental departments that would organize and facilitate communication among these far-separated settlements. Modernizing his government, he created offices of information, education, rehabilitation, security, religious affairs, and economic affairs. Women were encouraged to play an important part in Tibetan governance, and he reminded people that all positions should be filled based on qualifications, not gender. Refugees were given assistance in settling in their new country, orphans were housed and looked after, schools were established, and a parliament was formed to help the Dalai Lama improve life for Tibetans.

Though much of the money needed by the Tibetans was donated by the Indian government and international aid organizations, some of it came from the sale of Tibetan treasures that had been hidden in Sikkim in the 1950s. The sale generated eight million dollars on the open market. Unfortunately, unscrupulous people managed to swindle away most of those funds by convincing the Tibetan government-in-exile to invest in a paper mill and other schemes. The remaining one million or so was used to form the Dalai Lama's charitable trust, which aided thousands of needy people.

By 1965 the refugees had improved their lot considerably and were no longer living in utter desperation. Religious and cultural traditions were flourishing, and their economic situation was beginning to improve. Tibetans opened shops, established farms, learned English and Hindi, and began to take their case for independence into the world arena. But life for the Tibetans would remain hard (as it still does today), and the sadness of their enormous loss would always lie close to the surface. If not for the continual encouragement by the Dalai Lama, their most beloved leader and greatest strength, Tibetans readily declare that they never would have made it this far.

A key element in the Dalai Lama's enduring, immense popularity in all parts of the world is his straightforward and meaningful observations about the human condition. "We have, in my view, created a society in which people find it harder and harder to show one another basic affection," he writes in a recent book.

> In place of the sense of community and belonging, which we find such a reassuring feature of less wealthy (and generally rural) societies, we find a high degree of loneliness and alienation. Despite the fact that millions live in close proximity to one another, it seems that many people, especially among the old, have no one to talk to but their pets. Modern industrial society often strikes me as being like a huge self-propelled machine. Instead of human beings in charge, each individual is a tiny, insignificant component with no choice but to move when the machine moves. All this is compounded by the contemporary rhetoric of growth and economic development, which greatly reinforces people's tendency toward competitiveness and envy.[23]

People in the West, the Dalai Lama further observes,

> are so caught up with the idea of acquiring still more that they make no room for anything else in their lives. In their absorption, they actually lose the dream of happiness, which riches were to have provided. As a result, they are constantly tormented, torn between doubt about what might happen and the hope of gaining more, and plagued with mental and emotional suffering—even though outwardly they may appear to be leading entirely successful and comfortable lives. This is suggested both by the high degree and by the disturbing prevalence [in] materially developed countries of anxiety, discontent, frustration, uncertainty, and depression.[24]

It is not that the Dalai Lama has all the answers for lasting happiness. "It seems to me that you have very astutely outlined the basis of social problems in the West: intense competition, insecurity, isolation," I noted during one of our first meetings. "This is such an enormous dilemma to be overcome. Where do we begin?" I asked seriously.

The Dalai Lama paused. A smile flashed across his face, and he began laughing. "Hmmmm . . . it is much easier to see the problem than to find the answer!" he replied. Yet he challenges us to work together to find the answers and to find happiness in the cooperative effort itself.

The Dalai Lama encourages people to be something more than their titles, houses, cars, and incomes. He provokes people to recognize that it isn't their social position or their looks that are important but rather what they do to promote lasting happiness in their heart and in their society. He consistently calls for a consciousness of compassion and community, and he makes individuals he encounters, whether in a huge crowd or alone with him in a room, feel as important, worthy, and holy as he is.

Indeed, this was my experience during three separate meetings with him at his home. In Buddhist philosophy great masters are supposed to see the Buddha nature in everyone, but the Dalai Lama actually puts this into practice. Sitting there with him, I observed a person who was entirely accessible, down-to-earth, and brotherly. The truly remarkable experience, to me, was how he was able to make me feel his equal, to make me feel at ease and comfortable examining and even debating his views. He also told me repeatedly how much he enjoyed my sense of humor. "If someone comes to me and is serious," he said, "I too will be serious, and I will not feel very comfortable. It will not be so enjoyable. But you come to me smiling, laughing, and I feel comfortable and I enjoy it."

Unlike many religious leaders, the Dalai Lama does not make any effort to proselytize. He has no wish to swell the ranks or increase the wealth and power of Tibetan Buddhism. In fact, he often tells people that switching faiths is unnecessary and perhaps even harmful. "I'm not looking to turn anyone away from their faith, if they practice it with tolerance," he says. "I always say that people should not rush to change religions. There is real value in finding the spiritual resources you need in your home religion."[25] Buddhists, he says frankly and earnestly, "do not own the universal truth; we can only offer the results of a very long reflection, which is ours."

In fact, he advocates the creation of a new, worldwide spirituality that is centered not on any one faith but rather upon the notion that at the heart of every individual is compassion. "We need a new concept, a lay spirituality," he declares. "We ought to promote this concept, with the help of scientists. It could lead us to set up what we are all looking for, a secular morality. I believe in it deeply. And I think we need it so the world can have a better future."[26]

"In speaking of having a spiritual dimension to our lives," the Dalai Lama said in one of his public talks,

> we have identified our religious belief as one level of spirituality. Now regarding religion, if we believe in any religion, that's good. But even without a religious belief, we can still manage. In some cases, we can manage even better. But that's our own individual right; if we wish to believe, good! If not, it's all right. But then there's another level of spirituality. That is what I call basic spirituality—basic human qualities of goodness, kindness, compassion, caring. Whether we are believers or nonbelievers, this kind of spirituality is essential. I personally consider the second level of spirituality to be more important than the first. . . .[27]

Whether a person is Jewish, Christian, Muslim, Hindu, Buddhist, agnostic, or atheist, the important thing is that he or she live with compassion. "We can reject every form of religion," the Dalai Lama states, "but we can't reject and cast off compassion and peace of mind."

The Dalai Lama uses his own life as an example of the benefits of peace of mind:

> Every day I experience the benefits of peace of mind. It's very good for the body. As you might imagine, I am a rather busy

man. I take many responsibilities upon myself, activities, trips,
speeches. All that no doubt is a very heavy burden, and still I
have the blood pressure of a baby.... What's good for me is
good for other people. I have no doubt on that score. Good
food, a struggle against every excessive desire, daily meditation, all that can lead to peace of mind; and peace of mind is
good for the body. Despite all the difficulties of life, of which
I've had my share, we can all feel that effect.[28]

Though a champion of progressive social policy, such as using
birth control to curb population growth and redistributing wealth
to the underprivileged, the Dalai Lama remains steadfast in his
opposition to abortion. In his view, the fetus represents a living
being, and it is unconscionable for a Buddhist to take the life of a
living being. No argument, no matter how well intentioned, will
sway the Dalai Lama from his view in this matter. And though he
has admitted that the logical foundations are unclear, he upholds
the moral code formed in ancient India that includes strange rules
about the proper place and time for sexual intercourse and that pro-
hibits masturbation and oral sex. "But I am not the one to decide
these things," he concedes. "All leaders of Buddhism should meet
and decide whether the prohibitions are warranted."

That said, perhaps no religious leader has spoken more clearly
about the injustice of discrimination against religious or ethnic
minorities, women, and gays. And both in his plans for a free Tibet
and in his establishment of a Tibetan government-in-exile, he is
absolutely dedicated to democracy. As far as his office is concerned,
the Dalai Lama sees a day when his leadership is no longer necessary. "Of course," he adds, "if my people say that they need me, I
will be there for them. But I think the government should be run by
elected officials." Indeed, even now the Dalai Lama defers most
matters of governance to the *Kashag,* the cabinet, and the elected
parliament.

When I arrived in Dharamsala seeking an audience with the Dalai
Lama, I checked into my usual monastery guest house—a Spartan
room with a breathtaking view of the mountains but little heat and

plenty of noise from the surrounding houses. I called the Dalai Lama's private office, only to find that he was out of town. I was told that there was little chance that he would be able to meet with me since he had many commitments before a scheduled retreat. I could do little but wait for him to return and continue to pray for a private audience.

In the meantime, a fierce winter storm began. The thunder echoing through the mountains was so loud that it caused everything in my room to shake. The wind drove the torrential rains against my windows and through any crack it could find. Water was blown beneath my door and fanned out on the tile floor. I spent the better part of three days huddled under blankets, dressed in two undershirts, an outer shirt, a sweater, a vest, a knit hat, long johns and jeans, and two pairs of socks—and still shook from the cold.

When the storm finally ended, the mountains were covered with snow. They were brilliant white, emphasizing each jagged crag and peak. The end of the storm was not the only good news. A monk knocked on my door with a message. His Holiness's private office had telephoned and said that the Dalai Lama had an opening in his schedule and could receive me for a short meeting in a few days' time.

When I entered the Dalai Lama's compound I surrendered my passport to a Tibetan guard. Officially, protection of the Dalai Lama is carried out by soldiers from the Indian army, but agents from the Tibetan security office actually outnumber the soldiers. After being signed in, I was escorted to a waiting room, where an official searched my belongings and patted me down to ensure that I wasn't carrying any weapons.

About ten minutes later I was asked to follow an official who led me at breakneck speed up a path toward the Dalai Lama's reception room. Outside the room I was greeted by Tenzin Geyche, who informed me that His Holiness would be arriving shortly. Just a few seconds later I heard the telltale sound of the Dalai Lama's laughter.

The Dalai Lama smiled at me and nodded hello as he approached. With his robe draped over his arm, he extended his hand toward me. I bowed deeply and presented him with a few roses bound together by a yellow silk scarf, which he quickly took and handed off to his assistant. I greeted him in Tibetan, calling him Yeshi Norbu, the Tibetan equivalent of Your Holiness.

"Yeshi Norbu, Yeshi Norbu!" he repeated as he laughed. Few Westerners use these words. "Okay, okay," he said to me, clasping my hands in his effort to get me to stop bowing before him.

His assistant told him that I wished to have a few photographs of us, and he grabbed my hand and turned me so that the sunlight was in our faces. After a few pictures were snapped, I took the camera to take a few shots of him. He began to coach me on the best camera angles. "Turn it, like this," he said. "Okay, now take it," he commanded.

The Dalai Lama led me to his receiving room and motioned for me to sit down. He stood above his seat, folded his robe, and dropped down hard into his chair, breathing out heavily. I could see him collecting himself, becoming mindful of the present moment, and focusing his attention solely on our discussion. Within a few seconds he looked very content and welcoming. After thanking him for receiving me, I jumped right into my questioning.

"Your Holiness," I asked, "I'm writing about the future of peace, of how we can create it. So I want to ask you first of all what peace really is."

He nodded. "Peace is not just the absence of violence," he said resolutely. "Peace should be seen as much more. On the level of human interaction, peace involves satisfaction, happiness, and tranquillity. Peace is actually, I believe, an expression of compassion, a sense of caring. On this level, I think even the animals can enjoy peace. If they are not harmed and they have food, they can enjoy a life without fear. On the level of higher consciousness, peace is an inner achievement which is developed through practice, through meditation, by believing in either a Creator or one's own responsibility. And if you see there is violence, some problem existing somewhere, and you remain disconnected from that problem, then that is not nonviolence," he continued. "If you are seeing that there is a problem, but you fail to get involved, you are just watching the suffering of others, and that is not nonviolence. Nonviolence requires that you are fully engaged in the problem, fully involved, trying to solve the problem. But without adding any harm to the situation. And, so here, I think the main factor is compassion.

"If you have compassion," he continued, "a sense of caring, a sense of concern, even if you may use some harsh words, essentially you are nonviolent. Otherwise, with such motivation as wanting to cheat someone, or wanting to gain some bigger thing by giving some small thing, that is violent. For example, if you give one hundred rupees in order to get in return one thousand rupees, that is not really charity. It is not really giving. Using nice words, nice actions, nice smiles, and making gifts in order to cheat, to deceive, or to manipulate, that is violent."

"How are cheating and lying acts of violence?" I questioned.

"Because you are harming! Ultimately, you are exploiting!" he said emphatically. "You are disregarding a person's right to happiness. Even though the consequence of your actions causes others to have a painful experience, you have no feeling about them. You are just thinking about your own ability to gain. It is, I think, even the worst kind of violence. Actually, the animals cannot do it. Animals may adopt some tricks, very superficially, but in the long run, that kind of serious cheating animals cannot do; that kind of deep, sophisticated cheating is something only people do. So, I think we are wonderful!" he joked. "We can do all sorts of destructive things," he said, laughing. "We are experts in this line, because of our intelligence."

"That's the negative side of intelligence," I noted.

"Yes, that's the negative side. But on the positive side, only human beings can develop infinite altruism. Animals cannot."

"What do you mean exactly by 'infinite altruism'?" I asked.

"Well, you know, according to Buddhist practice, we think that all sentient beings—not just human beings, and not just sentient beings in this universe or this galaxy but in limitless galaxies—are trying to develop some sense of concern toward all other sentient beings. We always pray that all sentient beings will achieve permanent happiness. So, that's infinite altruism! Of course, at the beginning, these are just words. But then if you meditate on these things and practice, eventually you will develop some kind of deep feeling: you are ready to sacrifice your own life for the benefit of others.

That is infinite altruism. So, infinite altruism is possible because of human intelligence, because of wisdom. Without wisdom, that kind of altruism cannot develop. That is the positive side of human intelligence."

The Dalai Lama looked deeply into my eyes then smiled widely. He has a smile that brightens a room, that lifts one's heart. Yet I noticed that it is also tinged with a boyish mischievousness. I had heard that he likes to clown around, like the time at a conference when he kept trying to tip Archbishop Desmond Tutu out of his chair, to which Tutu responded, "You are a naughty boy!"

"Your Holiness," I asked, "I'm curious to know, who have been your greatest teachers about peace?"

He contemplated for a moment then answered. "I've had seventeen tutors, and each one of them taught me something. In recent times, of course, I had two principal tutors, and I learned a great deal from them, especially the senior tutor. Then also, in 1967 Khunu Rinpoche gave me teaching in that," he said, pointing to a book I had put on the table in front of me, *Guide to the Bodhisattva's Way of Life* by the Buddhist teacher Shantideva. "I received teachings on that text from him. As far as my practice of *bodhicitta* [enlightened mind, or altruism] is concerned, after I received the teaching on Shantideva's book, I myself meditated and put great effort into my meditation on peace and compassion."

"Did Gandhi influence your thinking about peace?" I asked.

"Gandhi. Yes, of course. In the freedom struggle in India, Gandhi implemented a nonviolent philosophy, very effectively and very wisely. In my own case, in Tibet's freedom struggle, there are similarities. I think at the last moment just before gaining independence from Britain Gandhi wanted India united. Right from the beginning he opposed the partition with Pakistan. He was even ready to offer the prime ministership to Jinna [the Muslim leader]. You see, it seems that he considered that peace was more important than political power. I deeply agree with him on this point."

"In fact," I noted, "Gandhi was killed by a Hindu who said that Gandhi had made too many concessions and given too much power to the Muslims. He was very conciliatory for the sake of peace."

"Yes. And I heard that at the time of partition, Gandhi wanted to go the border of India and Pakistan, but he was stopped by the people around him. I have been told such stories. He had great courage. Another fact which very much impressed me was that he remained at the forefront of the fight for independence, but when independence came, he remained outside of power. He was opposed to retaining a position in the government. Practically everywhere else, the leader of the freedom fighters retains some position of power after independence is achieved." The Dalai Lama laughed to punctuate his forthcoming point. "Gandhi, I think, was very clever. He knew that if he took some kind of power, he might ruin his reputation."

"Sometimes it's wise to know when you've done enough, isn't it?" I said.

"Yes, I think so. I think it was great that he didn't strive to gain power for himself. I was also impressed by his way of life. He was thoroughly educated in the West, but he never departed from the rest of the Indian people or the Indian way of life. I find that impressive."

"It seems to me, Your Holiness, that a great many of the conflicts in the world have been caused or worsened by religious sectarianism. Religious adherents seem to say, 'We're right and you're wrong.' And then attack each other. Do you, as a religious leader yourself, have a solution to this problem?"

"Yes. Since you and I are both Buddhists, to us Buddhism is best. Buddhism is the only religion, the only truth we follow. But now, on a human level, on the level of community and society, there cannot be a concept of only one religion or only one truth. There are many religions, and many religions are providing benefits to many different people. So, therefore, in a community we must say that there are many truths. There is pluralism. That, I feel, is the only proper way to work out the differences and confrontations between different believers. Several religions, several truths on the community level; one religion, one truth on the individual level. I admit that to me, Buddhism is the only religion. But that is merely *to me.* Because Buddhism is the most effective religion to me, I can't think about following the idea of a Creator. It is difficult for me to conceive of this. But to another member of the community, such as a

Christian practitioner, to him or to her, Christianity is the most effective belief. Therefore, to Christians, Christianity is the only religion, the only truth. So, if you put one Buddhist and one Christian together," he said, bringing his index fingers together to emphasize the point, "you have a pluralism of beliefs. That is the reality of the situation.

"Actually," he continued after a short pause, "I think when we talk about religion, about faith, that is primarily an individual's business. That's my feeling. But each of us must recognize that all other religions have the potential—whether it is the same potential or not, at least have some potential—to provide satisfaction or inner peace or tranquillity to humanity. To me, I have full conviction that Christianity and Islam and Hinduism—in fact all the great religions—have equal power to provide inner peace and tranquillity to millions of people. In the past several centuries, these great religious traditions have helped to provide inner peace and define the purpose of life. Today millions of people can benefit from these religions. And they can in the future as well. So, there are plenty of reasons to recognize the potential of all religions to help humanity. Therefore, I feel there is a real possibility to create harmony among the religious traditions."

"But what is the best way to promote harmony among religions?" I asked. "You can't just say it should exist. You must make it happen," I observed.

"Ah, yes," he replied. "I have five points, or five ways to improve this harmony. Number one, we should have meetings between scholars from different religious traditions to make clear on the academic level what are the differences and what are the similarities. Then, second, we should have meetings between people from the different religious traditions who have some inner experience as a result of their practice of their religious tradition. They can exchange their inner, special experiences. This is very powerful to introduce the helpfulness of the religious tradition on the individual level. I think some Christians as a result of meeting me, or meeting some genuine Buddhist, through this they change their attitude toward Buddhism. Similarly, as a result of my meeting Christian practitioners, reciting their prayers or participating in their different rituals, I can see that they are very good human beings. One can almost see the ultimate result: the expression of all the good human qualities in them. This is what happened during my meetings with the late Thomas Merton, with Christian monks in Spain, France, Austria, and America, and also of course with the late Mother Teresa. I think these are such great, wonderful people. This comes as a result of their practice.

"Third, we should take group pilgrimages to different holy places of the different traditions. Going together, praying together, or even in silent meditation, we understand each other better. With this belief, I visited Jerusalem, and Lourdes in France, and other places, not as a tourist but as a believer. In Jerusalem, in front of the rock at the blue-domed mosque, I wanted to put a *kata* there in respect. But the manager there was very reluctant to let me do it. But all right, it doesn't matter. I stood in front of the rock and reflected on all the millions of Muslims who get inspiration from this great tradition of Islam. Similarly, in Lourdes, in front of the statue of Mary and by drinking the holy water, I got this feeling that in this place, millions of people who are seeking some satisfaction get some inspiration. I myself, in that moment, joined that kind of feeling. Several years ago I adopted this practice, so I often tell of my experience to my brothers and sisters. Many of them really appreciate or agree with my positions, and now I think that this practice is catching on. One day, I think it would be wonderful if the heads of the different religious traditions started to make these pilgrimages. Like His Holiness the Pope, the head of the Christian Orthodox Church, a Muslim, and a Hindu leader all come together at Bodhgaya [the holiest Buddhist site in the world]. I don't know . . . ," he said, bursting into laughter.

"So, you have picked the spot already!" I teased.

He laughed. "If the Buddhist leaders, like the Someja of Thailand, go to Mecca, I think that would be wonderful too. Except, I must say, it must be without animal sacrifice!" he added with a volley of laughter. "But I fear that maybe in circling the holy site, we may not end up going the same way around. We may go this way and they may go that way, and," he paused, colliding his fists together and laughing, "we may have some confrontation anyway!"

"So, you spiritual leaders will need to pay attention to pragmatic concerns. You may need to bring traffic police with you," I joked.

He laughed heartily. "Yes!" When he stopped laughing he continued with his five-point plan. "The fourth point is that religious leaders should have the spirit, like the spirit of Assisi, to come together to talk peacefully in front of the eyes of millions of people. I think that is a very strong signal to the followers of the religious traditions who might be fighting somewhere. Exchanging bright words, in some cases perhaps very sincere prayers, I think that would be very good.

"And fifth is a point which has been suggested by Archbishop Tutu. We need to engage in volunteer work, in cooperative work involving the different traditions. That also gives us an opportunity to forget about our own tradition and work together as brothers and sisters. I think that is an excellent idea."

"That sounds very practical to me, and I think that would go a long way to end religious fighting. But I think that the trouble in establishing peace is not with the true believers who have a strong conviction that they should do right, but rather with those who don't sincerely believe in the teachings of their own faith about peace," I declared.

"True. That is true," he said, nodding. "So, here, I usually believe, or suggest, in order to reduce fundamentalism, we should do two things: One, the follower of the religious tradition should truly implement peace in his or her daily life. Through that way, you will gain some deeper experience, and as a result, once you get some spiritual experience, it is much easier to see the value of other religious traditions also. In many cases where people don't practice properly, instead of the religion overpowering the negative qualities of the human being—harmful attachments, negative aggression, hatred, manipulation—the negative qualities seem to overpower the religion. In that case, the practitioners are manipulating religion for their own purpose. Some, worst of all, manipulate religion for political power. They use religion. Once you use religion, you cloud it with emotion, emotion goes out of control, and you no longer have the ability to judge, to reason. In order to prevent this, the religious believer should implement the religious teachings as much as possible. That is one thing.

"Second, we must recognize our interdependence. Nowadays, the world situation has completely changed. It is a new situation. In reality, we live like one whole. Even in a small, remote place like Dharamsala, you can find things from all over the world: food, material, clothing items. So, therefore, if economic disaster occurs on one continent, for example, the share market in Tokyo or Hong Kong or Korea, these things have repercussions in London or New York. That is today's world. Now, therefore, since we have to live together with different religious believers, it is very essential to know the other religious traditions. And also now, we have much more opportunity to learn other religious traditions. So each of us should make acquaintance with other religious traditions. I think this is very helpful to help reduce fundamentalist thinking.

"For example, the Muslims of Indonesia, the Muslims of Malaysia, the Muslims of India, and the Muslims of Arab countries have big differences. Indonesia has Buddhist and Hindu influences there. In Malaysia, there are also many Buddhists—practically all the Chinese community, I think, is Buddhist. I think Hindus are also there. In India, especially in Kerala, a Christian community, a Muslim community, and a Hindu community live together. Because of those circumstances, because they are so used to one another, when they meet someone from another religious faith, they say, 'Okay, he is Muslim,' but nothing more than that. In Arab countries in the Middle East, however, when one Buddhist or one Hindu or one Christian comes, there is something very strange about it. Nowadays I think it is possible, and very important, to have closer contact with other religions. These methods, if implemented sincerely, and if we make more acquaintance with other religious traditions, I think will reduce fundamentalist attitudes."

"Of course, you'll never reach all the fundamentalists who believe that their god or their prophet told them that they have to go and change everyone else," I suggested.

"Yes, there will always be some who will remain fundamentalist. Our Tibetan community is now having a new experience with fundamentalism. Have you heard?" he asked, laughing.

His Holiness was referring to a controversy that arose in recent years in the Tibetan Buddhist community involving the worship of a figure called Shugden. "Some of them are really fanatic," he declared, shaking his head quickly.

Shugden worship is a complicated matter that is somewhat like the worship of an ancient indigenous deity by natives who converted to Catholicism. Unfortunately, according to the Dalai Lama, the practice flies in the face of Buddha's teachings. Therefore, all Dalai Lamas from the Fifth to the Thirteenth (and now the Fourteenth) have tried to stop the practice.

"I made it clear that as far as the Tibetan government is concerned, they are not to practice any rituals to Shugden. As far as a private individual is concerned, I did not interfere. But eventually the Shugden practice spread to England and America. So I saw a new danger. These young, new Buddhists in these countries, in many cases, come to follow Buddhism because they have some problems in their life. So they are in sort of a weak position, ready to accept almost anything. In their eyes, this spirit, Shugden, is very powerful, a very good protector. Then they put 100 percent faith in this practice, since they are seeking protection or are seeking help. Meanwhile, the Buddha is far away in their mind."

"I have to say, Your Holiness, worshiping a spirit at the expense of the Buddha is, for Buddhists, simply wrong."

"Yes! It is wrong! Absolutely wrong! Oh, yes, yes," he proclaimed adamantly. "As Buddhists, our protectors are Buddha, dharma, and sangha [the teacher, the truth, and the community of practitioners seeking truth]. Spirits are not included in these. Also to some extent in the Tibetan community, I think, due to lack of Buddhist knowledge, although there is a very strong Buddhist faith there, they do not truly know what Buddhism is. So as a result, they are in danger. Profound Buddhism eventually degenerates into spirit worship. In the Tibetan tradition, consulting spirits is simply what we call *dregpa*. We can ask them for some help, as a helper, that's all."

"This brings up another question in my mind. How do you react to sectarianism within Buddhism?" I asked.

"One time, many years ago," he answered, "twenty years ago, a sincere practitioner from Kulu came to see me, and he requested that I give him a teaching, some guidance about a meditation practice called *dzogchen*. I didn't feel that I knew enough about it, that I really didn't have enough knowledge about dzogchen. Today, I think I know a little bit about it, but still not so much." Here, in typical but sincere fashion, he was being humble, for he authored a book not long ago about dzogchen. "But at that time," he continued, "I told him I have no experience, so it's better to go to another teacher and ask him. Then, as a practitioner of *bodhicitta,* of altruism, I made a pledge to help, to serve every sentient being. Now, in this case, a human being, and someone from the Tibetan culture, a Tibetan Buddhist, was seeking advice from the Dalai Lama regarding a Tibetan Buddhist tradition, and I failed to provide him with information. I feel this was a mistake, and I feel very sorry about it. So, when we make a *bodhicitta* vow, there is no such vow as 'I will serve only the Gelugpa tradition.' No! I will serve all sentient beings. That is my duty."

We had already spent over an hour talking, and the Dalai Lama had to tend to other business. I was thankful that he had made time to see me at all. Yet I was quite surprised when he conferred with his private secretary then turned to me and said, "Come back and we will talk more. Come back next month. Okay?"

"Yes, of course. I'd love to," I said eagerly. "Thank you."

"I like talking with you," he said. "I enjoy it. Okay, good-bye now," he said as he walked briskly out of the room.

I had over a month to ponder my conversation with the Dalai Lama before I returned to see him again. His private secretary told me that it was unusual to be invited back for a second meeting on the same topic. I felt grateful for the opportunity.

I flew to Vietnam and spent four weeks exploring the country. I was deeply moved when I visited the museums housing weapons from the Vietnam War (what the Vietnamese understandably call the American War). The brutality of what was done in Vietnam takes on a whole new meaning when you are standing on Vietnamese soil.

Taking solace in the Dalai Lama's words, and praying that his wisdom takes root in all corners of the world, was the only way my heavy heart could leave the museums and enjoy the smiling faces of the children running around the streets.

Back in Dharamsala a month later, Tenzin Geyche escorted me to the door of the Dalai Lama's receiving room and motioned for me to enter. I had just sat down and opened my bag when the Dalai Lama strode in unexpectedly. I jumped to my feet. "Your Holiness! You surprised me," I said, clasping my hands together and bowing slightly in a gesture of reverence.

His Holiness reached out and took my hand. He squinted his eyes, leaned toward me, and said, "Good to see you again," as he motioned for me to take my seat.

I hurriedly reached into my bag and took out a *kata* and offered it to him. He took it and let it slip slowly through his hand onto the table in front of us. I presented him with an envelope containing a letter of appreciation and a monetary gift, which he held between his hands and stared at deeply before setting down. Then I took out a small box containing a glass pagoda from Thailand and also a small container of incense and a Buddhist tassel from Vietnam.

"I want to apologize for the state of the box," I said, showing the Dalai Lama its crumbled lid and small teeth marks. "The monkeys got into my room yesterday and bit your gifts!" He laughed robustly.

"It must have been Hanuman!" he joked, referring to the Hindu monkey god.

When our laughter subsided, he touched the glass pagoda to his head, set it down, then sat back in his chair with a warm smile on his face.

"Your Holiness, it seems to me that not everyone agrees that peace, avoiding violence and anger, is one of the most important aspects of life. Many people talk about the virtues of peace but also promote violence whenever it suits them. Why, in your opinion, is peace so important, first to the individual and, second, to society?"

"To answer your question, let me be clear that peace is a concept that involves sentient beings, animals and human beings, not such things as rocks and trees, which do not, I think, experience pain or pleasure.

There is also a third sort of experience, which is a neutral state, lacking either pain or pleasure, but this is not important in our discussion of peace. Peace is very much related with happiness. I think, generally speaking, the essential nature of happiness is constructive. So, therefore, I believe that peace is constructive. You may have some sort of happiness, some temporary satisfaction when you kill your enemy. This may give you an immense sort of satisfaction, but that is short-sighted and short-lived. True happiness is by its very nature constructive, and so peace is also constructive. They go together.

"Now we are talking about pain and pleasure. The question is peace and war. Of these two choices, nobody would naturally choose war. War means destruction, suffering. The importance of peace does not have to come from religious belief. I think that the very environment, nature, needs peace. When you have peace of mind, your physical functions are normal. Your mental functions are also normal. Under these circumstances, you can utilize fully your human values such as sense of compassion, sense of caring, and also the spirit of investigation, thinking. When you have peace, all these greatnesses of the human being can be utilized fully. When your own mind is under stress, is nervous, has no peace, then you can't practice properly. Therefore, I believe that peace of mind is very important for an individual's happy life and happy family and happy society."

"Most people will concede in theory that peace is a preferable way of life," I replied, "but these same people often carry out acts of violence. How do we change this fact?" I asked.

The Dalai Lama pondered his answer for a moment. "I think one weakness of the human mind," he said, "is that once the mind is conditioned or fixed with certain false beliefs or false convictions, then it is difficult to change. So, therefore, I believe it is very essential to introduce the importance of peace of mind or peace to people, to humanity, right from the beginning. Then, each family should always, twenty-four hours a day, try to keep a peaceful atmosphere in its home. That I think is a practical way to promote peace. Otherwise, as I said earlier, someone who has his mind fixed, even if he sees some reasons for our viewpoint supporting peace, he cannot bring himself to accept it."

I pressed further on the point. "But let's say that a general has his army on the border, and he sees the potential for a great military victory in which maybe he'll get more land, maybe he'll get more wealth and prestige among his countrymen. Maybe his countrymen are even pushing him to attack. How do we get through his fixed mind and show him that peace is a better course than the violent course he is set to take?"

"Of course, every issue, every action you take has a much wider relation than you might at first notice," he said. "Particularly in today's world, in modern times. Things are very much more inter-related, interconnected than they used to be." He paused quite a while before continuing. "For example, if you ask the Pentagon which is the best method for punishing Saddam Hussein, they may have a very simple idea. But then you ask the State Department. Their responsibility is not just military; they also have to look at all the possible diplomatic consequences. So they are more reluctant to use force. They don't just say, without hesitation, go ahead. So one party is looking at a limited area; the other party is looking at a wider perspective. I think because of Saddam Hussein's invasion into Kuwait, the whole nation for several years has been suffering, having difficulties, at the government level, and especially the level of the people. At the time of the invasion of Kuwait, I don't think Saddam Hussein calculated all these things. The same is true for Hitler, and all these historic generals and dictators. They think only about the immediate benefits of their actions. And once they have committed violence, it causes a chain reaction, which they did not predict. They were set on victory, but in reality they experienced defeat. Violence has unintended consequences. Leaders must keep that in mind."

"It seems to me that the mechanism in Gandhi's philosophy is to appeal to the human nature of the person who is committing vio-lence; by remaining peaceful yourself, those who are acting vio-lently will feel some sense of shame, some sense of deep-seated compassion. Do you agree?" I asked.

"Generally speaking, yes," he replied. "I recall an American pilot, who had experience in the Korean War. I think I met him here," he said, pointing to my seat. "He mentioned one of his missions, an air strike. Returning from the mission, he saw one lone North Korean soldier." The Dalai Lama extended his arms and pretended he was holding the steering wheel of a plane. "He could have shot him, quite easily. But then he thought, 'Poor soldier! It's just one soldier.' And he didn't shoot. This is, I think, the essence of human nature. Another example comes to mind. I think of one famous picture from the civil war in Spain. One soldier fell down wounded. The person from the other side, his opponent, helped him. That, I think, is the real expression of the responses of human beings. But then, when the individual mind, due to ideology or some other reason, becomes conditioned in anger or hatred, then compassion is suppressed. That pilot's other viewpoint could have been, 'I haven't killed any soldiers on my mission, I should kill at least one.'

"But then . . . I don't know . . ." His Holiness paused and leaned forward. "I'm not saying this with pessimism, but in reality, human society cannot be perfect. Mischievous people will always be there. They simply will always be there. I think what is important is that the general public achieve a certain mental attitude and awareness about peace. Then, a few individuals, a group of cruel people holding a different viewpoint, can't do much to harm society. Even if a violent person becomes a leader in a democratic society, his violent desires will be checked by the will of the people. In a totalitarian regime, it is more difficult, but I think that it is true even in a totalitarian regime, like China. So, therefore, if the public and the media change their viewpoint, their concepts, to be more positive, more reasonable, then the few individuals who are shortsighted or blindminded, they can't do much. That is what I believe."

"And is awareness about peace progressing?" I asked.

"Oh, yes!" he responded. "In fact, during the First World War and then the Second World War, whole nations proclaimed, 'Now we are in the war!' and mobilized to fight. The whole people, and with great enthusiasm, with no questions! They felt patriotic. They believed, 'Oh, what is individual life when we have to save the nation and destroy the enemy?' They had this feeling. Now, during the Korean War, there was less of this feeling. And then during the Vietnam War the feeling was even less. The moral resentment of many of the American people made the war very difficult for the

government. Similarly, in Afghanistan, the Russians at the beginning may have had enthusiasm for the Breshnev Doctrine, but
eventually they also encountered many problems. In the same way,
I think, the Chinese Communist military attitude during the
Korean War was different from their punitive action against Vietnam. I think that people's attitude has changed. So now, that kind
of attitude, where the whole nation mobilizes without question and
just blindly accepts the government's policy, that is now no more. I
think this is positive progress."

I was curious as to whether the Dalai Lama would be willing to
accept the common notion that humans are essentially violent creatures who must learn to control their aggressive tendencies. "I had a
professor at Harvard who taught human behavioral biology," I
noted, "and he said, from all his research, that we are predisposed as
humans to conflict, that we can control it but that we are biologically
predisposed to violence, anger, jealousy, and hatred. But you teach
that we are essentially not, that we are essentially compassionate."

"Yes, yes," he said, nodding his head confidently.

"How do you surmise differently than the professor did that we
are compassionate and not violent by nature?" I questioned.

"I believe that the very physical components of humans seem to
go well with peace of mind, not with anger or hatred," he replied
confidently. "Compassion is a strong emotion. When that feeling
arises, no matter if your own situation is difficult or easy, your mental attitude is, 'I'm okay.' You are not self-concerned but rather have
concern for others. That automatically gives you inner strength and
confidence. So, with compassion, there is no feeling of anxiety, no
sense of insecurity or fear. Now, the other emotion, anger, is very
much concerned with 'me,' with one's self. Emotions which come
on that basis lead to great disturbance to your mental peace. When
you focus on yourself, selfishly thinking of 'me, me, me,' then deep
inside you feel a weak self, you feel a sense of insecurity. But as soon
as you feel a sense of concern and caring for others, though you suffer in sympathy, you still feel strength. For example, in a group of
soldiers, one soldier feels a sense of concern for the others, and at
that moment he gets more confidence. Another soldier is worried
about what will happen to him, and he gets more worried, cries,

becomes more nervous. Although they both are under the same circumstances, the same situation of danger, because of their mentality, they respond differently. So, therefore, the negative emotion, I believe, has a very profound effect on our health."

The Dalai Lama sat back in his chair and stared into my eyes. "Health is very important!" he said finally with a hearty laugh. "The basic nature of humans is that peace of mind is good for us, and an agitated mind is not good for us. So, I think," he said, laughing, "that is the Creator's wish! I don't know whether there is a Creator or not; I think that is just nature. And then again I think"—here he paused a long while—"ah, perhaps, when we see things growing in the spring, we feel happy. Autumn, leaves fall, blossoms fade away, some things broken—although some artists find broken things beautiful, most people do not like them."

"People generally don't like seeing things dying away," I agreed.

"Yes. Hmmmmm, yes," he agreed.

"And the darkness. People generally don't like dark days, like in the winter," I noted.

"Darkness, yes." I saw a twinkle in the Dalai Lama's eyes, and I knew he was about to make a joke. "But in the heat, in the summer, with the moon, darkness is very pleasant," he said, laughing. "The sunlight is very, very, very hot," he added with more uproarious laughter. Turning serious again, he continued with his observation. "I believe that these are natural responses: seeing something growing makes us feel happy; feeling something decaying, dying, makes us feel unhappy. So war means destruction. Peace means growth. I think whether a person is educated or uneducated, whether rich or poor or religious minded or not religious minded, generally speaking the response is the same. In other words, without a particular reason, nobody wants to die. And also, without a particular reason, no one wants to become too old or ugly due to old age. Nobody wants that. Why?" he asked.

"Because it's frightening," I answered.

"Ah, yes! But why? Why is it frightening?" He paused before answering his own question. "It's a sign of ending. So war, destruction, is ending. Peace or construction is beginning, or sustaining. This is our natural belief. I believe it is much better, far healthier, to believe that basic human nature is positive. That way we will develop more optimism. That is better than being off in a corner, with pessimism, being isolated. I don't think that's happy at all."

"Speaking about anger," I asked, "the Buddhist saint Shantideva wrote that even if someone is trying to kill me, I should not become angry with him, because his actions arise from conditions. This is very similar to Christ's teaching that when someone strikes you, you should turn the other cheek. Can you speak about the importance of forbearance and forgiveness in the peacemaking process?"

"That's right. It is very much like Christ's teaching." I knew that the Dalai Lama sees many similarities between Buddhism and Christianity and views Christ as either a fully enlightened being, or a bodhisattva of a very high spiritual realization.[29]

"If you hold on to the spirit of revenge, you will not be a happy person," the Dalai Lama said. "You will not achieve peace of mind. If you get your revenge and destroy your enemy, I think that is a very temporary satisfaction. In the long run, generally speaking, you have to face the long-term consequences. So therefore, it is far better to give forgiveness. What was done against you is already done.

"The other day I met a Tibetan whose relative in Nepal was killed. He went there, and the police told him that they had a suspect and he should bring the suspect to court. And his response to the police was, 'My relatives—his wife and others—all four are already killed. If by bringing this murder case to court, my relatives can be brought back to life, then I will do it.' But that is impossible. So, he believed that bringing the case to court would cause more complications, more suffering to others, so he didn't want to bring the issue to court. He was not necessarily thinking that tolerance is great, and that he should practice tolerance. He just analyzed what were the benefits of retaliating. Through that way, he dropped the issue in the court."

"But some people derive some sense of satisfaction, they feel it rights some wrong, not to forgive, to remain angry, to have revenge," I pressed.

"Ah, but then appropriate counteraction is a different question. Tolerance does not mean that you accept what they have done. Say there are two families: your family all the time remains humble, but the other family all the time takes advantage of you. Once that kind of behavior becomes your neighbors' habit, then they may take advantage of everyone at every occasion, not just your family, but everyone. They become totally spoiled. As far as your own thinking is concerned, you can tolerate it, you can accept it. But that will eventually bring disaster or ruin on your neighbor. One day people will have enough and do some harm to your neighbor. So, under those circumstances, without a motivation of ill feeling, but with the motivation of trying to bring your neighbor to act correctly, you take a countermeasure. In a friendly manner you say, 'Oh, I love you, I respect you, but by behaving in this way, you eventually will lose, you eventually will suffer.' This is an appropriate countermeasure. Exactly in this way we are trying to deal with the Chinese invasion. We are not accepting the occupation and all the tortures and deaths. Instead, we are taking countermeasures. But we do so without losing our compassion. We maintain our sense of caring."

"And that countermeasure is based on the idea of hatred for the act but not hatred for the person who commits the act?" I asked.

"Oh, exactly! Exactly! And remember, a person always can change. If we think about it honestly, there is always someone from the early part of our life, or even more recently, who was our enemy, but after some time we became very good friends. And the opposite is true also. So this means that when a person's actions change, our attitude toward the person also changes."

"Your Holiness, some people say that violence is never permissible; never can you kill someone. But there is a story in Tibetan folklore about the killing of the bad king for the greater good of the nation, and Mahayana [the type of Buddhism that includes Tibetan] theory seems to support that perhaps killing—let's say Stalin or Hitler or Pol Pot—may be just, because millions of lives would be spared. What are your beliefs on this?"

"Now, first we have to know what is violence and what is nonviolence. We can't define it only on the basis of appearances. A harsh word or a harsh action, on the surface, can't be distinguished between violence and nonviolence. For example, if you have a sincere motivation, a sense of caring and sense of concern, you may use some harsh words to correct a situation. Like a teacher to his student, or parent to his children, with sincere motivation and sense of caring, being concerned about their future, they may use harsh words or actions. Because of the motivation, that action is essentially nonviolent. Another act, though, with the motivation to deceive, to cheat in order to gain something, that is violence. The motivation is not respectful to the other person, it is not a sense of love and compassion or a sense of respect. Instead, you are insulting, trying to deceive, trying to manipulate that person's mind. So, therefore, the demarcation between violence and nonviolence is mainly related to your motivation and goal. Now, if you undertake a harsh action, some wrathful action, with genuine motivation to save or to protect, or in order to achieve some great benefit for a great number of people, that action is essentially nonviolent. It is violent in appearance but not in essence."

"But how can one judge his own motivation, Your Holiness? I might think my motivation is good, but I might be deluded."

"Oh, yes," he replied, delighted that I had raised the point. "Sometimes, due to blind faith, a person sees himself or herself as having a very sincere motivation, but actually, due to a lack of awareness, his or her motivation is not correct. I think in the case of fundamentalists, in some cases their motivation may be very sincere, but due to ignorance, due to a lack of awareness, their motivation is actually wrong. But then, how do we judge that? I think it depends on knowledge. That is why Buddhists put such emphasis on learning instead of blind faith. It is similar to the story of the stupid son who bashed the head of his father because he was trying to swat a fly. If you don't have wisdom, you might choose the wrong method. Of course, I think yours is a very good question. How to know that your motivation is sincere, that your goal is positive, is very difficult to judge. Generally, every event is a mixture of positive and negative. So then, which percent is higher, the positive or the negative? A hundred percent right is almost impossible."

"That would lead me to conclude that if I can't be a hundred percent positive that my motivation is pure in committing an act of violence, then I should refrain from the violence altogether," I noted.

"Then again, it depends on the circumstances, whether there is no other alternative," he replied. "If there is an alternative to violence, then you should do as you said. But if you have no other alternative, if you have to do something or your failure to do something violent will create a disaster to many people, you must do something forcefully to stop it. However, if your motivation is simply 'for my country,' out of patriotism, then I think that is a difficult and dangerous attachment. I'm not talking about patriotism, but rather the people and animals of your country, in order to protect their peaceful life, if there is no other alternative except to use force, I think it is permissible. But first, tell those who are harming or threatening your people, 'This is my goal, and please don't harm us.' With respect, with a sense of caring, tell them this. Then, if they don't listen, and you have some force at your disposal, then I think it is permissible to use it. But then again, there is another important point that you have to keep in your mind: if I adopt this method, what are the consequences? It may be that you stopped this wrongdoing and your motivation was sincere, but due to this event, unexpected consequences may arise which are not good. In the long run you may perhaps make the situation worse. It is very difficult to predict," he concluded.

A smile spread across his face a moment later. "The best is not to act!" he said, lifting his arms. We both laughed for a long time. "The other day, I joked with some people," he said. "I told them my daily routine, that after 8:30 P.M. I sleep. That is my peaceful period. So if we want genuine world peace, then everyone should sleep. Then no one can act. Eventually we will starve, but for human beings, that is the guarantee for world peace," he roared with laughter.

"I like your intelligent questions. Your intelligence is very good," the Dalai Lama declared as he rose from his seat. His assistant brought him a *kata,* which he presented to me. I draped it around my neck. He took hold of my hand and rubbed it while we walked to the doorway. "I really appreciate this work. This is a very important book. It is very good work," he said to me. "I will see you again."

The Dalai Lama has begun to express his desire to retire from politics altogether. He only maintains his rigorous schedule of meetings with world leaders in order to gain autonomy for his suppressed people. But if he had his way, he would begin to go on long retreats, preparing his mind for his eventual death. He would also take on students and become a regular teacher in the ancient tradition of Buddhist education. And he has one other desire too: to continue to travel around the world to meet with other religious leaders, to take part in spiritual retreats and prayers, staying in monasteries and caves and kneeling before holy shrines. "Like the old Buddhist mendicants," he said.

On my way out of India, I had quite a difficult journey back to Delhi, encountering many obstacles. Yet in the face of each annoyance, each bump and jostle and impolite act, my mind was as relaxed as when I was in the small hill town of Dharamsala, in the Dalai Lama's sitting room, hearing his reassuring voice and robust laughter.

As Epictetus said, one can immediately become a better person by finding and emulating worthy role models. "Invoke the characteristics of the people you admire the most," he recommended, "and adopt their manners, speech, and behavior as your own. There is nothing false in this. We all carry the seeds of greatness within us, but we need an image as a point of focus in order that they may sprout."[30] Such advice put in me in good shape to face my immediate hardships, as I invoked the characteristics of the Dalai Lama and his interminable patience.

Before I had left India a high Tibetan official told me that the Dalai Lama had visited the Holy Land and was very saddened by events there. He was particularly troubled by the suffering of the Palestinians that he had encountered. "If you can," the official advised me, "go there. It really caused His Holiness sadness. Go and figure out what can be done," he recommended. My next journey took me deep into the heat of that question.

Three

THE PEACEMAKERS OF ISRAEL AND PALESTINE

The continuing battle between the Israelis and the Palestinians is one of the greatest tragedies of our time. There has been too much pain on both sides; too many rationalizations for hardening the heart and and growing numb to the suffering of the adversary; an endless stream of reasons for hatred, vengeance, madness, and despair. Every blame has a counterblame, every claim a counterclaim, every fact another equally compelling.

Many people have lost all hope that these two Semitic peoples who believe in the same God can ever live together in harmony. If peace is not found, however, then the Israelis and Palestinians will continue to live in the doubly damned state of insecurity and aggression, in fear and ferociousness. Neither people will be happy or safe or able to achieve its highest aspirations. Neither will be able to honor the goodness of their spiritual traditions, both of which call for *shalom, salamaat,* peace.

What remains above the fray is the wisdom of the spiritual masters who taught us that peace comes not through the capitulation of the foe, but rather through the righteousness of our own deeds. In his prayer called "Shalom Aleichem Malachey Hashalom" ("Peace unto You, Angels of Peace"), Faysal Al-Husseini pleads for enlightenment of the people of Israel and Palestine. "O God," he cries, "the chest is replete with bitterness. . . . Do not turn that into spite. . . .

The heart is replete with pain. . . . Do not turn that into vengeance. . . . the spirit is replete with fear. . . . Do not turn that into hatred." With this supplication for guidance, Faysal declares, "We wanted freedom for our people, we did not want slavery for others. . . . We wanted a homeland for our people to gather them, we did not want to destroy states of others, nor demolish their homes."

In his poem "I, May I Rest in Peace," the brilliant Hebrew poet Yehuda Amichai entreated:

I, may I rest in peace—I, who am still living, say,
May I have peace in the rest of my life.
I want peace right now while I'm still alive.
I don't want to wait like that pious man who wished for one leg
of the golden chair of Paradise, I want a four-legged chair
right here, a plain wooden chair. I want the rest of my peace now.
I have lived out my life in wars of every kind: battles without
and within, close combat, face-to-face, the faces always
my own, my lover-face, my enemy-face.
Wars with the old weapons—sticks and stones, blunt ax, words,
dull ripping knife, love and hate,
and wars with newfangled weapons—machine gun, missile,
words, land mines exploding, love and hate.
I don't want to fulfill my parents' prophecy that life is war.
I want peace with all my body and all my soul.
Rest me in peace.

In both Faysal's prayer and Yehuda Amichai's poem, we see the dual desire for freedom from antagonism and from complicity in wrongdoing. It is the desire to be liberated from the insidious animosity that painfully transforms the body into an instrument of hate and despair; and it is the desire to make right the wrongs committed against the other, to have the guilt of aggression lifted from the psyche. It is these two desires more than anything else that will bring lasting peace to Israel and Palestine.

For nearly two years now the "peace process," as the diplomatic wrangling is called, has been largely immovable, with both sides understandably (yet not convincingly) claiming that it is impossible to move ahead with peace while *their* people are being shot and killed.

As a result, sincere, bold, and generous measures are not made, and the violence seems to have no end. The present fighting is known to Palestinians as the Al-Aqsa Intifada. *Intifada* is an Arabic word that means "shaking off." It is used to describe the current battle to force Israel to withdraw from the territory that it has occupied by force since 1967. The United Nations, the United States, the European Union, and most of the rest of the world have called on Israel to withdraw from the Occupied Territories and to cease putting Jewish settlements there, but Israel believes it cannot do so (if it should do so at all) until and unless its national security is assured.

The latest Intifada began in earnest in September 2000, when Ariel Sharon went to visit one of the holiest sites in the Islamic world, the compound of the Al-Aqsa Mosque. Sharon has long done battle with Arabs, as a soldier and defense minister. He is a shrewd politician as well, and he undoubtedly knew that his visit to this holy site would be seen by the Arabs as a provocation. Yet he went anyway because, according to him, he simply had every right to do so. It is more plausible, though, that he saw it as a way to begin his challenge to the leadership of Prime Minister Barak. Sharon took at least a thousand armed officers with him as protection, virtually assuring that his visit would look like an invasion. Barak gave approval for the visit. It may have been precisely the pretense the Palestinians were looking for in order to begin a new uprising. In any event, violence erupted almost immediately.

It is difficult to lay blame for a particular armed clash, especially in Israel and Palestine, where each side claims that the other did something to provoke violence. This tit-for-tat quickly spirals out of control, well beyond reason. As Gandhi said, "An eye for an eye leaves the whole world blind." It certainly makes the genuine record of events very hard to see as well. Yet the historical narrative is quite important to understand, and in a manner that gives both sides—both descendants of Abraham—equal claim to live in peace in a homeland in the Middle East.

Many people in the West cling to a simplistic view of the conflict: that the Palestinian Arabs hate the Jews and want to destroy Israel because of this animosity. To be fair, some people believe quite the opposite: that all Israelis want to oppress the Palestinians and will never tolerate a Palestinian state. There are certainly some militant Palestinians who would love to see the Jewish state wiped out altogether, and there are high officials in Israel who want to evict all Palestinians from their traditional homeland in the West Bank and Gaza Strip. Yet neither view represents the majority view, and neither is helpful in the search for a peaceful resolution to the conflict.

While Americans seem to know the Israeli version of events quite well, peace requires us to understand also the other side's narrative and motivations. We must engage in an honest attempt to do so, however startling or uncomfortable that may be.

Israel's official position is that the Al-Aqsa Intifada began because "the Palestinian leadership decided to attempt to achieve through violence what they could not achieve through negotiations—a solution without compromise." According to Israel, "This is the source of the wave of Palestinian violence and terrorism that began in September 2000 and became known as the Terror Intifada." (To my knowledge, only the Israeli government refers to the present crises as the *Terror* Intifada.) The government concludes, "The violent events recently witnessed in our region are the result of a clear Palestinian decision to pursue violence as a political tool. Israel seeks to resolve its differences with the Palestinians at the negotiating table, while Yasser Arafat and the Palestinian Authority have chosen the path of ongoing confrontation." In short, "Israel's olive branch" is being "met with a hail of gunfire, rocks and firebombs."[1]

By contrast, a report by a Jewish peace organization states, "The conventional wisdom is that, even if both sides are at fault, the Palestinians are irrational 'terrorists' who have no point of view worth listening to. Our position, however, is that the Palestinians have a real grievance: their homeland for over a thousand years was taken, without their consent and mostly by force, during the creation of the state of Israel." The report concludes, "All subsequent crimes—on both sides—inevitably follow from this original injustice."[2]

Historian Benny Morris, a highly regarded professor at Ben Gurion University in Israel, offers the following explanation of the situation:

The cause of the [Al-Aqsa] eruption, which without doubt has scarred Jewish-Arab relations in Israel for many years to come, lay in the 52-year history of marginalization of and discrimination against the Arabs in Israeli society and their gradual radicalization, which has included a fast-growing Islamic fundamentalist movement and incendiary anti-Israel rhetoric by their elected leaders. More immediately, [former Prime Minister] Barak's studied indifference towards this minority and its leaders badly exacerbated existing tensions; after receiving 95 percent of the Arab vote in the 1999 elections, Barak failed to invite the Arab leaders into his coalition or even to consult with them, let alone offer redress for their various grievances, which included high levels of poverty and unemployment, a poor education system, and weak infrastructure.[3]

What is vitally important to note in Morris's account is that marginalization and discrimination against Palestinians are not based on ancient animosity. It is a widely held misconception that Jews and Arabs have always hated each other and that theirs is a type of antediluvian hatred that fuels incessant warfare. If this were the case, the problem would indeed seem rather hopeless.

In reality, Jews and Palestinians have not always been engaged in open hostility. The clash between the Israelis and the Palestinians is not an ancient one caused by religious intolerance, racism, or economic competition. In fact, notes scholar Sami Hadawi, one can "leaf through the pages of Middle East history and survey many eras of civilization and still find the same story of mutual respect between Arabs and Jews. In the Holy Land, as elsewhere in Arab lands, they lived together in harmony.... No community trespassed on the rights of another and each worshipped the One God in its own way."[4] Hadawi may paint too rosy a picture, for there were occasional transgressions against Jews by Arabs. Yet there was a remarkable amount of tolerance between Arabs and Jews, which was even codified into law. Certainly Arabs did not display the animosity and outright violence against the Jews that Christians did.

Historian Mark Tessler notes the "untarnished legacy" of Jewish-Arab relations that existed in Palestine before the conflict began.[5] If over the course of many centuries—and through not the most enlightened of times—the Arabs and the Jews could live and work together peacefully with relative tolerance and respect, then certainly they can do so again.

The conflict between the Jews and the Palestinians arose only in the past hundred years or so as a result of the collision between Jewish and Palestinian national aspirations. Jewish nationalism was expressed chiefly through the Zionist movement, which held that the Jews who were dispersed all over the world should be reunited in a homeland in which they constituted the majority population. Given the historical record of racism and severe abuse against Jews in Europe, these goals were certainly understandable.

Theodor Herzl, a Hungarian-born Jew, was the father of modern Zionism. In 1896 he published a book called *Der Judenstaat,* in which he proposed not only a Jewish state, but also a new society that would embrace and implement the ideas of freedom, democracy, and social justice. Herzl, it should be noted, did not declare that the Jewish state should be in Palestine. In fact, he did not much care for the climate of Palestine and preferred a Jewish state in Argentina. A year after the publication of his work, the First Zionist Congress (comprised of several hundred self-elected representatives) was held in Basel, Switzerland, and endorsed Herzl's concept, naming Palestine as the appropriate spot for a Jewish homeland.

The rabbis of Vienna were intrigued by the idea and dispatched a fact-finding mission to Palestine. After collecting information, the mission sent a cable back to Vienna stating, "The bride is beautiful, but she is married to another man." Herein lies the root of the conflict: much of the land that the Jews desired was already inhabited by the Palestinians. They had been well settled there for well over a thousand years; they comprised the overwhelming majority of the population; and, most important, they desired a nation of their own. At the time, they were under the rule of the Ottoman Empire.

Herzl was well aware of the fact that the Palestinians were native to the area, but he and his colleagues remained largely indifferent to their plight, concentrating instead on the plight of Jews who had suffered such great persecution around the world. Like most Europeans of his day, Herzl belittled native populations. According to

Avi Shlaim in his book, *The Iron Wall: Israel and the Arab World,* Herzl "viewed the natives as primitive and backward, and his attitude toward them was rather patronizing."[6]

Herzl was not alone. In fact, many of the Jewish colonists saw Arabs as "primitive, dishonest, fatalistic, lazy, savage—much as European colonists viewed the natives elsewhere in Asia or Africa."[7] Chaim Weizmann, who became the first president of Israel, said that Arabs were "dishonest, uneducated, greedy, and as unpatriotic as . . . inefficient."[8] Some Zionist leaders appear to have believed that their settlements in Palestine, with superior European ideas and technology, would benefit the Arabs and that the Arabs would peacefully and willingly blend into the Jewish state.[9] This is a classical view by colonists, that their superior skills will elevate and save the natives from their primitive ways.

The prevailing view among Zionists and their supporters, however, was a carefully cultivated myth that Palestine was an empty land. "A land without a people for a people without a land" was a falsehood purposefully advanced by Zionist leaders in an attempt to make the Palestinians and their own national aspirations invisible. Unfortunately, a good number of the Jews in Europe and elsewhere who had never been to Palestine actually believed that the land lay empty, just waiting to be cultivated.

Some prominent Jews, however, noted long before the creation of Israel that the rights of the Palestinians were being undermined or completely ignored by Jewish settlers in the region. When the prominent Zionist leader Max Nordau first learned that there was a sizable Arab population in Palestine, he ran to Herzl, crying, "I did not know that; but then we are committing an injustice."[10] Asher Ginsberg, who became the leading voice for spiritual and cultural renewal among Jews, visited Palestine in 1891 and wrote,

> We abroad, are used to believing that Eretz-Israel [Hebrew for Palestine] is now almost totally desolate, a desert that is not sowed, and anyone who wishes to purchase there lands, may come and purchase as much as his heart desires. But in truth this is not the case. Throughout the country it is difficult to find fields that are not sowed; only sand fields and stone

mountains that are not fit to grow anything but fruit trees, and this, also only after hard labour and great expense of clearing and reclamation—only these are not cultivated.[11]

Ginsberg was highly critical of Herzl's self-centered manner and the idea of rapid colonization of Palestine by the Jews. Ginsberg also believed that the Arabs in Palestine should be given greater consideration and treated with greater respect. Writing about the Jews who went to Palestine, Ginsberg said, "Serfs they were in the land of the diaspora, and suddenly they find themselves in unrestricted freedom, and this change has awakened in them an inclination to despotism. They treat the Arabs with hostility and cruelty, deprive them of their rights, offend them without cause and even boast of these deeds; and nobody among us opposes this despicable and dangerous inclination."[12]

On his first visit to Palestine in 1891, the Jewish teacher and writer Yitzhak Epstein declared that Jews should be extremely careful in their behavior toward the Arabs when Jews came to live among them once more, treating Arabs with justice and righteousness. Unfortunately, Epstein noted, Jewish settlers showed little love and respect toward the Palestinians, but rather acted shamefully and cruelly. He predicted that if such cruelty continued, then anger would persist in the hearts of the Palestinians and they would plot revenge:

> Can it be that the dispossessed will keep silent and calmly accept what is being done to them? Will they not ultimately arise to regain, with physical force, that which they are deprived of through the power of gold? Will they not seek justice from the strangers that placed themselves over their land? [13]

Morris writes that "though still a small minority, the settlers quickly began to behave like lords and masters, some apparently resorting to the whip at the slightest provocation. This was a major source of Arab animosity."[14]

Albert Einstein declared, "I should much rather see reasonable agreement with the Arabs on the basis of living together in peace than the creation of a Jewish state." He added, "Apart from practical considerations, my awareness of the essential nature of Judaism resists the idea of a Jewish state, with borders, an army, and a measure of temporal power, no matter how modest. I am afraid of the inner damage Judaism will sustain—especially from the development of a narrow nationalism within our own ranks, against which we have already had to fight strongly, even without a Jewish state."[15]

The Jews purchased as much land as they could (amounting to 7 percent of the land by 1947) while they pressed governments around the world to accept their idea of a Jewish state in Palestine. Meanwhile, Arab nationalism was also growing throughout the Middle East, and the Arabs of Palestine resented the growing number of Jewish nationalists who were coming to settle among them.

Unfortunately, the British greatly exacerbated the growing confrontation between Jews and Palestinians by promising the land to both sides—even before they had acquired it. Palestine had been ruled by the Ottomans since 1516, but when Turkey entered World War I on the side of Germany, the British reached a secret agreement with the French to carve up the Middle East into two spheres of influence in the event of victory. Meanwhile, searching for allies in every quarter, the British promised Palestine to the Arabs in return for their help in defeating Turkey. When Turkey was duly defeated, the British and French divided the Middle East between them, Britain alone adding over one million square miles to its empire. The borders of the countries imposed by the British and French were artificial and arbitrary, which created problems of stability we still see today. In any event, the Arabs in Palestine had every reason to believe that they would acquire their land as promised.

Yet the British promised the same land to the Jews in the now-famous Balfour Declaration of 1917. The declaration stated: "His Majesty's Government views with favour the establishment in Palestine of a national home for the Jewish people, and will use their best endeavours to facilitate the achievement of this object, it being clearly understood that nothing shall be done which may prejudice the civil and religious rights of existing non-Jewish communities in Palestine, or the rights and political status enjoyed by the Jews in any other country."

It is significant that the declaration never mentioned Palestinians or their right, much less their desire, for a state; it simply spoke of a vague non-Jewish community. This was no oversight. Speaking several years after the issuance of the declaration, Lord Balfour, its architect, asserted, "We do not propose even to go through the form of consulting the wishes of the present inhabitants of the country. Zionism, be it right or wrong, good or bad, is rooted in age-old traditions, in present needs, in future hopes of far profounder import than the desires and prejudices of the 700,000 Arabs who now inhabit that ancient land."[16] "In short," he concluded candidly, "so far as Palestine is concerned," the British government had "made no statement of fact which is not admittedly wrong [and] no declaration of policy" which it did "not always intend to violate."[17] Balfour's aims were primarily threefold: to enlist the support of Jews in the United States and Russia in the Allied war effort against Germany; to build, it was hoped, a non-Arab ally in the region that could protect Britain's vital access to the Suez Canal; and to reroute potential Jewish immigrants away from Britain into their own homeland.

The Balfour Declaration, then, was complicit in the Zionists' intention to completely ignore or, worse, to completely negate Palestinian national aspirations. Despite having made promises to both sides, the British nonetheless were supporting the Jews over the Palestinians.

Judah L. Magnes, an American Zionist who became the first chancellor and president of the Hebrew University in Jerusalem, tried to persuade his fellow Jews that a just division of the land should and could be found. "We seem to have thought of everything except the Arabs," he declared. Both peoples had a just cause, he said; both had a historical connection with and love for the land. He knew that peace required accommodation with the Arabs, as did Jewish spirituality itself.

Magnes's reasoned, moral, compassionate approach was not followed. Instead, Palestinians and Jews, both manipulated by the British, saw each other as uncompromising and therefore felt justified in taking a militant stance. From that point on, as one historian has noted, war between the two was inevitable.[18]

Between 1931 and 1936, the number of Jews in Palestine increased dramatically from 16 to 28 percent of the population.[19] This rapid rate of growth among Jewish settlers alarmed the Palestinians and, along with the clear support the Jews were receiving from the British, made them increasingly hostile and aggressive. In 1939 the Palestinians rose up against the British. The uprising was quashed and the British dug in their heels.

Soon the Jewish settlers, who had established enormous infrastructure and businesses under British support, also rose up against the British, resorting to acts of terrorism to drive them out. In one of the Jewish terrorists' most infamous early attacks against the British, they filled several milk cans with explosives and placed them in the basement of the King David Hotel in Jerusalem, a symbol of British colonial rule. Ninety-one people were killed when the bombs exploded.

Mahatma Gandhi did not fail to notice the situation in Palestine. "Palestine belongs to the Arabs in the same sense that England belongs to the English or France to the French," he declared.

> What is going on in Palestine today cannot be justified by any moral code of conduct. [Jews] can settle in Palestine only by the goodwill of the Arabs. . . . As it is, they are co-sharers with the British in despoiling a people who have done no wrong to them. I am not defending the Arab excesses. I wish they had chosen the way of non-violence in resisting what they rightly regard as an unacceptable encroachment upon their country. But according to the accepted canons of right and wrong, nothing can be said against the Arab resistance in the face of overwhelming odds.[20]

It is important to emphasize Gandhi's comment that the Palestinians were not angelic in their actions toward the Jews. They were certainly antagonistic, and some militants resorted to terrorism and acts of cruelty. Terrorism, whether by Palestinian or Jew, is equally abhorrent. Had the Palestinians followed the path of nonviolence, I believe that they would have garnered enormous international support and achieved statehood many years ago. By following the path of violence instead, Palestinians must now battle prejudice ("Arabs are militant") as well as Israel's incredibly strong military apparatus. Yet the Palestinians responded like native populations repeatedly have done in the history of colonization, resorting to violence to impede the encroachment of settlers and throw off the yoke of occupation.

The Palestinians' response was not unexpected in official circles. As early as 1919, Britain's chief military administrator, General A. W. Money, stated, "The Palestinians desire their country for themselves and will resist any general immigration of Jews, however gradual, by every means in their power including active hostilities." In August of that same year, Money's successor, Major General H. D. Watson, declared, "The antagonism to Zionism of the majority of the population is deep-rooted—it is fast leading to hatred of the British—and will result, if the Zionist programme is forced upon them, in an outbreak of serious character."[21]

Palestinian Arabs disliked foreigners and were especially put off by the Jewish colonists, who undertook construction projects without permission and forcibly denied shepherds the customary use of pasture land. "The settlers," Morris notes, "dressed differently, worshipped (if at all) differently, and acted differently. Their values were alien and antithetical to Arab norms. In short, everything about them was different and in some ways provocative."[22]

The British eventually tired of Palestine, which held no great strategic or economic advantages for them, and they turned the issue of its future over to the United Nations. On November 29, 1947, the United Nations voted to partition the land into a Jewish and a Palestinian state. At that moment the potential existed for a two-state solution that could have addressed the competing interests of the parties. However, the partition plan that was adopted generally followed the Zionist plan supported by the United States.

Writer David Hirst notes that the United States "went to the most extraordinary lengths of backstage manipulation" in order to pass the partition plan; a "deeply distressed" James Forrestal, the secretary of defense, called the U.S. behavior "coercion and duress on other nations [that] bordered on scandal."[23] This heavy-handed support for the Zionist plan flew in the face of U.S. State Department Middle East experts, but was nevertheless pushed adamantly by President Harry Truman. Why? In his memoirs Truman recalls the "constant barrage" of Zionist supporters. "I do not think that I ever had so much pressure or propaganda aimed at the White House as I had in this instance," he wrote. He plainly told a group of Arab ambassadors to the United States in 1945, "I am sorry, gentlemen, but I have to answer to hundreds of thousands who are anxious for the success of Zionism; I do not have hundreds of thousands of Arabs among my constituents."[24]

The proposed borders of the U.S.-backed plan were gerrymandered in order to create a Jewish majority in the proposed Jewish state.[25] Additionally, though the Palestinians comprised a clear majority of the population in the entire region, the Jews would be given a majority of the land of historic Palestine. It offered a two-state solution that could hardly have been seen as fair. By 1946 there were approximately 600,000 Jews, compared to nearly 1.3 million Palestinian Arabs, in Palestine.[26]

Eighty-five percent of the Jewish population was centered solely in the urban centers of Jaffa/Tel Aviv, Jerusalem, and Haifa. Jews comprised a majority of the population only in the subdistrict of Jaffa. In the subdistrict of Haifa, Jews made up 47 percent of the population. Yet in every other subdistrict, Jews were minorities by a wide margin. Arabs totaled 100 percent of the population in Nablus, Ramallah, and Jenin, 99 percent of the population in Beersheba and Hebron, 98 percent of the population in Gaza, 96 percent in Acre, 78 percent in Ramleh, and so on. Even in the subdistrict of Jerusalem, Arabs comprised 62 percent of the population. Statistically, then, the Palestinians should have received the majority of the land in Palestine.

The British told the Jews that British forces would complete their withdrawal from the region by July 31, 1948, but they kept the date secret from the Palestinians. And while the British disarmed the Palestinians, they permitted the Jews to arm and train themselves. Jewish military forces numbered over sixty thousand by May 1948, organized primarily as the Haganah, and they also included the terrorist groups Irgun and the Stern Gang.

Though Israelis often say that Israel was attacked by the Arabs without provocation on May 15, 1948, that rendition indeed shows, as one historian puts it, that "history is the propaganda of the victors."[27] Israeli accounts of the nation's creation emphasize a massive Arab coalition, hell-bent on throwing the Jews to the sea, descending upon innocent Israel and its pitiable forces. This is misleading; the Arab armies did not field superior military power over Israel. At each stage of the war the Israeli Defense Forces significantly outnumbered the combined Arab forces, and Israel enjoyed equal or better military hardware as well.[28] It is therefore hard to imagine that the Arab military strategists seriously thought that their outnumbered forces could completely dislodge Israel from its defensive positions and wipe the new nation off the map. The Arabs were fractured in their aims, but King Abdullah, who was put in charge of the Arab armies, sought not to destroy the Jewish state but rather to make himself the ruler of the Arab areas of Palestine.[29]

What is most overlooked, however, is Israel's own aggressive actions, which contributed to a state of war in Palestine even before the Arab invasion. In April 1948 the Jewish militant group Haganah launched major military operations throughout Palestine. The offensive, named Plan D, called for attacks, economic subversion, and psychological warfare in order to capture Arab villages.[30] In one assault by the Jewish forces in Deir Yassin on April 9, 1948, Jewish terrorist groups led by the future prime minister Menachem Begin attacked and massacred 250 men, women, and children, sending panic throughout Palestinian villages. Former Israeli Minister of Justice Dov Joseph called the massacre a "deliberate and unprovoked attack," and British historian Arnold Toynbee described it as "comparable to crimes committed against the Jews by the Nazis."[31]

Menachem Begin later noted, "In the months preceding the Arab invasion . . . we continued to make sallies into Arab areas. In the early days of 1948, we were explaining to our officers and men, however, that this was not enough. . . . It was clear to us that even the most daring sallies carried out by partisan troops would never be enough to decide the issue. Our hope lay in gaining control of territory."[32]

Well-planned and brutal attacks by the Jews led to Jewish control of Tabariyya, Haifa, Jaffa, West Jerusalem, eastern Galilee, Beisan, the Naqab villages, and the central plain between Latrun and Ram-leh. In his book *The Arab-Israeli War 1948,* Major Edgar O'Ballance notes, "It was the Jewish policy to encourage the Arabs to quit their homes, and they used psychological warfare extensively in urging them to do so. Later, as the war went on, they ejected those Arabs who clung to their villages."[33]

Historian Benny Morris notes in his book, *The Birth of the Palestinian Refugee Problem, 1947–1949,* that Prime Minister David Ben-Gurion

> clearly wanted as few Arabs as possible to remain in the Jewish state. He hoped to see them flee. He said as much to his colleagues and aides in meetings in August, September and October [1948]. But no [general] expulsion policy was ever enunciated and Ben-Gurion always refrained from issuing clear or written expulsion orders; he preferred that his generals "understand" what he wanted done. He wished to avoid going down in history as the "great expeller" and he did not want the Israeli government to be implicated in a morally questionable policy.[34]

In a 1954 publication on the history of the Haganah, Ben-Gurion admitted his goal of cleansing the land of Arabs. "In our country," he wrote, "there is room only for Jews. We will say to the Arabs: 'Move over'; if they are not in agreement, if they resist, we will push them by force." [35]

Brutalities toward Arab citizens continued, and the Arab states began to think about military interventions against the Jews. Morris concludes that the Deir Yassin massacre "seemed to push Jordan into the arms of those pressing for direct intervention by the Arab states, [and] it may also have contributed to the decision of leaders of other nations—principally Egypt—to join the fray. Certainly the news enraged Arab fighting men, and 'Deir Yassin!' became a rallying cry for combatants bent on revenge."[36] Faced with the loss of their ancestral land, continued aggression on the part of Jewish militant groups, and a disproportional split of the territory by the United Nations, the Palestinians joined the Arab states in their war against Israel. The day after Israel declared statehood, on May 15, 1948, the Arab armies attacked. The Israelis soundly defeated the Arab forces, and in so doing, captured an additional 21 percent of historic Palestine. They thereby controlled roughly 76 percent of the land, as opposed to the 55 percent called for in the United Nations partition plan.

It was at that time that Palestine ceased to exist. The promised Palestinian state was never created. Instead, Palestinians in the Gaza fell under Egyptian control, and Palestinians in the West Bank fell under Jordanian control. The dismantling of Palestine seemed to spell doom to the Palestinians' national aspirations.

After the Arab-Israeli war of 1948, only about 150,000 out of an estimated 900,000 Palestinians remained in the new state of Israel; 750,000 Palestinians became refugees. These refugees were civilians who fled their homes to escape the dangers of war; they never intended to leave their homes permanently. The United Nations recognized this fact in Resolution 194 passed in December 1948, which said that "the refugees wishing to return to their homes and live at peace with their neighbours should be permitted to do so at the earliest practicable date, and that compensation should be paid for the property of those choosing not to return and for loss of or damage to property which, under principles of international law or in equity, should be made good by the Governments or authorities responsible."

Meanwhile, to the victor went the spoils. Instead of recognizing Palestinian national aspirations and helping them create a viable state, the government of Israel began a policy of permanently appropriating Palestinian land. Palestinians were driven from their homes, and in all of the captured territories Palestinian homes, farms, and buildings of all sorts were demolished. In their place, the Israelis erected new towns with new names and gave the land to Jews who were now streaming into Israel from all over the world.

Jewish writer Nathan Chofshi, who had lived in the area since 1908, witnessed these events firsthand. He candidly wrote in 1959,

We, Jews, forced Arabs to leave cities and villages. . . . Here was a people who lived on its own land for 1,300 years. We came and turned the native Arabs into tragic refugees. And still we dare to slander and malign them, to besmirch their name. Instead of being deeply ashamed of what we did and of trying to undo some of the evil we committed by helping these unfortunate refugees, we justify our terrible acts and even attempt to glorify them.[37]

"Why should the Arabs make peace?" former Israeli Prime Minister David Ben-Gurion later questioned. "If I were an Arab leader, I would never make terms with Israel. That is natural: we have taken their country. Sure, God promised it to us, but what does that matter to them? There has been anti-Semitism, the Nazis, Hitler, Auschwitz, but was that their fault? They only see one thing: we came here and stole their country. Why should they accept that?"[38]

"There is not one place built in this country," former defense minister Moshe Dayan also later admitted candidly, "that did not have a former Arab population." Jewish villages, he said, "were built in place of Arab villages. You do not even know the names of these Arab villages, and I do not blame you, because these geography books no longer exist; not only do the books not exist, the Arab villages are not there either."[39]

I. F. Stone, an American Jewish journalist who was decorated by the Irgun, notes that "Jewish terrorism . . . 'encouraged' Arabs to leave areas the Jews wished to take over," and the Jews "tried to make as much of Israel as free of Arabs as possible; [but] the argument that the refugees ran away 'voluntarily' or because their leaders urged them to do so until after the fighting was over, not only rests on myth but is irrelevant." Stone asks, "Have refugees no right to return? Have German Jews no right to recover their properties because they had to flee?"[40]

It must be said that tiny Israel was magnificent in providing for the needs of the survivors of the Holocaust in Europe. It was able to house and clothe and feed the survivors and provide them with an opportunity to have some kind of normalcy after one of the most ghastly episodes in human history. Yet causing one people to suffer in order to alleviate the suffering of another is morally problematic.

There were four more major wars between Israel and its neighbors after 1948: in 1956, in 1967, in 1972, and in 1982. Of these wars, the one in 1967 is especially important to note here, for that is when Israel became unquestionably an occupying power. The Israelis took control of all the land that the United Nations partition plan had proposed for the Palestinians. Again thousands of refugees fled their homes, some leaving the region altogether, some emigrating to neighboring states, and others collecting in camps and enclaves in the Gaza Strip, the West Bank, and the Golan Heights.

As an occupying power, Israel has been in a difficult situation, both in managing its international image and in its own national discourse. Those Israelis who still believe that the entire region belongs solely to the Jews have advocated the establishment of permanent Jewish settlements dotted throughout the captured territories. One recent ultrahawkish cabinet minister supported the total deportation of Palestinians, repeatedly stating, "Let the Arabs go back to Mecca."

Former Prime Minister Barak and others advocated a "unilateral separation," a type of Chinese wall blocking out, or fencing in, the Palestinians, and recently work on such a wall was initiated. Internal Security Minister Uzi Landau said not long ago that he did not rule out expelling Palestinian leader Yasser Arafat to Tunis. He also accused the duly elected Arab members of the Knesset (the Israeli parliament) of being agents of the Palestine Liberation Organization (PLO) and Hizbullah. Landau openly espouses his party's opposition to a Palestinian state and any attempt to "concede" the "so-called Territories" to the Palestinians. "This readiness to hand over valuable territory marks an erosion in the social solidarity of Israelis," he says; it is a "withdrawal from the idea of Zionism" and a "total spiritual collapse."[41]

After decades of battles to protect the Israeli settlements from the Palestinian population surrounding them, however, a sizable portion of the Israeli public is ready to halt the expansion of the settlements. Some Israelis are even prepared to withdraw the settlers, and most acknowledge that Palestinians must be given the right of sovereign determination, but only if and when a comprehensive peace accord can be reached.

Yet extracting itself from the role of occupier has proven difficult for Israel, especially since the right-leaning government of Israel has no consensus on whether to permit the creation of a Palestinian state or what such a state would look like—except that any such state would be militarily eviscerated, chopped up into easily invaded territories, and dependent on Israel for water and other vital needs.

As with the United States in Vietnam, there seems to be no good way to get out of a bad situation. On the one hand, failing to withdraw perpetuates the conflict, leading to continued military and civilian deaths, enormous expense, and a measurable erosion of international support. On the other hand, withdrawing alone does not assure the end of the hostilities, as many Palestinian refugees still lay claim to the plots of land (now part of Israel proper) that they fled during previous wars. The fear is that granting the Palestinians complete control over the West Bank and the Gaza Strip will give them additional means to organize and execute a war against Israel.

Whether they are seen as freedom fighters or terrorists, groups like Hamas and Islamic Jihad, who use violent means to oppose the Israel occupation, not only have tarnished the Palestinians' image and undermined the strength of the Palestinian Authority but also have caused conservative elements within Israel to harden their stance against the proposed Palestinian state. Unfortunately, attacks on civilians within Israel led to a dramatic political shift in the electorate toward the right. Ariel Sharon, though once seen as an unlikely choice for prime minister given his uncompromising views and his forced resignation as defense minister after being implicated in acts of atrocities in Lebanon, was elected by a public desiring security above all else. Any spirit of accommodation seems to have exploded along with the militants' bombs.

I went to Israel despite the fact that the U.S. State Department dissuaded Americans from visiting the area because of daily hostilities. My friends and family were not keen on my going, but most of them had grown accustomed to my need to see things firsthand.

I spent my first few days in Tel Aviv in an expensive yet second-rate hotel across from the U.S. Embassy. Walking around town, I found Tel Aviv visually unimpressive. The architecture was uninspiring, plain, and even ugly. Yet the Mediterranean Sea and the beaches were beautiful and proved to be the city's most redeeming quality.

For three full days in Tel Aviv I visited cultural sites, lingered at cafés, restaurants, and pubs, talked with as many locals as possible, watched local television broadcasts, and read local papers. In my hotel, in taxis, and along the waterfront I engaged people in conversations about the state of affairs in Israel and the Occupied Territories. I truly wanted to know the Jewish perspective on what was taking place in and around their land.

Each opinion I obtained added to the picture of a country split between wanting peace and wanting once and for all to eliminate the Palestinians' ability to threaten Israeli security. But only a small minority of the people I spoke with, including those who identified themselves as progressive, placed any blame on Israel for the current conflict. Instead, it was nearly universally held that the Palestinians wanted to destroy Israel and take over the land for themselves. Palestinians were said to hate Jews most vehemently. There was also an overwhelmingly fatalistic view that peace was impossible to achieve in the foreseeable future. I was surprised by the uniformity of these views, even though I knew there was a Jewish "peace bloc" that at one time comprised nearly a third of the electorate.

On the fourth day of my visit I went to the train station and bought a one-way ticket to Jerusalem. I asked the man at the ticket counter when the next train left. "I don't know!" he snapped. "Ask information!" He gestured for me to step away from the window. I was the only one buying a ticket at that time, and no one was in line behind me, so I was a bit taken aback by his gruff manner. Yet an Israeli friend who now resides in the United States had told me repeatedly to expect this kind of rudeness and not to take it personally. It was just their way, he informed me.

There were many armed soldiers and security guards around the bus station, and nearly half of the passengers on my bus were uniformed soldiers. They looked tough and aloof, but who could blame them for that, I thought. I wondered what awful things they may have seen, what things they were ordered to do or, worse, took upon themselves to do in the name of peace and security. I always find abhorrent the things we ask our young men and women to do and how we later leave them to their own devices to deal with the moral, and often the physical, consequences. I said a silent prayer for their safety and happiness and hoped they would be lucky enough to finish their duty without ever aiming their rifles at another human being.

It took about an hour to reach Jerusalem. The first thing I noticed from the outskirts of the city was the consistent, sandy white color of every building in sight. Not a single building or house was made of anything but this sandy white rock, set against virtually the same color landscape.

I took a taxi to the King David Hotel, the same hotel that Jewish terrorists had bombed during British rule. Unfortunately, it was too early to check in, so I hired a driver to take me around the Old City's four quarters (Jewish, Christian, Muslim, and Armenian) and the various historical sites, including the main gates to the Old City, Mount Zion, the Church of the Dormition (where Mary is said to have died), the Mount of Olives, the Jewish Cemetery, the Church of the Ascension, the Church of Mary Magdalene, and Mount Scopus. From atop the Mount of Olives, I had a splendid view of the shining, golden Dome of the Rock, the site where Muslims say the prophet Muhammad ascended to heaven.

As we made our way into east Jerusalem, I recalled an important and courageous book I had read a week or so before leaving home. It was released by three Jewish writers in 1999, drawing attention to the inequalities that exist between the Jews and Palestinians in Jerusalem. Amir Cheshin was an Israeli army colonel and later a senior adviser on Arab and community affairs for Jerusalem mayor Teddy Kollek; Bill Hutman was a journalist with the *Jerusalem Post;* and Avi Melamed was an adviser on Arab affairs to Mayor Kollek and his successor. Their book, *Separate and Unequal,*[42] documents how the Israeli government and the municipality of Jerusalem intentionally set out to make life difficult for Palestinians in east Jerusalem.

Immediately after conquering Jerusalem in 1967, Israel tried to consolidate power there by rapidly increasing the city's Jewish population and decreasing its Arab population. Cheshin, Hutman, and

Melamed point out that despite condemnation by the United Nations and the United States, Israel carried out plans to take Arab land in east Jerusalem and build Jewish neighborhoods there instead. The American ambassador to the UN said, "The expropriation and confiscation of land, the construction of housing on such land, the demolition or confiscation of buildings, including those of historic or religious significance, and the application of Israeli law to occupied portions of the city are detrimental to the common interests in the city."[43] Yet Israel went ahead anyway; once Jewish neighborhoods were established, there was dwindling likelihood that Arabs would ever again gain the right to their land.

Jerusalem's non-Jewish residents have suffered greatly since 1967. "Although Israel has gone to great pains to show otherwise, the startling evidence of this policy is obvious to anyone who drives through east Jerusalem, and it is borne out by the statistics on the comparative well-being of Jewish and Arab residents."[44] Sewage, water, electricity, trash: all of these basic services are lacking in Arab neighborhoods while being taken for granted in Jewish neighborhoods. The streets in Arab neighborhoods are not even given names, as the municipality never has any need for them, failing to provide any services there.

Such ill treatment creates, as we have seen time and time again in history, a time bomb waiting to explode. I wonder, How long would it take any of us to become angry, seeing neighborhoods built on our former land with all the modern conveniences, while we had no running water, sporadic electricity, no trash collection, and sewage running into the street? Asking the question is important if we are to understand the massive disaffection of the Palestinians in Israel and the Occupied Territories.

"Don't believe the propaganda—the rosy picture Israel tries to show the world of life in Jerusalem since the 1967 reunification," the three Jewish writers say. "Israel has treated the Palestinians of Jerusalem terribly. As a matter of policy, it has forced many of them from their homes and stripped them of their land, all the while lying to them and deceiving them and the world about its honorable intentions." They conclude that governing properly would have led to more harmonious relations between the Israelis and the Palestinians.

"Indeed," they summarize, "it likely would have eased the growing conflict over Jerusalem's future. That massive error in judgment, we believe, is the tragedy of Israel's rule in east Jerusalem since 1967."[45]

We drove past a truck that had been firebombed and the driver (a Muslim who was working for the Israelis) murdered. It was an eerie monument, and at last I began to get a closer look at what I had seen on the news for many years. I asked my driver to take me into the heart of the trouble spots, including Bethlehem and Beit Jalla.

He smiled at me and shook his head, saying we couldn't possibly go there during the current crisis. "I can show you the crossing, though, if you wish," he said.

When we arrived at the army checkpoint, two heavily armed soldiers demanded that we turn back. I inquired why I couldn't go through. "Maybe you'll get killed there," my driver said. "They don't want you to get killed."

At lunch I insisted that I wanted to cross into Bethlehem. My driver, who was Jewish, said he would make some calls. He eventually arranged for a Palestinian to pick me up on their side of the checkpoint, if the soldiers permitted me to pass. After that, it was up to me where I wanted to go.

The cold wind ripped at my thin shirt as I strolled across the checkpoint on foot. On the other side, a Palestinian man approached me with a smile. His name was Ziad, and he would take me into Bethlehem in his old VW Golf. I was introduced to a man in the backseat who asked me what I was doing here. I told him. His name was Faiz, a professor of physics and math at a university in Jerusalem. Faiz told me that the soldiers had not let him cross the checkpoint for several weeks so that he could go to work. That morning they purportedly told him, "Palestinians don't need an education. Go home!"

"They just want us to be their servants," the professor told me.

In Bethlehem, a town of about twenty-two thousand people, we stopped at a small shop where I was introduced to a tour guide named Nidel. Nidel showed me around the streets of the Old City. Everything had been restored for the millennium celebrations. It was a marvelous place, clean and orderly and full of promise. Yet the streets were mostly empty and quiet.

I was quite impressed by the Church of the Nativity, one of the oldest churches in use in the world. It was built like a fortress over a small cave in which Jesus is said to have been born. The building has been modified over the years, but it mostly consists of the structure erected by Emperor Justinian around 530 C.E. A small door leads into the dark hall, to the front right of which is the entrance to the cave. On the day I visited the church was empty, except for a few monks chanting prayers. I knelt at the spot where Jesus was born and the spot where he was wrapped in cloth and placed in the manger. Amid the thick smoke of incense wafting from an ornate censer swung by a monk who circled the room and then departed, I said a prayer for peace in this land and throughout the world.

Outside the church, Nidel told me that the unemployment rate in Bethlehem was well over 85 percent, as there were no tourists these days. His statistics were anecdotal, as far as I knew. "We usually have two hundred tour buses a day come here," he told me. "Now look around. There is no one. It is very difficult to take care of my five children."

Nidel took me to his friend's shop, where he offered me a cup of coffee. The coffee was poured from a small pot with a long handle, called a *cezve,* into a small cup. It was traditional Arabic coffee, strong and spicy and delicious. Inside the shop seven Palestinian men sat around a makeshift table playing cards. "They are all tour guides," Nidel told me, "now out of work." They all greeted me with smiles and welcomed me to join in their game.

"No, I don't think so," I responded. "I would lose faster than you can believe." They laughed. I asked the men about the conflict with the Israelis and was a bit surprised by their calmness in replying. One of the men was from Beit Jalla, bordering on Bethlehem. He said his children lived in terror of the Israeli mortar shells. Some of his neighbors' homes had been destroyed in the shelling, though they had nothing to do with any of the fanatics who might have fired on Israelis.

"We didn't want any violence by Palestinians," Nidal said. "We began by protesting for human rights. The Israeli soldiers responded by shooting rubber bullets. Then some protesters threw rocks at the Israelis. Then the Israelis used regular bullets. Up to twenty Palestinians a day were dying. And then some fanatics came into Beit Jalla and other places and fired at the Israelis. We didn't want this, but it happened. But," he said, holding up his index finger, "the Israelis responded to each single bullet with a mortar shell from a tank. It was crazy. They responded with such vehemence. Whole houses were destroyed. You can go there to Beit Jalla and see for yourself. You already saw the Jewish neighborhoods. Not a single one of their homes was destroyed."

"We thought the Intifada would last only a few days," another man said. "Then we thought, perhaps it will last a whole month. We never expected it to last this long. We can't understand why the negotiators can't find a solution. There is nothing new to be said. So we don't know why they just can't agree and bring us some peace."

"Hey," another Palestinian called out to me, "when you get home tell the Pentagon that their weapons are really great. The Israelis use them against us with 99.99 percent accuracy!" How could I feel but saddened that American weapons were being used against Palestinian civilians, many of whom are children. Even some Israelis are horrified by this disproportionate use of force.

Nidal's little girl and boy arrived dressed in their school uniforms. They were shy but very sweet. "This is why peace is important," Nidal said to me as he pulled his children to his side. He leaned down and kissed his daughter's cheek and cupped his son's face in one of his hands. "If I must live without human rights and without peace, then so be it. But my children deserve better," he said spiritedly. "They should have peace."

The next day I returned to the West Bank, meeting Ziad at the border crossing. He had brought another guide along with him, and they took me to see a number of beautiful houses bombed out by Israeli artillery. I recalled that the Israeli neighborhood at the top of the adjacent hill had no such damage. The Israeli retaliation for Palestinian gunfire was surely out of proportion but was consistent with Israeli policy of swift and severe revenge.

Professor Edward Said of Columbia University in New York discussed the Israeli policy of retaliation in his book *The Question of Palestine*. He writes,

However much one laments and even wishes somehow to atone for the loss of life and suffering visited upon innocents because of Palestinian violence, there is still the need, I think, also to say that no national movement has been so unfairly penalized, defamed, and subjected to disproportionate retaliation for its sins as has the Palestinian. The Israeli policy of punitive counterattacks (or state terrorism) seems to be to try to kill anywhere from 50 to 100 Arabs for every Jewish fatality. . . . The number of Palestinian fatalities, the scale of material loss, the physical, political and psychological deprivations, have tremendously exceeded the damage done by Palestinians to Israelis.[46]

One thing that is certain is that the Israeli army can, and does, escalate situations, quickly resorting to live ammunition against rock-throwing teens. This fact was discussed rather comprehensively in the December 10, 2000, issue of *Time:*

Israel's loosely drawn rules of engagement permit soldiers regularly to shoot at children. In many cases, Israeli attacks can be indiscriminate, such as machine-gun fire into crowded neighborhoods. Children are frequently victims in these cases as well. Medical officials estimate that 40 percent of the Palestinian dead in Gaza in the latest violence were under 18. . . . The U.S. and the U.N. have both accused Israel of using excessive force.

One of the places I visited that day was Dehasha refugee camp. It was bitterly cold and raining, so most of the narrow, winding streets of the camp were empty. Nearly every building had a poster or graffiti dedicated to a "martyr" who had lost his life in clashes with the Israelis.

We stopped by the home of Akram. His mother answered the door, and my interpreter explained why we were visiting. She was wearing a dark green dress and a matching scarf over her head. She looked grim but invited us in. Several small children were playing loudly in the main room. I smiled at them, and the woman returned a slight smile to me. We sat in their sitting room, and the woman brought us coffee. A few minutes later, Akram came in, looking tired and frail, his eyes dark and sad.

My interpreter asked Akram to tell us about his ordeal with the Israeli army not many weeks before. He looked down at the floor and slowly recounted how he and his best friend had crossed the border to Israel that morning to go to work. Tens of thousands of Palestinians do this each day, providing Israel with cheap manual labor. After a long day of hard work, Akram and his friend were returning home when all of a sudden they heard gunfire coming from the Israeli army encampment on the top of the hill.

"I was with my friend Mustafah heading back from work in Jerusalem," he said in a low voice. "Of course, we didn't have permission to cross, along with many thousands of other workers. So, as usual, we had to come back by the bridge, bypassing the main crossing. It was around five o'clock. Israeli soldiers suddenly opened fire from the top of the hill. Six bullets hit us; three of them hit me, and three of them hit my friend. We remained on the ground for almost half an hour. No one came to help us. We had to wait while the Israelis coordinated with the Palestinian ambulance to get permission to take us. They took us to the hospital. I went into surgery. After six or seven hours I awoke. I immediately asked for my friend. They told me he was in the next room, so I thought he must be okay. Only the next day did they tell me that my friend had died. He had died immediately after being shot. He never reached the hospital alive. It is because of God that I survived. I must thank God. God loved both of us, but he wanted Mustafah by his side and he wanted me to keep living."

"What did you think while you were lying there waiting for someone to come to help you and your friend?" I asked.

He paused quite a long time. He looked very emotional as he said, "I don't recall thinking, but I really recall the smell of my friend's blood. Now whenever I see Mustafah's photo or see another victim on television, I recall the smell of his blood."

"After everything that has been done to you, could you live in peace with the Jews?" I asked.

"Not with Jewish soldiers. Toward Jews in general, I can get along with them, but never as close friends," he said.

I turned to Akram's mother and asked her what her aim was now. "Do you still hold out hope that you can return to your former village?" I asked.

"I remember how wonderful our life was there," she said. "The area was rich, with many olive trees, and we were very well off. We had a beautiful home and we were happy. We have not been happy since that time."

"If it is impossible to go back," I questioned, "then what will you do? Would you accept reparations or land somewhere else?"

"It is our right to go back," she said fervently. "If they make an agreement that does not let us go back, then we will not accept it. Such an agreement will only last a few years. We are willing to die in order to get our land back. Money comes and goes; even if you lose your lover, you can eventually forget and find someone else. But there is nothing that can replace your land. I still have the key to my house and the documents showing we own the land. If this happened to the Jews, that they were forced to leave their land, would they accept it? No. Never. So then why should we accept it?" she said, slapping her hands into her lap.

Akram walked me to the door.

"I wish you the best of luck," I said. "I hope you heal fully, and you can overcome the pain of Mustafah's death. Jews have died as well. Their blood smelled the same as your friend's blood. This whole conflict must end one day, and I pray it is soon."

He just looked into my eyes. I reached out and took hold of his hand, placing my other hand on his shoulder. "Don't despair too deeply. Peace will come. Thank you for letting me into your home and sharing your heart with me," I said.

He must have sensed my sincerity, for he squeezed my hand and said, "You are my friend. You are welcome in my home anytime."

As I was getting into the car, Akram stepped from his house into the rain. "Go in peace," he said in Arabic as he waved good-bye.

Driving back toward the checkpoint, I wondered how many people at home would believe my account of the situation in this land. The skeptics might be interested to know, I thought, that it was only a short time ago that the Israeli Supreme Court abolished the systematic use of torture to extract information and confessions from prisoners. Many studies have shown that information and confessions are unreliable when gained through torture. More important, the use of torture is strictly condemned throughout the developed world, and the fact that the United States' greatest ally, a supposed democracy that receives billions of dollars in aid from the United States each year, used torture routinely for decades without any public outcry from American taxpayers proves that the seemingly unbelievable does in fact happen.

Later that afternoon I made my way to the West Bank town of Beit Hanina, a suburb of Jerusalem on the road toward Ramallah. I had an appointment with Dr. Hanan Ashrawi, a prominent American-educated Palestinian leader who once served as the spokeswoman for the Palestinian delegation at peace talks with Israel. She is considered one of the most influential women, if not *the* most influential woman, in the Arab world, despite the fact that she is Christian, not Muslim. But religious labels are not important to Ashrawi, whose family has many labels: an Anglican mother, a non-practicing father, two Catholic aunts, one Greek Orthodox aunt, a Baptist uncle, a grandfather who was an Episcopalian minister, and a sister who married a Muslim.

Ashrawi earned her bachelor's and master's degrees in literature at the American University of Beirut. Afterward she had nowhere to go. She didn't have permission to stay in Lebanon, and Israel had denied her application to return to her home in occupied Ramallah. Fortunately, Ashrawi was awarded a doctoral scholarship by the American University of Beirut and she was accepted as a graduate student at the University of Virginia, Charlottesville.

It was not always easy for Ashrawi in the United States. "At that time," she remembers, "the word 'Palestinian' meant terrorist or nothing at all." Yet "as soon as people realized I was not going to jump up and start belly dancing between the salad and the main course," she recalls, "nor was I going to toss a grenade into the dessert, I began to make friends."[47] In 1973 she earned her Ph.D. in medieval and comparative literature.

After graduate school, Ashrawi returned to her homeland to set up the Department of English at Birzeit University on the West Bank. During her tenure at Birzeit University, Ashrawi established the University Legal Aid Committee in reaction to Israel's repeated closure of the university. She also helped form the first Palestinian-Israeli underground political organization, which advocated a two-state solution to the conflict. She also published many books, poems, short stories, and articles on Palestinian culture and politics.

In 1988, during the first Intifada uprising, Ashrawi joined the Intifada Political Committee and served until 1993 on its Diplomatic Committee. From 1991 through 1993 Ashrawi served as the Official Spokesperson of the Palestinian Delegation to the Middle East Peace Process. She was also a member of the Leadership/Guidance Committee and Executive Committee of the Palestinian Delegation.

After Palestinian President Arafat and Israeli Prime Minister Rabin signed peace accords setting up limited Palestinian self-rule in 1993, Ashrawi served as the head of the Preparatory Committee of the Palestinian Independent Commission for Citizens' Rights. In 1996 Ashrawi was elected to the Palestinian Legislative Council. From 1996 through 1998 she served as minister of higher education and research, and in August 1998 she established the Palestinian Initiative for the Promotion of Global Dialogue and Democracy, which she heads to this day. She also serves on many international advisory boards, including the Council on Foreign Relations, the World Bank Middle East and North Africa Region, and the United Nations Research Institute for Social Development.

Before making my way to Ashrawi's office, I reread the final few pages of her memoirs, published in 1995. "Often when I find the pain of self-inflicted wounds unbearable," she writes, "as on my inspection of interrogation cells where Palestinians used violence on other Palestinians, or when I investigate cases of dark deals concluded in secret, I am reminded of the words of an Old English poem, 'Deor.' As the poet catalogues a series of past disasters . . . he repeats at the end of each stanza a formula of consolation for the present misfortune: 'All that passed, so may this.' Our catalogue of disasters from a past almost beyond time is long, but it passed. So may this."[48] Ashrawi's career is completely dedicated to what she calls "a joy yet to come."

Ashrawi's workplace was in a small, new building just past the Israeli checkpoint. Inside I was greeted warmly by her assistant and given a cup of coffee. I waited for fifteen minutes before Ashrawi appeared. She wasn't ready to talk yet, though I was shown into her private office. When she did finally join me, I began by speaking of my visit with Akram.

"I went to Dehasha camp this morning," I told her, "and I met a young man who had been shot by Israeli snipers while he was returning from work."

"That must have been eye opening for you," she said.

"Well, it certainly is difficult to understand such violence toward someone who wasn't trying to cause trouble, someone who was just walking along the road, returning home after work."

"A Palestinian doesn't have to do anything to provoke Israeli violence," she replied calmly. "The mere fact that you are a Palestinian is a threat. This is a constant danger when you live here."

"I am eager to hear how you summarize the Israeli-Palestinian conflict," I said.

She responded immediately. "Primarily the conflict is an existential question, a question of legitimacy. In order to try to get legitimacy, Israel has wanted to negate our legitimacy, our existence, our culture, our reality. This stems from a basic sense of insecurity. Israel is an artificial culture created on Palestinian land through a tragic event for the Palestinian people. The conflict started by trying to rewrite history, by trying to fabricate myths and legends, dating back to the saying 'Israel, a land without a people for a people without a land.' When Jews found out that there was a people on the land and that they cannot not dismiss us, and that the ethnic cleansing that took place in 1948 cannot be repeated, then they came face-to-face with reality. So, this is a clash of legitimacy, this is a clash of versions of history, Palestinian and Israeli. And the Israelis want to claim exclusivity of pain, exclusivity of suffering, and exclusivity of victimization, while at the same time denying that what they are doing to others is the same as what has been done to them in their own history. They have now become the oppressor, yet they deny that they cause suffering and victimization."

"But do you see Israeli actions as a *calculated* effort to cause this suffering?" I asked.

"No, not necessarily," she replied, "but it could be a collective ethos; the ethos leads to the oppressive actions. And it could be calculated on the part of a few. But there are voices, of course, toward Zionism, new historians and so on, who are trying to really get back to the authentic historic narrative, who are beginning to understand that the only legitimacy that Israel can have is from the Palestinians, and can only come by empowerment of the Palestinians rather than by exploiting our weakness."

"There are people in Israel who are trying to do right by the Palestinians," I noted. "But that isn't as remarkable as the fact that most Israelis simply support the hard-line policies of the government. Why is that?"

"There is a sense of collective mind-set," she said, "an attitude in Israel, that has been exploited many times by hard-line, right-wing philosophical governments. These Israeli governments create security fears by delegitimizing the Palestinians, by creating a collective phobia among the Israelis, and they do so for political gains. It has always been the tradition of the right wing like Netanyahu and others to aggravate the fears of the Israelis and use them for their political ends. And they use them to justify their land grab. But now we've managed to demystify the conflict, not to make it a question of zero-sum game or of either-or. We've said, 'Let's legitimize sharing.' The land of Palestine can be divided, it can be shared by two peoples. So the question is what is the most equitable way of sharing. How do we create two states that can exist side by side as neighbors rather than on top of each other as occupiers and occupied? So that is why we launched the peace process. It is about creating a new Palestine."

"Everyone wants to know why the peace process hasn't worked thus far," I said.

"It hasn't worked so far for a variety of reasons. One reason is the mentality of the occupier. Once you are used to doing anything and getting away with it, with total impunity and total lack of accountability, you incorporate and internalize your power. And you become racist and you dehumanize the other, so you don't need to face the consequences of your own actions. And this is precisely what has been happening to the Palestinian people. The dehumanization of Palestinians began with the nonexistence of the Palestinians, the notion that this was a land without a people, continued with

Golda Meir's comment that there is no such thing as a Palestinian. 'Where are they?' she said. She made Palestinians totally invisible." Ashrawi was referring to Meir's statement in 1969 that "it was not as though there was a Palestinian people in Palestine considering itself as a Palestinian people and we came and threw them out and took their country away from them. They did not exist."[49]

"Then it underwent a metamorphosis of stereotyping and labeling with the most demeaning, dehumanizing labels," Ashrawi continued. "I documented this metamorphosis of racism. We were called the two-legged vermin, the cockroaches, the dogs, and then just an abstraction, the 'democratic problem.' And then later we became the snakes and the crocodiles and so on. Officials in Israel give themselves the right to be racists, and not to examine their own motivation, their own language, and the license to dehumanize and slander a whole nation of people. But this came to a head with this Intifada.

"When we launched the peace process," she added, "we began by recognizing the humanity of our objectives and saying that we would not do to them what they were doing to us, we would not dehumanize them as they dehumanize us, even though we are suffering as they occupy our land and demolish our homes. Though they kill people, torture people, imprison people, we still will not dehumanize them, and that is the only way to be. So we reached out to the other side in that manner.

"It is just incredible how they allowed the violations of Palestinian rights even during the course of the process. And they destroyed the very foundations of the peace process. This military occupation not only resurged but became more apparent. They impose upon the peace process this mentality of superiority, like the white man who tries to impose his will on the good little natives. But we don't act like good little natives, we are not grateful for these 'generous' offers that are 'given' to us. They don't seem to understand that there are requirements for peace: legality, justice, even practicality, pragmatism. You cannot set up a tiny state that is fragmented into a series of enclaves totally under Israeli control and call it a state. We do not have a viable Palestinian state."

I recalled hearing repeatedly that Arafat must not really want peace because the Palestinians rejected the eleventh-hour peace

proposal that Clinton and Barak fashioned, a proposal that most
Israelis and Americans saw as "generous" and the only hope for
peace. Yet anyone can call any offer generous; that doesn't make it
so. The so-called generous offer had onerous stipulations. Keep in
mind that the Palestinians had already agreed by the Oslo Accords
to accept the Green Line boundaries; that is, they had already
agreed they would give up any claims to 78 percent of historical
Palestine. Within the remaining Occupied Territories, Barak
demanded that Israel would maintain sixty-nine Jewish settlements. Each settlement would come with connecting roads and
protection zones that would effectively keep the Palestinian territories carved up into pieces. Moreover, Barak demanded that 10 percent of the Occupied Territories remain under Israeli military and
civil control for an indefinite period. What's more, Israel would
maintain roadblocks, supervision over border crossings, and a host
of other restrictions.

"It seems that most people in the United States see the Palestinians as the aggressor, as the fanatics, and as the obstacle to peace," I
noted.

"Yes, we have always been presented through the eyes of the
Israelis. We were always the other, the aliens, the Muslims, the terrorists, so many labels. We were not human to them. Now this
dehumanization came to a head when they once again started
blaming us for all the violence. They robbed us of the most elemen-
tal of human feelings, the love of parents for their children, when
they said, 'Palestinians don't have feelings for their children so they
send them out to die.' In Israel the horrendous application of these
statements was never addressed by the media. And the Western
media swallowed this hook, line, and sinker."

"It does often seem," I noted, "that the United States has uncon-
ditional support for Israel. Do you think this stems in part from a
Western sense of guilt about not doing anything to stop the Holocaust? I wonder how much that plays into it."

"Oh, there are many reasons. First of all, Israel is trying to confis-
cate the conscience of the West when it comes to the Jewish people.
And now many brave Jewish voices are saying no, that this is *not* the
case, Israel does *not* speak for them, this is *not* the heir to the Jewish

tradition. Israel does not hold the key to our conscience. It is a state. It claims to be the heir to the legacy of the horrible cruelty to the Jews by the West, and therefore that has been internalized in the West, and the label *anti-Semitism* has become extremely convenient."

"What about the corruption by officials in the Palestinian Authority?" I asked.

"Yes. There is some corruption, and some repression too. And we detest it. I said to the Palestinian leaders who were in Tunisia that when they return to set up and occupy positions in the Palestinian Authority that they had better not bring their corruption and non-democratic practices here. I implored them not to do that. We in Palestine had spent decades setting up local democratic institutions, small elected bodies, with incredible openness and participation, and we didn't want to see that work destroyed. But some of the leaders from Tunisia didn't listen and they came here with their negative practices, and so, yes, we have some problems to sort out. But this doesn't mean that the whole system is bad or that we can't sort out our problems democratically while we remain under military occupation."

We spoke a bit longer about the present situation in Palestine, then talked about more personal issues: her family, how I came to be writing this book, things I had seen during my travels. She was soon called away to appear on an international television broadcast. I realized while returning to my hotel that Ashrawi is often given ten or fifteen seconds on news broadcasts to present or defend Palestinian goals, largely after coverage of the violence by Palestinian militants that Ashrawi deeply opposes. But those who give her more than a few seconds to speak find in her a clear and courageous voice for "a joy yet to come."

The next day I returned to Tel Aviv to visit Uri Avnery, a man who consistently has sought a just solution to the Israeli-Palestinian problem. For backing the idea of a Palestinian state and for advocating the right of the Palestinian refugees to return to their ancestral land, Avnery has been denounced by some Jews as a traitor and belittled by others as a left-wing nut who would give Tel Aviv to the Arabs if he were given half a chance. These ridiculous attacks against his character fly in the face of Avnery's long and devoted service toward the Israeli state.

Avnery, a Jew, fled Nazi Germany with his family (a very well off, established Jewish family in Westphalia) to Palestine in 1933. Avnery was ten years old. The family lost its wealth, and soon Avnery's father and mother had to resort to hard manual labor to make ends meet. Avnery attended school in Nahalal (a famous communal village) and in Tel Aviv, but because of his family's poverty he was forced to leave school and find a job.

At the age of fourteen, Avnery joined Irgun, one of the main Jewish militant groups that carried out acts of terrorism against the British in an attempt to create the Israeli state. He left Irgun four years later in protest of its anti-Arab policies and reactionary social positions. Avnery, even then, was of the opinion that the Jewish and Arab national movements should form an alliance. In September 1947 Avnery published a booklet entitled *War or Peace in the Semitic Region,* which stated that it was only natural for the Semitic peoples (Jewish and Arab) to stand together to oppose colonialism in the Middle East and to support one another in their national ambitions.

When war broke out, however, Avnery joined the Israeli army, fighting in the Giv'ati brigade. He volunteered for what later became a legendary commando unit called Samson's Foxes, battling on the Egyptian front. Avnery's reports from nearly every major battle on the Jerusalem and southern fronts were printed in the *Ha'aretz* evening paper and were later published as the best-selling book *In the Fields of the Philistines, 1948.* Avnery was twice wounded in battle. In the waning days of the war he was gravely wounded, and after months of convalescence was discharged in the summer of 1949 with the rank of squadron leader.

He spent the next year or so working on the editorial staff of *Ha'aretz,* feeling, he recalls, unable to truly express his opinion about the mass expropriation of Arab land being carried out by Prime Minister Ben-Gurion's government. Avnery decided to buy a failing family publication and turn it into an aggressive magazine of investigative journalism. For the next forty years *Haolam Hazeh* would expose many acts of government corruption and push

Avnery's agenda of better treatment of Israel's Arab minority, Jews from non-European countries, and women. The government never appreciated the criticism (even branding the magazine and Avnery as "Public Enemy No. 1") and tried to silence the magazine in 1965. The magazine office was also bombed several times, and Avnery himself was ambushed and had his hands broken after criticizing the government.

Avnery fought the government's heavy-handedness by forming a political party called Haolam Hazeh (the New Force Movement) and pulled off a historic victory, securing himself a seat in the Knesset. Although he became widely regarded as an outstanding parliamentarian who contributed greatly to the institution, Avnery was often the lone voice in the Knesset arguing that Israel should make peace with the Palestinians by permitting a Palestinian state in the West Bank and Gaza Strip.

In 1974 Avnery established secret contacts with senior officials of the PLO. At the time this was an unthinkable sin in Jewish circles around the globe. For Avnery it was a necessary step in establishing peace between the two peoples, and he briefed Prime Minister Yitzhak Rabin on the meetings. Although there is no hard evidence establishing a connection between the two events, an attempt was made on Avnery's life in 1975. Fortunately, he escaped with only severe knife wounds. Avnery's counterpart in the PLO was not so fortunate; extremists who objected to the meetings assassinated Sa'id Hamami in 1978.

On July 3, 1982, Avnery created an uproar when he openly crossed the lines during the battle of Beirut and met with Yasser Arafat. This was the first time Arafat had ever met with an Israeli official. Several cabinet ministers called for Avnery's arrest and trial for high treason, but a small but growing number of Israelis saw the move as the beginning of a new peace movement.

In 1992, Israel expelled 415 Palestinians from the Occupied Territories without trial. Avnery protested this contravention of international law (specifically the Fourth Geneva Convention), which culminated in the creation of Gush Shalom, one of Israel's most active peace organizations (for which Avnery and his wife won the

Right Livelihood Award, the so-called Alternative Nobel Peace Prize, awarded in the Swedish Parliament). Gush Shalom continues to push for the creation of a Palestinian state, the release of political prisoners, the dismantling of the Jewish settlements, and the recognition of Jerusalem as the joint capital of both the Palestinian and the Israeli states.[50]

I went to Avnery's apartment in the late afternoon. The building was unimpressive, like most of the buildings in Tel Aviv, but it boasted a magnificent panoramic view of the Mediterranean Sea and the entire city.

Meeting me at the door, Avnery invited me in and offered me a seat. The apartment was small but well furnished, bright, and cheery. Avnery was a thin man, very handsome and gentle, like a kindly grandfather with shiny white hair and a matching beard.

"It is difficult for most people in the West to understand the conflict in the Middle East," I began. "Can you help us understand the situation?" I asked.

"In order to understand the whole business," he said, "you must go back to the beginning. What we have here is a clash between two great national movements. The Zionist movement, on one side, was a national liberation movement created in Europe. It began during the gathering storm of anti-Semitism when national movements became the dominant culture in Europe. Every European people became nationalistic from the time of the French Revolution onward, but mainly throughout the nineteenth century. And all the national movements, without exception, were more or less anti-Semitic. Some where outspokenly anti-Semitic, such as the Polish national movement and the Lithuanian national movement and the Slovakian, and so forth. But the French and the Germans were equally anti-Semitic. So the idea grew that if none of the nations of Europe wanted to accept the Jews as part of their nations, then the Jews should constitute themselves as a nation. Incidentally, that did not mean that a nation would be in Palestine. The leader of the Zionist movement didn't want a nation in Palestine; he didn't like the weather in Palestine. He actually wanted to go to Argentina. But the Jewish people were culturally conditioned to want Palestine, so they decided to create a Jewish homeland in Palestine. Two hundred Jewish delegates met in Switzerland, elected by themselves, and though only perhaps one of them had ever been there, they chose Palestine for a future homeland."

"Since they had not been there, to them the Palestinians must have been truly invisible," I remarked.

"They were invisible in two senses," he replied. "They hadn't been to Palestine ever. Therefore, they knew little or nothing about Palestinians. On another level, one should understand that the Zionists were Europeans of their time. They came from European cities and towns, and they shared the European views of their time. For the Zionists of that time, then, black people, brown people, yellow people, red people were not really people. So Palestinians were invisible as people, a people with rights and so forth. Remember that the first Zionist Congress took place fewer than thirty years after the slaves had been liberated in America. Now, at the very same time that the Zionist national movement began in Palestine, influenced by Zionists from Europe, the Arab national movement began locally, of which the Palestinians were a part. Two great movements were now aiming to fulfill their dreams in the same country, carried out by people completely ignorant of each other. The Zionist Congress didn't give a damn about an Arab national movement in Palestine. And the Palestinians couldn't dream that a little congress in Europe would one day threaten their land. So the Zionists came here with the idea of a country, and the moment they arrived here both movements immediately began to clash. It was inevitable."

"I have heard it said that the Palestinians deserved to lose their land because they did not accept the United Nations' partition of Palestine into two states, one Jewish and one Arab. They attacked Israel, so they deserved to lose their state. What do you say to this argument?" I asked.

"Well, it was the clash of the national movements that was the real cause of the war in 1948. The war of 1948 started because the Palestinians, and the Arabs in general, objected to the partition of Palestine. The United Nations decided to divide the land into a Jewish state and an Arab state, with Jerusalem and its vicinity belonging to neither the Jewish nor the Arab state. At that time, the

Jews received 54 or 55 percent, the Palestinians were supposed to
have 45 percent. The Palestinians objected to this. It was natural
that they would object! If you don't have half a loaf of bread, then
you are willing to accept half of the loaf. For you it is a gain. But if
you have already a whole loaf of bread, then you don't want to give
any of it away. Why should you? It is natural. So the war came. The
war broke out between two communities: 1.2 million Arabs and
630,000 Jews; nearly two to one exactly.

"Each community considered all the land to be its natural homeland," he continued. "It was not a war in which each nation claimed
the right to the land that lay in between them, but rather each side
claimed all the land of the other. In this sense it was a real ethnic
war; it was very cruel. It was quite natural for us to drive out the
Arabs. It was also quite natural for the Arabs to drive us out. And,
in fact, not a single Jew remained in any of the land conquered by
the Arabs. Fortunately for us, not very much land was conquered
by the Arab armies. We drove out the Arabs, partly because of military necessity. We expected the Arab armies to march in, and we
did not want to leave any hostile population at our back. But somewhere in the middle of the war it became the deliberate policy of the
government to drive out the Arabs. Many Arabs were driven out.
Many villages were driven out. But I would say that the majority of
Arabs were forced out by the war. When there is shooting in your
village, you take your children and wife and move to the next village. The same thing happens to the next village and the next. That
is what happened. Then, suddenly one day, there was an armistice,
and a new border. So, when the Israelis say that we did not drive the
Arabs out, it is partly true and partly untrue. Yet it is not really so
much a question of how the Arabs were displaced from their
homes, it is more a question of why they are not allowed to come
back after the war. Okay, let's imagine that we had no choice but to
drive the Arabs out because of the necessities of war."

"Sure. We'll assume that war is hell," I replied.

"But when the war was finished, we could have allowed a small
percentage of Arabs to return to their homes, and we could have
achieved a true peace agreement with the Arabs. However, the
main achievement of the war for the Israeli government was not

that they went from having 55 percent of the land to having 87 percent of the land, but rather that our land was free from Arabs. We were now almost completely devoid of Arabs. That was a great success for the government."

"Was that just the government's feeling, or did everyone feel that way?"

"Everybody felt that way," he said. "It was a great sense of exhilaration. We had won the war, we had escaped from mortal danger. We had won an incredible victory against five Arab armies, and we had won the land. And the land was now empty so we could really start building."

"But the Palestinian land was not actually empty of structures. It contained Arab houses and farms and buildings of all sorts," I noted.

"Yes. But [Prime Minister] Ben-Gurion in 1949 and 1950 destroyed about 450 Arab villages. Jews destroyed them to such an extent that even the Arabs can hardly find their former villages. To find them, you really have to search quite hard. Some villages still contained Arabs. We ordered them to leave and told them they could come back in a few weeks. But when they were gone, we totally destroyed the villages. These are the facts."

"But what did the Israelis expect to happen to the Palestinian refugees?" I asked. "Did they think that the other Arab states would take them in and that the refugees would be happy with their new lives in a new place?"

"Ben-Gurion believed," he responded, "in fact everyone believed—except perhaps the number of people you could count on the fingers of one hand—not that the Palestinians would go away. The general idea was that the Palestinian people had ceased to exist. Palestine itself ceased to exist. The West Bank was annexed to Jordan. The Gaza Strip was held by Egypt. The refugees had therefore ceased to have an identity. The idea, then, was that in five or ten years the refugees would simply be absorbed by the Arab states. Israelis did not think that there was a Palestinian problem. What Palestinian problem? The Palestinians no longer existed."

"Was this an authentic belief or just a justification?" I questioned.

"It was a mixture. It is my personal opinion, which I have written about many times, that somewhere in the national unconscious there was, and still is, a feeling of guilt, which led to aggressiveness, which led to the conviction that we are justified in what we do. You know, Moshe Dayan was a typical Israeli; perhaps *the* typical Israeli of my generation. Moshe Dayan was an interesting person. He used to make three speeches a day, and in each one he would say contradictory things with deep conviction. You now might call him a pragmatist. But there was one famous speech in which he really spoke his mind. It was a beautiful speech. There was something almost poetical about it, spoken in really beautiful Hebrew. A good friend of his was killed on the border of Gaza, and he made this speech at his friend's funeral. He said, 'Look at the hatred from the Gaza Strip. They are the people whom we have driven from their land. We have turned their land into our homeland. They will never forgive us, they will never live in peace, and therefore we are condemned to live with the rifle in our hand. Let the hand not weaken, for then we will lose our lives. We cannot build our houses without the cannon.' It was a completely fatalistic view by Dayan that we would never have peace with the Arabs.

"Ben-Gurion was not quite so fatalistic. He thought that within three generations the Palestinians would disappear. 'Just give it time and they will vanish,' he said. 'There is no Palestine.' The general view was that we had to stand fast, let time pass, and hit the Arabs on the head if they tried to gather too much military power. Every ten years we could hit them on the head, have a war and destroy their military power, and let them slowly vanish."

"I would like to better understand the process by which the unconscious guilt, the collective guilt, leads to violence," I said.

"Deep down," he responded, "there is a profound uneasiness that rationalizes itself by projecting on the other what you yourself are feeling. For instance, one says, if *I* were in their place, *I* would never make peace; so it follows that *they* will never make peace with me. So with this thinking there will never be peace. Those who think there can be peace are called crazy, naive, stupid, or whatever. I think that there is something similar in the American psyche with the way that they treated the Native Americans. They have not forgotten them. The whole ideology of the Wild West still exists today. I believe that the whole unnatural tendency toward violence in

America, that we see on the television and read about in the paper every day, that streak of violence comes from the myth of the Wild West and also justifies what was done to the Native Americans. It was simple genocide. It has had a profound impact on the American culture, even today two hundred years later. What we have in Israel is, I think, similar. The whole Zionist movement was a very moral movement. And I think the morality of Zionism has led to a psychological dissonance. If Zionism had been just for the sake of the settlement of people and the use of power had no moral implications, then there wouldn't be any psychological problem with what we have done. Yet Zionists believed in beautiful ideas. They believed in Tolstoy, they believed in kibbutzim, they believed in a totally just human society. And this created a dissonance, which we have had to try to deal with, to wish away or to try to totally forget. So we say, 'They attacked us, they tried to kill us, they wanted to throw us into the sea,' and so on. Today, after a whole group of new historians has written about it, published in Israel in scientific papers and in books, by Israeli sources, one knows exactly what we did to every Arab village in 1949. But you have such denial and justification and negativity in Israeli politics, and this negativity prevents looking for a real solution to the problem.

Avnery's comments reminded me of something the Zionist leader Nahum Goldmann wrote in his memoirs: "[T]he ideological and political leaders of the Zionist movement always emphasized—sincerely and earnestly, it seems to me—the Jewish national home must be established in peace and harmony with the Arabs. Unfortunately these convictions remained in the realm of theory and were not carried over, to any great extent, into actual Zionist practice."[51]

"We should consider the incredible, glorious achievement of the new state of Israel," Avnery continued, "which had 635,000 Jews managing to absorb 2 million new Jews—all the Jewish remnants from the Holocaust and those that came from the Arab lands. The mood the day after the war of 1948, then, was, 'My God, there are 750,000 refugees. If they come back, it would be like a tidal wave coming from the sea.' We had only 635,000 Jews. The tidal wave would render Israel an Arab state, would make Jews a minority in their own country. This apocalyptic view was not unjustified in

1949; that was the reality. Yet today, after there are 5.5 million Jews in Israel, the problem is still viewed the same way. If you bring back the refugees, *any* refugees, it brings about fear and hatred among Israelis. I wrote about this key question long before you were born, in 1952 or 1953. I made innumerable appearances and spoke lots, in the Knesset and in other places. When I spoke about the settlements, which today nearly everybody hates, it wasn't such a big problem. If I spoke about Jerusalem, I received criticism. But when I spoke about the problem of the Arab refugees, nearly everyone hated me. I became very cautious to keep my comments on the refugees in small doses. This problem of hate, of apocalyptic fear of turning Israel into an Arab state, today it is as fresh as it was many years ago. Many facts of the conflict have not changed at all."

"Explain to me how Israeli Jews could treat Palestinians so poorly, so oppressively, when Jews themselves have suffered so much persecution throughout history," I said.

"Well, it is nice to think that persecuted people become better people. Unfortunately, it is not borne out by psychology. If a child is beaten, he probably will become a child beater when he grows up. Years ago a high school principal sent to me writings done by students whom the school had taken to Auschwitz. The students had been asked to write down their feelings about the terrible experience. And the writings confirmed what I had suspected they would, that there were two distinct reactions. The first reaction was, this was terrible, what was done to Jews, it is incumbent on Israel to behave differently, to treat minorities differently, to show the whole world we are better than those who treated us so badly. But this was a minority reaction. The majority had another reaction, that what was done to Jews was terrible and that we should take any action without hesitation that safeguards our people. Both reactions are natural, and sometimes even both exist within a single person. I am very much against forcing people to have a type of endless concentration on the Holocaust in all its terrible details. The reason for doing so—and it is the official doctrine of Israeli education and politics to remember the Holocaust every day—is that if you forget the victims of the Holocaust they will be forgotten forever, and it is our duty to remember them, and so on. What it brings about is all this anxiety; all this need for security becomes a national obsession, becomes a malignant growth. It is a need for absolute security, but there is no such thing as absolute security in the world today. Security is our holy cow. Barak only talked about our security, not about true peace. But there is no security without peace."

"The obvious question now is, What are the prospects for peace?" I questioned.

"It will come," he replied without hesitation. "It will come because peace is inevitable. In the last fifty years the basic facts have not changed. There is a Palestinian people, there is an Israeli people, we can't dispose of them and they cannot dispose of us. In the end we have to live together; of course, not in one state, but in two states. So the solution in my mind is quite clear and inevitable. The question is when. We are in the middle of the conflict of two national movements that goes on for five generations. It was too naive to expect that Rabin could have achieved peace in one big move, which he was afraid to do. It is a movement, forward and backward, like a river to the sea, not in a straight line. We will have a few years of a Likud government, which could lead to a war with a lot of casualties. But in the end, we will reach the same point. The basic circumstances will not change. I am an optimist, in a way. We can make peace tomorrow morning. I can write out a peace agreement in the morning, and put it away, and it will be the agreement that will eventually be reached. There is nothing prophetic about it, it is just that there is nothing new about what must be agreed. Nothing more needs to be discussed. Jerusalem will be the capital of Palestine; there is no question about it. Most of the Jewish settlements will have to be removed and the settlers will have to come back to Israel. The borders will more or less follow the Green Line of 1948. Thousands of Palestinian refugees will come back to Israel, although most of the refugees will not come back. So, this is quite clear.

"In a sense I am very optimistic, but I am old enough to remember how things looked after the war of 1948. No one would have believed that Israel would be ready for a Palestinian state and would daily negotiate with the PLO and Yasser Arafat. It was unthinkable."

"And what accounts for this change?" I asked.

"People learn from each other and from their own experience," he replied. "They learn from their relatives who served in the army. And one day a fellow like you is doing his job, working in an office, and they call you up and put you in a uniform and the next day you wake up in the middle of nowhere in the Gaza. People shoot at you, people throw stones at you, and people shout at you, and you shoot back and see children fall. It is not what you want to do forever. When we left Gaza in 1994, it freed us from a foreign occupation. It was a big relief, and most people do not want to go back there. If they are sent back to Gaza, within a year or two they will be fed up. Most people will make peace not because they are for peace but because they are fed up with war. When people are fed up with war, then peace can take over."

He became somber and looked down. "You see on television a lynching of an Israeli by an Arab mob, and it is infuriating. But then again, you also see a Palestinian child killed by an Israeli bullet. These things are horrible," he said slowly.

I told him that I admired how he had stuck to his convictions all these years. "Well, some people support me," he replied, "but many others think I am terrible. I just have to do what I think is right." With that I said good-bye and made my way back to my hotel.

The next morning I went for a walk along the coast to Jaffa, a former Arab village that had been taken over by the Jews. Compared to Tel Aviv, it was a gem—romantic and quiet and charming. There I sat and wrote and wished that I could somehow make a difference in this place, that I could be sitting here with Arabs and Jews in a single place, without dissension, without violence, learning about their shared history and culture.

Later that afternoon I called on Shalumit Aloni. Aloni was recently awarded the prestigious Israel Prize for a lifetime of service to her country. I wanted to know her perspectives on the issues dividing the Palestinians and Israelis and how peace might be achieved once and for all.

Aloni, born in Tel Aviv in 1929, is unapologetically secularist in a conservative Jewish state. Often described as "colorful and outspoken," she infuriated Orthodox Jews when she declared that schoolchildren should no longer be taught the Bible's view that the world was created in six days and refused to adhere to strict Orthodox rules. For her obstinacy she has been called a "Jezebel," a "harlot," and "a stinking offense against God." Her political views have also led to her denouncement as a "traitor."

But Aloni doesn't deserve any of those ridiculous labels. During the War of Independence in 1948, Aloni fought with the Hagana to defend Jerusalem and was captured by Jordanian forces in the Old City. After her release she worked as a teacher, a lawyer, a columnist, and a radio producer. She also founded the Israel Consumer's Council, which she chaired for four years.

From 1965 through 1969 Aloni served as a member of the Knesset as part of the Labor Party. Later, Aloni left the Labor Party because of her difference of opinion with Golda Meir. In 1973 she founded the Civil Rights Movement Party, advocating electoral reform, laws protecting human rights, and the separation of church and state. From 1974 to 1996 Aloni returned to the Knesset. She served briefly in 1974 as a cabinet minister and again briefly as minister of education in 1992, when a dispute with Orthodox Jews forced her to move to the position of minister of communications and the arts, science, and technology, which she held until 1996.

Outside of her government positions, Aloni established shelters for battered women and victims of rape and was one of the founding members of the International Center for Peace in the Middle East. Perhaps one of her most remembered remarks is, "The fight should be for all human rights—religious, ethnic, sexual. We have to stop grouping people. They aren't pickle bottles, and you can't stick labels on them."

Aloni lives in a quiet and well-to-do neighborhood outside Tel Aviv. I reached her house a few minutes early, so I waited in her yard for a while before knocking on the door. She did not answer immediately. When she did, she peered out at me, looking rather stern.

"Come in," she said in her deep voice, showing me into her living room. A lovely aria was playing in the background. "I think we'll go outside," she said.

I sat down at a table on her patio, and she brought me a drink.

"So what do you want to know?" she asked as she took a seat and placed her hands on the table. I smiled at her frankness, and she smiled in return. I could see that despite her reputation for being tough as nails she was really quite a kind person with a good sense of humor.

"In talking with Palestinians, I haven't found confirmation of the Jewish view that Palestinians want to destroy Israel, that they want to kill Jews," I noted.

"No, they don't!" she replied firmly.

"But nearly every Israeli I have spoken with tells me that that's what Palestinians want to do. What is this overwhelming perception by Jews in Israel that says, 'The Palestinians want to kill us, they want war, they don't want peace and the problems that we have today are because of the Palestinians, period'?" I asked.

"This is nonsense!" she said. "This is the way to justify what we are doing to them. You see, the Jews are playing, or believing, that they are the ultimate victim in the world. So, as the victims we have the right to do whatever we want, and no one can tell us what to do! So we can blame the Palestinians for everything that happens. We pretend to be their victims as well. You know, fifty-three years ago we were under the British mandate, and they were not occupiers. They had a mandate to govern from the League of Nations. Whatever they did here, the British were angels compared to our occupation of the West Bank. Under the British there wasn't collective punishment, they didn't kill people without a trial—although in those days there was capital punishment, but it was never carried out without a trial. We were fighting for our independence, and Begin with his people and Shamir with his people—the two of them later became prime ministers—they used to throw bombs to kill Arabs and British, and they were hailed as 'freedom fighters.'

"Now, the resolution of the United Nations in November 1947 said that in so-called Palestine there will be two entities: the Jewish state and the Arab state. And the Arabs didn't accept it and there was a war and after this war, in 1949, there was an armistice agreement where our borders were enlarged, and we were very happy. Then came the Catastrophe, the Six Days' War in 1967, when we became occupiers. And no one can say that the Occupied Territories belongs to us because we took it under military administration, which means it is occupied. We are the occupiers of the Arab Palestinian people. But because we Jews choose to see ourselves as the victims, no one can tell us what to do and how to do it. So against every international law and against every international agreement and against every international convention—and including Israeli law—we started to put Jewish settlements in the Occupied Territories. And greediness made us put more and more settlements in the Occupied Territories, in the middle of the land which is not ours. We took more and more land so we could settle our people there. We have these zealots, armed groups, who in the name of God say that they had the right to take everything which belonged to the Palestinians: their land, their water, and even the right to destroy their agriculture. They treat Palestinians like servants, and worse, the policy of collective punishment—the closing of their towns, not letting them leave those places, and cutting them off from Jerusalem, knowing that the whole West Bank is a hinterland of Jerusalem. In Jerusalem today there live 220,000 Palestinians. According to a law in Israel, when 20,000 people live in a place it becomes a town. So 220,000—it's a big town. We have said that we annexed it, and therefore Palestinians are under Israeli jurisdiction, not the military administration. Nevertheless, they are not given equal treatment but are treated like second-rate human beings.

"Now, once we took over all this land, we settled people there, we started to believe that God is with us and the land belongs to us because two thousand years ago it belonged to the Jewish people, and now we are the strongest ones. So instead of showing generosity and building peace, we behaved like colonialists. I would compare what we are doing there to the most brutal imperialistic attitudes of the nineteenth century.

"So, at the beginning they started to talk peace and we were talking very highly. But Barak is not God, you know. When God said let there be light, there was light, but if Barak says I want peace, it doesn't mean that there is peace. Unless he gives something back. I said it to him, and he is afraid of the zealots, and the zealots are the people who are carrying this country to another war in this terrible conflict. We say we offer peace, but this is just doublespeak. The way Israel wants peace is to prevent Palestinians from having a truly sovereign state. It means that all the Palestinians in Jerusalem will be disconnected from the hinterland. So how can they accept such an offer? So, no, they don't want the kind of peace that Israel is offering today.

"What bothers me most is that people become so happy with the power they have that they never think of the consequences of their actions, of what the chain reaction can be. The fact is that people can suffer pain for a time, and they can suffer hunger for a time, but they cannot suffer humiliation for very long. And Israelis are humiliating Palestinians again and again. Every Israeli soldier, even at the age of eighteen, is treating the Arab women, men, and children as second-class human beings, not even as human beings."

"You are frequently denounced by the right wing in Israel, especially the settlers," I noted. "They say that you and people like you want to give away Israel to the Arabs, that you are therefore a traitor to your people."

"Yes. I got a letter from one of the settlers who lives in the Occupied Territories saying that I am worse than anything. He says he curses me for what I am saying and I should go to hell. That is an understatement of what he says. And then he finishes his letter saying, 'I have the right to say this to you because I have a number from Auschwitz tattooed on my hand.' Well, my mother was in Auschwitz," she pointed out. "I couldn't resist and I wrote an open letter about how I understand that he had the number from Auschwitz and so forth, but I cannot understand why he cannot live, for example, in the Jewish areas of Negev or in the Galilee. Why does he have to live in the Occupied Territories?"

"There still persists a huge fear," I said, "that making the Palestinians stronger, by giving them a homeland, will pose an enormous security risk for the survival of Israel."

"What has happened," she said, "is that the leadership of Israel— the rabbis, the teachers, all the books, the army—they are all brainwashing the people that the Arabs want to throw us to the sea. Now here you have something which is not understandable. We have the strongest army in the Middle East. We are not any more a minority.

We are more than 6 million people. [Former right-wing prime minister] Netanyahu just came to Israel for a few weeks, and said don't forget that Arafat wants to throw us to the sea. Just imagine, for instance, that Arafat did want to do this. So what? We are here, with all our power and our army! So what we are really saying is that because of the threat that they want to destroy us, that's why we have the right to do against them as a group whatever we want. It is a tragedy and it's shameful!

"Since 1988 the Palestinians have recognized the state of Israel at the border of the Green Line—which is the only agreed-upon line dating back to 1949. What the Palestinians want is the West Bank and the Gaza Strip, and we sit there on every hill and in every place, destroying their towns. I especially can't understand how we are destroying their fields and their agriculture. You see all the Israeli settlers recite the Jewish law: 'Don't ever pluck something from the earth which has been growing there.' But what they are doing is plucking everything which doesn't belong to us. The settlers want to be natives. How can you be native in a land where you are destroying whatever grows? Natives do not do this. So it is a sad story. The way the settlers speak today and the way they behave, it's pure fascist."

"For me, it seems that in the end the only way to understand this conflict is to understand the psychology of imperialism," I said.

"That's what we are doing!" she exclaimed.

"You have an occupying force," I continued, "and you have a people who lived here for centuries, and they're being displaced and denied their basic rights."

"Yes. That's exactly the same thing that we have done. We don't call them 'natives'; we call them 'the people of the place.' But no matter what we call them, we have colonized them just the same."

"It seems true to me that the oppressed naturally, because of human psychology, will resist suppression and ultimately will resort to violence to try to throw off that yoke," I said.

"Yeah. That's why I say that people may tolerate humiliation for a time, but they will not forever be humiliated, they will not tolerate it for very long."

"Anyone who points out the facts, as you do, becomes marginalized as an extremist, don't they?" I asked.

"Yeah, that is what happens. I know that's what they are trying to do to me too, but I am not marginalized in Israel any more. Although there was a time they wanted to kill me and I had guards, and so forth. It may sound nice to say that I am marginalized in Israel, but I am not. Because of so many years in the public eye and because of fighting so many years for human rights, and because I established a successful political party in 1973, I am not marginalized. Now, when I started to speak of human rights in Israel twenty or thirty years ago, it was like speaking Chinese! Today everyone knows what Chinese is, but think of forty years ago before Nixon went to China," she laughed.

"I cannot say that I am marginalized, and I am invited more than I am ready to go to TV programs and for lectures and so forth, and people listen. So I would say that people like me are accepted, but only a few of us dare to speak openly the way I do. There are many who think the same way. There are many who are happy when I speak on the radio or on television. But only a few—especially members of Knesset from the left, you won't hear them speaking the way I do. But even in the Labor Party they are happy that I say it, you see."

"Is the peace movement primarily a movement from the left wing of the political spectrum in Israel, or is widely based?" I asked.

"Well, on the Israeli spectrum, comparatively speaking, the peace movement comes from the left end. But I wouldn't say that they are left. We don't have a left in Israel. What we call left are the dovish people in the peace camp. But the politicians are afraid of the right wing, and they cater to them. I mean, who cares about what they call the rock of the mountain—what do you call it?"

"Temple Mount?" I interjected, referring to the Muslim holy site of which Al Aqsa is a part.

"Yes, Temple Mount. Suddenly, it became an urgent need for us to have sovereignty over it. Since the seventh century it has been in the hands of the Muslims. But suddenly today it became the most holy place for the Jews. And every time a grave of a sheikh is found the Jews decide that this is an old *Jewish* prophet or whatever it is, and you can see how they adapt and take it from the Muslims because we are the strong one. Not even the Labor Party, or even these days the party that I founded, dares to speak openly that these holy places are not ours. Such is the power of the right wing."

"It is said that Arafat is a dictator," I noted, "and his government is corrupt. He and his comrades seemed to have gained a lot through the Oslo Accords and subsequent agreements, but the average Palestinian feels that they have nothing to hope for and that talk of peace is irrelevant. I have heard Americans and Israelis using the corruption of Arafat's government as an excuse, or as an example, of why the Palestinians cannot rule themselves, much less uphold agreements with Israel. The average Palestinian may stop caring whether an agreement is reached or not."

"Well, the Palestinians must have some agreement with Israel or they won't have water, they won't have work, they will starve. They need this peace process in order to survive. And they need this peace process so that every day they are not surprised by new settlers taking away their land. Then, later, they will fight for changing this dictatorship, but only they have their sovereignty. What really needs to be fixed even more than the Palestinian government's corruption is the way Jews treat the Palestinians. The Jews always say that for two thousand years we were suppressed and oppressed and executed and made to bear all the troubles in the world. We say only we can know the troubles in the world. And all the while the way that we treat the Palestinians is unbelievable. We are humiliating them. It's true that many officials in the Palestinian Authority are corrupted. They are corrupted! I have connections with many of the Palestinians, and none of them really ignores that this leadership which came from Tunis is corrupted and is treating their own people in a terrible way. But during this time they cannot fight Arafat. In the time where every one of them is under the Israeli occupation and every day he can find himself humiliated or be stripped of whatever he has, this is not the time to fight Arafat."

"I have noticed that Israelis do not bother to distinguish between the common Palestinian, who does not want to destroy Israel, and the extremists who do," I observed.

"Now the question is whether we cannot distinguish or we don't want to distinguish," she replied. "And the answer is that we don't want to distinguish, because then we can justify our use of collective punishment. If we can distinguish, then we have to bring the people who are making those troubles to jail, to bring evidence against them, and we cannot just kill them the way we have been killing them. In Israel, we don't have capital punishment. In Israel, you have to bring people before the court and you have to bring evidence. And this is very complicated for the army to do, so the easiest way is to put the collective blame on all Palestinians, and then you can use collective punishment against them all."

"I still find it difficult to figure out how this can be done in a democracy," I said.

"You see, people in the United States are confused by this because you have fallen for the propaganda by Israel that we are a real democracy. We are not! And we cannot be, because the people who came to this country came from Eastern Europe and the Middle East. They never lived in a democracy. They don't know what a democracy is. We don't have a written constitution, we don't have a bill of rights. We adopted the Ottoman system of segregation from cradle to grave. We are divided into twelve ethnic religious groups under the jurisdiction of the clergies—Jewish, Muslims, and so forth—which are the worst and the most backward in the world. So we do not have a real democracy. Your situation is quite different in the States. People may immigrate there from all over the world, but the moment they come they have a Constitution, and the Constitution has a meaning. It is a kind of umbrella which gives a code of norms to everyone, and everyone knows to become an American this is what they have to respect and follow. And you give to it a kind of a power and flavor which is above every other law, and people know that this is what they have to respect, and this is what they have to accept. But we don't have a written constitution, and we have people coming from Eastern Europe and the Middle East with all the troubles and with all the feuds and with all the systems of being terribly ethnocentric because they were minorities there. And then also by law we are divided and segregated. So everyone can push around whomever one wishes. In this system, people rarely show generosity to others."

"That is something I hadn't thought about," I said. "Somehow not having a bill of rights, and having an institutionalized system of segregation, and feeling that it is normal to compete with and push around other minorities seems to betray the memory of the Holocaust," I said.

"It has nothing to do with the Holocaust," she said firmly. "We use the Holocaust just to emphasize that we are the victims of the world. You see, we teach our kids the Holocaust was solely a Jewish issue, not a universal issue of genocide. These allies of Sharon say that they will close off water to the Palestinians so that they won't have anything to drink. Others say that they will destroy Palestinian towns. That's why I brought up the name Lidice." [Lidice was a Czech town that was brutally razed by the Nazis in World War II to demonstrate that no mercy would be shown to would-be rebels against the Third Reich.]

"A few years ago a girl was killed, not by a Palestinian, but by one of the Jewish settlers, who is a crazy one. And still they said in the Knesset that we must wipe the Palestinian town off the map. I said, 'Yeah, you want to have a Lidice?' And so they became quiet. But it is unbelievable how ready they are to kill, to destroy, to shoot."

"Where does that come from," I asked, "this readiness to violence?"

"In the Bible they say that there are two things that the land cannot bear: a slave who becomes king, and a lowly person who becomes a master. Those are people that the land cannot bear because they behave so badly. We are not even aware, most of us, that we are now the kings and the masters and we behave so badly. The settlers and zealots say openly that we haven't finished the War of Independence. We will finish the war, they say, the day that we clean the land of the Arabs altogether. These people still say that the Arabs have twenty countries so let the Palestinians go there, but this is the only country Jews have, we chose it, and it belongs to us. And they think that we can clean the whole country of Arabs the way that we cleaned Jaffa and Haifa during the War of Independence."

"It is so difficult in my country to criticize Israel because then you are called anti-Semitic. I'm not at all anti-Semitic. Why can't I criticize the state of Israel?" I noted.

"Yeah, this is something that we use to our advantage. For instance, in Europe, whoever says something criticizing Israel, we say that he is anti-Semitic and we remind him there was a Second World War and a Holocaust and so forth. It is very effective because the Christian world has a kind of a guilty feeling toward the Jews. And we are using it very efficiently. I'll give you an example of how we are using this and are being the ultimate victim. When Israel invaded Lebanon in 1982, we were criticized in Europe. Then the prime minister stood up and said that the British and the Germans and the French, not one of them can tell us what to do; not one of them has the right to criticize us. Those people did not save us from the Nazis, these people ruthlessly bombarded Dresden when the war was almost over; how dare they to tell us what to do and how to do it? I was listening to him, and I thought, here we go, the way he is talking we will certainly destroy Beirut. In fact, after this speech he gave the order to bombard Beirut, which means that civilians would die. But, again, no one can tell us what to do because we are the ultimate victims of the world."

"Did it feel like a vindication when you received the Israel Prize?" I asked. "After all, you have been criticized so often over the years."

"I don't care about the criticism. I never wanted to be loved by everyone," she said with a laugh. "I have always wanted my voice to be clear and to make people think. But they don't have to love me for it."

"Are you hopeful that the center is growing and that awareness is growing?" I asked.

"Yes, yes. I look in favor that the younger generation is fed up with the war and with all this conflict and arguing and so forth. If you go to the high schools, you'll see this."

"Well, I don't want to take up your whole day," I said. "It has been a great pleasure to talk with you."

"Okay, go away, go away," she replied, causing me to laugh. She smiled.

At her front door she said, "I hope you have met some nice people in Israel. There are some very nice people here. Not many," she said with a grin, "but there are some."

"Well, I certainly have now," I said playfully in a transparent attempt to be charming.

She laughed. "Have a safe trip home," she said as she closed the door.

There was one thing I needed to do before my trip home. On my last full day in Israel, I emerged from my hotel and asked several cab drivers to take me to the Erez checkpoint where I could cross over into the Gaza Strip. They refused. One driver told me that he had lived in Israel all his life but had never heard of Erez. I seriously doubted his sincerity, as the Jewish settlement of Gush Erez takes up most of the Gaza Strip's northern border. When I asked him to take me to whatever crossing leads into Gaza, he replied that the border to Gaza was closed.

I returned to the front desk and asked them to call a cab that would take me to Erez. Another hotel guest overheard my request and approached me. He did his best to try to dissuade me from going. He said it was a near certainty that I would be shot by Palestinian gunmen, who hate Americans just as much as the Israelis. "You supply the weapons, the money, and they hate you for that," he reminded me. "You'll be shot for sure," he said, shaking his head.

Another driver, though willing to take me, said he thought I was nuts for trying to go to Gaza. He said that the soldiers wouldn't let me in, but he was happy to take me there to see for myself. Talking to one of his friends on his cell phone, the driver looked back at me when we were halfway there and said, "My friend said you are crazy. You'll be shot. You shouldn't go." I just smiled and returned to looking out the window.

I noticed many new housing developments along the way. The bright sand-colored buildings seemed to be sprouting up everywhere outside Tel Aviv. This has been made necessary by a steady increase in the population on account of emigration of Jews from Russia, Ethiopia, and elsewhere.

At the checkpoint, which consisted of several large parking lots, many barricades, and various stations staffed by soldiers with automatic weapons, the driver let me off and wished me luck. I was stopped by a friendly, handsome soldier who smiled at me in disbelief that I wanted to go into Gaza. "What will you do there, he asked, "except for being killed?"

"I want to have a look around Gaza," I replied.

"Are you a journalist?" he questioned.

"No. I'm not a journalist. I'm a writer."

He seemed reluctant to allow me to pass. I then told him I had met with Shulamit Aloni the day before and I wanted to see some of the things that we had discussed.

"Aloni?" he responded sarcastically. "Okay. Go ahead. It's up to you," he said, shaking his head and pointing to an office where I had to check in.

I went to a small building that looked very much like customs at international airports. I was the only one trying to cross into Gaza. A female soldier asked for my passport and gave me the same line of questioning and the same discouragement I had heard repeatedly.

"I don't understand why anyone would want to go into Gaza right now," she said. "Are you sure you know what you're doing?"

The question was not a bad one. To be honest, I wasn't 100 percent sure that I knew what I was doing, except that I knew I should see with my own eyes the conditions in the Gaza Strip.

The soldier typed my passport number and name into her computer, then gave it to another soldier who eventually issued me a pass. "Present this to the soldiers," he said, pointing down the road.

It was about a hundred yards or so to the next station. The soldiers there simply took the pass and waved me through. Then it was a long walk down the road, lined with walls and barricades, to the Palestinian Authority checkpoint. They took down my name and passport number and said I was free to enter.

I found a taxi driver who spoke English and asked him to take me around Gaza, to show me exactly what conditions are like there, both good and bad. He had apparently served as a guide for several European journalists and knew what I wanted to see.

We went through Beit Hanun, Beit Lahiya, and Jabaliya before arriving in Gaza City. The distance between the towns is very short, perhaps a kilometer or two. It is less than ten kilometers from the crossing to Gaza City.

I noticed right away that conditions were much worse, that the area was in a state of disrepair as compared to the Israeli side of the border. That wasn't surprising to me, as the border had been fenced off, sealed by military posts and patrols, and the Palestinians had been subjected to severe restrictions in their ability to move.

Again, I have no doubt that there are legitimate security issues presented in the Occupied Territories. But the basis of the insecurity most surely comes from the ways in which the Palestinians are forced to live. I was happy to see my feelings confirmed by Secretary of State Colin Powell, who noted that the "siege" of the Palestinian territories by Israel should be ended and that economic deprivation there does not further the cause of peace.

The main road was blocked off by the Israelis. We came first to a Palestinian police outpost that had been shelled by the Israeli army the night before. The policemen were busy replacing sandbags and repairing structural damage the best they could. Apparently the Israelis claimed that someone had been shooting from the outpost. That seemed highly unlikely to me, but perhaps the gunman was nearby and the outpost a convenient target for retaliation.

Across the street from the outpost a small group of policemen huddled around an open fire to keep warm. The oldest policeman, who must have been in his late sixties, greeted me after my driver explained what I was doing in the area. He gently took my arm and pulled me past the fire. "All of this land," he said, sweeping his arm across the horizon, "used to be olive trees. People made their living from the trees. But the Israeli soldiers came in with bulldozers and plowed them down. They said it was for security reasons."

The old man shook his head. I watched him intently, looked deeply into his eyes, and saw his pain. He was old enough to remember when all this land was Palestinian and relatively prosperous. It appeared that he choked back his emotions, then he turned to me and asked if I wanted some tea. Though I would have loved to warm up by the fire and have something hot to drink, I had too much to see in a short period of time. I said good-bye and got back in the car.

Passing through Nezarim was very saddening. It was the place, sandwiched in between two Jewish settlements, where a young Palestinian boy was shot and killed in his father's arms as they were caught in the crossfire between Palestinian gunmen and Israeli troops. The image has been widely broadcast around the world and may, in the end, finally cement in people's minds that the common Palestinian is suffering badly, caught between the power of the Israeli state and Palestinian zealots. People around the world are beginning to see that between the combatants live the civilians, many of them dispossessed of their ancestral land, forced to live in military zones in a constant state of battle, with very few jobs and few opportunities to enjoy life for any extended period of time.

A long row of trucks lined a road leading to Israel. "That is how we get food and supplies here," my driver informed me. "So much of what we consume comes from Israel. When they close the borders and stop the trucks, we can't get as many supplies. They have a stranglehold on us," he said, shaking his head.

The settlements from the outside look like prisons. The olive orchards, which had been cultivated by the Arabs for generations, have been plowed down to create wide-open fields for better security; the same has been done to houses, unless the military has taken them (without compensation) for its own use. Barbed-wire fences and barricades surround the settlements. Roads between the settlements are reserved for military and Jewish use only. I watched as a bus was escorted by military jeeps from one settlement to the next, all the vehicles making haste to get within the protection of the next settlement.

Just why a Jew would like to live like this, I cannot fathom. I thought of what Aloni had said to me the day before: "Why do you have to live in Arab land? Why can't you live in the Jewish areas of Negev . . . ?" Yet many of the settlers say that God promised them not just a land, not just Israel, but this land, *all* of this land. Some even claim (and claimed before 1948) that all the land from the sea to Iran belongs to the Jews.

In the refugee camp at Khan Yunis I got out of the car and walked along the street, making my driver rather anxious. "We can drive, we can drive," he implored. But I wanted more freedom to see the streets and talk to the people. The conditions in the camp are bad. I talked with three young men who were reading magazines. They had no jobs and nothing to do, they told me. A crowd gathered around me, and I began to shake hands with everyone. A young man grabbed my arm and pulled at me. I asked him to stop, but he kept pulling. I didn't want to create a scene, so I stopped resisting and went with him. He led me to a group of men who were sipping coffee. They had told him to bring me over so they could say hello and thank me for making the troublesome journey to see how they lived under Israeli occupation.

After fifteen minutes or so I thanked the men for the conversation and got back into the car. We went down the road a bit farther and came across a crowd of young men. I got out to see what they were up to. Apparently a young man had been shot and killed the night before, and they were meeting to remember him. They now considered him a martyr and spray-painted his name on the sides of buildings. Virtually every building had such paintings.

A group of about ten men approached me, looking quite tough and angry. For a moment I felt slightly threatened, but I resisted the feeling and walked toward them. When we met face-to-face I extended my hand and smiled. My hand seemed to linger forever there in midair, but finally one of the men took my hand and shook it firmly. My smiles were returned as my driver told them in Arabic that I was there to explore conditions in Gaza. Several of the men led me farther down the road to a makeshift barricade of concrete rubble, tires, and scraps of metal piled eight or nine feet high. Atop the barricade I observed the damage inflicted on the camp. From this spot, Palestinian boys (and I mean boys, as young as eight and most not older than eighteen) throw stones at Israeli forces who try to keep the Palestinians from approaching the Jewish settlement of Gush Katif.

I have no doubt that gunmen have also fired upon the Jewish settlement, but I seriously doubt that they lived in the houses that have been destroyed by Israeli mortar shells and guns. Again, the average Palestinian pays the price for zealots on both sides. Yet most Israelis I spoke with don't care about what gets destroyed during acts of retaliation; an eye for an eye is an official and popular policy of the Israeli state. The United States did the same during the Vietnam War, before massive anti-war demonstrations and vigilent press coverage changed the situation.

After Khan Yunis we drove to Rafah on the border of Egypt. There wasn't much to see, except the border crossing and an Egyptian flag flying in the distance. On the way back from Rafah, we stopped at the new international airport, which was quiet and empty of passengers. I got out of the car for about twenty seconds to take a photo. Unfortunately, that caused Palestinian security police to detain us and inquire what we were doing. They never asked me a single question, but they grilled my driver. Lately there has been a concerted effort by the Palestinian Authority to uncover and punish collaborators, and it seemed to me they were trying to ascertain whether my driver was helping an American or Israeli agent. Of course, I kept trying to tell the officers that a picture of the airport could pose no security threat. Israeli tanks, armored vehicles, and attack helicopters were within minutes of the airport; if the Israelis wanted a picture of the airport, they'd come and take one. Yet the officers didn't care to hear from me at all.

They finally let us go, and we proceeded back toward Gaza City. Along the way we were stopped in a long line of vehicles. A single Israeli soldier in a tank directed traffic, stopping cars at will from a strategic bend in the road. He ordered our car to halt, but my driver pretended not to notice and stepped on the accelerator. The soldier yelled at us, and when we got down the road a bit we laughed. For me, it was a release of tension; for my driver, it was a minuscule victory over Israeli occupation.

I returned to Tel Aviv that night with a new understanding of the situation in Israel and Palestine and a conviction that peace would be far closer if the Israelis used their power to create more habitable conditions in the Occupied Territories. After all, what stake do the Palestinians have in peace at the moment? They have lost everything and are now herded into desperate camps, juxtaposed by Israeli settlements on the choicest land; they have few jobs, no large industry, very few luxuries; and they are not even considered as equal humans by most Israelis that I spoke with during my stay.

That evening back in Tel Aviv, I went to the late-night cafés and walked through an area near the marina that contained a number of nightclubs. One street was packed full with thousands of young Israelis, all decked out in their trendiest and most expensive clothes,

forking over plenty of shekels to get into the clubs. It was an amazing contrast for me, a day in the absolute poverty of the West Bank
and Gaza Strip, that evening in the well-off district of Tel Aviv.
There was not a single Arab counterpart to this area; Arab youth
would have to make do with sitting on the sides of streets, in
bombed-out buildings and disintegrating apartment blocs, while
Israeli youth enjoyed the high life, so near but so far away from the
Occupied Territories.

I felt sorry for the young Israelis too, knowing that many of them
would serve in the military. Some of them would be wounded,
some of them would die, and all of them would be forced to participate in subjugating civilians in the Occupied Territories. It would
be a psychological burden that none of them should ever bear.

A few months after my return from Israel, a bomb exploded in
one of those Tel Aviv discos that I strolled past, killing many young
people. I was so saddened by the news. A Jewish friend of mine,
who deplores the violence on both sides and who certainly deplored
the terrorist attack on the Tel Aviv disco, wrote to me after a great
deal of contemplation, "Bombing from the air is no less a terrorist
activity than blowing up a bomb in a marketplace. The only difference is that each side [because of available weapons] chooses a different means."

Violence always begets violence. It creates animosity whose
embers burn for decades. When a small group of Palestinian terrorists kills Israelis, the Israeli state responds with attack helicopters,
mortar shells, and missiles. They raze homes and uproot orchards
and assassinate suspects without a trial. They call it self-defense,
and they truly believe that is what it is. Yet when the Israelis use this
force, the Palestinian terrorists gain popular support, undermining
the power of the Palestinian Authority. With each attack by Israel,
the radical group Hamas gains popularity among the Palestinian
people, who see Hamas as defenders of Palestinian land and honor.
Ordinary Palestinians, especially young males, aid groups like
Hamas, and the cycle of violence is perpetuated.

As our wise spiritual leaders have told us for centuries, only
through love, only through sensible acts of compassion, can peace be

achieved. Many people in Israel today know this. Many in Palestine know it as well. Unfortunately, their voices are infrequently heard over the chorus of hatred.

Yet there are signs of hope in the Holy Land today, and these signs will continue to grow until peace is finally achieved. Prime Minister Sharon promised the Israelis public security through military might, but his policy of overwhelming force and escalation has failed. A popular conservative newspaper in Israel has taken the unusual step of criticizing Sharon's policy of assassinating Palestinians, calling it an unwarranted escalation of hostilities. The paper notes that even when the Palestinians bent over backward to halt violence against Israelis (an Israeli prerequisite to further talks), Sharon ordered assassinations of Palestinian leaders, thereby restarting the cycle of violence. Sharon's failed policies simply cannot be sustained.

Meanwhile, tens of thousands of peace activists have been reorganizing and staging demonstrations for an Israeli withdrawal from the Occupied Territories. A group of one thousand top-level military reserve officers and intelligence officials has publicly called for Israel to withdraw from virtually all of the West Bank and Gaza Strip and for an immediate creation of a Palestinian state, leaving other unresolved issues to be decided during the resumption of negotiations. And nearly five hundred reservists have signed a petition declaring that they would not participate in Israel's "missions of oppression" in the Occupied Territories.

A welcome overture has come from Saudi Arabia: a proposal to grant Israel full recognition by the Arab world in exchange for an end to Israeli occupation of east Jerusalem, the West Bank, and Gaza Strip. Arafat praised the proposal as a "historic opportunity" to establish lasting peace in the area.

The United States can do a lot for peace in Israel and Palestine and must surely start by being more fair in its treatment of the Palestinians. My observation here could be dismissed as naive, except that the same conclusion has been reached by leaders throughout Europe. *The Economist*—no one's idea of a liberal publication—stated, "What does seem to be true is that the Middle East will burn, with American interests and even lives going up in flames, unless the United States intervenes swiftly and much more neutrally in the conflict."[52]

The magazine also concluded, correctly I think, that Sharon's Operation Defensive Wall (as the ongoing incursions into the Occupied Territories are called) "will almost certainly fail to . . . uproot Palestinians' terrorist 'infrastructure,'" but rather will supply "bitter men and women willing to kill and be killed on Palestine's behalf; and the bitterness can only grow after Israel's onslaught."[53] Moreover, President Bush's long-awaited initiative unveiled in June 2002 was "a disappointment" that provided "a thicket of contradictory, and arguably impossible, conditions" on the Palestinians, while providing Israel with everything it wanted. "Even Israelis admitted," *The Economist* noted, "that the peace plan George Bush and his divided administration set forth . . . could just as well have been written by their own prime minister, Ariel Sharon."[54] Such bias toward Israel may be good politics in the United States—as Truman noted many years ago—but it is lousy for the future of peace in the Middle East.

Peace will eventually come, of course, after much needless loss and suffering on all sides. Yet we can be assured that even after a political peace is found in Israel and Palestine, a deep wound will remain. This will be the unfinished business of violence: how to forgive, how to heal. As Aung San Suu Kyi said in an earlier chapter, forgetting is not an option. Reconciliation will require that the current players step aside. New leaders, and most probably spiritual ones, will then have to help bring their peoples together.

In the United States we are still trying to heal one of our greatest national wounds. Unfortunately, many in America would like to forget our involvement in the Vietnam War. Yet we have never finished our business there. We have never properly atoned for our actions, nor have we done much over the past three decades to help the people of that country. It is to Vietnam, and an extraordinary peacemaker who lives there, that I turn my attention next.

Four

THICH QUANG DO: VIETNAM'S CHAMPION OF HOPE

My uncle was a young man, just a year or so out of high school, when he arrived in Vietnam. It was 1965, when America was already well engaged in the conflict but before amassing huge numbers of casualties. He was an intelligent soldier, a technical specialist who manned and maintained a Hawk ground-to-air missile system on a small island in Cam Ranh Bay, opposite the port city of Nha Trang in central Vietnam.

My uncle recalls that neither he nor the other servicemen around him really knew the root causes of the war or the reasons for widening and continuing it year after year. Today his reluctance to talk about the Vietnam War comes more from regret about his lack of knowledge at the time than from any horrors he may have encountered there. "I was stupid for not knowing why I was over there," he told me with great candor recently. All he and his comrades knew at the time was that their country wanted them to defeat the enemy, the North Vietnamese and their Communist collaborators in the south.

Had the American people known more about Vietnam's past, I truly believe we could have avoided a war there; the American people would have shied away from direct military intervention, which led to the longest war in our nation's history. Nearly sixty thousand American soldiers died in Vietnam. The Vietnamese lost over 2 million people, neighboring Cambodia lost more than a million, hundreds of thousands died in Laos, and thousands of soldiers from Thailand, the Philippines, Korea, and Australia were killed there as well.

Surprisingly, many Americans either do not know or have forgotten exactly what the United States was doing in Vietnam. Public polling shows that two-thirds of all Americans regard the Vietnam War as a mistake, but half of our people do not know what our goals were, and a third of our people cannot recall which side we supported. This is troubling for several reasons.

First, how we perceive our involvement in the Vietnam War can greatly affect our future choices about military engagements. Given that we have continued to use our power throughout the world, often in an arrogant and irresponsible way, it is important that we remind ourselves of the limits of force and the propensity for a powerful nation to act in cruel and repressive ways. It certainly shows great strength of character to contemplate what we do incorrectly and then apologize, atone, and try not to repeat the same mistakes going forward.

Second, perhaps in an attempt to regain lost pride, our society has created a few powerful myths about its involvement in the war. One myth says that we simply didn't try to win in Vietnam, that we fought with one hand tied behind our backs, whereas we should have conducted ourselves like the strategists Clausewitz and Machiavelli instructed, using all available resources to ensure victory. In my mind, there was never a chance that the United States and its corrupt, unpopular puppet government in the South would prevail in Vietnam.

Sitting on the bow of a small boat on the Thu Bon River outside the ancient city of Hoi An, I stared at the thick vegetation along the banks. I couldn't image chasing an enemy into such terrain, especially when the terrain was the enemy's own yard. I felt the same way winding up the road through the Hoi Van pass between Hoi An and the former imperial city of Hue; while staring at the steep mountains across the turquoise lagoon at Lang Co Island; while boating along the coastline around Nha Trang. It was apparent to me just by seeing these places that the only way to defeat an enormously popular nationalist movement would have been to defoliate nearly every forest and jungle, to strip bare every mountain, and to raze every village and intern every villager. Even then, nearly all civilians would have had to be seen as potential combatants and treated accordingly. In other words, victory would have meant the total destruction of Vietnam.

My uncle reached the same conclusion on his own: "There was a lot of propaganda coming out of Washington, and it wasn't real and it didn't make any sense. General Westmoreland said he could defeat the enemy. But there was no way to overcome guerrilla warfare there. It wasn't realistic. There was no way to win the war, short of killing all the Vietnamese. And then, how could that be called winning? There would have been no country left."

Another popular myth that has arisen about Vietnam is that the United States became "entangled" in Vietnam for noble reasons. I am sure this would make us feel better about the sixty thousand American deaths in Vietnam. True, many of our soldiers died fulfilling a duty, and that can be seen as admirable, but the notion that our government went to Vietnam with the intention of promoting justice and democracy is simply not true.

Our involvement was not initiated in order to defeat a tyrannous power that posed an imminent threat to the United States, though it was often hawked as such. Nor was our aim to halt a genocide or some such other just cause, which arguably could have justified the enormous military power brought to bear against the indigenous population. What we hoped to do was to halt the perceived menace of the Soviet Union and China and thereby to project and enhance our power in the world.

Justice and democracy would have called for supporting free elections in Vietnam, as mandated by the 1954 Geneva Accords, after the French were all but defeated by the North Vietnamese. However, since the United States knew that free and fair elections would result in a Communist victory, and since the government saw all Communism as a political threat, we decided to oppose the popular will. The United States instituted a massive plan to create a country in the south of Vietnam, which was headed by a corrupt and repressive regime.

Consider also that Vietnam is a nation with a past and a future. As we continue to find how to be morally involved in the world, we must be willing to examine what is taking place in the country upon which we dropped tons of bombs. Vietnam today is a nation that is still not at peace with itself. Radicalized by the war and driven by more than a thousand years of foreign occupation, the regime in Hanoi continues to deny the Vietnamese people common freedoms. We cannot, especially given our involvement there, turn a blind eye to the people of Vietnam.

What should the American people have known about Vietnam when our government began to send troops there? We at least should have known about the country's history, particularly its history of resistance to foreign domination. Vietnam was dominated by China for over a thousand years, from the second century B.C.E. until the tenth century C.E. Nam Viet, as it was called in 208 B.C.E., was composed almost exclusively of the Red River Delta area bordering on China; only later did the country expand to include the former Cham kingdom in central Vietnam and the former Khmer region in south Vietnam.

Nam Viet was defeated by the Chinese in 111 B.C.E. and renamed Giao-chi. The new Chinese overlords set out to integrate Vietnam into the Han Empire by supplanting Vietnamese culture, sending ethnic Chinese to settle in Vietnam, imposing Chinese as the official language, and replacing Vietnamese nobility with Chinese leaders. The Chinese also remodeled political institutions in accord with Chinese models, established Confucianism as the official ideology, and advanced Chinese art, architecture, and music. The Chinese even imposed their written characters as the written form of Vietnamese. (Interestingly, these policies bear a striking resemblance to China's current practices in Tibet.)

The Vietnamese absorbed a great deal of Chinese culture and technology. Yet the Vietnamese resisted the loss of their cultural identity and rebelled against China whenever they were able. The most famous act of resistance against the Chinese came in 40 C.E., when the Chinese executed a high-ranking feudal lord. His widow and her sister, known as the Trung Sisters, organized tribal leaders, raised an army, and launched a rebellion against the Chinese. The Chinese governor was forced to flee, and the sisters were proclaimed queens of an independent Vietnam. But just three years later, the Chinese counterattacked and defeated the rebels. The Trung Sisters threw themselves into the Hat Giang River rather than be captured.

In 679 C.E. the Chinese named the Vietnamese country Annam, meaning "Pacified South." But the Vietnamese would not be pacified permanently. In 938 C.E., in the wake of the collapse of the Tang Dynasty in China, Ngo Quyen led the Vietnamese to victory over the Chinese army in a battle along the Bach Dang River. The country was in anarchy when Ngo Quyen died, but in 968 C.E. Dinh Bo Linh reached an agreement with China in which Vietnam would be independent while still paying tribute to China. A fully independent Kingdom of Vietnam (Dai Viet) was established in 980 C.E.

In 1284, during the Tran dynasty, the feared Mongol warrior Kublai Khan sent 500,000 troops to Vietnam. Under Tran Hung Dao, the greatly outnumbered Vietnamese bogged down the Mongol forces, cut off their supply lines, and drove the invaders back into China. The Mongols returned to Vietnam again with 300,000 men. In Tran Hung Dao's campaign against the second invasion, he used guerilla tactics and lured the Mongols deep into Vietnam. As the Mongol fleet sailed on the Bach Dang River, Tran's forces attacked. He then ordered a tactical retreat before launching a massive counteroffensive, impaling the Mongols on steel-tipped bamboo stakes that had been hidden in the riverbed. The Mongol fleet was destroyed and the Mongolian invasion defeated.

The Chinese continued to control Vietnam either directly or through a tributary system for hundreds of years. Their rule was harsh, characterized by burdensome taxes, enslavement, and intolerance of Vietnamese culture. It was hundreds of years before the Vietnamese were to gain control of their country again.

The next major invaders of Vietnam were the French, who tried their hand at ruling the country beginning in 1847 when they attacked Danang. In 1861 the French defeated the Vietnamese at the Battle of Ky Hoa, although a particularly strong guerrilla movement persisted until 1867.

In 1885 the Vietnamese were forced to accept the Treaty of Tientsin, which subdivided Vietnam into the French colonies of Tonkin (North Vietnam), Annam (Central Vietnam), and Cochin China (South Vietnam). The French also colonized Kampuchea (Cambodia) and Laos, completing their control over all of Indochina.

Colonialism was a major blow to Vietnam. Colonialism is often thought of as a purely economic system in which a powerful country sends settlers to dominate and control the natives of a lesser developed country. But, as political historian Edward Said has noted, European powers had a commitment to this system "over and above profit." Colonialism was a system that "allowed decent men and women from [Europe] to accept the notion that distant territories and their native peoples should be subjugated." These decent people readily accepted the empire "as a protracted, almost metaphysical obligation to rule subordinate, inferior or less advanced peoples."[1]

Le Marechal Lyautey, commissioner general of the 1931 Exposition Coloniale Internationale de Paris, which showcased the people and materials of European and American colonial possessions, unabashedly declared, "To colonize does not mean merely to construct wharves, factories, and railroads. It means also to instill a humane gentleness in the wild hearts of the savannah or the desert."[2] This belief, which became known as the *mission civilisatrice,* or mission to civilize, was widely accepted in French society.

French humanist Frantz Fanon notes in his brilliant work *The Wretched of the Earth* that the mission to "civilize" natives, indeed the whole structure of colonialism itself, dehumanizes the subjected and "turns him into an animal." In addition, the colonial enterprise itself, he argues, is a Manichaean one. Manichaeism was a movement in the ancient world that saw things as either wholly evil or wholly good. "As if to show the totalitarian character of colonial exploitation," Fanon writes, the colonial power "paints the native as a sort of quintessence of evil.... The native ... represents not only the absence of values, but also the negation of values. He is, let us dare to admit, the enemy of values, and in this sense he is the absolute evil."[3]

In pursuit of its economic and social policies, France developed the most extensive colonial empire in the world. Forty-seven countries had some form of allegiance to France. Colonialism brought technological advancement to Vietnam and created a limited bourgeoisie among the natives. Even Vietnamese nationalists at the time conceded that "the French have built roads and bridges; they have improved communication through the construction of railroads and steamships; they have established post offices and telegraph lines: [and] all these works are indeed very useful to Vietnam, and anybody with ears and eyes can hear and see them."[4]

Yet the technological advances in Vietnam were accomplished by strangling and subjugating every aspect of Vietnamese life. Whereas the majority of Vietnamese peasants owned land before the arrival of the French, by the 1930s nearly 70 percent of them owned no land at all. Capital was consolidated in the hands of very few people at the top of the social ladder, and the French treated Vietnamese workers abysmally. Between 1917 and 1945 one rubber plant in Vietnam alone saw twelve thousand out of forty-five thousand workers die from appalling working conditions. Taxes extracted from Indochina as a whole increased tenfold in the first decade of French control.

During World War I some fifty thousand Vietnamese troops and fifty thousand Vietnamese workers were compelled to go to Europe to assist France's war effort. The French also imposed upon the Vietnamese additional heavy taxes to help finance the war. Rebellions arose during this time but were easily suppressed by the French troops in Vietnam.

While the Vietnamese were forced to support France with their blood, labor, and all material means at their disposal, France continued to deny the Vietnamese the most basic civil liberties. In 1915 Vietnamese nationalist Luong Lap Nham observed,

The French authorities do not allow Vietnamese citizens to read foreign newspapers, nor do they permit them to study foreign languages. Vietnamese from North Vietnam cannot go to Saigon without a passport. We are forced to smoke opium and to pay a high tax to the government for opium.

The country is strewn with opium dens. We are obliged to consume cheap alcohol and to pay a high tax on it. Access to education is very limited. For the Vietnamese, there are no universities nor specialized superior schools. Vietnamese soldiers cannot be promoted to high officer ranks.[5]

Accounts of French abuses against the Vietnamese were not merely revolutionary propaganda; they were well established in historical records. In fact, as historian George Herring notes, even President Franklin D. Roosevelt "regarded the French as 'poor colonizers' who had 'badly mismanaged' Indochina and exploited its people."[6]

In August 1940, just a month after France fell to Nazi Germany, the Japanese pressed the German-backed Vichy government in Paris into ceding control over Indochina. In September, as Japan officially assumed control, it also invaded Vietnam from China and drove the French south.

The Japanese had already invaded and taken control of Korea and important parts of China. (By the end of the year, Japan had invaded Siam, Hong Kong, Burma, North Borneo, the Philippines, and many other Pacific islands.) The brutality of Japanese occupying forces in other lands should have told the Vietnamese what kind of treatment to expect from their new overlords. But the Vietnamese initially welcomed the Japanese, believing that they would be better governors than the French had been. It soon became apparent, however, that the Japanese did not intend to liberate the people from colonialism; the Japanese were extremely brutal against the Vietnamese people, and they left in place the French civil servants to carry out Japanese policies.

In 1945 the Japanese military forces used rice as fuel to operate their machinery and halted the supply of rice from South Vietnam to the north. This, along with floods and the Japanese policy of forcing farmers to grow industrial crops, caused more than 2 million people to die of starvation. Neither the French nor the Japanese did anything to alleviate the widespread suffering.

Having endured Chinese domination, French colonialism, and now Japanese occupation, the Vietnamese understandably harbored nationalist intentions. The most successful group of nationalists was led by Ho Chi Minh, who brought various factions together and established the Viet Minh (short for Viet Nam Doc Lap Dong Minh, League for the Independence of Viet Nam) as the preeminent freedom fighters in Vietnam. Ho Chi Minh's own faction within this coalition was Communist.

It is crucial to point out that the chief goal of the revolutionaries in Vietnam was not to spread Marxist ideology but rather to liberate Vietnam from foreign domination. The United States apparently understood this at the time, and American intelligence provided aid and support to the Viet Minh freedom fighters and their army of five thousand. The Viet Minh carried out constant military harassment of their new overlords. When the Japanese surrendered to the Allied powers in August 1945, after atomic bombings of Japanese cities, the Viet Minh took over Hanoi and the northern part of the country. Ho Chi Minh triumphantly declared the independence of Vietnam from Japanese and French rule on September 2, 1945. In his declaration, he quoted heavily from the U.S. Declaration of Independence and the French Rights of Man, and he listed Vietnamese grievances against France as the Americans had done against the British nearly two hundred years earlier:

> For more than eighty years, the French imperialists, abusing the standard of Liberty, Equality, and Fraternity, have violated our Fatherland and oppressed our fellow-citizens. They have acted contrary to the ideals of humanity and justice. In the field of politics, they have deprived our people of every democratic liberty.
>
> They have enforced inhuman laws; they have set up three distinct political regimes in the North, the Center and the South of Vietnam in order to wreck our national unity and prevent our people from being united.
>
> They have built more prisons than schools. They have mercilessly slain our patriots; they have drowned our uprisings in rivers of blood. They have fettered public opinion; they have practiced obscurantism against our people. To weaken our race they have forced us to use opium and alcohol.

In the fields of economics, they have fleeced us to the back-bone, impoverished our people, and devastated our land.

They have robbed us of our rice fields, our mines, our forests, and our raw materials. They have monopolised the issuing of bank-notes and the export trade.

They have invented numerous unjustifiable taxes and reduced our people, especially our peasantry, to a state of extreme poverty.

They have hampered the prospering of our national bour-geoisie; they have mercilessly exploited our workers.[7]

In the declaration Ho Chi Minh put forth both a hope and a warning: "We are convinced that the Allied nations which at Tehran and San Francisco have acknowledged the principles of self-determination and equality of nations, will not refuse to acknowledge the independence of Vietnam." He added, "The entire Vietnamese people are determined to mobilise all their physical and mental strength, to sacrifice their lives and property in order to safeguard their independence and liberty."

American military officers were present at the reading of the Vietnamese Declaration of Independence, standing side by side with the Vietnamese victors they had supported. General Giap, a former history teacher who became the supreme commander of Vietnam's military, spoke about Vietnam's friendly relations with the United States. Ho would later repeatedly ask for American support, offer Vietnam as a "fertile field for American capital and enterprise," and even raise the possibility of an American naval base in Cam Ranh Bay.[8] When Mao emerged victorious in China, Ho made an enormous overture to the United States, specifically stating that an independent Vietnam would remain neutral in America's growing conflict with the Communist bloc.[9] It was a great opportunity for the United States to establish constructive relations with an independent Vietnam.

The United States, however, had fallen deeply into a Manichaean trap, which was to consume its foreign policy for years to come, viewing Communism as a monolithic evil that threatened the West. The Soviet Union had just tested a nuclear weapon, and China had "fallen" to the Communists. Both of these were seen as serious threats to U.S. national security. Ho's offers of friendship and cooperation were completely ignored by Washington. Only after being snubbed by the United States did Ho feel compelled to seek closer relations with China and the Soviet Union. Disregarding the cause of Vietnamese nationalism, the United States now chose to see the Viet Minh as part of the growing international Communist plot to take over the world. The loss of Vietnam was feared by most U.S. leaders as the tip of the balance of power in favor of the Communist monolith.

The U.S. view of the Viet Minh was simply wrong. The Viet Minh was not a puppet movement sponsored by the Soviet Union or China. As noted above, the Viet Minh aimed to liberate their country, not cede control to another outside power, Communist or otherwise. U.S. diplomats in Hanoi clearly recognized this fact and stressed that Ho enjoyed broad support in all regions of Vietnam.

Yet the United States, preoccupied with its view of the Communist threat to the free world, sided with France over the Viet Minh. "Despite the glowing professions of friendship on September 2," historian George Herring notes, "the United States acquiesced in the return of French troops to Vietnam and from 1950 to 1954 actively supported French efforts to suppress Ho's revolution, the first phase of a quarter-century American struggle to control the destiny of Vietnam." In so doing, Herring states, "the United States was attaching itself to a losing cause."[10]

The French, with the help of British troops and the acquiescence of the United States, expelled the Viet Minh from the southern part of the country. Then in November 1946 the French set out to regain control of the entire country; a French cruiser shelled Haiphong, a Vietnamese port about sixty miles southeast of Hanoi. The shelling killed six thousand civilians, outraging and energizing the Viet Minh, who already enjoyed widespread popular support. This was the beginning of the Vietnamese war for independence.

Try as they might, the French could not defeat the Viet Minh. Constant attacks on French positions drained French resources and manpower, and the Viet Minh came to control two-thirds of the countryside by 1950. General Giap was confident enough of his troops' strength to launch an offensive against the French. In one engagement, at Cao Bang, the French lost six thousand troops and massive amounts of supplies.

The United States gave France billions of dollars' worth of military assistance, but French control in Vietnam remained extremely tenuous.[11] In March 1953 the Viet Minh accomplished what U.S. and French military leaders said was impossible. They hauled heavy artillery up to the high grounds around the French garrison at Dienbienphu, putting twelve thousand French troops under siege and constant attack. On May 7 the Viet Minh forced the French to surrender, ensuring that France would now cede the northern part of the country to the Viet Minh.

In Geneva, the parties to the conflict agreed to split Vietnam into North and South, divided at the eighteenth parallel, until free elections could be held in the summer of 1956. Neither entity was supposed to join in a military alliance with a foreign power.

President Eisenhower's secretary of state, John Foster Dulles, admitted that the loss of North Vietnam to Communists was "something that we would have to gag about" but that the U.S. could still "salvage something" in Southeast Asia "free of the taint of French colonialism."[12] The United States would assume France's role as "protector" of Laos, Cambodia, and southern Vietnam. Eisenhower and Dulles believed that France had failed to hold North Vietnam because the French were trying to perpetuate colonialism there whereas the United States would succeed throughout the world by befriending anti-Communists and helping them protect the independence of their countries. This meant, of course, that the United States would construct an anti-Communist state in South Vietnam.

The United States set about to build the nation of South Vietnam, which it would support, arm, and protect at all costs. The United States never intended to allow free elections in accordance with the agreement it had made in Geneva in 1954, for to do so would certainly result in a Viet Minh victory. Instead it would pour billions of dollars in aid into the country in an attempt to create a new client state in the region. A client state by no means necessitated a democratic state. "The men who ran the American imperial system," writes Neil Sheehan, winner of the Pulitzer Prize and the National Book Award, "were not naïve enough to think they could export democracy to every nation on earth." Instead, "their high strategy was to organize the entire non-Communist world into a network of countries allied with or dependent upon the United States. They wanted a tranquil array of nations protected by American military power, recognizing American leadership in international affairs, and integrated into an economic order where the dollar was the main currency of exchange and American business was preeminent."[13] In fact, South Vietnam, writes historian Louise Brown, "existed as a national entity only on the balance sheets of the US Treasury."[14] By 1966 upward of 65 percent of South Vietnam's budget came from United States aid. The United States handpicked the leaders of South Vietnam and either turned a blind eye or encouraged their corruption and repression.

Not all U.S. leaders thought we should be sending troops there, but very few took any rigorous action to stop it. Contrary to the current popular sentiment that the United States simply didn't try hard enough to win in Vietnam, the U.S. military and its civilian leaders demonstrated that they were prepared to annihilate large parts of Vietnam in pursuit of victory. The United States alone dropped more bombs on the tiny country than had been dropped by all sides in the entire course of the Second World War. This amounted to 250 pounds of dynamite for every person living on the entire Southeast Asian subcontinent.[15] Pulitzer Prize–winning journalist Stanley Karnow notes that American firepower brought to bear against the Vietnamese Communists was "unprecedented, awesome, almost beyond the bounds of imagination."[16] Hundreds of thousands of land mines were buried, and one hundred million pounds of herbicides (Agent Orange being the most famous) were sprayed on a million acres of forests, killing half of the timberlands of South Vietnam.[17] The United States also designated large areas to be free-fire zones, meaning that the areas were subjected to massive bombings without regard to the status of the inhabitants or other such limitations.

Already in January 1969 the war in Vietnam was claiming the lives of two hundred Americans each week and around $30 billion per year.[18] Nixon said that he would not end up like President Johnson, who was forced into early retirement from politics by the unpopularity of the war. Nixon therefore aimed to end the war quickly through the application of more force. In March 1969 he ordered the expansion of the fighting into neutral Cambodia. He wanted the North Vietnamese to know that he would use as much force as possible, at any time and in any place necessary, to assure that the United States would not lose face in its war effort.

Before launching one aerial campaign in 1972, Nixon said, "The bastards have never been bombed like they're going to be bombed this time." In June of that year 112,000 tons of bombs were dropped on North Vietnam. In October 1972 the United States delivered more than $1 billion in military equipment to the South Vietnamese, giving the tiny nation the fourth largest air force in the world. During twelve days of the Christmas season of 1972, Nixon ordered the dropping of 36,000 tons of bombs, "the most intensive and devastating attacks of the war."[19]

Perhaps "war is hell," and terrible things simply happen during combat. Yet it seems to me that the U.S. military in Vietnam carried out programs with extraordinarily devastating consequences to civilians. One search-and-destroy operation was called Cedar Falls, in which the United States surrounded and bombed an area called the Iron Triangle, sent in thirty thousand specially trained U.S. troops, forced out all the villagers, leveled the area with plows, set it on fire, and bombed it again. Though some seven hundred Vietcong (short for Cong San Viet Nam, the Vietnamese Communists fighting for liberation of the south of Vietnam) were killed in the campaign, the main enemy force escaped.

A fairly typical search-and-destroy operation was described by Jonathan Schell in his book *The Village of Ben Suc*. The village was suspected of assisting the Vietcong. It was therefore surrounded and attacked. The houses and other structures were leveled, and all the inhabitants were forced off their ancestral land. A man riding his bicycle was shot during the attack, as were three people picnicking by the river.

The worst example of search and destroy, and of American inhumanity during the war, came to be known as the My Lai Massacre.

On March 16, 1968, soldiers of the Charlie Company, which had experienced heavy losses in the preceding weeks, entered the tiny village of My Lai in Quang Ngai Province. All the inhabitants, about five hundred people—mostly elderly, women, and children—were ordered into a ditch, shot to death, and then set on fire by the American soldiers.

Credible sources claim that many units carried out acts like those at My Lai. "That's why so many civilians were killed," my uncle tells me. "American soldiers just didn't know who was and who wasn't the enemy. They didn't know who to trust." The Phoenix Program, carried out by the CIA, claimed to have killed twenty thousand Communists. Yet no one knows how many of these were simply civilians in villages that had supported the Vietcong.

The United States marched 2 million troops through Vietnam over the course of the war. At the height of the war, the United States had 500,000 soldiers there—a number equal to the army of Kublai Khan that the Vietnamese had defeated centuries before. One can offer many reasons for why the superior power of the United States was not able to overcome the North Vietnamese (an inept ally in South Vietnam and a growing antiwar sentiment in the United States being chief among them), but Vietnamese nationalism was not about to be stopped. "Westmoreland was wrong to count on his superior firepower to grind us down," Vietnamese General Giap recounted to journalist Stanley Karnow. "We were waging a people's war, *à la manière vietnamienne*—a total war in which every man, every woman, every unit, big or small, is sustained by a mobilized population. So America's sophisticated weapons, electronic devices, and the rest were to no avail. Dispite its military power, America misgauged the limits of its power."[20]

The fall of South Vietnam and the end of the fighting in 1975, however, did not bring happiness to the people of Vietnam. The North Vietnamese, who had fought so fiercely against the abuses of colonial France and the corrupt U.S.-backed regime in the south, soon became the new masters of repression under a unified Vietnam. That they became a repressive force, however, does not justify the United States' attempt to build an unpopular state in the south and to deny by force free elections, which certainly would have resulted in Ho Chi Minh's victory years earlier. Had he been allowed to rule the country after a free election, and had the United States tried to influence his regime to embrace democratic principles, it is quite possible that Vietnam would be a much freer place today and certainly much of the misery experienced by its people would have been avoided.

Despite memories of colonial and American abuses, the Communist victors had the option of reconciling with their former enemies and showing by their superior conduct the righteousness of their efforts. Yet a Communist state incorporating the south now required an enormous effort to pacify the people who had received so much aid and indoctrination from Americans. The Communists sent tens of thousands of South Vietnamese collaborators to "re-education" camps and began clamping down on freedoms of every kind. Hundreds of thousands more fled Vietnam by land and sea, fearing reprisals by the new government.

Steve Tue Nguyen, a friend who accompanied me on my first journey through Vietnam, came to America by way of Thailand after a harrowing but typical escape from Vietnam. One night his mother led four-year-old Steve and his baby sister, Jady, on a long hike through the mud toward the seaside. Steve was given a last meal of rice, which turned out to be terribly undercooked. Hard as it was for him to swallow the meal, it would be his last for a number of days.

Aboard the tiny boat, the passengers were packed well beyond capacity below deck. They set out into the open sea, eluding patrol boats, which would have jailed the passengers, or worse. At one point Jady began to cry, and the other passengers threatened to throw her overboard lest she give away their whereabouts to a patrol boat. Her mother had to wrap her and Steve in her sweater and fend off the other passengers.

Thai pirates, who cruised the waters looking for easy targets, boarded their boat, stole their supplies, and robbed the passengers. One man became delirious and jumped off the ship to his death. The boat's engine, which had been fixed several times, eventually gave out for good. From that point on the boat took on water and passengers drifted without supplies. They were fortunate to be saved by

Thai fishermen, who brought them to shore. Steve remembers being carried on someone's back along the beach and through the jungle.

Steve's family was among the lucky ones. Many died on the open seas, were captured and returned to Vietnam, or were attacked, robbed, raped, and killed by the pirates who fed on the suffering of the Vietnamese. Others languished in camps throughout Southeast Asia for years on end.

Steve's father, who had been a medic in the South Vietnamese army, remained in Vietnam in a so-called reeducation camp. Hundreds of thousands of prisoners were detained in these camps. In theory, reeducation was a positive first step in reintegrating the former enemy into the new state—a more humane approach, it was argued, than death sentences or life imprisonment. Yet thousands of former prisoners' accounts of the camps detail a different story: life in the camps was characterized by extreme hunger and malnutrition, inadequate or no medical treatment, forced hard labor, strict regulation (often enforced by beatings and torture), and intense indoctrination. The camps, in practice, were (and continue to be) vehicles of revenge and repression. It is estimated that after 1975 approximately 500,000 people were sent to roughly 150 camps, and from 10 to 15 percent of them died while incarcerated.

In 1992 the Communist regime granted a general amnesty for former South Vietnamese military officers. Yet, as the United Nations Commission on Human Rights Working Group on Arbitrary Detention noted in 1994, many rank-and-file soldiers remained in the prisons for many years after the amnesty for officers. One prisoner interviewed by the working group had been imprisoned without trial for seventeen years.

Not just former South Vietnamese civilian and military collaborators were forced into camps. Thousands of civilians also have been imprisoned there for expressing or exercising democratic beliefs. Hundreds of writers, artists, poets, and professors have been sent to the camps, as have monks and priests and political reformers.

Today, despite significant gains in education, public health, and infrastructure and forward strides to liberalize the economy, promote tourism, and fight corruption, Vietnam continues to severely limit freedom of expression, freedom of worship, and freedom to change the government through peaceful means. "The Government's human rights record remained poor," the U.S. Department of State concluded in its February 2001 report.[21] "Vietnam continued to restrict significantly civil liberties on grounds of national security and societal stability." The report lists human and civil rights abuses such as being detained for expressing political and religious views; beatings during arrest; limits on freedom of speech, the press, assembly, and association; and harassment of dissident religious groups and outspoken political opponents. It specifically mentions Thich Quang Do as one person subjected to "periodic questioning and close monitoring by security officials."

Human Rights Watch has also reported on detentions of religious leaders and harsh prison conditions. "Prison conditions continued to be extremely harsh. Human Rights Watch received reports of the use of shackles and solitary confinement in cramped, dark cells, and the beating, kicking, and use of electric shock batons on detainees by police officers."[22]

Several months before making my second trip to Vietnam, I contacted an international organization, which communicated on my behalf with the Most Venerable Thich Quang Do, Vietnam's leading dissident who was under house arrest for advocating human rights and freedom of religion in Vietnam. From the time of the fall of the South in 1975, Thich Quang Do used his position as one of the country's preeminent Buddhist scholars, teachers, and religious leaders to work tirelessly for human rights for the Vietnamese people, and he has paid for it dearly.

Thich Quang Do was arrested the first time in 1977 for speaking out against the systematic dismantling of the Unified Buddhist Church of Vietnam (UBCV), a two-thousand-year-old organization that had the support and loyalty of the vast majority of the nation's population. Thich Quang Do was the head of the church's executive arm, the Institute for the Propagation of Dharma, second in the UBCV only to the Patriarch of the Church. Fearing the UBCV for its strict adherence to the separation of church and state, and its advocacy of individual freedom, the Communists set out to destroy the it. The government seized UBCV property, including temples, hospitals, orphanages, and schools. It then sanctioned a new Buddhist organization, strictly regulated its activities, and forced monks to denounced the UBCV and join the state-sanctioned church.

Thich Quang Do was charged with trying to foment unrest and subvert the government and was held in prison under extremely harsh conditions without trial for nearly two years. Faced with mounting pressure from foreign embassies and nongovernmental organizations, the Communists finally released Thich Quang Do from prison. In 1982, however, he was rearrested for publicly protesting the Communists' expropriation of the UBCV property throughout South Vietnam. This time he was sentenced and exiled to Vu Ban village in Nam Dinh Province of North Vietnam, which he was forbidden to leave.

Yet the outspoken and seemingly fearless master would again defy the government. He later returned to Saigon without permission and quietly resumed his work for religious freedom and human rights. In 1994 there was a devastating flood in the Mekong Delta. The UBCV, in keeping with its tradition of helping society, organized a relief effort and began to distribute food, clothing, and medicine to the victims. The government chose to see this independent relief effort as a threat to its stability and arrested the UBCV organizers.

The aging Thich Quang Do was arrested on January 4, 1995, charged with "undermining the policy of unity," and detained at T82 interrogation camp until his trial in August 1995. In a one-day trial, Thich Quang Do was found guilty of "sabotaging solidarity" and sentenced to five years in prison.

He was imprisoned at Thanh Liet Prison Camp near Hanoi. Conditions were appalling, and the old monk developed a variety of illnesses, including chest pains, a stomach ulcer, a lung condition, and migraine headaches. Again international pressure proved to be effective in securing his release from prison in September 1998, although he was placed under house arrest, closely watched, and repeatedly harassed by authorities.

In March 1999 he was summoned for questioning and ordered

to return to Ho Chi Minh City after he traveled to central Vietnam to visit the church patriarch, Thich Huyen Quang. In early August 1999 Thich Quang Do was again interrogated. Officials tried to force him to sign a confession that he had acted illegally when he wrote a letter to European Union ambassadors meeting in Hanoi in July 1999. In his letter, Thich Quang Do conveyed "the concerns of all Buddhists who, because they speak out in the name of their conscience and human dignity, are being mercilessly silenced by an intolerant political regime." Thich Quang Do declared that fundamental and inalienable rights are not respected in Vietnam and pledged that "despite all the restrictions imposed upon us, we Buddhists strive our utmost, and shall never cease to strive, to make these universal rights the foundation-stone of all international relations and the basis of all interchange between communities, peoples and nations. Civilized society shall never allow any Government, whatsoever its ideology or political creed, to derogate from universal human rights and isolate their people behind an iron curtain on the pretext of 'non-interference' into their nation's internal affairs."

In mid-August 1999 a squad of police officers came to his pagoda after midnight and demanded to see him, threatening to break down the door before they eventually left. In September 1999 he was again summoned several times for questioning by the police. Thich Quang Do and several of his fellow monks were told that warrants for their arrest had already been issued and that their arrests were imminent. They were also told that they were the subject of continuing investigations for their alleged "subversive activities."

During another interrogation in September 1999, Thich Quang Do was confronted by ten officials, including members of the Ho Chi Minh City police, the Ho Chi Minh City section of the Communist Party of Vietnam, the Fatherland Front, and the state's official Vietnam Buddhist Church.

Yet if government officials believed that the old monk was too ill or too dispirited to continue his campaign for freedom and human rights, they were wrong. Their harassment and threats did not shake his inner conviction; they have not been able to make him fade away in silence and fear.

In late September 1999 Thich Quang Do wrote a letter to the Communist Party and government officials criticizing the distortions of Buddhist philosophy, and Vietnamese Buddhism in particular, as published in government-sponsored books and documents. Though Thich Quang Do, a superb scholar and teacher, asked permission to refute these distortions in print, the government never answered the letter.

In another controversial letter written to the Communist Party and the government in January 2000, Thich Quang Do noted that "even earlier in the North, and since 1975 in the South, the Party and the Government have confiscated pagodas; destroyed Buddha statues; mistreated, imprisoned, and exterminated Buddhist clergy and followers. The entire policy, from actual treatment to the laws, aims at a total destruction of Buddhism in Vietnam." These actions have occurred, Thich Quang Do pointed out, despite the fact that in July 1947 Ho Chi Minh himself stated that "only in an independent nation can Buddhism blossom easily. The French colonists want to rob our country. They burn pagodas, destroy statues of Buddha, mistreat clergy, and kill lay people. They aim to exterminate Buddhism."

In recognition of his sustained efforts, twenty-five U.S. members of Congress, ninety-five parliamentarians in Canada, seventeen parliamentarians in Belgium, fifteen members of the National Assembly, and twenty-six senators in France, as well as several Nobel Peace Prize recipients and various professors, nominated the Most Venerable Thich Quang Do for a Nobel Peace Prize in 2000. "Like the Reverend Desmond Tutu of South Africa, and His Holiness the Dalai Llama of Tibet," said the U.S. members of Congress, "the Venerable Thich Quang Do has exemplified the best of the human spirit in his quest for one of the most basic of human rights, freedom of worship."

I was eager to meet this outlaw, this old monk battling the government for the survival of his church and, more important, for the establishment of basic human rights for all Vietnamese. Within two weeks of my request word came back that Thich Quang Do had agreed to meet with me at his pagoda in Saigon. I was warned on several occasions, however, that the secret police had Thich Quang

Do under strict surveillance and there was no telling how they would treat me when I tried to see him.

I knew that conditions in Vietnam were not as bad as in Burma, yet the authoritarian regime was still firmly in control and could easily thwart my attempt to meet with this great symbol of perseverance and compassion. My contact informed me that in April 2000 a French journalist tried to see a lesser-known dissident in the country. She was arrested, interrogated, and expelled from the country, after having her notes confiscated. "It would be a shame if the same thing happened to you," my contact noted. "You can be sure that your room will be searched in your absence," I was cautioned, "so make sure no traces of your mission are apparent."

We arranged for the meeting just before Tet (Vietnamese New Year), as the city would be packed with Vietnamese who were visiting from abroad to celebrate with family and friends. This meant that the authorities would be busy watching the activities of hundreds of people they viewed as possible security threats, lessening the chance that I would be targeted by the secret police.

I stayed at an apartment complex in downtown Saigon, spending my first few days as a tourist, visiting various pagodas and mingling with locals. I rose early each morning to have a breakfast of *pho* (a delicious noodle soup eaten by just about every Vietnamese) and to say prayers. The morning tranquillity was a counterpoint to the evenings I spent soaking up the Saigon nightlife.

I had met a woman named Natasha on my flight. She was of Russian ethnicity, born in China and now living in Australia. She had been to Dharamsala and practiced Tibetan Buddhism, so we had much in common. It was her first visit to Vietnam, and I was able to show her some of the sights of Saigon. I eventually told her that I was there to meet a Buddhist dissident and asked her if she might take a backup disk out of the country for me if, and only if, there appeared to be no danger in it later on. She readily agreed.

On the appointed day I walked several blocks from my apartment building, went through the lobby of a large hotel, walked out a side door, down several more blocks, then flagged a taxi. I told my driver to take me to the intersection of two streets not far from the temple.

"Okay, okay," he said as we zoomed off.

About ten minutes later he looked at me in the rearview mirror. "Where do you want to go?" he asked.

"I already told you. Haven't we been driving there?" I asked sternly.

"I don't know where you are going," he replied.

I tried to tell him several times the street names that intersected in the place I wished to be dropped off, but he said he had never heard of such an intersection. I showed him the piece of paper on which I had transcribed the street names exactly as they appeared on the map I had used, but he still claimed he didn't know where to take me.

In frustration, and fearing I would be late, I finally asked him if he knew of the pagoda I was trying to reach.

"Oh, yes, yes, yes. I know it," he said happily. "Do you want to go there?"

"No! Not there. But close to there. Drop me off several streets away from there. Do you understand?" I asked.

He lowered his eyebrows, confused at why I should want to be let off there.

"There is nothing to see there," he said.

"Don't worry. Just drop me where I told you," I said firmly.

As I approached the temple I wondered whether I would encounter the police. I took out my guidebook and looked around frequently, doing my best impression of a tourist who just happened to be looking for one of Saigon's temples. When I came upon the temple I quickly entered the gate.

Inside I found a nun and told her that I was there to see Thich Quang Do.

"Is he expecting you?" she asked quietly in a heavy accent.

"Yes, he is."

"Okay. I'll tell him you are here," she said, smiling politely. "Please sit down."

After five minutes I was shown into a small room lined with chairs. I took out my digital voice recorder and turned on my laptop. I would download each hour of our conversation to my computer, then hide the electronic files before leaving the temple grounds.

Several minutes later the Most Venerable Thich Quang Do came into the room. He was wearing the customary brown robe of a Vietnamese monk. He was smiling, and his face seemed to shine with light. I rose to my feet to greet him.

"It is very good to see you," I said.

"Yes, yes. Please sit here next to me," he said, taking both my hands and leading me to the chair next to his. "I don't hear so well, so we should sit close," he said, laughing.

"So this is your home now? You must stay in the pagoda all the time?" I asked.

"Oh, yes," he grinned. One of his front teeth was missing. "I have to stay here all the time. But I have full freedom in my study, and in my sitting room. And I have full freedom here," he said, pointing to his head.

His laughter was infectious. Each time he chuckled I found it impossible not to laugh with him. I was charmed by him and could see why other people call him charismatic.

"That is perhaps the most important thing we have," I observed, "the freedom to think."

"Oh, yes. They cannot imprison my mind. I close my eyes, and in my mind I fly everywhere. Of course, I can only do so in my thoughts." He sat back in his chair, placing his left arm on the armrest, his right hand resting gently on my arm.

"I rarely have an opportunity to meet a foreigner like you," he told me. "I rarely have the opportunity to speak English either. I have great difficulty speaking English, because for more than fifty years I did not speak English. I have forgotten almost all of what I learned," he cautioned me, "so sometimes I will not find the words to express my ideas fully. So please speak slowly and clearly."

I promised to try to be clear and also told him that he could speak in Vietnamese if he found it necessary. But I was surprised to find that his English was very good and he had quite an extensive vocabulary. Even the few times that he spoke Vietnamese, he simply repeated what he had already said in English.

"It is my pleasure to be in your book," he said smiling. "You know, I cannot call outside. I can receive calls. But I am cut off from the world. The Communists try to keep me apart from people."

In fact, Thich Quang Do does not have many visitors these days. Many of his colleagues fled the country, and the ones in Vietnam do not bother to come to see him. "They are afraid of the police," he told me. "If anyone comes to see me they will be asked to go to their People's Committee and will be questioned about why they came and what I said. So no one comes to see me. It is too troublesome for them."

"Well, I am here, Most Venerable. I want to learn from you. I want to ask you about peace. And I hope that people all over the world will read your words and understand your message," I said. "You know, you are popular with many people in the Vietnamese community outside of Vietnam."

"Yes, but not here," he replied. "In Vietnam, no one dares to speak my name. Before 1975 I had published books here, but now they are published secretly with my name blotted out. One man wanted to republish a dictionary I translated from Chinese to Vietnamese, but the government told him he must take it to Taiwan to publish it."

Before he let me begin asking questions he wanted to get to know me better. He asked me where I was from, how many times I had been in Vietnam, what I had seen, what other countries I had gone to, and so forth. He was especially intrigued that I had ventured to Burma to see Aung San Suu Kyi.

"Was it difficult to get to see her?" he asked.

"Yes, quite. It was quite an ordeal," I said. "But it was well worth it."

"So now you are prepared for the regime in Vietnam!" he mused. "One reporter who came to see me before took some pictures of me. Before she left she hid the film in her shoe." He laughed. "I said to her, 'I see you are used to dealing with the Communists.' That is how it is in such a state."

"Venerable, let me ask you a tough question. Why should people care about what happens in Vietnam? There is a growing amount of capitalism here, many tourists come here, the Vietnamese who escaped from Vietnam now return here as tourists, they send lots of money here, they buy land and businesses here, even President Clinton came here. So many people may wonder why they should be concerned with a country that seems to be on a course of vast improvement."

He paused for a time, thinking about how to answer. "I'm not sure how to put my answer in words," he finally said.

"Well, let me make the question more personal first. Why do *you* care so much?"

"It is my duty!" he replied instantly. "I am a Buddhist monk. I have to take care of my people's happiness! That is my purpose."

"But many monks are very quiet. You are not."

"Because the most important thing for a human being is freedom," he replied. "If you have no freedom, life becomes meaningless. All the Vietnamese people are living under a yoke, the yoke of dictatorship. So we must do something to bring about real freedom for Vietnamese Buddhists in particular and the Vietnamese people in general. That is why I care."

"I understand. Yet many people around the world believe that there is plenty of personal freedom here," I remarked. "There are karaoke bars, modern discos, many shops; lots of people have motorcycles and drive around looking quite happy."

"That is not freedom!" he retorted. "That is not *real* freedom. Freedom is the ability to express one's ideals openly without being controlled. And whatever it is that you think in your mind, you have the right to speak. Freedom means you are not afraid to speak out. But we don't have that freedom here. Yes, you can go to a cinema and enjoy it without problem. But if you say anything that the government dislikes, then you will be in trouble. Freedom of expression and freedom of belief—nobody has the right to take those freedoms away from you."

"Now, let me ask again, why should people care about Vietnam?" I questioned. "And why should people care if the inhabitants of Tibet and Burma and Palestine have freedom?"

"Everybody has different qualities," he replied, patting my arm. "You have a compassionate heart. If someone else is happy, then you are happy. If someone else is sad, then you are sad. That is your nature, and it is an ideal way to be. But not everyone has that quality, that compassion. For those who don't have that quality, who don't have compassion, your going around traveling and spreading understanding about freedom and working for peace, to them it is in vain, it is useless. But to you it is very important. So, again, the way you are is an ideal way to be, but on this earth not everyone has this quality. It is a rare quality. You can rarely find people like you."

"I don't know if I'm so rare, Venerable. But I know that we can rarely find people like you," I responded.

"No, it is rare. Most people," he declared, "all they can think about is eating until they are full, wearing clothes to stay warm. They only think about keeping their bodies happy. They don't think about happiness or sadness or other people's feelings. If it doesn't have anything to do with themselves, it doesn't concern them. They only think about what is theirs, and not other people's. In other words, people are selfish. They don't have a heart of compassion.

"Everywhere around the world," he continued, "especially among youth, people have only one idea: to enjoy life. In the West, many people are trying to find something to feed their starved mind in this scientific age. They are coming East to find something in this culture that will help them find peace in their mind."

"Yes. I suppose I am an example of that," I said. "Unfortunately, though, drugs like heroin and ecstasy are becoming popular among Asian youth, and MTV and fashion and discos are wildly popular, even though most of the people can't afford the lifestyles of the West. At the same time, I notice that few young people really know much about the Buddha's teachings."

"I'm sad to see that in Asia people are trying to Westernize life, to learn the Western way of life. They believe their own ways are no longer good enough. They are not in fashion. We have a long history of compassion, of respect for human rights and freedom. But the young people born since the war know nothing of these traditions. The government wants them to be content with karaoke and discos and these things. They are not supposed to worry about freedom," he said. "And you are right, the youth know nothing of Buddha's teachings. Especially under the Communist regime, where they want to take out every religious feeling in people's mind. They want to reeducate people to think only of food and clothing. In general, young people are not allowed to go to the temples. For the

Communists, religion is just like a drug. Marx said so. So they try to destroy all religion. Mao started the counterrevolution in China and tried to destroy everything cultural, all the temples, even Confucian ideas." He laughed. "And now the Chinese Communists are destroying all of Tibetan culture because it is a Buddhist country. That is how the Chinese believe they can control Tibet forever."

"Yet the Tibetans still love the Dalai Lama. They cannot destroy that," I noted.

"Yes. In Vietnamese we have an expression, 'Man proposes but God disposes.'" He smiled. "The people in power cannot do whatever they like, even if they think they can."

"When Ho Chi Minh was fighting the Japanese, most Buddhists gave him support," I stated. "Venerable, is it proper for Buddhists to support war?"

"No," he said immediately. "At the time the Japanese were on the offensive. Vietnam was not a threat to them. When the French came in, like I said before, the people were unified. The Buddhists did not support using weapons and killing people; they wanted the happiness of society to prevail. They didn't want a confrontation. They just wanted Vietnam to belong to Vietnam. Even though they were Buddhists, they were also Vietnamese, and their nationalism, their want for independence, what they felt for the country, came first. Our Buddhist belief says that we cannot kill, but we wanted to support independence. We did not directly enter into killing. We only took part in social, economic, educational, and health services."

"To the Americans, who saw that Ho was in Russia and in China, automatically he was a Communist. But to the Vietnamese, they saw only that he was a freedom fighter. Is that correct?" I asked.

"Yes, that is right. We could not imagine that after we gained our freedom from the French yoke, we would be put under the Communist yoke," he said.

"Yet the Viet Minh promised more freedom. They could have delivered on their promise," I noted. "Even the Communists could have delivered the freedom that they preached."

"Yes, in order to unite the entire Vietnamese people, they did not interfere into individual life. But now, they interfere in all matters of individual life: what we are allowed to eat, to think, to say."

"Were people surprised by the actual policies of the Communist regime?" I asked.

"Oh, yes," he said, laughing. "But by then it was too late."

"Once Ho Chi Minh took over the north, what should have been done, do you think?"

"Well, no one could do anything to liberate the north once he took it over. It was impossible to rid the north of Communism. It was too late."

I paused and thought for a moment. "When I think about the war I become very sad," I observed. "I am sad for all those young American boys who died, for all the other soldiers as well. It astounds me that there were 3 million Vietnamese casualties during the war. It is such a tragedy."

"Yes. At the time we were victims of the international struggle between the Soviet Union and the U.S. We were just like chess pieces in a game. When they wanted war, they had war; when they wanted to settle it, they settled it. It was another example of how the strong exploit the weak. The superpowers exploited Vietnam. We Vietnamese killed each other for the interests of foreigners. We are very, very sad about that. It was an ideological war between the blocs, and it was the Vietnamese people who suffered.

"I do not mean all American people think the same way," he added. "Some of them have real ideals for freedom. Some came here to bring real freedom to Vietnam. To those we have to express our deepest, heartfelt thanks. But some came here to serve their own interests." His smile was gone and he shook his head slowly from side to side. "It was a situation like we say, in Vietnamese, where the heart is broken but nothing can be done to repair it."

"There were many instances during the war in which American soldiers fought in ways that are against American ideals: killing civilians, killing women, killing children," I said.

"That is why war is so horrible," he replied. "These things happen during war. We should do whatever we can to stop these things, but they will only end when we stop war itself."

"When Ho Chi Minh took over the north, what did he do to Buddhism?" I inquired.

"Oh, many, many big, beautiful Buddhist temples were destroyed. Buddhist social services were destroyed as well. The Communists are atheists, you see. They respected no religion, only money and rice. They took the temples as storage for oxen and rice and even fertilizer."

"Venerable, how are people suffering in Vietnam today?" I questioned.

"Poverty in the countryside. No rice to eat, but rice to export. The population is growing too fast. No right to think or express ideas. Close surveillance every day. You know, the secret police are watching me at all times, every day. You came here, and they know. They will follow you now to your hotel.

"You are very happy people living under a democracy," he observed. "It is much better. Nothing in the world is absolutely good, but it is much less bad than it is here. We Vietnamese suffer because we have less freedom, you Americans suffer because you have too much freedom." He paused, then began laughing. "I have no freedom at all, but Americans have so much!"

"Venerable, why do you laugh and smile so much? Why are you so happy?"

"No one can imprison my mind. That's why I'm happy," he replied, his eyes gleaming.

"It is an inspiration to me to see someone who has been so mistreated retaining a sense of joy about life," I told him. "Can you tell me about your imprisonments?"

"I was arrested the first time in 1977 because I denounced in a letter the destruction of Buddhist property. I requested that the Communist government stop this destruction. So they denounced me for trying to start a revolution, for trying to topple the government, trying to cause a coup d'état," he said, laughing heartily. "So I was sent to prison for nearly two years without trial. Twenty-three months without trial."

"What were the conditions in prison like?"

"Oh, very, very bad," he said, shaking his head. "I had a cell, not a room. It was one meter twenty centimeters by just over two meters. That's all."

"Did you have a chair? A bed?" I asked.

"No. No bed. It was just the cement. No mat. Just cement."

"Just the bare cement? No pillow, no blanket?" I asked in surprise.

"No, nothing. Not even a curtain. The iron door had a small window which they pushed food and water through."

"Did you get to leave the cell for exercise?"

"No. I was only permitted to leave my cell when they interrogated me. They would do so for three or four days at a time. The rest of the time I was in the cell, for twenty-three months."

"During the interrogation," I asked, "do you think they felt ashamed of what they were doing to you?" I just couldn't imagine interrogating an old monk, especially one with such a kind disposition.

"No. They didn't care at all. They simply thought that I was trying to topple the government, so they didn't care for me. But I told them that even if I was asked to take a chair in the government, I couldn't do that. If I was asked to be the director of the government, I couldn't do that. 'What I demand from you is that you give me freedom of worship,' I said to them, 'freedom of religion, freedom of teaching Buddhists. That's all.'"

"What did you do during your days? Meditation?" I asked.

"Oh, I had nothing but time. They didn't allow me any pens, any paper, nothing. They allowed no Buddhist literature, no prayer beads, no robe. I wore prisoners' clothes with a number on it. And in the cell they put a red light. The red light was always in my eyes, all day and all night. That was their way of torturing my mind. But I meditated and went to the pagoda in my mind."

"Why did they finally let you out of prison?"

"People in other countries were campaigning for my release, and the authorities apparently cared about world opinion. So they eventually let me go," he said.

"So without the pressure from human rights groups you would still be there?" I asked.

"Without the pressure, we would have had no hope at all."

I was delighted to hear how effective groups like Amnesty International can be. Here was a concrete example.

"What happened after prison?" I inquired.

"They sent me to the north in a small village temple for ten years. I was not allowed to leave that village, and no one from the outside was allowed to come and see me. The village was mainly old people. The young people in the village were not allowed to see me. But after ten years, I came back here."

"You mean, you came back without approval?"

"I came back myself. I decided I should come back. I informed a local official to inform Hanoi that I would leave there within thirty days." He laughed.

"You were brave to defy the government like that," I declared.

"Well, what was my crime? If I had committed a crime, they should put me on trial. But they never brought me before the court."

"But what happened when you returned to Saigon without approval?"

"Nothing happened. They left me alone. I did things quietly, behind closed doors. I made Buddhist translations. But in 1994 there were floods in the Mekong, and I organized a relief team to give relief parcels to the flood victims. For that the police arrested me."

"Why should they arrest a monk for helping his people?"

"They accused me of trying to overthrow the government, of trying to incite the flood victims to stand up against the government. But I replied, 'They can't lift their heads. They are nearly dead. How can they do that?'" he said loudly and laughing intensely. "This time they brought me to court and I was sentenced to five years in prison and five years' house arrest. They took me to Hanoi. I was released in 1998 under a general amnesty."

"And again, while in prison you were in solitary confinement the whole time?"

"Yes," he said. "All the time."

"I read that this last time you were very sick in prison," I noted.

"Yes. I was very sick. But now I've recovered."

"When Nelson Mandela was in prison he said the guards respected him. He demanded that they respect him. Did they respect you?" I asked.

"Well, I am happy by nature," he said, leaning forward in his chair. "My nature is to be happy. My guards and interrogators used to ask me, 'Why are you always laughing?' I told them, 'Well, what else can I do now? What do you want me to do? Weep? No, I do not weep. Instead, I will laugh. I will laugh with you.' And finally this made them laugh, and we would laugh together. You know, according to Buddhist doctrine, Buddha is in your mind. When we are free, when we laugh, we are Buddha. When we are suffering, we are in prison. When we are happy and there is nothing to worry about, we are in nirvana—free from greed, fear, hatred. If we deeply hold on to things, then we are in hell."

"When you see the Communist officials, the policemen and the soldiers, what do you see?" I questioned.

"Human beings!" he replied. "Ones just like you and me. I have no bad feelings against them. I have compassion for them because they have no wisdom. They have common knowledge, but no wisdom. We must train ourselves to achieve wisdom. It is not gained through studying or reading books, but by meditating, by getting rid of hatred and anger and fear and self-cherishing. Only by ridding ourselves of these things can we become wise. With advanced wisdom we can acquire even the power to read people's minds!"

"Do you have that power?" I asked with a smile.

"No, not yet. But if I had that, I would use it to help others. I could use it to teach the Communists," he laughed.

"Venerable, I have heard that some Vietnamese living in the West have criticized you. Is that true?" I asked.

"Oh, I get letters under false names from some people asking me, 'Why are you fighting the government?'" he replied. "You know, there are many Vietnamese secret police serving in the diplomatic corps in the United States, especially in California. They are trying to divide the Vietnamese community. There is trouble within the Vietnamese community. Even from 1975, they sent spies with the refugees when many people were leaving Vietnam. Now we have so many agents in the U.S.!"

"I didn't know that," I replied. "But that makes a lot of sense. Totalitarian regimes can be very clever. So what would you say to those critics if you met them face-to-face?"

"I would tell them, No, I'm not fighting the government. I am asking them something. I am asking them to permit freedom. I never do anything political. I don't do anything for money. What I do is to ask for freedom of worship. That is all. I do everything with nonviolence. I am not violent like them."

"Venerable, I have taught my students that liberation is joy, and since truth is liberation, it is also joy. Isn't that so?" I asked.

"Yes. If you acquire wisdom, you become happy."

I smiled. "I can see that you are a happy man," I said.

He laughed. "Well, I often say that I am the most free man in Vietnam. The government has made me an outlaw. Now I have no obligation. They have no right to make me act according to their law. I have full freedom now!" he said, roaring with more laughter.

He fell silent for a moment and then continued. "The Buddha says that by necessity this body will die," he said, pointing to his chest. "We can even burn ourselves for the right cause. But when it isn't necessary, we must not harm even a single hair on our body. So, I am careful to protect myself. I will not die now. I must continue to live in order to work for freedom."

"Are the Communists eager for you to die?" I questioned.

He howled. "Of course! I'm now seventy-two years old already. According to Oriental philosophy, the man who reaches seventy can die without any regrets. But for me it is like being at a cinema. I do not want to leave before the curtain comes down. When Vietnam has freedom, then I will die."

"What will happen with your church when you die? Is there anything left of it now?" I wondered.

"They have taken the pagodas, the hospitals, the orphanages. They just passed a law that everything that the government has acquired is permanently government property. All the pagodas belong to the government-sanctioned Vietnamese Buddhist Association."

"But are they good people, the monks in the government-created church?" I asked.

He lifted his eyebrows. "Some good, some bad. Some are very sincere, some follow the Communists for their own interests."

"That is like any organization, I suppose. Venerable," I said, changing the subject, "were you happy to be nominated for the Nobel Peace Prize?"

"Oh, I didn't hope for that," he replied instantly. "I know it was very difficult to get that. But to be nominated is very important. I was nominated by nearly three hundred people. I was later told that there were three finalists left: Mr. Clinton, me, and Mr. Kim Dae Jung. Mr. Kim Dae Jung won because he made a very good journey to North Korea. He was very worthy of the prize. He is making peace between north and south. He has been nominated fourteen times, and now he received it. I too have been nominated before. In 1980 I was nominated for the prize. Last year was the second time. But I can't hope to be nominated again. It would be greedy of me," he said, laughing.

"You know," he added, "it is not the money that I would want. That is not important for me. If I got the prize I would be able to speak out more. The most important thing for me is how to bring about freedom and human rights and democracy for all the Vietnamese people."

"What will you do now while you are stuck here in this pagoda?" I asked.

"I will continue to work for freedom," he said. "But then after it is won, I will withdraw. I will retire very happily and completely to do something for myself, to try to earn more wisdom. Yet time is not on my side. I am old. Though I have time in which to do things now, I am not allowed to preach in the temple."

"Can you teach monks?" I inquired.

"No. I cannot teach even one monk. Even my books have my name blotted out. The government fears that people will follow me. If you have many supporters, then the government makes it difficult for you. They fear you. You see, almost all of the Vietnamese people are opposed to the Communist government. The Communist Party, according to their reports, has two and a half million members. Not all of them are good Communists. It is very corrupt. Many join the party just to make money. Not more than 10 percent of them are real Communists. Besides that, they have no one. In general the Vietnamese people belong to Buddhism, to Christianity, to Cao Dai, to Hoa Hoa. Communists have no one. So they believe they must control religion very tightly. If a political group wants to topple the government, they cannot. The political groups have been crushed. There is only a handful of them left. Only the religious groups can do it. The people are loyal to religions. So religious groups are very difficult for the government. If they were to crush all the religious groups now, the world would cry out against the Communists.

"Followers listen to their preachers. Communist propaganda is useless now. The Communist paper is not read. People don't listen to their radio broadcasts. They would rather karaoke. When the news comes on, they turn it off.

"Much of the country has been destroyed by thirty years of war. And now there is a new war against the jungle forests. They destroy the forests. In the countryside the Vietnamese people remain in poverty. Foreign investment comes only to the cities. But even in the cities it is difficult for foreigners because it is so corrupt. Wherever you go, corrupt officials say, 'Let Uncle Ho show you the way!'" he said with a laugh, referring to the Vietnamese currency, which bears a picture of Ho Chi Minh.

"How long will Communism last in Vietnam?" I asked.

"Not long. Sooner or later we can reach our goal. I cannot predict the exact time, but it will come sooner or later. One day the Communists will go out. They cannot occupy the same stage for their entire lives. I deeply believe this. Belief is hope. Confidence is hope. No one can live without hope. I hope we will have freedom, human rights, and democracy. Right when the Communists took over in 1975 I began my struggle, and I do even now. I continue my journey because I have deep hope and deep belief that we can achieve freedom here.

"Ten years ago no one could imagine how quickly the Communist bloc would collapse, especially Soviet Communism. According to Buddhism, nothing exists without changing. What exists must change. What does not change does not exist at all. That is the law of impermanence. Vietnam was under the Chinese yoke for one thousand years. Then it was under the French for eighty years. Now we have been fifty years under Communist rule.

"The Communist culture has destroyed our Vietnamese culture. The poor fight against the rich; the ignorant fight against the educated. They create classes. Ho said every citizen must be a policeman and believe only in Ho and the Communist Party. They have a religion without God! Actually Marx and Lenin are their gods and Marx's book is their dogma! But the people hate the Communist government. If the Communists do not take a backseat, to withdraw, the people will force them to withdraw. The government is very afraid of the people now."

"Do you think the party officials know their days are numbered?" I asked.

"They know. They are busy trying to strengthen their position. They are not ignorant. They saw what happened in Russia, in the entire Communist bloc. I know that even the highest ranking officials don't believe in Communism now, just in their self-interest. They fear for their lives too. The hatred among the people, especially in the north, is very great. Land reform killed 700,000 people, landlords and peasants. Their relatives remember this and have great hatred toward the Communists. They would kill the Communists if they could. Conservatives and radicals are fighting in the government now. We hope that it will happen just like Russia, that the government will change from the inside."

"But Gorbachev thought he could remain in power," I pointed out. "Yet he was brushed aside."

"Yes, the hard-line Communists want Communism until they die. After they die, they don't care what happens."

"Of course, people cannot simply wait and hope," I declared. "They must work for freedom now."

"Yes, yes," he replied. "But only through nonviolence, strict nonviolence. I cannot do anything violent. I follow nonviolent means, according to Buddha's teaching."

"You have more freedom than they do, not because you are an outlaw," I observed, "but because they have to worry about their lives. They have to worry all the time. But you are free from these worries."

"Yes, yes, this is true," he responded.

"Such freedom must help you have peace in your heart."

"Yes," he replied. "But it is not the same for everyone. Almost all the people in Vietnam are greedy. With that, how can you have peace? They must become real spiritual people first," he declared.

"That's why we need masters like you to show us the way," I said, "to teach us how to overcome our greed."

"Yes, but here I cannot do as much as I want to do. But I can tell you, relatively, we can have peace, we can have progress. A peaceful mind, that lasts forever. That is what we must achieve—a peaceful mind," he said, looking deeply into my eyes.

I sat for a moment and absorbed his words. "Venerable," I finally spoke, "I feel that the biggest problem in the world today is the lack of faith, the lack of self-confidence that you can change yourself, and by coming together with others, you can change the world."

"Yes. But many people cherish hatred," he noted.

"But the hope is that hatred is very thin," I countered. "And when you take it off, when you peel away the hatred, one's deeper nature is cleared and love is released."

"Oh, yes," he said, taking hold of my hand again. "What is easily gained is not precious. If you teach one man to give up greed and to replace hatred with love, that man becomes a precious man."

We sat silently for a few moments before he continued to speak. "Even now there is not one truly enlightened being, one Buddha in the world. Buddhism believes in rebirth, so if in this life we don't become a Buddha, we hope to become one in the future. It is a long journey. Today we walk, we try to train ourselves, so we can reach our goal. Buddhism makes people hopeful, because in this moment you are greedy, but in the next you may become a Buddha. It is not far away. Therefore Buddhism makes people hopeful. We Buddhists are very optimistic. I have never been pessimistic. I always hope for good. Even the Communists are lovable people. We just have to change their way of thinking; make them think of goodwill, not hatred, give up their policy of power. We are the same people, and we must love each other. We are all the same people, we must stop fighting each other."

We had been talking for three hours when Thich Quang Do stood up. "I can't believe the time has gone so fast," he said. "I have been enjoying talking to you so much."

When I finished collecting my things from the table in front of me, Venerable took my hand and led me downstairs to the court-yard, where we continued talking.

"One thing I ask you to do," he said. "Help us bring freedom and human rights to Vietnam by writing and talking. Add to the world discussion about Vietnam. We want our people to be happy. Right now we are regressing, not making progress. It is still a poor, backward country. As long as the Communist regime remains, we will remain poor and backward. They keep the people in ignorance so that it is easier to rule. If you want them to follow you, you must keep them in poverty, in hunger—just like an ox, if you keep him hungry and put a bundle of grass before him. Relatively speaking, if we have real freedom, human rights and democracy, the world will have peace. In all the world, if every country becomes free, we will not have fighting. Economically, we will have to make people more equal. Then we will have peace.

"But," he added, "as long as you have greed, anger, suspicion, fear, and hatred, you will not have peace. The Buddha says that when you have peace in your mind, the world will have peace. But if you want to have peace in your mind, you must get rid of all greed, anger, suspicion, fear, and hatred and replace them with love and goodwill. When you do, then peace will come naturally."

Just beyond the gate we were being watched by men in civilian clothes who were obviously members of the police. We ignored them and continued walking hand-in-hand.

"Violence is the inheritance of many generations of man," he said. "It is deeply part of man. You cannot in one day or two days get rid of it. It will take time. Not only do people and nations act violently, but they also think violently." He laughed. "But nonviolence will bring happiness to mankind."

"Why are you so hopeful about the world?" I asked.

"The human heart contains a good seed," he said, smiling and once again looking deeply into my eyes. "It is concealed deep within the heart. It is always there. When this concealed seed is realized, the whole world will be better. When you have peace in your mind," he repeated, "there will be peace in the world."

A young monk came over to us and offered me some water. I declined but asked him to use my camera and take a few pictures of me with Thich Quang Do.

"I hope to see you again, Venerable," I said, holding his hand.

"Yes. Come and see me anytime," he replied. "I welcome you. Now I must go and have lunch with the abbot. See you next time," he said as he walked out of the courtyard.

The nun who had greeted me earlier came to me and asked if I wanted her to call a taxi. I thanked her, and the car arrived a few minutes later. I told the taxi to take me to a hotel. In the heavy traffic I couldn't tell if I was being followed, but I decided to wind through several downtown hotels just to be sure.

I hopped out of the taxi at the first hotel and went into the men's room. After a few minutes I walked away from the front entrance and into a restaurant. After pretending to examine the menu, I exited the restaurant onto the street. I then went through another hotel, a gift shop, and finally into an office building that was connected to where I was staying.

Once inside my room I downloaded the digital recordings of my conversation with Thich Quang Do onto my laptop and encrypted the files. I downloaded a copy of the encrypted files onto a compact disk and embedded the files within innocuous-looking operating system files.

There was a knock at my door not long thereafter. It was the hotel manager and someone from the front desk. He handed me an envelope quite shyly.

"I'm sorry, Mr. Hunt," he said, "but we must spray the room for bugs. It is an order by the Ministry of Health. We must do it tomorrow morning, so you will have to leave the room. Will this be too inconvenient for you?" he asked.

I opened the letter. It said exactly what he had just told me. "No," I replied, "it will be all right. I don't think I have a choice anyway, do I?" I asked.

"Well," he smiled nervously, "there is nothing we can really say about it. It is an order by the government."

"I see," I responded. "Okay. That's fine." I started to close the door but then opened it again. "Excuse me," I said. He returned to my door. "Is it just this room which is being sprayed?" I asked.

He paused a moment before answering. "Yes."

"So, none of the other rooms? Just my room has bugs?"

I could see that he didn't know how to answer. He just smiled again. "Okay," I said. "It's no problem."

I guessed that the secret police already knew where I was staying and were coming to search the room under the pretext of routine pest control. It wouldn't matter much, because the files were now already encrypted. There was the chance, however, that they would completely erase my computer's hard drive and destroy my disks and tapes.

That evening I met Natasha for dinner and gave her the disk. It was safe to do so, since even if the disk was confiscated for any reason, there was extremely little chance that the authorities would find anything on it, and if they did, there was only a remote possibility they could decrypt the files. In any event, it was highly likely that the entire conversation with Thich Quang Do had been monitored electronically by the authorities outside of the monastery, so the only issue was how interested they were in preventing me from taking the conversation out of the country.

Before I left the next morning, I put tiny markers around the room in places where neither the maids nor the sprayers would move them by accident. I was quite clever in this scheme. I took my laptop with me, since it fit easily into my bag. Later, I returned to find all of the markers moved, indicating to me that the authorities had done a thorough search of my things, including the things inside my luggage.

But I was quite happy that they did, as there was nothing incriminating, nothing to suggest that I had any connections with any foreign agency or government or that I meant Vietnam any harm.

I was still a bit unsure what it would be like for me upon leaving the country, recalling my experience at the airport in Burma. But other than the many long lines, I encountered no problem whatsoever.

During my flight to Thailand I reflected on my meeting with the Most Venerable Thich Quang Do. I had been deeply inspired by his irrepressible spirit. If he can face the deprivation of his freedom, the severity of interrogation, harassment, and denouncement, the systematic dismantling of his church, and the distortion of Buddhist teachings, how can we who are free to roam the planet complain about the inconvenience of taking time to do small things to help others? We can certainly not be too inconvenienced by writing to our leaders to press them to change unjust policies or by lending a few hours to Amnesty International or some such organization, which, as I saw in the case of Thich Quang Do, contributes enormously to getting dissidents released from prison. Yet the more personal gift that Thich Quang Do gave me was his brilliant, joyous, uncomplicated smile.

It is often said in the United States that our failures in Vietnam created a national malady called the "Vietnam syndrome." This refers to an alleged failure of the United States to use its military power in pursuit of its national interests around the globe. There is implicit in this remark a sense that Vietnam crippled us and prevented us from pursuing military actions that we otherwise would and should have—in Iran when our citizens were held hostage, for example.

In 1991 a jubilant President George Bush declared that our military victory against Iraq meant that, finally, "We've kicked the Vietnam syndrome." To me, that is just another way of saying that we no longer need to apologize for using force whenever we deem it necessary and just. Yet in my reading of recent history, the United States has not learned to apply its military power in more prudent and just ways; rather, the government has learned to hide its actions more and to rely on proxies to do its bidding. The United States continues to arm the world at an alarming rate, and has used its military and secret intelligence forces to set up and maintain repressive regimes around the globe.

As we will see in the next chapter, the United States in fact played out its Vietnam War angst in our own backyard, in Central America. If not for the courage and leadership of a great peacemaker in that region, hundreds of thousands of more lives would have been lost and hundreds of millions of dollars would have been spent zealously pursuing nebulous national interests.

Five

OSCAR ARIAS: CENTRAL AMERICA'S AMBASSADOR OF PEACE

I stood and wiggled my toes into the fine, warm sand. The beach stretched out in a crescent moon shape, the white sands framed perfectly by the clear blue water and the lush, deep green forest. I breathed in deeply and listened to the sound of the waves rumble and roll gently to the shore. What a blessing to be here in this peaceful place, I thought to myself. In times such as these we see that life is a precious and magical opportunity, not a crisis to be managed or a burden to be borne.

A little farther down the beach I turned fully toward the ocean. I wished deeply that such peacefulness would be carried across every sea and every land, and people could finally stand on their beach or their mountain or their field and contemplate how to fulfill their highest potential, to discover what their work should be and then attend to it with all their heart.

I had seen the beauty of Costa Rica before. It is a magnificent country of friendly people, with a remarkable tradition of democracy, activism, and environmental awareness. Costa Rica's wilderness areas have been protected not just by law, but also by custom, with pride, and these areas are now a gift to the entire world.

I wasn't here to sightsee this time, however. Rather, I was here to seek out a peacemaker who could address the pragmatic aspects of peace that I may have missed in my other discussions. I arrived already certain that to establish lasting peace we must disarm nations and at the same time strengthen the global bodies designed to respond to international disputes. I think it is inevitable as we grow in awareness and interdependence that an international body will be adequately empowered to protect the peace among nations. The great imagination of Albert Einstein aptly described the purpose and character of such a world body:

> It must be a combination that by its composite nature will greatly reduce the chances of war. It will be more diverse in its interests than any single state, thus less likely to resort to aggressive or preventative war. It will be larger, hence stronger than any single nation. It will be geographically much more extensive, and thus more difficult to defeat by military means. It will be dedicated to supranational security, and thus escape the emphasis on national supremacy which is so strong a factor in war.[1]

This supranational security arrangement, however, would be quite ineffective if nations failed to disarm. By maintaining independent armed forces nations could act unilaterally, whenever they saw fit, in their limited national interests, thereby triggering wars. Einstein recognized this fact and suggested "all the nations forming the supranational state pool their military forces, keeping for themselves only local police."[2]

For some people, and particularly the self-described "realists" of international relations, a world without national armies is a ridiculous, naive, and even dangerous idea. What is present in the thinking of these critics is cynicism, and what is absent is imagination. Their cynicism is based on a view of the world as a violent brew of selfish and conflicting desires, in which a strong army is necessary to make people and nations behave themselves. Their lack of imagination means they have abandoned the vision of humanity in which spiritual and ethical considerations are finally elevated above selfish desires. Believing in the worst of human nature, the realists continue to push our societies to arm and prepare for coming, inevitable conflicts. Failing to envision a world of higher consciousness, therefore, ensures that peace will always be short-lived, sporadic, and unequal.

"Striving for peace and preparing for war are incompatible with each other, and in our time more so than ever," Einstein said. Of course, this flies in the face of conventional thinking. Even in antiquity it was the popularly held belief that we must be ever vigilant in preparing for war. Quintus Horatius Flaccus (65–8 B.C.E.) recorded the accepted adage that "in time of peace, as a wise man, one should make suitable preparation for war." Flavius Vegetius Renatus, the Roman author of *Epitoma rei militaris,* likewise held that "he who would desire peace should be prepared for war."

Karl von Clausewitz, the famed Prussian general and military strategist, followed this Roman maxim and held that war is, in fact, a normal extension of pragmatic politics. He echoed Lao Tzu and Machiavelli in stating that when war is pursued, leaders must be prepared to use all possible resources at their disposal to ensure the most complete military victory possible. Such beliefs continue to pass for wisdom in the capital cities of the world and are used to justify enormous military expenditures on all types of horrific weapons, as well as aggressive and provocative political and military posturing.

Our political leaders have spoken of peace so frequently, in an attempt to clothe themselves in morality and appear laudable, that they have anesthetized the electorate to the significance of the word. Politicians consistently preach peace while tapping on the drums of war. All of America's most prominent leaders over at least the last six decades have praised peace while they presided over enormous military organizations, controlled and meddled in the affairs of foreign governments, funneled aid to repressive regimes, gave military support to nations in volatile regions, and protected "national interests" at the expense of the mass of humanity living in dire poverty. This is not the peace envisioned by our spiritual and moral teachers, and it is not a peace with which any of us can be satisfied. Our leaders can do much, much better, and we must demand that they do so.

Of course our nation has done good things as well, but the good things are not what we need to change. What we need to correct is the behavior that adds to the cycle of conflict in the world. We need to use our superpower status to truly implement a culture of equality, respect, and peacefulness.

Political leaders around the world could well take their cue from the actions of Oscar Arias Sanchez, the former president of Costa Rica and the 1987 recipient of the Nobel Peace Prize. Arias has earned a reputation as one of the greatest living peacemakers through his tireless advocacy of an end to poverty and strict control over the production and transfer of weapons. As we shall see, Arias has earned this reputation through deeds, not merely through academic writings and speeches.

In order to understand Arias and his accomplishments, we must first understand something about the relationship between Latin America and the United States. One historian says that the relationship "is about the way a powerful nation treats its weaker neighbors."[3] It exposes the "might makes right" mentality, which often creates long-term conflicts and hinders the creation of a culture of peaceful resolutions to problems.

The American public traditionally has had little interest in Latin America. Most Americans today would be hard-pressed to name and place on the map the major countries of the region. There still lingers in the minds of Americans the same racism and cultural bias exhibited by John Quincy Adams, who said that Latin Americans were clearly inferior. The area is often dismissed as backward, poor, and weak and its citizens ridiculed as inept, corrupt, or slavish. In short, these nations have typically been disparaged as the "banana republics" in which the culture of the crude prevails.

In contrast to this view, Latin America has fascinated me for quite some time. Even in my childhood it was not simply a place of poverty and problems, it was a place of enchantment. I was captivated by the imaginative scenes in a book I'd been given on Latin America: landing at the beaches of northern San Salvador, ascending the Great Pyramid built by the Aztecs at Cholula, climbing the mountain Popocatepetl, exploring the Mayan ruins at Chichén Itzá, sailing to the holy island of Cozumel, and so forth.

The United States' involvement in Latin America, however, has showed far too little respect for these cultural treasures and the people to whom they belong. Our first involvement in Latin America was primarily military. We had an imperialist fever that we called Manifest Destiny, in which we sought to take as much land as we could. Latin America was the prime target of our expansion. The term *Latin America* was a mid-nineteenth-century French invention to stress the area's former close ties with the Romance-speaking Latins of Europe and an attempt to curb American expansionism by asserting that the area did not belong indisputably to the sphere of American influence—something that would be asserted later in the Monroe Doctrine.

Latin America is vast in geographic area, population, ethnicities, and cultures. It comprises all the Spanish-, Portuguese-, and French-speaking countries of North America (except Canada), South America, Central America, and the West Indies. Today it is twice the size of the United States in population and land area (including some twenty republics) yet six times smaller in economic terms. It is an ancient land with ancient traditions, some of its cities being continually inhabited for a thousand years and its farms producing maize and bananas for longer still. Yet it is not just part of the developing world; it is also Western. Nine out of ten people in Latin America speak a European language and practice a European religion (most of the world's Roman Catholics are Latin American).

Latin American history is anything but peaceful. It "was born in blood and fire, in conquest and slavery," says historian John Charles Chasteen.[4] The Spanish were the greatest conquerors in the region, while Portugal subjugated a vast area in South America. In Central America, Spain dominated the landscape from the sixteenth until the nineteenth century. Later France, Britain, Germany, and others played significant roles as well.

In North America, U.S. expansion led to the annexation of the territories now comprising Texas, New Mexico, Arizona, Colorado, Nevada, Utah, California, and parts of several other states. Americans had little legal claim to the areas, but by defeating, bullying, and frightening Mexico, the United States had acquired most of the western continent by the mid-1860s. Theodore Roosevelt, the great embodiment of American imperialism, observed, "It was out of the question that the Texans should long continue under Mexican rule;

and it would have been a great misfortune if they had. It was out of the question to expect them to submit to the mastery of the weaker race."[5]

In 1899 Roosevelt wrote an enormously telling article about our imperialism, and about American attitudes toward peace in general, called "Expansion and Peace." In the article Roosevelt declared, "Every expansion of civilization makes for peace. In other words, every expansion of a great civilized power means a victory for law, order, and righteousness.

"This has been the case in every instance of expansion during the present century, whether the expanding power were France or England, Russia or America."

He praised the westward expansion of American settlers across the North American continent and into Alaska, claiming that it brought an end to the wars of frontier life, which he said were caused simply by the fact "that we were in contact with a country held by savages or half-savages. . . . In North America, as elsewhere throughout the entire world, the expansion of a civilized nation has invariably meant the growth of the area in which peace is normal throughout the world." Roosevelt concluded, "It is only the warlike power of a civilized people that can give peace to the world."[6] The "great colonizing nations" of England and Germany were his examples of the "civilized powers," the selfsame powers that fought so fiercely and brutally in the First and Second World Wars.

The wars against the Native Americans and the Latin Americans were extremely patriotic and popular events. The continual battles, the victories, the expansion showed energy and vigor, unlocked resources, and focused our disparate political ideologies against a common enemy. We were all pointed in the same direction: the perpetual expansion of American power and prestige, and the unending battle against anyone who would oppose our interests. Unfortunately, once started, this fervent and perpetual expansion became a very addictive habit, lodging itself firmly in the American way of doing things.

In 1898 the United States accomplished its longtime aim of defeating the Spanish and taking possession of the territories of Cuba and Puerto Rico (along with Guam, and the Philippines for a nominal sum of money). In 1903 President Theodore Roosevelt swept aside objections to his site for a new canal across the isthmus of Central America and decided to create a new nation that would accommodate the United States' desires. Consequently, the United States encouraged the northern part of Columbia to rebel. Roosevelt deployed U.S. military forces to prevent Columbia from putting down the rebellion, leading not just to the creation of an independent nation of Panama, but also to the United States' sovereignty "in perpetuity" of a ten-mile-wide swath of land across the whole of Panama.

Having conquered these territories, the United States then began pursuing a policy of economic and political domination in Latin America. Between 1898 and 1934, the United States launched more than thirty military interventions in Latin America in order to protect economic and hegemonic interests, all the while proclaiming its intent to spread democracy.[7] The United States saw Latin America as a new and expansive market and believed that its own economic health depended on growing markets. "What has remained unchanged over time," notes historian Lars Schoultz, "has been the desire of U.S. producers to help expand in order to make money, and the desire of U.S. political leaders to help them in order to win elections."[8]

As a result, the U.S. government not only encouraged businesses to set up shop in Latin American countries, but it also assisted them aggressively. "U.S. entrepreneurs would have discovered Latin America's markets and resources without government assistance," Schoultz concludes, "but for more than a century the process of economic integration has been accelerated by U.S. officials' consciously seeking to tie Latin America's economies to the United States."[9]

As the Cold War between the West and the Soviet bloc heated up, Latin America became a leading battleground. Unfortunately, the United States' methods in protecting its interests were often as bad as those that it was supposedly protecting the region against: dictatorship and repression. The United States supported a series of "friendly" dictators who would bend to the will of Washington and oppose the evil of Communism at all costs.

One example of the United States' pursuit of power and profits is demonstrated in its support for the United Fruit Company in

Guatemala in the 1950s. The United Fruit Company was formed in 1899 when the first major importer of bananas to North America and the first railroad baron of Central America (both hailing from the United States) merged their respective businesses. The combined company owned huge tracts of land and made incredible profits. In Guatemala, the United Fruit Company was heavily involved, and uncompromisingly so, in political affairs in order to protect its vast holdings.

"Companies like United Fruit," Chasteen explains, "reserved managerial positions for white U.S. personnel and hired 'natives' for the machete work. . . . And when they pulled out—because of a banana blight or a new corporate strategy—all that these multinational installations left behind was ex–banana choppers with no job, no land, no education, and a lot of missing fingers."[10]

When a populist leader named Jacobo Arbenz was elected president of Guatemala in a free election in 1950, he kept his promise to initiate agrarian reform. Arbenz was the second president in a row popularly and freely elected after a long string of dismal dictators who enjoyed the support of the United States. Arbenz took the reins of a country plagued by wide economic disparity and poverty. As Chasteen notes, half the people of Guatemala were illiterate Mayan peasants, treated more or less like animals by plantation owners.[11] The agrarian capitalism that fueled the economy did not significantly improve the lives of the landless masses.

In 1952 the Guatemalan Congress approved Arbenz's Agrarian Reform Act, which lawfully expropriated about 1.5 million acres of uncultivated farmland. The land would be given to peasants in plots of between eight and thirty-three acres, and in return they would pay the government 3 to 5 percent of the land's yearly assessed value.[12]

Much of the expropriated, unused land was owned by United Fruit Company, yet Arbenz himself had seventeen hundred acres expropriated from his own estate. According to the laws of expropriation, the owner of the land had to be compensated, and the government of Guatemala tried in good faith to fulfill this legal obligation. The government used United Fruit Company's own tax records to determine that the company should be paid over $600,000 for the land. United Fruit Company, however, which had grossly undervalued the land on its tax records, demanded some $16 million in compensation. The government naturally refused to pay such a sum.

The United Fruit Company had powerful links throughout the Eisenhower administration. John Foster Dulles, the secretary of state, had been the chief legal counsel in a major United Fruit Company transaction. His brother, Allen Dulles, was the head of the CIA and later became a board member of a United Fruit Company subsidiary. John Moors Cabot, brother to the assistant secretary of state, had been the president of United Fruit Company. UN ambassador Henry Cabot Lodge was a stockholder and outspoken defender of United Fruit Company. Eisenhower's personal secretary was married to United Fruit Company's public relations director. Undersecretary of State Bedell Smith was being considered for an executive position at the company and was later named to its board of directors. The U.S. ambassador to Costa Rica had close ties with United Fruit Company and would also become a member of its board of directors.

On at least two occasions Arbenz had risked his very life for democracy. Even U.S. aid officials considered Arbenz's land reform program to be a moderate and constructive program that adhered to democratic principles.[13] Yet the top-level U.S. officials mentioned above—the ones with close ties to United Fruit Company— branded Arbenz a Communist sympathizer. They also completely trumped up charges that the small number of Communists in Guatemala posed a threat to U.S. national security—something that the State Department analysts themselves did not believe. Eisenhower decided that Arbenz must be deposed. Not only did the United States use the CIA and the State Department to orchestrate and execute a coup against Arbenz, it also handpicked the "liberator" who would oppose the indigenous political reform movement that the United States spuriously called "Communist." In short, the new leader would protect United Fruit Company's interests and thwart "radical" politics such as land reform measures.

In the end, after a great deal of planning and covert action, the coup was a relatively easy operation. Arbenz had little support in

Guatemala's military. A few bombing raids on the capital, and Arbenz resigned and fled the country. Arbenz openly proclaimed that the United States had orchestrated the coup, which the State Department denied as "ridiculous and untrue"—a denial the American press readily accepted and proclaimed as fact.[14]

"Most American commentators now admit, with hindsight, that the intervention was a mistake," writes political scientist Piero Gleijeses.[15] It was a mistake not only because it thwarted an honest attempt to remedy the severe disparity that kept so many people in poverty, but also because—true to the nature of violence—it had the unintended consequence of entrenching the country in violence for years to come. "As the decades passed," Chasteen observes, "and the grisly death toll mounted, U.S. diplomats began to view the intervention of 1954 as a tragic overreaction."[16]

Our interventions and overreactions would continue in Latin America. In the 1980s all of Central America was caught in one of the most deadly, most complicated, and most hopeless situations in the world. Right-wing dictators, who had been kept in power for decades with U.S. assistance, clashed with left-wing partisans, whose actions were as cruel as those of the dictators they opposed. The people of these countries were caught in the crossfire and suffered horribly as a result. Had this merely been a regional crisis, it may have been resolved sooner. But as mentioned above, the region had become a battleground of Cold War ideology between the United States and the Soviet bloc. Each side chose its favorite zealots and armed them to the teeth. In simple terms, both superpowers poured gasoline on the fire and fanned the flames, hoping that out of the ashes would arise a region committed either to democracy or to Soviet-style communism.

In 1984 President Ronald Reagan proclaimed, "The defense policy of the United States is based on a simple premise: we do not start wars." Despite incontrovertible historical evidence to the contrary, Reagan said,

> We will never be the aggressor. We maintain our strength in order to deter and defend against aggression—to preserve the

freedom and peace. We help our friends defend themselves. We Americans should be proud of what we're trying to do in Central America, and proud of what, together with our friends, we can do in Central America, to support democracy, human rights, and economic growth, while preserving the peace close to home.[17]

The Reagan administration repeatedly told the American public that Communist insurgency in Central America threatened to turn the region red, right up to the border of Texas. The nations of Central America were dominoes that could fall to the Communists one by one. The majority of the American public swallowed the claim whole.

Inherent in Reagan's actions was an attempt to overcome the so-called Vietnam syndrome, the supposed reticence to use military power overseas for fear of becoming entrenched in a quagmire or experiencing defeat. "Perhaps it was inevitable that Americans would have to finish the debate over Vietnam in Latin America," historian William LeoGrande writes, "where the United States had long been the predominant power. Vietnam was 12,000 miles away, but Latin America was our own backyard," he continues. "If Washington's commitment in Vietnam was a mistake because it was too far away, because the culture was too alien for Americans to understand, or because the interests at stake did not justify the sacrifice, none of these reasons applied in Central America."[18]

At the same time that Reagan was full of pride about American actions in Central America, the might of the United States, under the guise of democracy, was helping rip the region apart. As part of its zeal to combat political movements that threatened U.S. business and political authority in Central America (most of which were handily deemed Communist), the United States operated the School of the Americas (SOA), a training school for Latin American soldiers. The school, nicknamed by critics as the "School of Assassins," was based in Panama from 1946 until 1984, when the Panama Canal Treaty forced it to relocate. Thereafter it was run from Fort Benning, Georgia, where its successor continues to operate. Former Panamanian president Jorge Illueca declared that the SOA was the "biggest base for destabilization in Latin America."[19]

Over 60,000 Latin American soldiers were trained at the SOA, learning counter-insurgency, military intelligence, commando warfare, psychological warfare, and enemy interrogation techniques. As many human rights groups have noted, this training was widely and consistently used by the soldiers to wage brutal warfare against insurgents, political opposition, and civilians. An organization called School of the Americas' Watch states, "Hundreds of thousands of Latin Americans have been tortured, raped, assassinated, 'disappeared,' massacred, and forced into refuge by soldiers trained at the [SOA]. Among those targeted by SOA graduates are educators, union organizers, religious workers, student leaders, and others who work for the rights of the poor."[20]

According to excerpts from the SOA training manuals released by the Pentagon, students were instructed in the use of "motivation by fear," paying bounties for enemy dead, executing opponents, subverting the press, and using torture, blackmail, and injections of truth serum to obtain information. "These tactics come right out of an SS manual and have no place in a civilized society," Congressman Joseph Kennedy declared after investigating the SOA. "They certainly have no place in any course taught with taxpayer dollars on U.S. soil by members of our own military."[21]

Congressman Jim McGovern helped investigate the murder of six Jesuit priests, their housekeeper, and her teenage daughter in El Salvador. The priests were active in promoting peace and human rights in their country. McGovern recalls that the victims were "forced out of their beds in the middle of the night, forced to the ground with high-powered U.S. rifles put to their heads, [and] their brains blown out across the yard. These images haunt me. They should haunt all of us. And they should certainly haunt the U.S. Army School of the Americas. Because when the facts of the case came out, 19 of the 26 Salvadoran soldiers who murdered these men and women were graduates of the School of the Americas. In the past ten years, not once have I heard anyone from the School of the Americas, the U.S. Army, or the Pentagon express any regret or concern about any possible role they might have played in relation to these murders. Not on or off the record. Not in private. Nothing."[22]

U.S.-backed Guatemalan military leaders in the early 1980s began to sweep the countryside in areas thought to be pro-guerrilla. As many as one million people were displaced, and many killed. Intellectuals and civic organizers were gunned down in assassinations.[23] "The United States did not murder Guatemalans, and it did not urge the Guatemalan army to slaughter, rape, or burn," Professor Gleijeses notes. "But the United States armed the murderers." Successive American administrations since the early 1960s had supplied and trained the Guatemalan military and had provided military advisers. Of all these administrations, "the most brazen was the Reagan administration." But our military support did not end in 1988. "In 1996 ... the Clinton administration released a report admitting that the CIA had worked closely with Guatemala's security and intelligence services through the Reagan, Bush, and first Clinton administrations, had funded them to the tune of several million dollars, and had kept a number of Guatemalan officers on its payroll who were 'alleged to have been involved in significant human rights abuses.'"[24]

The U.S. complicity in the violence that consumed Guatemala was by no means a rare occurrence in Central America. Journalist Mark Danner writes a chilling account of a massacre that occurred at El Mozote, El Salvador, in December 1981. The U.S.-backed and U.S.-trained Atlacatl Battalion of the Salvadoran army, trying to root out guerrillas and their support network, entered the village of El Mozote and murdered more than five hundred men, women, and children. Many were killed by decapitation. The brutality of the event is almost incomprehensible. Children were hacked to death with machetes or had their skulls crushed by rifle butts, had their throats slashed, were herded together in rooms and machine-gunned, or were bayoneted or hanged to death in the trees.[25]

Two hundred and forty-five rifle cartridges unearthed at the scene were from U.S. M-16 rifles, most of which were discernibly stamped as manufactured for the U.S. government at Lake City, Missouri.[26] Nevertheless, the Reagan administration said that reports of the massacre were merely Communist propaganda, and it continued funding, supplying, and training the Salvadoran army as if nothing had happened.

Murders such as those at El Mozote were far too common at that time in El Salvador. As Danner notes,

> The most visible signs of the "dirty war" were mutilated corpses that each morning littered the streets of El Salvador's cites. Sometimes the bodies were headless, or faceless, their features having been obliterated with a shotgun blast or an application of battery acid; sometimes limbs were missing, or hands or feet chopped off; or eyes gouged out; women's genitals were torn and bloody, bespeaking repeated rape; men's were often found severed and stuffed into their mouths. And cut into the flesh of a corpse's back or chest was likely to be the signature of one or another of the "death squads" that had done the work. . . .[27]

Throughout the western part of the country, where an abortive rebellion had been centered, members of the National Guard, along with civilian irregulars, lined peasants up against walls and shot them. Before the purge was over, they had murdered well over ten thousand people. (Some estimates put the number at four times that.) Again, the United States continued to arm the Salvadorans who committed these gross violations of human rights, with full knowledge of the events. Later, in 1993, the U.S. State Department would admit that the massacre occurred and that "the U.S. statements on the case were wrong."[28]

A small but significant group of citizens all over the United States began openly to oppose the U.S. tradition of military intervention in Latin America. Their efforts have been chronicled by writer Christian Smith in *Resisting Reagan,* which shows how a broad coalition of people and organizations began to speak out against the United States' role in the wars in El Salvador, Honduras, Nicaragua, and Guatemala. Three nationwide organizations— Sanctuary, Witness for Peace, and the Pledge of Resistance—mobilized thousands of Americans to oppose the government's actions in Central America. In what became the biggest popular political protest of the 1980s, well over one hundred thousand citizens became a vocal and ardent opposition to the extremely popular president, and more than ten thousand people went to jail after committing acts of nonviolent civil disobedience.[29]

The epitome of Reagan's zeal in opposing any semblance of Communism in Central America was his support for the anti-Sandinista movement in Nicaragua. The Sandinistas had been a guerrilla movement opposing the often-brutal regime of the U.S.-backed dictator Anastasio Somoza. The other main opposition to the Somoza regime was led by the well-known journalist and political figure Pedro Joaquín Chamorro, but Chamorro was assassinated on January 10, 1978. More than fifty thousand people joined the funeral procession, and strikes and violence broke out everywhere. The dictator's house of cards was coming down.

The Sandinistas attacked Nicaraguan National Guard positions, often striking from temporary bases set up within densely populated neighborhoods. The National Guard responded with mortar fire and aerial bombardment without regard to noncombatant casualties. The Organization of American States (OAS) concluded that the "Nicaraguan National Guard not only used its firepower indiscriminately, causing a great number of casualties and tremendous suffering to the civilian population, but that it also ordered the people to remain inside their homes before the bombing, without even allowing them to evacuate, thus violating a basic humanitarian norm."[30]

After one major offensive, with the Sandinistas driven back, the National Guard initiated Operation Mop-Up, designed to wipe out any remaining resistance forces. Again, the OAS found that "the Nicaraguan National Guard's actions during the phase called 'Operation Mop-Up' were marked by complete disregard for human life, that they shot numerous people, in some cases children, in their own homes or in front of the same and in the presence of parents and siblings." The National Guard killed people simply for being in the areas that the Sandinistas had once occupied. Yet the National Guard did not stop there. Even after Mop-Up was over, the National Guard rounded up hundreds of teenage boys and summarily executed them in case they were or would become supporters of the Sandinistas.

President Jimmy Carter wanted Somoza out of power, but he was determined to ease him out; after all, Carter feared that the repressive regime of Somoza would simply be replaced by a repressive Sandinista regime. This not only would fail to protect the Nicaraguan people, but it also would fuel Carter's domestic critics. Though limited sanctions would be imposed against Somoza, economic aid continued unabated, and Washington would not publicly call for Somoza's resignation. In July 1978 Carter sent a letter to Somoza praising him for promising to improve human rights. Unfortunately, the letter was leaked to the press and seen as a statement of support for Somoza. Somoza then became steadfast in continuing the brutal methods that kept him in power.

Meanwhile, the strength of the Sandinistas grew. By mid-June 1979, the Sandinistas controlled much of the country. Effectively, the national government collapsed and the country fell into lawlessness. During this period, there would be grave human rights violations on both sides. For their part, the Sandinistas would be heavily criticized for summary executions of captured enemies. By July 17, 1979, Somoza and nearly all his senior military officers were forced to flee the country. On July 19 the Sandinistas marched into the capital, Managua, and declared an immediate cease-fire.

The Organization of American States would spend more than a year conducting an extensive investigation into the human rights situation in Nicaragua after the Sandinistas took power. Its human rights commission concluded that though abuses by the Sandinistas existed and responsible parties needed to be punished, the new regime was sincerely trying to respect human rights in a country torn apart by civil war and the legacy of human rights violations by the military.[31] To his credit, President Carter—a man hated in Central America by the right wing, who opposed his policy of denouncing human rights abuses and withholding military aid to those responsible for the abuses—was able to forge a constructive relationship with the Sandinistas and prevent them from becoming either radical revolutionaries or threats to their neighbors.

Once President Reagan took office in 1981, however, things changed dramatically. Reagan would erase Carter's "naive experiment" in Central America. As historian LeoGrande put it, "The new administration seemed determined to replace Carter's policy of coexistence with one of hostility."[32] It was time to get tough, Reagan believed—to use the military expertise and equipment of the United States to bolster right-wing regimes in their fight against Communists. No longer would we try to contain the Communists or simply oppose them; rather, we would use our might to roll them back all over the world. To accomplish this Reagan would return to Henry Kissinger's policy of supporting friendly dictators. And he would appoint as his secretary of state General Alexander Haig Jr., who was so intimately involved in the U.S. war in Vietnam. On Reagan's inauguration day, Haig immediately fired or reassigned the core of the Latin American bureau of the State Department, replacing many of them with officials who had learned their trade in Southeast Asia during the Vietnam War.

Reagan reaffirmed that no more U.S. aid would go to Nicaragua. Instead, the United States would immediately marshal $10 million to create the *contras,* a paramilitary army of Nicaraguan exiles who would fight to liberate their homeland from the Sandinistas. Most of Reagan's plans were initially secret, issued in executive findings, and kept from all but a select few in Congress. It was the beginning of the United States' newest proxy war, fought by others who were encouraged, trained, supplied, and funded by us.

For the contras, Reagan would support dictators, bully democrats, lie to the U.S. Congress and the American people, and ultimately break the laws of the United States. It would weaken his presidency toward the end of his second term, but he never wavered in his support for the army that the CIA had built by his direct order.

The United States sent new weapons to the armed forces of Honduras, Nicaragua's neighbor, with the understanding that its old weapons would be passed to the contras. As a reward, the United States dramatically increased military aid to Honduras, despite the fact that Honduras's human rights record was incredibly dismal. Contra training camps were set up in the United States, and contra bases were established in Honduras, from which they executed attacks against the Sandinistas in Nicaragua.

For their part, the contras committed grievous human rights

abuses in their war against the Sandinistas. They were also corrupt and were implicated in drug trafficking. None of these things dissuaded Reagan, however, and because of his immense popularity with the American public he was able to keep funding for the war alive in Congress, to the tune of $100 million.

Facing an all-out war designed and funded by the United States, the Sandinistas in fact did develop closer ties with the Soviet Union and Cuba, though the amount of contacts and the number of Soviet arms were grossly and purposely exaggerated by the Reagan administration. The Sandinistas also began to repress domestic opposition and committed human rights abuses. Though these were largely the consequence of Reagan's war, such abuses nevertheless served as useful propaganda for Reagan, proving that the war was just in its aims to stop Communism and tyranny.

Despite the CIA's attempt to disrupt them, national elections were held in Nicaragua in 1984, giving Daniel Ortega, leader of the Sandinistas, 67 percent of the vote. The elections were remarkably free and fair and were certainly not a rubber stamp of Soviet Communism. By comparison, elections held by the U.S.-backed regime in El Salvador were highly corrupt, despite being praised by the administration (and much of the U.S. press) as a triumph of democracy.

Reagan remained undeterred in his zeal to unseat the popularly elected Sandinistas. Though Congress eventually voted to restrict U.S. funds to the contras, Reagan's deputies carried out his wishes in secret, against the law. Reagan said, "We're not going to quit and walk away from [the contras] no matter what happens."[33] Reagan issued orders that violated the laws, and as would later leak out, part of his clandestine operations diverted profits from secret arms sales to Iran to fund the contras. (Reagan himself escaped criminal prosecution, and President George Bush would later pardon all of the principals in the illegal activities supporting the contras.)

For Reagan and his deputies there were only two types of people in Latin America: our friends and our enemies, the anti-Communists and the Communists' cronies. The enemies of our enemies were our friends. This left no room for neutral parties or for individuals who believed that a solution to the region's problems could be solved by the people of the region themselves.

To thwart domestic criticism, Reagan pursued a halfhearted peace discussion known as the Contadora peace process. In November 1986 the Contadora peace discussions fell apart. Nicaragua filed complaints against Honduras and Costa Rica in the World Court for harboring contra guerrillas and promptly stopped participating in the discussions. The United States was opposed to any deal that would end outside support for the contras.

While the fighting throughout Central America continued to rage, Oscar Arias began his campaign to become president of Costa Rica. It was a long shot. At the age of forty-four, Arias was opposed by a much older and better known candidate, President José Figueres, one of his main mentors. Though Figueres eventually decided not to seek a fourth term, he backed another candidate against Arias. Fortunately for Arias, his party had changed its selection rules, permitting all party members to cast a vote for the party nominee, not just the party elite. Arias handily won the vote to represent his party in the upcoming elections in 1986.

Arias's opponent was Rafael Angel Calderon, who was the choice of the Reagan administration for his strong support of the contras and Reagan's military policies in the region. He also advocated reinstating the army in Costa Rica, which had been abolished by the country's new constitution after a civil war in 1948, an idea Costa Rica was already being pressured to accept by Washington, which threatened to pull all U.S. aid to the economically strapped country if it did not agree. Already a U.S.-backed Costa Rican guerrilla group patrolled the border of Nicaragua, and the contras set up shop in the supposedly neutral territory. By contrast, Arias was the peace candidate, opposing rearmament and advocating regional peace based on agreement, not escalation of war. "Roofs, jobs, and peace!" was his campaign slogan in 1984.

Arias's candidacy troubled the Reagan administration. Arias pledged that "Costa Rica will not be converted into a dormitory for the contras." Calderon's campaigned was secretly funded by the Reagan administration,[34] and it appeared that he would beat Arias by an ample margin. Yet Arias pulled out a stunning come-from-behind victory and was inaugurated in May 1986.

Immediately after entering office, Arias showed that he was will-ing to take courageous action for peace. He denounced the contras and said that U.S. money should be flowing into economic develop-ment projects instead of military operations, prompting swift com-plaints from U.S. officials. Arias demanded that all contra bases and operations in Costa Rica be closed and all combatants leave the country. Within two weeks of taking office, Arias also met with the presidents of Honduras, Guatemala, El Salvador, and Nicaragua, seeking ways to foster peace and development in the region. At that meeting Arias bluntly told the Nicaraguan president Daniel Ortega that his country would have to have free and fair elections and respect human rights.

The U.S. ambassador to Costa Rica had promised Arias that the contras' supply airstrip at Santa Elena in Costa Rica would be closed, but the United States secretly kept using it for months. When Arias found out in September 1986 that the airstrip was still in operation, he ordered the police to raid it and keep it closed.

The Reagan administration was furious with Arias. His trip to the White House was postponed, vital aid to Costa Rica was threat-ened (and some of it was actually held up), and senior officials con-tinued a full-court press to pressure Arias to support U.S. operations in the region. Despite the fact that Arias was highly edu-cated and a proven leader, he was derided at the highest levels in the Reagan administration as the "Boy." Retired General Richard Secord, who was assisting White House national security adviser Oliver North in supplying the contras with secret aid, dispatched a message to Washington regarding Arias: "Boy needs to be straight-ened out by heavyweights."[35]

The heavyweights who tried to straighten him out included the assistant secretary of state, Eliot Abrams. Reporting back to Wash-ington, Abrams said, "We'll have to squeeze his balls." Abrams's brand of ball squeezing was to engage in heated arguments with Arias. Arias found Abrams's tone imperious and retorted, "Not even [Margaret] Thatcher, the closest ally you have, supports your policy. Doesn't that tell you something?"[36] Reagan's special envoy, Philip Habib, warned Arias that U.S. aid would be cut off unless he became more cooperative, and CIA director William Casey flew to

Costa Rica to lecture Arias. Arias, however, refused to meet with Casey and continued his pursuit of a Central American solution to the region's problems.

On February 17, 1987, Arias brought together the presidents of Honduras, Guatemala, and El Salvador. The assembled presidents agreed to the principles that all military aid to the region should stop, that there should be an immediate cease-fire and an amnesty for political prisoners, that free elections should be held as soon as possible, and that human rights should be respected and military forces reduced. Each country also agreed that it would set up a National Reconciliation Commission to adjudicate disputes, and each would receive foreign observers to monitor elections and human rights. These leaders knew that they would face intense pressure and intimidation by Washington to continue supporting the contras, yet they were tiring of the war and the enormous costs to their people, their economies, and their personal reputations.

The president of Nicaragua, Daniel Ortega, however, did not attend the meeting, and getting him and the rest of the Sandinistas to agree to the peace plan was essential for it to succeed. Within a month, Ortega signaled that he also was willing to accept the agreement.

Reagan did not support the proposed peace agreement, for it would abolish his beloved contras. Arias was invited to the White House in June 1987, where Vice President Bush, Chief of Staff James Baker, and other senior officials berated his peace efforts. President Reagan then scolded Arias and tried to persuade him to accept the need for the contras. Yet Arias did something that no other leader in Central America, or indeed any ally in the world, had done: he told Reagan explicitly that the contras could not win, that their fight was not a necessary and moral crusade, and that U.S. policy in Central America doomed the region to continual bloodshed. Historian LeoGrande provides the following account of the meeting:

> His quiet demeanor notwithstanding, Oscar Arias was not easily cowed. He retorted by lecturing Reagan for thirty minutes on the failings of U.S. policy. "I told him the U.S. has been left completely alone on aid to the contras," Arias recalled.

"'You're totally isolated,' I said. 'Nobody is backing Washington. . . . By no one, I mean Contadora, the Latin American Support Group, Western Europe. You're betting on war. Why don't we bet on peace?'"

Reagan hung tenaciously to his conviction that only military force could dislodge the Sandinistas. When Arias tried to point out that the contras were not strong enough to win, Reagan countered that reports of the contras' weakness were the product of "disinformation" spread by the "press and leftist groups." Communists, Reagan insisted, had never in history left power voluntarily.

"We all know history, Mr. President," Arias replied, "but no one is obliged to repeat it."[37]

Reagan continued to pursue a new round of funding for the contras in Congress. He even tried to create a plan with the Democratic Speaker of the House, Jim Wright. Yet Arias held that the best solution would come not from the United States but from Central America itself.

On August 5, 1987, Arias assembled all four presidents, including Ortega, at Esquipulas, Guatemala. For two days they hammered out the language of a peace accord, producing what became known as the Arias Peace Plan. The plan followed the broad principles agreed upon previously but also set out a timetable for each stage of implementation.

Though Reagan continued to work to defeat the Arias Peace Plan, calling it "fatally flawed," two months after the plan was signed Arias was awarded the Nobel Peace Prize. Arias was vacationing with his family when his brother called to inform him of the award. A stunned Arias wasted no time in using his new prestige to further peace in the region. When Ortega called Arias to congratulate him on receiving the award, Arias got Ortega to agree to negotiate directly with the contras to initiate a cease-fire.

A changing of the guard in Washington helped the cause of peace in the region immensely. Reagan was succeeded by George Bush, who was much less ideologically driven and made far fewer ideological appointments in his administration. Though this did not by any means assure peace in Central America, it did increase the ability of the Central Americans to sort out their own problems.

In February 1989 Arias again called together the presidents. Reacting to a near collapse in the agreement, Arias reminded them that democracy was the only hope for peace in the region. Ortega surprised the other presidents by announcing that he would allow free and fair elections once again in Nicaragua. This gave the other presidents a strong impetus to continue to meet the goals of the Arias Peace Plan.

When elections in Nicaragua were finally held the following year, Ortega lost to Violet Chamorro, the widow of martyred newspaper editor Joaquim Chomorro. With all eyes on Ortega, he peacefully handed over power to the victor, who promptly praised Arias for helping restore democracy to her grateful nation.

It was late morning when I arrived at Arias's house in a quiet, affluent neighborhood in San José. I had taken a taxi from my hotel about five minutes away. All I had to tell the driver was, "Casa de Oscar Arias, por favor." I was surprised that there were no noticeable security measures at the sprawling single-story home. I walked through an open gate, rang the doorbell, and was greeted by a butler who had been expecting my arrival.

I was shown through a sitting room well laden with antiques into a formal room, full of more antiques, with a dark, polished wood ceiling.

"Please have a seat," he said, pointing to a leather chair in an adjacent room.

A few minutes later the butler brought me an embroidered napkin atop a silver platter. I thanked him and he left the room. I had plenty of time to look about the room, as Arias did not appear for at least twenty minutes. Two sides of the room were glass walls with a view of a courtyard containing a fountain, a small, well-manicured lawn, and shrubs. Along another wall were walnut-colored bookcases, highly polished and filled with books, pictures of Arias as a boy, and one of him sitting next to Reagan in the White House.

I was on one of five or so maroon leather chairs, flanked by a large couch of the same material and color, all facing a black-and-white marble table. Several art books, a book about Arias, a collection of his *discursos,* and a Rodin sculpture of a nude woman sat atop the table.

The opulence surrounding Arias was a reflection of his family's wealth. He was born in 1941 to wealthy parents in Heredia (a prosperous small town near San José); his grandfather was a well-known government minister and legislator, and his father was head of the Costa Rican Central Bank. His mother also came from one of Costa Rica's most affluent coffee-growing families. Yet despite his enormous privilege, Arias was a sickly boy, suffering from chronic asthma. One of his longtime friends later told me about Arias's inability to play and socialize with other children. He was always a bit of a loner—quiet, shy, and serious. His main activity was reading, which he did voraciously. In his high school yearbook Arias made it known that he would one day be president, but few of his classmates could see the awkward and timid young man filling such a prestigious role.

Arias initially entered Boston University to study premed, hoping to go on to medical school. Yet before the end of his second year he decided that he was much more interested in economics and politics, and he dropped out of college in the United States. While still in Boston, however, Arias wrote a letter to President John F. Kennedy, who had greatly impressed Arias during the 1960 campaign against Richard Nixon. Arias titled his letter, "This Is How I See It." In his letter he presented Kennedy with a Central American view of relations with the United States. Arias was stunned when he received a reply inviting him to join the president at the Kennedy home in Hyannis Port. One can only speculate about the effect of the letter on Kennedy's policies toward Central America, but as it turned out his administration had some of the most enlightened policies toward the region.

While finishing his education in law and economics at the University of Costa Rica, Arias met another of his political heroes, José Figueres Ferrer. Figueres returned the country to democracy after a civil war and presided over the dismantling and outlawing of the country's army, the extension of voting rights to women.

Arias's thesis, *Grupos de Presión en Costa Rica* (Pressure Groups in Costa Rica), earned him the 1971 National Essay Prize. Figueres read the book and was impressed by the young thinker. In 1974 Arias received a doctoral degree in political science at the University of Essex, England. After serving as professor of political science at the University of Costa Rica, Arias was appointed by Figueres as his minister of planning and economic policy. From there on, Arias's rise to the top was meteoric. He won a seat in Congress in 1978, was elected secretary-general of the National Liberation Party in 1981, and became president in 1986.

Arias finally entered the adjacent room and walked toward me, waiting until he reached me before extending his hand. He was wearing blue dress pants and a pullover shirt. True to form, and despite the costly furnishings of his home, he disdains ostentatious displays and pomp and circumstance.

"Thank you for taking this time with me," I said.

"No, not at all. It is my pleasure," he replied, gesturing for me to sit.

"I was examining the details of your home," I told him candidly. "It is quite beautiful."

"Oh, thank you," he replied, gazing around. "It is perhaps too big. When I was running for president, I bought a piece of land there and had the house expanded," he explained, pointing to the far end of the courtyard at a part of the house containing a swimming pool, a secondary library, and a number of other rooms. "I wasn't aware that I was going to be president for only four years," he joked wryly. "I thought, like Napoleon, I was going to be president for fifteen years! So I expanded my house, and now it's too big. It's just too big.

"But, at that time," he added, "as you might know, many people used to come to Costa Rica. Every single week I used to receive one or two senators or congressmen, people from all over the world. Vice President Bush, then he became president, stayed here at my home. Vice President Quayle and Jimmy Carter and so many people from all over the world stayed here. So I used to receive them in my home instead of the Presidential House."

We chatted for a while about my journeys and the people I had met. When I mentioned the Dalai Lama he said, "I told the Dalai Lama that he should read more."

"I understand that *you* read quite a lot," I observed.

"Yes. I always have," he replied, offering a story. "Senator Bradley was here once, sitting where you are now. We were discussing foreign policy, and he said that I didn't really understand what he was telling me. He suggested a book that I should read. I got up from the table, went into my study, and returned with the book he had mentioned. I opened it and flipped through the pages for him to see: every page had my notes written on it." Arias smiled. "Yes, I read quite a lot."

"If you were writing a book on peace," I asked, "what would you say that peace is?"

"I believe that peace is a dynamic concept that involves *much* more than the absence of violence," he replied. "I spoke about this in my Nobel address. I said that peace is not a matter of prizes or trophies. It is not the product of a victory or of a command. It has no borders, no time limits, nothing fixed in the definition of its achievements. Peace is a never-ending process; it is the result of innumerable decisions made by many persons in many lands. It is an attitude, a way of life, a way of solving problems and of resolving conflicts. It cannot be forced on the smallest nation, nor can it be imposed by the most powerful. It can neither ignore our differences nor overlook our common interests. It requires us to live and work together. Peace is not a matter of noble words or Nobel lectures. We already have an abundance of words, glorious words, inscribed in the declarations of the United Nations, the World Court, the Organization of American States, and a network of international treaties and laws. We need deeds which respect these words, which honor the commitments avowed in these laws. I have often spoken about this subsequently as well. I stress that we need to understand ideas like violence and security in new ways— to embrace the broader concept of human security."

"Since you are a professor, an observer, a peacemaker, what would you say are the chief causes of violence?" I asked.

"I think that you have to look at this historically," he said. "Of course, there have always been many types of conflicts: territorial conflicts, ethnic conflicts, border disputes. Then, especially during the Cold War, conflicting ideologies were given as reasons for war. But now more than ever, with the end of the Cold War, we see that

violence arises as a result of unattended human needs. I believe that
the exaggerated levels of poverty and inequality, if not remedied,
will inevitably lead to conflict in the future. Already, we can see that
inequalities give rise to waves of immigration and that societies
have great difficulty dealing with these constructively. There is a
saying that 'poverty needs no passport to travel.' Indeed, we cannot
achieve true peace and human security in a world with such a dramatic divide between those who have and those who have not."

"Is this the key to peace? Is this inequality the chief cause of
war?" I questioned.

"I think that it has always been a question of values," he said.
"Greed, cynicism, unchecked individualism, and hypocrisy are all
values that impede peace. Unfortunately, they are too often
accepted as norms in today's world."

"And are greed and so forth inextricably tied to the human experience? Is violence an inevitable expression of human nature?" I
asked.

"I do not believe that we, as a society, cannot overcome violence,"
he replied. "We can overcome it, but it will involve many structural
changes in the political and economic systems that govern our lives.
Moreover, it will involve changes in consciousness and culture. It
begins with education, teaching our children the values of peace: to
be honest, to have politics with principle, and not to resort to violence. Just earlier this week, I spoke at a ceremony commemorating
the fiftieth anniversary of the abolition of the armed forces in Costa
Rica. Before, who would have thought that eliminating the military
would be possible? As Costa Ricans, we hope to present our nation
as an example of the type of steps that human societies can take in
creating a new culture of peace. In our country, we do not believe
that acts such as abolishing armies are utopian or ridiculous. It is the
horrific levels of world military spending that are ridiculous, especially in light of the tremendous human needs that exist. In this context, Costa Ricans merely want to be reasonable; that is why we
insist on declaring peace in the world."

"It strikes me that in order to declare peace we must also be willing to put the past behind us emotionally. I am quite struck in my

conversations with peacemakers about the role of forgiveness in the peacemaking process. Can you comment on this?" I asked.

"Yes, I believe that forgiveness is an important part of any peace process. Forgiveness is necessary so that people can look to the future instead of always to the past. I believe that Mandela's and Bishop Tutu's efforts in South Africa provide a good example of how forgiveness and reconciliation can facilitate progress, even in a very difficult situation. But although we must forgive, we cannot forget, and let the past repeat itself. Nor can we grant immunity to those who have committed crimes against humanity."

"Pragmatically, how do we convince the man who beats his wife or the gang member who kills his rivals or the politicians and army generals who start wars or repress their country that peace is better than the immediate gains derived from violence?" I questioned.

"In this case, I would not focus on the agency of the general but rather on that of common people. These people are so often the victims of violence, but it is they who must stand up and demand that it stop. In creating peace, we cannot wait for the generals to have a change of heart. Instead, we must focus the democratic will on creating a more just society, a society in which warmongers will not be accepted as legitimate authorities. Popular, democratic resistance to all forms of violence cannot be underestimated; you will find this sentiment at the heart of almost any concept of nonviolence."

"Yet so many people are resigned to the inevitability of violence," I observed. "What do you say to them?"

"I say in my speeches that many of our global problems seem impossibly daunting to people and that, in this context, it is easy to become resigned or apathetic. We need leaders who can address this despondency, generate hope, and help people find solutions. Ultimately, though, people must come together and organize because it is through joining in movements that they will be able to accomplish great things."

Arias was speaking, of course, from his own experience, especially his long-shot campaign for the presidency and his peace plan opposed by Reagan. Arias offered to show me a videotape of his campaign and major achievements.

As I watched the tape, I periodically glanced at Arias, who stared at the screen as if it were the first time he had seen it.

"How does it feel when you watch that?" I asked when the tape was finished.

"It almost makes me want to cry," he said candidly. "It gives me chills. How do you say it? It makes me *tingle,*" he added with a smile. "Come," he said, "let's have lunch now, and later we'll go to my office."

We ate in a small dining room. It was a simple but tasty meal: hearts of palm with dressing for an appetizer, followed by sautéed fish served by his butler. Afterward we had strong Costa Rican coffee.

We talked about our mutual admiration for one of Arias's long-time assistants who had recently died. I had been stunned to hear of her death. Arias was visibly upset as I spoke about her kindness to me during my previous trips to Costa Rica.

When we had finished chatting, Arias showed me a letter from John F. Kennedy in his study. Then he picked up a package and said we should get going. In the driveway Arias jumped into a small car and told me to get in. I was surprised that he didn't use a driver. I had never driven with a former head of state, and I wondered how well they did behind the wheel.

We came to a red light at an intersection on the other side of town. Arias glanced out his window. I turned my head just in time to see a woman's face undergo the realization that the famous former president was seated behind the wheel right in front of her.

"Oscar Arias, Oscar Arias!" she yelled out in delight. A crowd instantly gathered and waved at him. He smiled and blew the women a kiss, to the cheers of everyone.

"You haven't lost any popularity," I said, laughing. He just smiled broadly.

In a posh neighborhood we stopped in front of a house, and Arias got out of the car. "It is one of my friends' birthday," he informed me. "I just have to run in and give her a gift. I'll only be a moment." I noticed now that the bag contained a blue box, unmistakably a gift from Tiffany.

No more than ten minutes later a smartly dressed servant came out of the house and said eloquently that my presence was requested inside. When I reached the door I was met by a handsome woman who extended her hand in greeting.

"I am Maria," she announced, motioning for me to enter and slipping her arm under mine. "Please come in and join us."

The living room was filled with fashionably dressed women, sipping champagne and wine. They were all laughing and poking fun at Arias, who sat there eating up their attention.

"Oh, good, another man," one woman exclaimed as I entered the room. I felt shy as I was being searched up and down by many pairs of eyes. Some of the remarks being made were a bit off color, but I could only understand bits and pieces of them in Spanish.

"He speaks Spanish!" Arias warned them.

One woman checked to see if it was true. I replied as best I could.

"You know, Oscar Arias is quite a ladies' man," one of the women said.

"That's true," another said, causing everyone to laugh.

"Don't say that," Arias said half sternly, half sheepishly. "He is writing about me," he said pointing to me. "Don't say bad things."

Everyone howled with laughter.

We drove to the headquarters of the Arias Foundation for Peace and Human Progress, which runs three centers: the Center for Human Progress, the Center for Peace and Reconciliation, and the Center for Organized Participation. Despite its many achievements, Arias told me he wasn't satisfied with the clout of the organization.

"We also want to build a museum of peace in San José," he said. "And extend our projects in many communities around the world. But we need more funding in order to do that. We need to have more money. I've got to find a way to make that happen," he said.

One of the main projects of the Arias Foundation is the promotion of the International Code of Conduct on Arms Transfers. In 1995 Arias invited his fellow Nobel peace laureates to develop and promote a code of conduct for the arms trade. Each year the United States alone transfers billions of dollars' worth of weapons and military aid to repressive regimes. Believing that such aid only strengthens and encourages undemocratic regimes and destabilizes volatile regions, the Code of Conduct on Arms Transfers calls on nations to permit weapons sales only when the recipient abides by international human rights standards and humanitarian law, respects democratic rights, abides by international arms embargoes and military sanctions, opposes terrorism, works toward regional peace and stability, and, very important, continues to undertake human development programs. For Arias and the other leaders supporting the code of conduct, it is merely a first step in establishing a new era of peace; the longer-term goal would be to end the arms trade altogether.

"It is so hard for people to envision a world without militaries to protect the borders of their countries," I observed. "Tell me about your work in this regard."

"A main focus for me over the past several years," he replied, "has been my work convincing countries to abolish their armed forces. Increasingly, this is not a utopian dream but a most practical and viable alternative. All that is required is political will. Indeed, in the past few years Panama and Haiti have both effectively eliminated their militaries, joining Costa Rica. The Arias Foundation for Peace and Human Progress is actively working in sub-Saharan Africa to encourage countries to disarm and even, in cases such as Sierra Leone, to consider abolition in the very near future. This is not to say that abolition is easy in all cases. In Costa Rica the armed forces were rather small to begin with. Clearly, immediate abolition is most feasible in similar countries, where the prospects of demobilization, retraining, and reinsertion of soldiers represent manageable challenges."

"In most countries, however," I noted, "it is part of conventional thought that military power actually deters wars. The fact that the Soviet bloc and the U.S. bloc did not engage in a world war, it is argued, was because nuclear weapons were an effective deterrent to war. What do you think of this deterrence argument? And is total disarmament practical and desirable?"

"The deterrence argument, so often invoked in the age of intense ideological conflict, may have had some validity in the case of nuclear arms," he said. "Concerning conventional arms, however, the argument is absurd. I am glad to say that the terms of international dialogue about peace and security have shifted substantially in the past twenty years. Personally, I try always to put forward a concept of human security—the idea that peace will be achieved not by nationalistic posturing and arms races, but rather by addressing fundamental human needs."

We drove from the foundation headquarters to another office he maintains. Along the walls were many pictures of him with various heads of state and public officials, alongside many honorary degrees and awards.

"Who have been your most influential teachers on peace?" I asked him. "Are there any texts or experiences that have particularly influenced or inspired your thinking about peace?"

"You must understand that I was not born a peacemaker," he replied. "Rather, I became president in a time of great conflict, a time when I felt that peace was the only viable alternative for my country. Before, when I was an economic minister in the government, peace was not my goal. This was in the 1970s, before the conflicts in the region had really escalated. My goal then was to make Costa Rica the Denmark of Central America: a country with many businesses controlled by many different people; a prosperous nation where land and property were well distributed among the people; a land where wealth was not concentrated in the hands of a few, nor power in the hands of large, transnational corporations. By the time I ran for president, however, the regional conflicts were a major issue. At that point, the government of Costa Rica was claiming to be neutral in the conflicts, but this was not the case; the contras were already operating on our soil. A major claim of my campaign was that we should not be spectators but actors; I said that the government must become 'an active agent for peace.' I argued that we should not continue to be the peons of the superpowers because, as it was, we were the great losers of the Cold War. It was just as in El Salvador, where Archbishop Romero had said, 'The superpowers provide the weapons; we provide the dead.' I argued that none of our other goals for the region—education, development, health— could be achieved without peace. Thus it was this resolve, from my campaign, that I followed during my term. And it was this that led to the peace plan and regional negotiations. I will say, however, that

Gandhi did have a profound influence on me. Clearly, he is a very important teacher of peace for many people."

"Do you believe, as Gandhi did, that nonviolence is ultimately more powerful than violence? And are there situations in which violence is, in fact, necessary?" I inquired.

"I believe that there are situations when violence may be necessary. Stopping the evil of Hitler is frequently used as an example in this regard," he said. "But this does not mean that we should jump to military solutions in a premature way. Violence should only be a last resort, one that we use with great reservation. As it is, we don't try hard enough to find peaceful solutions. I think an important example of this is the Gulf War. President Bush was very proud of his use of force. He made a great effort to Satanize Saddam Hussein. Speaking from a Central American perspective, I wonder if the U.S. was still not obsessed with restoring its military image, after having been unsuccessful in winning the contra war against the Sandinistas. President Bush, perhaps, needed to overcome the Vietnam syndrome of defeat at the hands of a developing country. More concretely, all I would say is that we could have tried harder before using military force."

"In one of your speeches I recall you read a quote by Eleanor Roosevelt. She was a champion for universal rights that are inviolable for every human being. Yet not every nation believes in such rights. I think of China, for example. Doesn't peace require a universal set of human rights?" I asked.

"As a philosophical question this is very complicated. But I do believe that, morally and politically, the rights outlined in the United Nations Universal Declaration of Human Rights are very important. A few years ago I spoke at an Amnesty International festival in London and stressed the importance of upholding social and economic rights—how these must be the fundaments of a concept of human security. Very simply, however, we must remember that the right to life is the most basic human right and that violence always risks violating this right."

"And is democracy the only form of government that can truly promote peace?" I asked.

"There is much that could be said on this subject," he replied. "In general terms, I would say that democracies do not fight among one another. Also, dictatorships are clearly more prone to violence than democracies because there is much less accountability and far fewer controls on decision making. In the case of Central America, I believed that democracy was the only direction for peace—that it needed to be a central element in the peace plan. Here, there existed a long tradition in which the voice and the will of the people were not respected. This lack of representation fueled many of the civil disputes in the region. And because of this, I argued that true democracy was a necessary precondition for the end of conflict— that it would be the very essence of a just and lasting peace.

"The United States is a democracy, a very advanced democracy in many ways," he added, "but clearly not a perfect one. I am often critical of the U.S., even domestically. This is because I believe that democracy, most fundamentally, is a distribution of power—economic as well as political power. It is quite clear that a main shortcoming of U.S. democracy can be found in its failure to distribute economic wealth among its citizens. Internationally, the U.S. has often not supported democracy. Instead, it has overlooked its principles when convenient. One could cite a plethora of examples from the past: U.S.-supported dictators such as Somoza in Nicaragua, Marcos in the Philippines, or the shah in Iran. Even today, one could argue that the U.S. pursues contradictory human rights policies in different parts of the world. U.S. officials argue that open trade will help democratize China and thus are willing to overlook human rights abuses, but they make the opposite argument in regard to Cuba. The U.S. continues to support autocratic governments, like that of Saudi Arabia, and send military aid to countries that abuse human rights, such as Turkey, Indonesia, and a number of African countries. Thus the U.S. has been very inconsistent in its support for democracy. Similarly, one only has to look at how quickly the U.S. resorts to the use of force to see that a similar case could be made about its commitment to peace."

"I have read much about the United States' involvement in Latin America. What is the Latin American perspective about U.S. involvement in the region?" I asked.

"We have a joke in Latin America saying 'the only reason there are no coups d'état in Washington, D.C., is because there is no U.S.

embassy there.' The history of U.S. intervention in Latin America is a long, complicated, and nefarious one. To mention just one instance from our recent past, I spent an enormous amount of energy trying to convince the Reagan administration that the U.S.-backed contras were the problem, not the solution, in terms of creating peace and democracy in Central America. Indeed, following up on the idea that Costa Rica should be an 'active agent for peace' rather than a 'neutral observer,' I decided, once elected, that Costa Rican policy should be very open and very clear. I wanted to show that my government and I practiced what we preached. Thus I told all of the contra *commandantes* operating in Costa Rica that they must either leave or renounce their military posts. All of them left except one.

"Clearly, the U.S. was in profound disagreement with Costa Rica's new policies, and I did receive much pressure," Arias recounted. "I was told by some U.S. officials, very straightforwardly, that Costa Rica was not a viable country because we had no armed forces. My reply was 'nonsense.' I believe that our actions in removing the contras from our soil, as well as Costa Rican involvement in the regional peace process, vindicated my position on this point.

"To speak a bit more about my motivations in engaging the struggle for peace," he continued, "I would point to two factors. The first might be called altruistic: thousands of people were dying, thousands more lost their homes and became refugees, many innocent civilians were killed, and it was evident that there was no chance of a military victory that would end this. Reagan was simply obsessed with the contras, but it was ridiculous to think that they could win. I wanted to silence the guns—to find a diplomatic, democratic solution. The second factor motivating me was more pragmatic: I had promised that I would advance the development of my country. But in a region so small, and with so many refugees, no one would invest a penny to assist Costa Ricans. The conflict impeded progress for all of the region and it made it impossible to fulfill my pledges of increased development."

"I have read that in 1989," I noted, "a Costa Rican congressional investigation concluded that the U.S.-backed contra resupply network in Costa Rica [that Oliver North coordinated from the White

House] doubled as a drug smuggling operation. 'These requests for contra help were initiated by Colonel North to General Noriega,' the congressional investigation reported. 'They opened a gate so their henchmen could utilize Costa Rican territory for trafficking in arms and drugs.' I understand that you then banned Oliver North, CIA agent Joseph Fernandez, Ambassador Tambs, Admiral Poindexter, and Richard Secord from Costa Rica. Is this correct?"

"This is true that I banned these individuals. I did so because I believed they were undermining our peace efforts. This is not to mention that, in so many of their contra-support operations, the United States was operating in clear violation of international law. As for the drug-trafficking charges, it was always reputed that the CIA turned a blind eye to the contras' narcotics connections. But I cannot speak to any specifics; others have done much more detailed work in this area."

We returned to Arias's home in the late afternoon, and I made my way to my hotel from there. He asked me to meet him in the morning so that I could go with him to a student peace rally being held in a nearby town.

The next morning I was greeted by Arias and two of his assistants from the foundation. They all sported Arias Foundation T-shirts and asked me to slip one on too. Decked in our uniforms, we drove to the rally of several hundred children. Arias gave a speech then led a short parade to the town square, where more speeches were given. Arias continually looked after me, ensuring that I kept up in the crowd. It was then that I noticed most of all how his understated manner and yet thorough self-confidence make him a charismatic figure. I noticed also that behind his self-controlled exterior, he was a man of great compassion and warmth.

I got the sense that at some point he accepted me not as a tag-along observer, but as a friend of sorts whom he willingly invited into his circle. It was not at all a conscious attempt to cast himself in a good light but rather an honest expression of his friendly nature.

Arias had spent the better part of two days talking with me, ensuring that I understood his work. Before we parted I asked, "What is the most significant thing you would like the people of the world to know?" His answer was thoughtful and telling.

"Ultimately, I want to tell people that we can end poverty," he said. "At the present time, the clear way to do it is by cutting military spending and redirecting funds to human development. Currently, there are 1.3 billion people in the world living in tragic poverty. This can change. The decisions that we make in our personal lives affect many others in the world. The United Nations development program tells us that at the same time that Americans spend $8 billion a year on cosmetics, only $6 billion annually would be sufficient to provide basic education for everyone. Europeans spend $11 billion each year on ice cream, but for only $9 billion annually, we could provide clean water and safe sewers for all of humanity. Institutionally, our culpability is much greater. World military spending accounts for $800 billion every year, but just 5 percent of that annual sum over ten years would provide each person on this planet with an income level above the poverty line for their country.

"But just as each of us participates in systems which perpetuate poverty and injustice, each of us can work for change. There is so much suffering generated by the focus on purchasing weapons and bolstering militaries. And there is so much potential for progress that could be realized if these funds were redirected. In this context, I believe we have an ethical mandate to alter the warped, militaristic priorities displayed in so many national budgets. We have the moral authority to eliminate armed forces. Costa Rica has shown that this is not just a utopian dream but a real option. It has long been my ambition to make Central America the first demilitarized region of the world. I still believe that this is possible. Moreover, in war-torn and poverty-stricken regions like sub-Saharan Africa, demilitarization is perhaps the only truly humane and reasonable option.

"Steps like the International Code of Conduct on Arms Transfers are significant in promoting global security and protecting human rights, but they are not ends in themselves. This is because the struggle for human security will not end until the world undertakes a comprehensive and humanitarian demilitarization. It will not end until all people enjoy fundamental liberties. And it will not end until all public policy embodies a thoroughgoing affirmation of human dignity. Demanding significant changes requires a movement of many people in many walks of life, all working together. By speaking out and by offering my vision, I hope to stand as one person in this larger movement. I hope to stand with these people, in spirit if not in person, on the day that these just ends are realized."

"I hope to see you again," I said to Arias as I was leaving.

"Yes, I do too," he replied graciously. "Have a safe trip home, and let me know if I can help you with anything."

Of course, in my mind, it was the other way around. I wanted to help this man spread his message to as many people as possible. Reading something he had written recently, I was more assured than ever that this man pointed the way toward the future of peace. "Terrorism is one evil that should not exist in the world today," he wrote in a document he gave to me,

> and there are many others, including poverty, illiteracy, preventable diseases, and environmental destruction. We have the resources—both material and spiritual—to eliminate many of these ills. Let us channel them according to the needs of the poorest and most vulnerable among us. Instead of building bunkers and shields that fail to protect us, let us build goodwill and harmony, human capacity and understanding, and in this way we shall build the world we want to live in. We must be the change we wish to see, as Gandhi once said, and not the darkness that we wish to leave behind.

Arias certainly has lived his life as the change he wishes to see, and I was honored to have spent so much time with him. Another person who blessed me with this same gift, who has freed himself from the darkness of ill will unlike any other person I have ever met, is the central figure in my next journey, to Cambodia.

Six

MAHA GHOSANANDA: THE GANDHI OF CAMBODIA

Tears rolled out of my eyes, slowly at first, but then with such volume that they dripped onto the floor. I was standing in Phnom Penh in a former high school known now as Toul Sleng. In 1975 the Khmer Rouge regime in Cambodia turned the school into a prison and interrogation center, which they called Security Prison 21, or simply S-21. I stood alone in one of the twenty rooms of Building A and stared in sorrow at a large black-and-white photograph on the wall. The photograph showed a man on his side, shackled to a bare, iron bed frame, his feet tied together and his hands tied behind his back. His body, gruesomely blackened and mangled, was left to rot above a thick layer of dried blood on the checkered tile floor. The iron bed, an interrogator's desk, and the bloodstains are still visible in the room today.

I had come to this place on the back of a hired motorcycle. It was late afternoon. Children were playing in the street outside the compound, and birds were fluttering about in the trees. As I walked across the peaceful, grassy yard alongside my motorcycle driver, he told me in a quiet voice that his father had been a prisoner here. He never saw him again. Twenty thousand men, women, and children came through these gates, twelve hundred to fifteen hundred at a time.[1] No more than seven prisoners total came out of Tuol Sleng alive. Many would die from brutal torture or execution and be buried in mass graves in the compound; the rest would be tortured and marched to the killing field of Choeung Ek outside of Phnom Penh, where they would be bludgeoned to death with shovels and hoes in order to save ammunition.

To be sent to Tuol Sleng for interrogation meant that you were already considered guilty of some political offense or trumped-up charge against the Khmer Rouge revolution, and it meant certain death. Nonetheless, the Khmer Rouge pretended to have some kind of justice system, and all prisoners were brutally coerced into giving confessions about their crimes, especially their alleged ties to the CIA or the Vietnamese or other enemies of the regime. Prisoners were also coerced under extreme physical pain and fear into implicating their family members, friends, and neighbors, who would soon follow in their footsteps into this chamber of hell.

In the hallway, sealed off with barbed wire, a sign proclaimed in Khmer and English the ten "security regulations" that each prisoner had to follow during interrogations. Among them were: "You must immediately answer my questions without wasting time to reflect"; "While getting lashes or electrification you must not cry at all"; "Do nothing, sit still and wait for my orders. If there is no order, keep quiet. When I ask you to do something, you must do it right away without protesting"; and "If you disobey any point of my regulations you shall get either ten lashes or five shocks of electric discharge." More than one thousand soldiers guarded this prison, among them many twelve- to fifteen-year-olds.

In other rooms hundreds of photographs of the former prisoners lined the walls. This wallpaper of misery was made possible because the Khmer Rouge were meticulous in keeping records of their deeds. The look of terror or silent resignation on the victims' faces haunted me. Some of the victims had been badly beaten and tortured, and all of them looked hungry, tired, and unimaginably vulnerable. I remember staring into the face of one handsome youth in a photograph that captivated me. His crime could have been nothing more than being the son of someone whom the regime mistrusted. His hands were tied behind his back, he had received a nasty blow under his left eye, and his shirt was tagged with a number. "Under other circumstances he might have become my best friend," I thought, deeply imagining what that might be like. "I might have loved him dearly," I said to myself. "But I will never know him."[2]

Many of the classrooms of the Khmer Rouge had been subdivided with shoddy brick walls and barbed wire, forming small cells in which they jailed political prisoners. The only furnishing in each cell was an empty ammunition can, which the prisoner had to use as a toilet. How people survived in such confinement, in the stifling heat, in the stale, rank air, without water when they needed it, with very little food, and often with open wounds and broken bones, I could not comprehend. Prisoners who were workers, peasants, and simple soldiers were jammed into larger cells on the upper floors, each person manacled by the leg to a long iron bar. Everyone slept on the bare floor, without a mattress, pillow, or blanket.

In another room are displayed the instruments of torture used by the Khmer Rouge to gain "confessions" from the victims: a barrel in which a victim was shackled headfirst while water was slowly introduced until his or her face was submersed; a platform to which the victim was shackled while a cloth hood over his or her head was drenched from a watering can, preventing the victim from drawing air; and other such horrendous devices. Some of the thousands of documents maintained at the prison mention torture by beatings with sticks, branches, and bunches of electric wires, cigarette burns, electric shocks, being forced to eat spoonfuls of excrement or drink urine, jabbing under the fingernails with needles, crushing the fingertips in a vice and pulling off the fingernails, scratching, suffocating with a plastic bag or in a bucket of excrement, and various forms of water torture.[3] In an adjacent room, skulls and femur bones of several hundred victims are arranged on a wall in the shape of the nation of Cambodia as a grisly memorial to those who perished.

Most Americans know little about the Khmer Rouge genocide or about the history of Cambodia in general. This is a shame for several reasons. First, I think it is important that each of us know the details of one of the darkest episodes in human history, taking time to reflect on how such a thing was possible and how it might be prevented. Second, I believe that it is important for the people of the

United States to recognize the role our country played in destabilizing Cambodia, and failing to try to stop the genocide. The United States seems slow to learn that its use of force to protect questionable "national interests" often has unintended negative consequences. The people of our country, I believe, must be determined to exert maximum effort to prevent our leaders from using the nation's power in callous and unwise ways. We must remind them when they tell us about the world's great complexities and complications—all of which are supposedly beyond our comprehension—that we prefer the simple wisdom of kindness to their labyrinth of political perceptions; we prefer open and honorable actions to manipulative, covert ones; we prefer our nation to do what we know is right; that we treat others as we would have them treat us; and that we avoid hostility and cherish the lives of all people everywhere.

Another good reason for Americans to know about Cambodia is that this tiny nation shows us how goodness survives even the darkest deeds of evil. It is an example that tells us that we should never give up on the human spirit and that every single individual has the ability to effect peace. No one within Cambodia provides a clearer example of this than a humble, soft-spoken monk named Maha Ghosananda. After coming to know him, I concluded that he is perhaps the one person alive today who is most deserving of the title conferred years ago on Mohandas Gandhi: the *Mahatma,* or "Great Soul."

Before discussing Maha Ghosananda and his incredible contribution to peace, we should first understand his country better. The history of this small Asian nation is not effortless reading, but it will be of benefit to know it and the often harsh details it provides. The best way to encounter such difficult facts is not to let them make us feel depressed or hopeless but rather to let them serve as a powerful impetus to ensure that we establish lasting peace in the future. This is something implicit in Maha Ghosananda's message.

The Kingdom of Cambodia, as it is officially known, is a small country, slightly smaller in size than the state of Oklahoma, with over 12 million people. Ninety percent of the population is Khmer, the rest are

Vietnamese (5 percent), Chinese (1 percent) and others (4 percent). The country lies between Thailand (to the west) and Vietnam (to the east) on the Gulf of Thailand. Laos is its other neighbor, which borders on the northeast. The land is mostly flat plains, with some mountains in the north and southwest. The Mekong River winds its way down the eastern part of the country, entering through Laos and exiting into Vietnam. It is along this river, in the south central region, where its capital, Phnom Penh, is located.

The majority of the land, despite rampant illegal logging activities, is forests and woodlands. The combined area of pastureland and arable land is less than 25 percent. Besides timber, the nation is rich in gemstones and has some deposits of iron ore and other metals. The illegal logging activities along the border of Thailand have resulted in significant environmental destruction, including soil erosion and the loss of biodiversity.

Most of the population is rural, and a majority of people have no access to potable water. There is little seasonal temperature change; tropical heat rules year-round. The rainy season from May to November brings heavy downpours, and floods are not unusual. In the dry season, there is the ever-present danger of droughts and crop loss.

According to an Indian legend, one day a Brahman named Kaundinya sailed by a water-spirit princess whose father ruled the watery kingdom. Kaundinya desired the princess and frightened her into marrying him by shooting an arrow into her boat. As a gift to his bride, Kaundinya gave the princess beautiful clothes to wear, and as a dowry, her father created a country for them by drinking up all the water covering the land. This new kingdom became known as *Kambuja*.

This creation myth mirrors the actual geologic process that created the terrain of Cambodia. Half a millennium ago the Mekong River carried silt from the high plateau of Tibet and deposited it into a bay formed by two peninsulas jetting into the South China Sea. Gradually, the bay filled with this silt and a new land mass emerged.

Scholars continue to debate the origins of the Cambodian, or *Khmer,* people. It is not certain whether they originally came from China, India, or the islands of Southeast Asia. Yet it is known that the people of *Kambuja* (later known as *Kampuchea* in French and *Cambodia* in English) inhabited caves in the area as early as 4200 B.C.E. By the beginning of the common era the people of the region spoke languages related to modern-day Khmer and developed a sophisticated culture.⁴ Indian colonists intermarried with the Khmer, and the Khmer adopted Indian religions (both Hinduism and Buddhism) as their own. They also adopted and adapted profusely from Indian customs, dress, jewelry, music, writing, architecture, science, and art.

From the first through sixth centuries C.E., which is known as the Funan Period,⁵ Cambodia's political center was located south and east of present-day Phnom Penh. During this period trade with India and China was well developed, and political life centered on the village and small groupings of villages rather than on a tightly bound kingdom. By the sixth century C.E., the population began to shift away from coastal trading areas and concentrate along the Mekong and Tonlé Sap Rivers. The small inland principalities, sometimes collectively referred to as "Chenla," grew in population primarily because of the development of wet-rice agriculture. Society in these principalities was highly stratified, with absolute rulers at the top and impressed laborers at the bottom.

In 802 C.E. Jayavarman II united the kingdoms of Cambodia through military campaigns and alliances and proclaimed himself supreme ruler. This is generally considered the beginning of Cambodia as a unified country, and it marks the beginning of an ancestral identity for the Khmer people. Jayavarman II, like most Cambodian kings who would follow him, was said to hold a close association to the Hindu deity Vishnu, thereby providing his claim to a divine right to rule.

For the next 630 years or so, Cambodia was one of the most powerful countries in Southeast Asia. Though this power waxed and waned over this so-called Angkor Period, it was the golden era of Cambodia's power and wealth. After Jayavarman II, the next king to exercise great power was Yasovarman, who reigned from 889 to 910. He established the capital of Cambodia at present-day Angkor and extended the kingdom into the Malay Peninsula, Laos, and much of Burma.

King Suryavarman II also added to the kingdom during his reign (1112–1150). It was he who commissioned the famed Angkor Wat, a temple, tomb, and astronomical observatory dedicated to the Hindu god Vishnu. The temple complex was built by tens of thousands of slave laborers and was maintained by a priestly class who appropriated grain surpluses from the peasants.

Of all the kings of the Angkor Period, King Jayavarman VII, who reigned from 1181 to 1201, was arguably the most powerful. In 1178 Jayavarman VII soundly defeated the Cham invaders from central Vietnam who had sacked Angkor in 1177. Unlike his Hindu predecessors, Jayavarman VII was a Mahayana Buddhist, and when he ascended the throne he displayed his devotion to Buddhism by building enormous public works projects, including roads, temples (such as the grandiose Angkor Thom temple near Angkor Wat), reservoirs, hospitals, and rest houses. Though Jayavarman VII may have wanted to be seen as a benevolent ruler, he never tried to dismantle the traditional class hierarchy or slavery. His public works were carried out by hundreds of thousands of conscripted laborers, and he was ruthless and even punitive in the use of military might to preserve his kingdom.

After Jayavarman VII, the Khmer empire began to fade. Angkor's influence over the principalities in Thailand and Laos diminished, while the Thai kingdom of Ayudhya began to grow in strength. In 1431 the Thais invaded Cambodia and sacked Angkor. The Khmer elite abandoned the capital and its environs and migrated toward Phnom Penh, where they carried out trade with China.

Internal rivalries, a divided elite, and Thai invasions characterized the next several centuries. In 1594 the Thais captured the Khmer capital. Thereafter, the Thais would repeatedly exert influence over Khmer internal affairs, and they annexed many of Cambodia's western lands.

A hundred years later another foreign force began to exert substantial influence over Cambodia. In the 1690s the Nguyen overlords of south Vietnam broke off from the Le dynasty of the north and permanently took over lower Cambodia. As part of this annexation, the Vietnamese took over the Khmer city of Prey Nokor, which later became known as Saigon. All of Cambodia's seaports on the South China Sea where thereby taken away, and huge numbers of Khmer now fell under Vietnamese control, resulting in an intense hatred toward the Vietnamese that persists to this day.

Eighteenth- and nineteenth-century Cambodian history is one of repeated invasions by the Thai and Vietnamese. Internal strife prevented the kings of Cambodia from gaining much power and thwarted them from repelling (except in a very few cases) foreign invasions. In fact, the kings and their would-be usurpers frequently called upon either the Thai or Vietnamese for assistance in maintaining or gaining power.

Thailand and Vietnam also frequently battled each other on Cambodian soil. The Thai and Vietnamese, however, were quite different from one another in how they treated the Cambodians. The Thai thought of the Khmer as Buddhist little brothers who should be loyal and friendly to their Thai elders. This sense of kinship with the Khmer made the Thai rather accepting of Khmer customs. The Vietnamese, on the other hand, viewed the Cambodians as barbarians who should bow to the superiority of Vietnamese civilization.

Vietnam's view toward Cambodia is well illustrated in its attempt to mold the country into a Vietnamese protectorate. From 1835 to 1840 the Vietnamese tried to turn Cambodia into a buffer against Thailand and to raise a Khmer army to fight the Thai. General Minh Mang, who was in charge of the "Vietnamization" of Cambodia, stated that Vietnamese "military convicts and ordinary prisoners, if kept in jail, would prove useless. Therefore, it would be better for them to be sent to Cambodia and live among the people there, who would benefit from their teaching." Moreover, the emperor of Vietnam called the Khmer ignorant and lazy and instructed that they be taught to speak Vietnamese and adopt Vietnamese dress and table manners. "If there is any out-dated or barbarous custom that can be simplified, or repressed," the emperor declared, "then do so."[6] The Vietnamese attitude toward the Khmer only added to the hatred of Vietnamese in Cambodia.

As discussed in a previous chapter, the French defeated the Vietnamese in 1861, although a strong resistance movement continued in Vietnam until 1867. With the defeat of Vietnam, the French began to pay closer attention to Cambodia, its neighbor. French naturalist Henri Mouhot also brought the country to wider attention when he ventured to Siem Reap and stumbled upon the magnificent Angkor ruins.

In 1863 the French established a protectorate over Cambodia, promising to defend the country against the Thai in exchange for timber and mineral exploration rights. The Vietnamese were already constrained by the French, so the Thai were Cambodia's main concern. France initially allowed considerable self-government in Cambodia and lent the king military assistance in suppressing internal rebellions. The French extracted rice and timber and used peasants much as the Khmer kings had done for centuries.

But by 1884 the French were instituting reforms throughout Indochina, and Cambodia was increasingly made into a traditional colony controlled either by French or by French-installed Vietnamese administrators who carried out French policies. France recouped its considerable administrative costs by imposing heavy fees for government services and levying onerous taxes on imports and exports and on salt, alcohol, opium, and agricultural products.[7] The tax burden on peasants was substantial (especially when France pressured its colonies to produce more funds for its war efforts in World War I), though it was adjusted at times to hinder possible uprisings.

Unlike Vietnam, which resisted colonialism, Cambodia remained largely passive and acquiesced to France. The French maintained the prestige of the Cambodian king, the Cambodian king maintained the authority of the Buddhist monks, and for the peasants, very little changed. As David Ayres notes,

> The impact of French control on the lives of Cambodia's peasants, in the main, had been insignificant. Preoccupied with their day-to-day survival, with the food on their table, with rice cultivation, and with their Buddhist lifestyle, Cambodians continued to be locked into a cycle of localized patron-client relationships. They continued to pay taxes to a higher authority as they had always done, supporting the

lifestyle of an elite whom they rarely saw and with whom they had little in common.[8]

But make no mistake about it; this was a colonial system. As former *New York Times* correspondent and author Henry Kamm declares,

> France's colonization of Cambodia was of a most condescending and patronizing kind. Hardly any Cambodian was trained to perform functions of authority. Little was undertaken to educate Cambodians to take their place in the modern world. Significant administration functions were held by Frenchmen; economic life in the largely agrarian country was dominated by Sino-Khmers in commerce and imported Vietnamese as skilled artisans and office personnel.[9]

This system of control began to unravel when the Japanese staged a *coup de force* throughout Indochina on March 9, 1945. The Japanese immediately dissolved the colonial government of Cambodia (as they did in Vietnam and Laos) and allowed King Norodom Sihanouk (whom the French had installed) to declare an independent government under Prime Minister Son Ngoc Thanh. It was because the Japanese allowed immediate independence (though they used French administration to prevent "confusion and instability") that during this time Khmer nationalism grew rapidly among the Khmer elite, and anti-French sentiments began to be more freely expressed.[10] Once independence had been experienced, the nationalist genie was out of the bottle.

The French, unfortunately, reasserted dominance over Cambodia in September 1945 after Japan was defeated by the Allied powers. France deposed Son Ngac Thanh and convicted him of treason, with full support from Sihanouk. Many of Son Ngac Thanh's supporters, however, took up arms and formed a guerrilla movement called Khmer Issarak, demanding full independence from France. France recognized nominal independence of the Kingdom of Cambodia, but in reality it continued to run nearly all aspects of the Cambodian government.

The king hastened France's decision to grant full independence to Cambodia by dissolving parliament, declaring martial law, visiting foreign capitals in search of support, and finally declaring his father regent and going into self-imposed exile. France, now preoccupied with Communist insurgents in Vietnam, knew that its control over Cambodia had to end and granted full independence on November 9, 1953. This independence was later affirmed in the Geneva Conference of 1954, in which the Viet Minh agreed to stop using Cambodia as a base from which to attack the French in Vietnam.

Sihanouk, much to the consternation of the Eisenhower administration, and especially Secretary of State Dulles, declared Cambodia a neutral state. Sihanouk (who ran the country as an elected autocrat) initially accepted aid from the United States, but while doing so he steadfastly refused to align with Washington. However, believing that the Vietnamese Communists would eventually prevail and threaten the sovereignty of Cambodia, Sihanouk decided to confirm Cambodia's neutrality in 1963 by rejecting all American aid.[11] This neutrality, however, did not stop Sihanouk from allowing the Viet Minh to be supplied through the Cambodian port of Sihanoukville.

Sihanouk's decision to reject American military aid angered many members of the Cambodian elite, especially the army and police force. U.S. military aid constituted 15 percent of the national budget.[12] Sihanouk also closed privately owned banks and nationalized import-export business, further alienating the civil service, large landholders, and international traders. The United States exploited this social rift, supporting with direct aid rightist groups that might draw the Cambodian army into the Vietnam War on the side of America. At the same time, opposition to Sihanouk's authoritarian rule grew in the middle class and among leftist groups such as the Communist Party of Kampuchea (CPK). The CPK was led by Son Sen, Ieng Sary, and Saloth Sar (later known as Pol Pot). Sihanouk labeled the CPK the Khmer Rouge, or "Red Khmer."

In the spring of 1967 U.S. general William Westmoreland and the Joint Chiefs of Staff pressed hard to widen the Vietnamese war by sending ground and air forces into Laos and Cambodia to attack North Vietnamese supply routes. Though the Pentagon repeatedly requested an expansion of the war, President Johnson repeatedly resisted. When Nixon entered the White House, however, he and his special assistant for national security affairs, Henry Kissinger, decided to try to frighten Hanoi into accepting American proposals for an armistice. They were looking for a way to end the war in Indochina but only on "honorable" terms. In other words, they were looking for a way to save face, to prevent American humiliation and loss of prestige among current and potential allies.

The Nixon-Kissinger plan was to conduct guerrilla raids against the Vietnamese Communists and bombard their sanctuaries within Cambodia. Over a fifteen-month period beginning in March 1969, American B-52 bombers flew 3,630 missions, dropping 100,000 tons of bombs on Cambodia. Many of the missions were flown from air bases in Thailand, a staunch client-state of the United States. The air strikes were called Menu, after having gone through Breakfast, Lunch, Snack, Supper, and Dessert.[13] Such American feasting on Cambodia would have dire consequences for that country.

Nixon insisted that the bombings in Cambodia be held in the strictest confidence. Only senior officials in the administration and the Pentagon would be told. To Nixon, it was imperative that the American public continue believing the myth that he was ending, not widening, the war. (Later Nixon and Kissinger would wiretap senior administration officials and members of the press to find out who leaked news of the bombings.)

The bombings, however, were ineffective from a military perspective. The North Vietnamese soldiers simply retreated farther into the Cambodian interior and began training local Communists (including the Khmer Rouge) in guerrilla warfare. In fact, during the bombing campaign the government actually reported an *increase* in the number of Vietnamese Communists within Cambodia.[14]

The people of Cambodia were enraged at the destruction of their homes and farms by American bombs, leading to anti-American sentiment, which aided the North Vietnamese and local Communists. Intelligence reports in Cambodia revealed that U.S. "aerial bombardments against the villagers have caused civilian loss on a large scale" and that peasant survivors of the bombings were turning to the CPK for support.[15]

The increased war effort in Vietnam also led to the draining of Cambodian rice crops, as the elite smuggled the rice to Vietnam, where they could fetch higher prices. The government responded by trying to take rice crops forcibly and pay only government-set prices, infuriating the farmers.

For its part, Hanoi was not intimidated by the American bombings of its supply lines in Cambodia. Hanoi believed that the American position in Vietnam was simply untenable and would ultimately result in America's defeat.

Rightist general Lon Nol became prime minister of Cambodia in 1969, with the support of Sihanouk. Lon Nol returned the favor by deposing Sihanouk in March 1970. Historians disagree on whether the CIA helped orchestrate the coup. Yet Lon Nol certainly knew that the United States would be friendly to his regime, and U.S. assistance, including weapons, soon began flowing into Cambodia. Lon Nol proved to be as autocratic as Sihanouk, and his government was incredibly corrupt. Yet Washington supported him anyway.

Cambodia was now in utter chaos. The Vietnamese Communists had retreated into the heart of Cambodia, Lon Nol's regime was corrupt, the army was poorly trained and equipped, and the various insurgent groups were unified in their opposition to Lon Nol. The National United Front of Kampuchea, which fought Lon Nol's forces, consisted of an unlikely coalition of supporters of Sihanouk as well as opposing groups of local Communists, some loyal to Vietnam, some loyal to China. The National Unified Front was quite successful in raising peasant support. This was greatly facilitated by Sihanouk's plea for the peasants to rise up against Lon Nol, as they were traditionally loyal to the royal house.[16]

The Communists soon controlled the five northeastern provinces. Kissinger was certain that a Communist offensive would topple Lon Nol, and on April 22, 1970, Nixon told his security council to come up with a plan to save Lon Nol because "the only government in Cambodia in the last 25 years that had the guts to take a pro-Western and pro-American stand is ready to fall."[17]

On April 30, 1970, Nixon, who had continually promised to bring American troops home, astonished the nation by announcing that he had ordered thousands of American soldiers into Cambodia to seek out and destroy Communist bases there. Nixon flatly lied to the American public, saying that since 1954 "American policy . . . has been to scrupulously respect the neutrality of the Cambodian people." Nixon completely covered up that fact that months earlier he had ordered massive clandestine bombings of neutral Cambodia. He also said that the United States had not provided any military assistance to Cambodia for the last five years and that the U.S. invasion was in the interests of American lives and South Vietnamese lives and that "the future of . . . 7 million people in Cambodia is involved."[18] Indeed, 7 million lives were at stake, but Nixon cared little about them.

Historian George Herring writes, "The ultimate tragedy was that from beginning to end, the Nixon administration viewed its new ally as little more than a pawn to be used to help salvage the U.S. position in Vietnam, showing scant regard for the consequences for Cambodia and its people." Kamm agrees. "The interests of Cambodia did not seriously enter into the Nixon-Kissinger strategy," he notes. "This country of seven to eight million people became a lightly regarded pawn in a game whose objective was to put an end to the effects of an arrogant miscalculation and ease America's way out of a no-win war [in Vietnam], cutting its losses in lives and prestige."[19]

The United States and South Vietnamese invaded Cambodia in May 1970 with twenty thousand troops. The Vietnamese Communists were driven deeper into Cambodia but were not destroyed. The U.S. "incursion" had little, if any, measurable benefit for the United States except perhaps giving the United States a little more time to try to strengthen the South Vietnamese forces to fight the North Vietnamese by themselves (Nixon's so-called Vietnamization of the war). Hanoi boycotted the Paris peace talks until the Americans withdrew their troops. Moreover, as David Chandler states, "The invasion . . . probably spelled the end of Cambodia as a sovereign state."[20]

The Communist forces, pushed deeper into the interior, were able to garner the support of the peasants, attack town after town, and ultimately control the heartland of Cambodia. Lon Nol's forces waged several campaigns against the Communists in 1970 and 1971, but his troops were decimated and were never able to mount another serious offensive. The United States had no intention of sending troops to bolster Lon Nol's government. Yet in an attempt to keep it alive, Nixon resumed massive clandestine bombings in Cambodia in February 1972. Throughout the rest of that year, U.S. B-52 bombers dropped thirty-seven thousand tons of bombs on Cambodia. Despite the incredible brutality of the bombing, Lon Nol's government continued to lose territory. By the end of the year he controlled only Phnom Penh, Battambang, and a few provincial capitals.

During March through May 1973 alone, the United States dropped 140,000 tons of bombs in a campaign that David Chandler calls "in its intensity . . . as brutal as any conducted during World War II."[21] In July through August, the bombing increased even further.

It is clear that, had they known about it, the antiwar groups, as well as congressional leaders, would have mounted enormous protests against the resumed bombing. In May, when U.S. troops invaded Cambodia, massive protests had erupted on college campuses, four protesters were killed and nine injured at Kent State University, and one hundred thousand demonstrators poured into Washington. When the members of the Senate Foreign Relations Committee learned, in Kissinger's words, that the United States was "bombing the bejesus" out of Cambodia in violation of prohibitions on U.S. participation in combat operations there, they were furious. In May and June 1973 angry congressional leaders demanded an end to the bombing. At the end of June 1973 Nixon was forced to agree to stop the bombing campaign by August 15.

Meanwhile, the Khmer Rouge, supported by the Chinese, began to purge the Communist insurgency of centrists, pro-Vietnamese, and pro-Sihanouk members. They saw victory, and they wanted to ensure that their agenda emerged on top. By 1973 the Khmer Rouge had gained control over the insurgency movement and mounted attacks on government forces unaided by the Vietnamese Communists. They even battled the Vietnamese forces in order to ensure control over as much territory as possible. Soon they controlled nearly 60 percent of the country's territory and 25 percent of the population. As bombs continued to rain down on the countryside, the Khmer Rouge became more and more radicalized, less open to negotiations, less constrained by normative conduct in war, and more ruthless in purging centrists.

We must keep in mind that in bombing Cambodia the United States was acting to preserve its "honor," nothing more, since protecting Cambodia itself from Communism was not vital to U.S. interests. Kissinger to this day argues that he and Nixon made the right decisions in the Vietnam War (including the bombing of Cambodia). Because the United States had given its word that it would protect our allies, he argues, if we had let them down they and potential allies would have turned away from our bloc toward the Soviets or the Chinese. No matter that our allies were corrupt and repressive regimes; in Kissinger's view we had a duty to protect them, and our prestige and influence in the process.

Cambodia scholar Stephen Heder said in 1973, "There's certainly a major American responsibility" for the civil war in Cambodia. Former Cambodian ambassador Jonathan Ladd said much the same thing in 1973: "I can't help [but have] a sad feeling that Cambodia is a little country that we have used and for which we must now bear a moral responsibility."[22]

It is estimated that 600,000 Cambodians were killed as a result of the U.S. extension of the Vietnam War into Cambodia. Other sources say the U.S. bombs alone killed 150,000 peasants, while hundreds of thousands more died as a result of ground battles, starvation, and disease. While the U.S. war in Cambodia may have temporarily disrupted or inconvenienced North Vietnamese supply lines, the American bombing neither broke the North Vietnamese will nor stopped their war effort. It also failed to prevent the collapse of the inept and corrupt U.S.-backed Lon Nol regime in Phnom Penh.

Yet the massive and brutal bombing did devastate the straw huts, temples, clinics, and rice fields of villages in the countryside, killing many innocent civilians, destroying normal village life, and causing an enormous refugee problem. By April 1975 at least 2 million refugees poured into the cities. The huge influx of refugees caused an enormous breakdown in the traditional social structure. The population of Phnom Penh ballooned from 600,000 residents to 2 million, causing widespread and persistent deprivation that only foreign deliveries of aid could help alleviate.

Yet the full effect of the U.S. bombing, and its support for the corrupt Lon Nol government, was not considered at the time. That is the main problem with the use of violence: once unleashed, it has unintended consequences, which can spiral out of control. In this case the bombing certainly aided and radicalized the Khmer Rouge, helping to boost them as the main opposition force in Cambodia. "In 1969 the Khmer Rouge numbered only about 4,000," writes author Jonathan Glover. "By 1975 their numbers were enough to defeat the government forces. Their victory was *greatly helped* by the American attack on Cambodia, which was carried out as an extension of the Vietnam War."[23]

Cambodian scholar Ben Kiernan states clearly that the Nixon-Kissinger strategy in Cambodia was "largely responsible" for the dominance of the radical Khmer Rouge faction over the other insurgent forces that opposed the Lon Nol regime. Evidence can be seen in, for instance, a Khmer Rouge document aimed at recruiting the support of Cambodian women. The document argued, "Every day their planes pour millions of tons of bombs on our territory, killing men, women, old and young indiscriminately, devastating and systematically flattening the houses and rice fields of the peaceful populations, as well as historic monuments such as Angkor Wat, and monasteries."[24]

"What Kissinger and Nixon began, Pol Pot completed," highly acclaimed historian John Pilger concludes. He continues,

> Evidence from U.S. official documents, declassified in 1987, leaves no doubt that this U.S. terror was critical in Pol Pot's drive for power. "They are using [the bombing] as the main theme of the propaganda," reported the CIA Director of Operations on May 2, 1973. "This approach has resulted in the successful recruitment of a number of young men [and] the propaganda has been most effective among refugees subjected to B-52 strikes."[25]

Those who survived the bombings and napalm took refuge in the forests, where the Khmer Rouge recruited them. Fueled by their hatred of those who had destroyed their property, they readily joined the insurgency. Chhit Do, a Khmer Rouge leader from northern Cambodia, recalled,

> The ordinary people . . . sometimes literally shit in their pants when the big bombs and shells came. . . . Their minds just froze up and they would wander around mute for three or four days. Terrified and half-crazy, the people were ready to believe what they were told. . . . That was what made it so easy for the Khmer Rouge to win the people over. It was because of their dissatisfaction with the bombing that they kept on cooperating with the Khmer Rouge, joining up with the Khmer Rouge, sending their children off to go with them. . . . Sometimes the bombs fell and hit little children, and their fathers would be all for the Khmer Rouge.[26]

Sihanouk, reflecting on the rise of the Khmer Rouge, laid the responsibility at the feet of Nixon and Kissinger: "[They] gave the Khmer Rouge involuntary aid because the people had to support the Communist patriots against Lon Nol. . . . They demoralized America, they lost all of Indochina to the Communists, and they created the Khmer Rouge."[27]

That the United States bears a significant amount of the responsibility seems clear. The North Vietnamese, the Chinese, the United States, and other Khmer groups all share blame in the dominance of the radical Khmer Rouge. Why is this important? Because had the United States acted differently—not extending the fervent anti-Communist war into Cambodia, strengthening the peasants instead of bombing them, supporting an honest and competent regime in Phnom Penh, and of course, not becoming involved in a ruthless war in Vietnam in the first place—the Khmer Rouge probably would never have come to power. The consequences of the Khmer Rouge reign were devastating to Cambodia—and to humanity in general.

On April 17, 1975, the Khmer Rouge forces captured Phnom Penh and declared the foundation of Democratic Kampuchea

(DK). Lon Nol had left the country on April 1 at the behest of the American government, which paid him between $200,000 and $1 million to do so. Kissinger hoped that with Lon Nol out there was the possibility of negotiating a last-minute deal with Sihanouk and China. But the fall of Phnom Penh to the Khmer Rouge was now inevitable. On their way out, the Americans took only 159 Cambodians, leaving the rest of the civil servants and military officers to fend for themselves. Virtually all of them were summarily executed by the Khmer Rouge.[28]

Democratic Kampuchea was in chaos. Staple crops such as rice and corn were decimated. Nearly 75 percent of all domestic animals had been destroyed, and the urban population, which had depended almost entirely for its survival on American rice shipments, was in danger of starvation. Thirty to 40 percent of the roads and bridges were blown up, rice and paper mills destroyed, and cement and textile factors severely damaged. The hospitals were packed and lacked supplies, and the refugee slums were filled with disease.

The people in the cities welcomed the Khmer Rouge troops as the victors over the corrupt Lon Nol government and were delighted at the end of a long, devastating war. As author Teeda Butt Mam notes in *Children of Cambodia's Killing Fields,* a moving collection of memoirs by survivors of the Khmer Rouge regime,

> I was fifteen years old when the Khmer Rouge came to power in April 1975. I can still remember how overwhelmed with joy I was that the war had finally ended. It did not matter who won. I and many Cambodians wanted peace at any price. The civil war had tired us out, and we could not make much sense out of killing our own brothers and sisters for a cause that was not ours.[29]

Yet the Khmer Rouge would soon show their true face. They took the astounding step of clearing the cities completely, in order to consolidate their authority by separating families and groups and scattering the population throughout the countryside. "They forced millions from their homes," Teeda Butt Mam remembers.

They separated us from our friends and neighbors to keep us off balance, to prevent us from forming any alliance to stand up and win back our rights. They ripped off our homes and possessions. They did this intentionally, without mercy. They were willing to pay any cost, any lives for their mission. Innocent children, old women, and sick patients from hospital beds were included.[30]

Another means of consolidating control was the summary execution of doctors, lawyers, teachers, business leaders, and anyone else suspected of opposing the revolution, and of course civil servants and military officers of the Lon Nol government. Other people were sent to Tuol Sleng, where they were tortured and forced to confess to crimes they had not committed before being executed.

Survivor Savuth Penn recalls the fate of his father, who had served in Lon Nol's military. As soon as the cities were emptied, the Khmer Rouge, he learned, took all officers to a remote area of the city. "They asked all the officers to stand in formation and then they mass executed them, without any blindfolds, with machine guns, rifles, and grenades. Then they shot one by one at anybody who moved."[31]

Sihanouk, who returned from exile, was declared the head of state, and foreign governments believed for several months that he was actually in control. In reality he was kept under house arrest in the royal palace. Pol Pot, followed by a handful of other top officials, presided over *Angkar* (the "organization"). Angkar was highly secretive and didn't even confirm the existence of the Communist Party of Kampuchea until much later. For months the average Cambodian never even heard of Pol Pot.

The Khmer Rouge aimed not to transform the existing society but rather to smash it to bits. They declared Year Zero, the start of a new society, abolishing money, private ownership, freedom of movement, markets, and formal education. They also outlawed religion, banned books, records, modern furniture, and musical instruments, and dictated a uniform style of dress. Nearly everything contemporary was prohibited. Even family connections were dissolved. *Angkar,* the Khmer Rouge said, was a person's true family.

Ninety to 95 percent of the country's population was forced onto collective farms or collective labor details. The masses were divided chiefly between the peasants, who had long supported the revolution, and the *neak phnoe* (or *neak thmei*), the "new people," who came from urban areas. The new people were considered untrustworthy and inherently disloyal because of their love of private property and individual rights. Young, uneducated soldiers, as well as local leaders and party members, exercised fanaticism and intolerance in their new roles as overlords.[32]

How did these young cadres become so cruel? It was largely through training. Young children were taken from their families and friends and taught to be cruel. François Bizot, a French ethnologist, was captured and kept in bondage by the Khmer Rouge. He witnessed firsthand the conditioning of young children by the Khmer Rouge. He had befriended a young girl who was separated from her father. The two played together and grew fond of each other. Yet she changed after attending Khmer Rouge indoctrination classes. Upon finding that she could slip her finger between the rope and Bizot's ankle, she called the guards over to tighten the ropes. Ben Glover notes that this became "a regular spiteful routine" and a "demonstration of the vulnerability of children to conditioning in cruelty."[33]

Of course it was even easier to indoctrinate teenage boys, who were encouraged to exercise ruthlessness in their newfound power. The Khmer Rouge hoped to create soldiers who loved to fight. In time, a great many of them killed innocent civilians without any remorse and even became addicted to torture and killing.

It was the new people, Khmer Rouge cadres were told, who supported the American bombing of the peasants' farms and villages. The new people, the Khmer Rouge said, must learn to live in fear, they way the peasants did during the civil war. "Keeping you is no profit; losing you is no loss," the new people were told. They were placed in the most abject conditions within the collectives. Initially not even provided with shelter, the new people were forced to do the harshest work and given inadequate food and medicine.

Executions were widespread and frequent. People marked for death, for any minor infraction against the Khmer Rouge leaders, were usually taken out in the night and beaten to death with axes, shovels, or hoes. Horrifyingly, many people were told to report to a mass grave site (a killing field) that night, and they would spend the remainder of the day knowing that their murder was only hours away.

Ranachith (Ronnie) Yimsut, a boy who survived the Khmer Rouge, was forced to relocate at least twenty-four times. By the time he was ordered to march with eighty-seven others from the forced labor camp in Siem Reap Angkor Province, it had become routine to him. They were all pressed into service at a labor camp at Tasource Hill. There thousands of malnourished people were forced to dig a canal; many of them died from heat stroke, starvation, and exhaustion. The bodies often lay there among the living, rotting in the tropical heat. One day the remaining seventy-nine people from Yimsut's original group were marched south. The men who could walk were ordered to separate from the rest, and unbeknown to the women and children, the men were executed. The women and children and a few remaining elderly men were then led to the edge of a canal in a field. Ronnie Yimsut describes what happened after that:

I was beyond horrified when I heard the clobbering begin. Somehow, I knew that was it. Oum's elderly father was next to me, and his upper torso contracted several times before it fell on me. At that moment, I noticed a small boy whom I knew well get up and start to call for his mother. And then there was a warm splash on my face and body. I knew it was definitely not mud. It was the little boy's blood and perhaps brain tissues that got scattered from the impact. The rest only let out short but terrifying sputter sounds, and I could hear their breath stopped cold in its track. Everything seemed to happen in slow motion, and it was so unreal. It happened in a matter of seconds and very fast, but I can still vividly remember every trifling detail. I closed my eyes, but the terrifying sounds continued to penetrate my ear canals and pierced my eardrums. The first [blow] that came was when I was lying face down to the ground with a body partially covering my lower body. It hit me just below my right shoulder blade. I remembered that one very well. The next one hit me just above my neck on the right side of my head. I believed it was the one that put me to sleep that night. The rest, which was at least fifteen blows, landed everywhere on my skinny body.[34]

Ronnie Yimsut was left for dead underneath a pile of bloody bodies. A second group of victims was brought the next day, and Ronnie Yimsut had to watch and listen while they were clubbed to death. The following day, when a third group came to meet the same fate, Ronnie managed to crawl along the canal on his elbows and knees and escape. He hid in the forest for the next seventeen days and eventually made his way to Thailand, were he was put in a squalid jail by the Thai authorities.

The Khmer Rouge intended not only to eradicate the upper and middle classes, but also to cleanse the country of unwanted races. The Islamic Cham, for example, were targeted, and only a third of their population survived the Khmer Rouge regime. The Chinese also suffered, but not as intensely as other groups, given that China was the chief supporter and supplier of arms to the Khmer Rouge.

Yet the most intense racism was aimed at the Vietnamese. Most Vietnamese civilians were driven from Cambodia through intimidation and deportation. Of the ten thousand Vietnamese who failed to flee Cambodia, not a single one survived the Khmer Rouge genocide. Border skirmishes between Cambodia and Vietnam took place frequently. Meanwhile, Pol Pot dreamed of retaking the ancient lands of Cambodia that Vietnam had held for hundreds of years. His plan was to whip up national hatred of the Vietnamese so that the Khmer Rouge would annihilate them from the land.

Pol Pot believed that the Khmer Krom (the Cambodians living in southern Vietnam) would rise up to overthrow the Vietnamese, so in January 1978 he ordered, "Each Cambodian is to kill thirty Vietnamese, in order to move forward to liberate, to fight strongly in order to take southern Vietnam back." Tensions with Vietnam escalated over the coming months. By June three-quarters of a million Vietnamese civilians had fled their homes along the border, seeking safety from Khmer Rouge attacks by relocating to other parts of Vietnam.[35]

In December 1978 the Vietnamese announced the formation of the Kampuchean United Front for National Salvation, headed by Heng Samrin, calling for the overthrow of Pol Pot's regime. They broadcast to the Cambodians that a liberated Cambodia could return to normalcy, ending the collectivizations, repopulating the cities, reestablishing money and private property, and reuniting families. On Christmas Day they sent twelve to fourteen divisions of well-trained, well-equipped soldiers into Cambodia from the poorly protected northeast. Vietnamese forces numbered over 100,000 soldiers, aided by 15,000 Khmer resistance fighters. In the face of such superior force, the Khmer Rouge army quickly crumbled.

Phnom Penh fell on January 7, 1979, and the People's Republic of Kampuchea (PRK) was declared under the leadership of several individuals, including Hun Sen, a former Khmer Rouge leader who had been retrained by Vietnam. Hundreds of thousands of refugees fled the fighting, many relocating to makeshift camps along the Thai border and inside Thailand. The Khmer Rouge began retreating, taking tens of thousands of refugees with them at gunpoint. Others who fled the collectives and returned to their homes were massacred by the remaining Khmer Rouge as traitors.

The Khmer Rouge were pushed back and routed nearly everywhere, except a few isolated jungle strongholds along the four-hundred-mile border with Thailand. They would have been completely defeated but for a strange turn of events. The United States declared that Democratic Kampuchea, the genocidal Khmer Rouge, was the legitimate government of Cambodia! Never has *realpolitik* been so transparent. The United States had waged a war against the Khmer Rouge that devastated Cambodia; now it was siding with them simply because its old enemy, the Vietnamese, had invaded.

It is estimated that between 1.5 and 2 million Cambodians had been killed during the Khmer Rouge rule, yet this is the regime that the United States chose to recognize as the legitimate government of Cambodia. The U.S. support of the Khmer Rouge permitted them to retain Cambodia's seat in the United Nations for years to come, and tens of millions of dollars, from the pockets of American taxpayers, went to keep the Khmer Rouge resistance alive.

With the Vietnamese invasion, millions of Cambodians could now return to their homes, try to find any remaining family members, and strive to rebuild a normal life. That did not mean, however, that the fighting was over. The Khmer Rouge continued to threaten a major port and the second largest city and also ruled the night in many camps and villages in the countryside. They would raid refugee camps, shooting people from palm trees, capturing and executing refugees.

The United States joined China in denouncing the Vietnamese invasion as a violation of international law, no matter that the Khmer Rouge had provoked it in repeated acts of violation of international law, or the fact that the invasion ended the horrendous genocide that neither the United States nor China did anything to stop. The Chinese, as noted previously, in fact aided the Khmer Rouge with full knowledge of the genocide, even observing operations at Tuol Sleng. Now, the Chinese funneled weapons to the Khmer Rouge forces through the Thai military, with the support and approval of the United States. Food, medicine, and other supplies donated by international aid organizations for the refugees fleeing the fighting were doled out by the Thai military and disproportionately channeled to the Khmer Rouge.[36] Additionally, though tens of thousands of Cambodian refugees were forcibly repatriated (resulting in many deaths), the Khmer Rouge guerrillas would be permitted to freely enter Thai territory to escape the Vietnamese and the troops of the government they installed, the PRK.

There is a saying in Cambodia, "A journey of ten thousand miles begins with a single step." The journey to bring peace and reconstruction to Cambodian society would indeed be a long and arduous one. Though it is difficult to mark the first step in this lengthy process, one could say that the rebuilding of Cambodian society began when a small, smiling monk stepped into a Khmer refugee camp in 1978.

While the barrels of the guns still smoldered, Maha Ghosananda, who later earned the nicknames "the Gandhi of Cambodia," "the Living Treasure," and "the Living Truth" for his tireless efforts and boundless compassion in trying to restore peace and normalcy to Cambodian society, made his way from Thailand into Cambodia. From their strongholds along the border of Thailand, the Khmer Rouge leaders remained defiant and committed to their revolution. Monks were fair game for execution. Yet Maha Ghosananda felt a sense of compassion even toward the Khmer Rouge soldiers, though they had murdered his own family and plunged the country into such darkness. His compassion for them seems incomprehensible at first. Perhaps it can best be explained by his understanding of the words of his former master: "When this defilement of anger really gets strong, it has no sense of good or evil, right or wrong, husband, wives, or children. It can even drink human blood." Maha Ghosananda has written,

> I do not question that loving one's oppressors—Cambodians loving the Khmer Rouge—may be the most difficult attitude to achieve. But it is a law of the universe that retaliation, hatred, and revenge only continue the cycle and never stop it. Reconciliation does not mean that we surrender rights and conditions, but rather that we use love in all of our negotiations. It means that we see ourselves in the opponent—for what is the opponent but a being in ignorance, and we ourselves are also ignorant of many things. Therefore, only loving kindness and right mindfulness can free us.[37]

"Both the noble and the good are embraced because loving kindness flows to them spontaneously," Maha Ghosananda also declared. Yet the "unwholesome-minded," he added, must also be embraced because "love embraces all beings, whether they are noble-minded or low-minded, good or evil." The unwholesome-minded are, after all, "the ones who need loving kindness the most. In many of them, the seed of goodness may have died because warmth was lacking for its growth. It perished from coldness in a world without compassion."[38] If the Khmer Rouge could be shown once again the warmth of virtue and love, then they could again learn to differentiate between right and wrong, good and evil, and live in peace. In other words, they were redeemable, and Maha Ghosananda would quite literally bet his life on it.

The roads to Sakeo Camp were choked with men, women, and children fleeing the fighting between the Khmer Rouge and the Vietnamese. It was a procession of unbelievable suffering in the scorching heat. These people, who had lost so much during the genocide, had nothing but a single hope to stay alive and perhaps to be reunited with any surviving members of their family.

"The camp was stark," it says in the introduction to Maha Ghosananda's book *Step by Step*. "Streets were crowded, sewage flowed in open gutters, food and water were scarce, and most refugees huddled inside their tattered cloth tents.

"Passing through the checkpoint, Ghosananda walked slowly toward the center of the camp, and as he did so the gloom that had enveloped the camp instantly turned to excitement. Refugees rushed to gaze at his saffron robe, the long-forbidden symbol of Buddhist devotion. Many peered from a safe distance, overwhelmed with anxious memories. Ghosananda reached into his cloth shoulder bag and pulled out a handful of tattered pamphlets—copies of the *Metta Sutta*, the Buddha's words of compassion and forgiveness for the oppressor. He offered one to each refugee within reach, bowing his head in the traditional gesture of respect.

"In that moment, great suffering and great love merged. Centuries of Buddhist devotion rushed into the consciousness of the refugees. Waves of survivors fell to their knees and prostrated, wailing loudly, their cries reverberating throughout the camp. Many say that the dharma [the teachings of Buddhist truth], which had slept gently in their hearts as the bodhi tree [a symbol of Buddhism] burned, was reawakened that day."[39]

Maha Ghosananda oversaw the construction of a large, makeshift temple out of bamboo. When it was completed, thousands of refugees gathered together and wept as this lone Buddhist master sat and chanted melodiously the ancient words of the Buddha:

Hatred never ceases by hatred
but by love alone is healed.
This is the ancient and eternal law.

"The whole world has been supplying guns to our people to help us kill one another," Maha Ghosananda declared. "Now it is time for peace, for a nonviolent resolution to all of our problems."[40]

Maha Ghosananda was born in 1929 in a small farming village in the Takeo Province of the Mekong Delta. At the age of eight he impressed the monks of his village with his eagerness to learn Buddhism. Five years later the young boy asked his parents if he could become a novice monk, and they agreed.

After completing his novice training and reaching the level of *bhikkhu,* a fully ordained monk, in 1953 Maha Ghosananda pursued his doctoral-level degree at the famed Buddhist college, Nalanda, in India. A few years later he was chosen to be part of the Cambodian delegation to a rare and very important gathering of Buddhists from various countries, a high honor for such a young monk.

Maha Ghosananda received teachings in both the Mahayana and Theravada traditions (the two major divisions of Buddhism). He received training in nonviolence and peacemaking from Japanese Master Nichidatsu Fujii, a close associate of Mahatma Gandhi. He also was one of a very few monks chosen to take instructions directly from the Supreme Patriarch of Cambodia. In 1969 he received his doctoral degree from Nalanda, at which time his name Maha Ghosananda ("Proclaimer of Joy") was officially bestowed.

Maha Ghosananda had earned a reputation as a gifted monk. He traveled widely and became proficient in a number of languages, including English, French, German, Vietnamese, Laotian, Thai, Hindi, Bengali, Sanskrit, Pali, Sinhalese, Burmese, Japanese, and Chinese. At the age of thirty-six, Maha Ghosananda decided to enrich his spiritual training by venturing into the forests of southern Thailand and studying meditation. There he became a disciple of a famous meditation master named Ajaan Dhammadaro.

Dhammadaro was a renowned teacher who explained difficult concepts simply. Yet life for his disciples was not necessarily a

simple affair. They were taught to sit in meditation and concentrate
on their breath and the sensations of the body as they slowly raised
and lowered their arms. They did so all day, hour after hour, every
day, year after year. "If your mind doesn't stay with your body in the
present," Dhammadaro told them,

> all sorts of evil things—all sorts of distractions—will come
> flowing in to overwhelm it, making it fall away from its inner
> worth, just as a vacant house is sure to become a nest of spi-
> ders, termites, and all sorts of animals. If you keep your mind
> firmly with the body in the present, you'll be safe. Like a per-
> son on a big ship in the middle of a smooth sea free from wind
> and waves: everywhere you look is clear and wide open. You
> can see far. Your eyes are quiet with regard to sights, your ears
> quiet with regard to sounds, and so on with your other senses.
> Your mind is quiet with regard to thoughts of sensuality, ill
> will, and harm. The mind is in a state of seclusion, calm and at
> peace. This is where we'll let go of our sense of "me" and
> "mine," and reach the further shore, free from constraints and
> bonds.[41]

This training within Buddhism is known as mindfulness, and it
is something at which Maha Ghosananda became a supreme master. He would eventually explain the importance of mindfulness in
this way:

> *The thought manifests as the word.*
> *The word manifests as the deed.*
> *The deed develops into the habit.*
> *The habit hardens into the character.*
> *The character gives birth to the destiny.*
> *So, watch your thoughts with care*
> *And let them spring from love*
> *Born out of respect for all beings.*[42]

Four years after entering Dhammadaro's monastery, Maha
Ghosananda heard rumors of the U.S. secret bombing in Cambo-

dia, which was devastating villages and killing many civilians. The country was also being ripped apart by the ensuing bloody civil war. Though Maha Ghosananda recalls weeping for his country every day, Dhammadaro instructed him to try to prevent the suffering from destroying his rigorous training. "Having mindfulness," Dhammadaro told his followers, "is like knowing when to open and when to close your windows and doors." Maha Ghosananda could do nothing to stop the atrocities in his homeland. Instead, his teacher told him to fight the impulses toward sorrow and anger and to prepare himself for the day when he could truly be of use to his society.

For nine more years Maha Ghosananda practiced meditation in the Thai forest, secluding himself in his hut and entering into the highest stages of mental concentration. With the clarity and stability that arise from deep contemplation, Maha Ghosananda also gained profound control over his emotions. During this time, the war took hundreds of thousands of lives, the Khmer Rouge revolution and genocide raged, and Vietnam invaded and took over much of Cambodia after numerous provocations by the Khmer Rouge. Maha Ghosananda was not isolated from the events; his parents, brothers and sisters, other family members and friends were murdered, as were most of his fellow monks and nuns (as many as eighty thousand of them). Temples were desecrated and used as granaries and sties or destroyed outright, along with their precious contents of ancient religious texts, art, and objects.

When Maha Ghosananda eventually returned to Cambodia he toured the country and helped reestablish traditional Cambodian society, building temples and healing hearts. Meanwhile, battles continued between the remnants of the Khmer Rouge, anti-Vietnamese factions, the Vietnamese troops, and the Vietnamese-installed government forces.

Vietnam withdrew from Cambodia in 1989, when the pro-Vietnamese government seemed strong enough to stand on its own. With the Vietnamese out of Cambodia, the United States finally stopped supporting the Khmer Rouge. In 1991 a peace accord was signed between the different factions, including the Vietnamese-installed government, the king, the Khmer Rouge, and an opposition party. The accord provided for power sharing among the different factions with Sihanouk as the head of government until free and fair elections could take place. The United Nations sent thirteen thousand soldiers and seven thousand civilians into Cambodia to help the nation rebuild and to implement the accord.

In July 1993 elections were held and a coalition government formed between Sihanouk's son, Prince Rannaridh, and Hun Sen. The Khmer Rouge during this time became more violent and committed many atrocities against civilian and military targets. Their antipersonnel mines, which they planted increasingly in civilian areas, caused hundreds of casualties each week. But in August 1996 Ieng Sary, one of the highest ranking Khmer Rouge leaders, defected and was given a royal pardon. He was permitted to stay within his protected stronghold, surrounded by his loyal supporters, so long as he stopped fighting the government. Many other Khmer Rouge soldiers were given amnesty and absorbed back into the ranks of the Cambodian army.

In July 1997 Hun Sen staged a bloody coup and executed many of the coalition government leaders. Heavily armed soldiers loyal to Prince Rannaridh continued to fight Hun Sen's troops, as did Khmer Rouge guerrillas. This civil war continued as I flew into Phnom Penh.

I arrived in the morning and checked into a clean but no-frills hotel a few blocks from Sisowath Quay Boulevard along the Tonlé Sap River. I was eager to make some phone calls, so I ventured into the center of town. It was incredibly hot in the sun, and my shirt was quickly dampened with sweat. I made several calls to the United States, which I would later be shocked to find out cost about five dollars per minute.

The local currency is officially the *riel,* but in fact everyone uses American dollars. Getting around town is done on the back of a motorcycle, dodging the many potholes on gravel side streets. A ride usually costs from three to five dollars. As the city was completely empty of tourists and all but a few businessmen during this tumultuous time, I was a favorite target of the motorcycle drivers.

One unscrupulous driver charged me twenty dollars for a few hours of shuttling around town, whereas an air-conditioned car and driver can be rented for the entire day for that amount. Yet I never got angry in Cambodia. Not only were the people very kind and friendly, but I always had in my mind the great devastation and suffering that had occurred in this tiny country.

I noticed almost immediately that the population was young and that the city was much less crowded and much slower paced than most cities in Asia. Most of the architecture consisted of the horrendous modern concrete structures found all over Asia these days, but a number of French colonial and traditional Khmer buildings are scattered around town in various states of repair. After visiting the beautiful Royal Palace, the mustard-colored art deco Central Market, and the National Museum, I ended my first full day in Phnom Penh at the Foreign Correspondents Club of Cambodia. This is a place I would visit nearly every day in Phnom Penh, as I could send and receive e-mail and faxes downstairs before taking lunch or dinner in the comfort of the colonial-style bar on the top floor overlooking the river.

A few days after arriving I went to meet Maha Ghosananda. His temple, Wat Sampho Maes, was about twenty minutes away, along very bumpy roads that nearly unseated me from the motorcycle a number of times. I was relieved when I finally arrived and could stand with my feet on the ground once again.

I had called Maha Ghosananda's office from New Delhi, India, several weeks before and told the person who answered that I'd like to come to Cambodia and meet the Supreme Patriarch.

"Yes," the man replied in a soft voice, then went silent.

"So, will he meet with me if I come to Phnom Penh?" I inquired.

"Yes," he said.

"That's wonderful. Is he there now?" I asked, meaning whether he was in the country.

"Yes," came the reply. "I am Maha Ghosananda. Please come and visit."

As I walked into the temple grounds I at once heard the soothing murmur of chanting in the distance. I stopped briefly at the main temple and looked in at the young, saffron-robed monks. Then I proceeded to the office below a large sign reading Samdech Preah Maha Ghosananda (*samdech* is the highest title that can be given to a person who is not part of the royal family) and Dhammayietra Center for Peace and Nonviolence, his main peace organization in Cambodia. There I found Maha Ghosananda's assistant, who asked me to wait for the Supreme Patriarch. I sat back in my chair, listened to the melodious chanting in the background, and looked out into the tranquil courtyard.

A group of elderly nuns in their white shirts and with shaved heads came in and sat on the floor. They opened up a few boxes and took out large banners made of shiny yellow cloth, which they stitched in preparation for an upcoming Dhammayietra, a peace march that Maha Ghosananda has led for a number of years.

These marches, or pilgrimages, for peace began in 1992. The first march was planned as a onetime event to promote peace and reconciliation between the still-warring factions. As the fighting continued year after year, however, so too did the marches. Now nearly a decade later, the marches have come to symbolize the fearlessness and engagement of Buddhism in modern society, much as Catholicism played an important role in combating the violence in Central America in the 1980s.

One ever-present danger during the marches, in addition to bullets and shells, which killed several marchers one year, has been land mines. Cambodia is a country littered with land mines. Each faction that waged war in the country for thirty years buried mines as part of its war effort. The mines were placed near bridges, outside of villages, along riverbanks, near wells, in rice paddies, and along paths—wherever they could impede the movements of enemy troops. Not even the soldiers who buried the mines can now remember where they put most of them. As a result, exploding mines have given Cambodia the highest rate of physical disability in the world: approximately one in every two hundred people has had to have a limb amputated; more than forty thousand victims since 1979. In a largely agrarian society, where the ability to carry out hard work is essential, amputees face a particularly harsh future. Maha Ghosananda's peace marches through heavily mined areas help draw attention to this terrible problem.

At the appointed time I was shown upstairs to Maha Ghosananda's office and apartment. I was seated on a cushion in front of a low table and waited there while Maha Ghosananda finished a late morning shower. (I noticed that Cambodians tend to take frequent showers to stay fresh in the heat, and I too learned to do so during my visit.) Maha Ghosananda emerged from behind a curtain with a bright and delightful smile.

"Hello," he said.

I rose to my feet and bowed deeply, smiling all the while. When I sat again, I felt a great sense of joy, and I laughed aloud.

He started to laugh with me. "Welcome, please be comfortable. Have some tea," he said.

When he had taken his seat on a cushion on the other side of the low table, I presented him with a few gifts. I then told him, "The Dalai Lama has asked me to give you his warmest greetings."

"Yes, thank you," he said, smiling.

"I'm very impressed by the people in Cambodia," I commented. "Everyone has been very kind to me."

"Yes," he replied, "the people are very kind. Khmer people are very gentle."

"Yes, they seem so," I said. "And yet," I added a moment later, "the leaders have not been gentle at all. They have caused the deaths of so many people."

"That is because they cling to hatred, so they are fighting always," he answered in his slow and calm speech. "They are pushed by the desire for power." He laughed. "They want to become prime minister or something. They want name and fame," he said, laughing more. "And they want money. That is why they are always fighting."

"Your family was murdered by the Khmer Rouge," I noted. I watched for a reaction, but the peacefulness of his face did not change. No emotion of anger or sadness was apparent. "How have you forgiven them for their cruelty? How can anyone forgive another for such crimes?" I asked.

"We always say, 'Hatred is never pacified by hatred. Only through love is hatred pacified.' That is an eternal law. I also remind people that the wars of the heart always take longer to cool than the barrel of a gun." He paused and smiled gently. "We must heal through love," he added, "but it also takes a bit of time. We must go slowly, step by step.

Maha Ghosananda's incredible patience has been honed through a lifetime of spiritual practice. "In Cambodia, in Thailand and Laos we have the same tradition," he said. "When we are young we become a novice, when we grow up, we become a monk. Including the king. He must become a monk, according to tradition. Even if it is for a short time, to learn something about Buddhism." I knew that many young people in those countries enter the monastery as novices, gain an education, and then leave to carry on their adult lives.

"But you stayed more than a few weeks," I noted.

"Yes," he said with a chuckle, "I stayed my whole life."

"How old were you when you became a monk?"

"I was eight years old," he said.

"The Dalai Lama said he was sad when he went to the monastery as a child. He missed his parents, and he was frightened."

He laughed. "Yes, he was very young."

"Did you also miss your parents?" I questioned.

"No. The temple was very near our house. I saw them often."

"You were privileged to have amazing teachers who contributed greatly to your understanding," I said. "Your Thai teacher has some unusual practices, doesn't he?"

"Yes. He taught that every action could be felt in the hand. We concentrated on the hand. Raising and lowering the hand. All day. Concentrating on the movement of it."

"Was it a powerful practice for you?" I inquired.

"Yes. It made you always aware of the present moment. Your mind did not wander."

"Do you teach it still?"

"Yes. I myself did it for ten years in southern Thailand."

"It didn't rely on any texts?" I asked.

"No," he said with a giggle. "My teacher was illiterate. When he was a layman, before he became a monk, he had six wives. They would come to him and he could not concentrate." He laughed harder. "So he developed this technique. He taught this deep concentration on the hand movement. He is still doing it. He is over ninety years old, his eyes have become dark [blind], and he still does this meditation."

"Do you recall your first teacher?" I asked.

"Yes, it was the *Sangharaja* of Cambodia," he said. *Sangharaja* loosely translates as the king (the *raj*) or supreme leader of the Buddhist fellowship (the *sangha*), which means Maha Ghosananda's teacher was the Supreme Patriarch of Cambodia.

"That was quite a great honor for such a young monk," I noted. But he wasn't attached to the honor at all. "Do you recall what you first studied when you became a monk?" I asked.

"As a novice, we followed the Three Trainings: in morality, concentration, and wisdom," he replied. "These three things go together like the head, the body, and the limbs. And we learned the Eightfold Path," he said, slowly ticking them off: "right understanding, right thinking, right speech, right action, right livelihood, right effort, right mindfulness, and right concentration. That is the path of the Buddha, to overcome these three things: greediness, anger, and ignorance.

"All the Buddha's teachings are about 'compositing,'" he continued, meaning that all seemingly solid items are actually a composite of many tiny items. Even a person does not exist as a solid, unchanging person but is actually an everchanging composite of water and bone and chemicals and bacteria and so forth. "Everything in life follows four formulas: when *this* is existing, *that* comes to be; when *this* is not existing, *that* does not come to be; with the arising of *this, that* arises; with the ceasing of *this, that* ceases. Every moment is like that; it is the universal law. It is dharma (truth)." Maha Ghosananda was describing the Buddhist belief that all things made of many elements are ceaselessly changing and impermanent. The four formulas essentially demonstrate that everything in life is relative, interdependent, and interconnected. "Only the Buddha has escaped this cycle of life," he added. "Morality was taught to us by five precepts (or vows): to refrain from killing, to refrain from stealing, to refrain from adultery, to refrain from cheating people by word (that is, telling lies), and to refrain from intoxicants. This always goes together with compassion, right livelihood, good conduct, loving speech, mindfulness, and clear comprehension. This is Buddhist morality."

"Many people in the West say that humans are essentially violent creatures, that we are prone to violence. Do you agree?" I asked.

"No," he replied instantly. "There are four categories of man. Some are violent, and some are very peaceful. We compare these to light and darkness. Some people come from light and again enter into light. Some people come from light but go into darkness. Some people come from darkness but then go into light. And some people come from darkness and return to darkness. These are the four kinds of people."

I realized as I was recording his remarks and listening intently that I would never be able to capture the incredible peacefulness that seemed to emanate from his body. I have never witnessed another human being who seemed—how can I put it?—to glow with serenity. His skin appeared to be luminescent, and his eyes seemed so radiant with love that I found myself wishing that I could remain in his presence as long as possible.

"What decides whether a person goes into light or into darkness?" I asked.

"According to the teachings of Buddha, it is decided by mindfulness," he said. "Here! Now! This!" he proclaimed, as if making a sacred incantation, followed by the words in Pali. Then he continued, "You are here, now, in this present moment. When I am speaking, you are listening. When you are speaking, I am listening. We are nowhere else but here. And when we are here, together, you and I have to speak the truth: right speech, lovely speech, timely speech, and useful speech. When these things happen, then we are happy."

"But why," I asked, "are some people so drawn to the darkness instead of the light? Why aren't they mindful?"

"You know, we have thirty-eight blessings," he replied. "First among them is to associate with a wise man. You are who you associate with. In Buddhism this actually has many meanings: We are what we eat, we are what we drink. If we drink good things, we become healthy. If we drink poison, we will die. If you eat the world, you are the world. If you understand it, you understand the dharma." He fell silent and smiled at me lovingly.

"Did you find that these teachings were always easy for you to understand?" I asked.

He laughed. "Buddhist teachings are very easy! There is no need to make them complicated. You must do three things only: to refrain from evil, to do what is good, and to purify the mind. That is all."

I smiled. "And yet we see examples of violence even in the Buddhist countries."

"Yes. These people do not know about the essential teachings, or they do not know how to apply them. Theory, practice, and enlightenment go together. Theory without practice is useless. If you write very good things, but you do not follow the teachings, then it is useless," he said, laughing.

"Some people are more controlled by greed and anger—the defilements of the mind—so they can't even understand plain teachings," I observed.

"Yes. But if you are mindful, you are Buddha. Mindfulness is in the present. The past is already gone, the future has not yet come. You must take care of the present moment. The present moment is the mother of the future. You and I speak at this moment about peace, and in the future it will give birth to many benefits, many children, in many countries."

I wasn't certain if his words were a prayer, prophecy, or simple statement of fact, but I found them to be quite profound. I sat silently and pondered their import. He was quite content to sit silently with me.

After a time I began to laugh quite hard, and I could see through his smile that he wanted to know what I found so amusing. "Here I am," I said, "sitting before a renowned master who has trained his mind to focus on the present, on this very moment, but I want to ask you all sorts of questions about your past. It doesn't seem that the past is very interesting to you at all!"

He joined me in laughing.

"Do people ask you about the past too much?" I asked.

"The past is our teacher. It teaches us. The past is the mother of the present," he replied.

"Do you recall any particular teachings that have inspired you over the years?" I asked.

"Yes," he replied, then paused. "We always recite *Namo Buddyaa sitan*, 'Homage to the Buddha, Success!' Success is self-confidence and understanding. In Buddhism, we have no self which exists on its own; we only have truth. We take the time to investigate the reality of who we are, we don't just accept the conventional belief in self. We are here speaking, but it is not about this concept of you or me. It is about action. No *you*, no *me*. If you listen to me, that is the action of listening, not about this concept of *you*. And if we have good action, then we become good, and if we have bad action we become bad. What we must develop is the courage to avoid bad things and to do good things. We must employ compassion, esteem for right things, self-confidence, and self-acceptance. We must speak with confidence, and we must accept our role in life."

"People frequently ask me," I said, "whether we come into this life with a certain predisposition that will either add to or take away from our success. How would you respond to this issue?"

"Yes, we do have predisposition. We have seven aspects of karma: if you kill people, you will have a short life; if you do not kill people, you will have a long life. If you are angry by nature, you will become ugly; if you have a lovely nature, you will become beautiful, always smiling and happy. If you harm other beings, you will become ill. If you do not, you will be healthy. If you are jealous, you will become forlorn and friendless and no one will be able to approach you. If you are not jealous, you will have many friends everywhere. It is like you coming here," he laughed, pointing to me. "You have come for peace, and now you have many Cambodian friends. You are not a jealous person. You have the goal to help, and therefore people love you." He laughed robustly before continuing. "People have become your friends. If you are a miser, then you will become very poor. If you are not a miser, then you are very well off. If you look down upon people, are very proud and haughty, your mind will become ignorant. If you respect everybody, because the whole world is your house and all human beings are your mother, then you will become very wise. You must have *su, chi, po, li. Su* means to listen, *chi* means to think, *pu* means to question, and *li* means to record. To listen, to think, to question, and to record, these make you become very wise. If you don't have them you become ignorant. That is the law of dharma."

"It seems quite important to have a teacher like you," I said.

"Yes, you are what you associate with," he said again, smiling. "Wisdom comes from listening."

"So, what about individuals who don't believe in karma?" I asked.

"Every moment is karma, physical karma, mental karma. Karma simply means action. It is simple truth. We are speaking. If I speak good things to you, you will become happy. If I insult you, you will become unhappy."

"Yes, please don't insult me," I joked. "I would be very sad."

He laughed heartily. "Yes, it would be very bad if I insulted you! You would quickly return home!"

"What about non-Buddhists who don't believe in karma, not as it is used to mean action, but as it is often used to mean retribution for an action? Without fear that your action will come back to you, that you will be accountable, then why would you act in peaceful and loving ways?" I inquired.

"All religions copy from each other," he said. "Buddhism copied some things from Hinduism. Christianity copied from Buddhism. Islam copied from Christianity. The old ones are copied by the new ones. But we all believe that a person will receive the effect of his action. We all fear our bad action. Fear goes with wisdom. We know the result of our bad actions. And we also know that wisdom and compassion go together, like two wings on a bird. You need both in order to fly."

"How would you advise people to put wisdom into action?" I asked.

"Take care of the present moment. In speaking, be rightful, lovely, timely, and useful. This is the right verbal action. And in physical action, don't kill, don't steal, don't commit adultery. And develop compassion, right livelihood, right conduct. Create mindfulness and comprehension. Don't drink poison, so that your mind can become clear."

"It is fascinating and sad to me," I said, "that many so-called religious people seem to have poisoned minds. All religions seem to fight and to justify fighting. Christians, Muslims, even some Buddhists fight."

"This is because they do not really practice their religion," he declared. "All religions call for peace. If they are truly practiced, then they will not fight and peace will come."

"And how do we bring peace to a world that has many differing beliefs and different religions?" I asked.

"We do it step by step," he said. "Begin with yourself. A person makes a peaceful community, a peaceful community makes a peaceful state, a peaceful state makes a peaceful world. You spread peace by coming here!" he laughed. "Your book will spread it further! But the first step is to take care of the present moment. Our friendly meeting here today will make a friendship in the future. Be mindful of the body, of your breathing. Take care of your senses, in the eye, nose, mouth, and so on. Recognize that if I shout, you become unpleasant in your mind. If I bite you, you will feel unpleasant in your body. What is Buddha? Buddha is the man who can control his feelings!"

"All over the world," I said, "we see passions arise. Someone steals, someone is violent. At that moment when anger arises, what do you do?"

"You know the driver: mindfulness," he replied. "If the driver is not there, then everyone in the car is harmed. If your U.S. president is mindful, then the world can have peace. If he is not, then he can drop the atomic bomb, and the world will be harmed!"

"What does mindfulness tell the person who is angry?" I asked.

"There is good action and bad action. Mindfulness tells you that anger is fire, which will burn you and will burn those around you," he replied, sipping at his tea.

"Why is it so difficult for people to see the harm they will create for themselves when they act out of anger?" I questioned.

"They don't have mindfulness. As our friends and our mother always tell us, 'Take care.' If you take care, you will be happy. I didn't take care once while I was walking. For a moment when I was in Switzerland I didn't take care, and I fell and broke my leg." He laughed. "It is still painful now. I was in the hospital for a long time.

The pain is now my teacher," he said, laughing even harder. "It reminds me to take care, step by step, to watch every step always."

"What do you say to the general of an army who is planning to attack another country or his own people?" I posed to him. "If a person's mind is already focused on power and riches, how can we persuade such a person to focus on virtue?"

"The Buddha dealt with this very situation," he replied. "His family was fighting over water to build a rice field. He went to them and told them, 'If you make war, there will be no end to it. Those who claim victory will be met with hatred by those who lost. Those who won will also feel hatred toward the ones who lost. Hatred itself will kill you. There is no need for another enemy. Hatred will kill you.'"

"And it will kill you through your thoughts?" I questioned.

"Yes. It will kill you through your thoughts. You will have no peace."

"Do you believe that the world is understanding this principle more and more? Are we growing in awareness?" I asked.

"Yes," he said. "Many people understand. Like you."

"You have said that in Thailand, when you heard the news of Cambodia, your teacher told you to concentrate on your meditation," I noted.

"Yes. We thought about the killing, but the dead were in the past. And we thought about the future, but it wasn't time for us to be able to do anything. We took care of the present, so we stopped crying. We went back to our breath; breathing is never in the past or the future."

"So, there is no such thing as sorrow in the present moment?" I asked slowly as the truth of it was seeping into my mind.

"No. Sorrow is about regret of the past or fear of the future. How can there be sorrow in the present moment?"

"This is very clear to me now, as never before," I said. "There is also absolute equality in the present moment, isn't there? Titles and praise and pomp mean nothing at all in the present."

"Yes. Everyone is the same. Everyone is equal. If you don't breathe, you die. We are all equal in that fact."

"Master, what would you most like people to know about your work?" I asked, having a sip of the tea that his assistant put before me.

He smiled and looked into my eyes. "We want them to know that we want peace for all of them," he said succinctly. Coming from someone else (and certainly from a politician), these words might have seemed trite. But from this man they were sincere.

I waited for him to add something more, but he didn't. Having answered my question, he was content to sit in silence. "But," I pressed, "is there anything specific about the work that you do that you would like to bring up? How people might help you?"

"Yeah," he replied, smiling broadly, "we tell them to be mindful in every moment, in every step, according to this book, *Step by Step*." The book was his gift to the world. In it he declares, "Peace is a path that is chosen consciously. It is not aimless wandering but a step-by-step journey." We reach it by following the path of compassion.

> Human rights begin when each man becomes a brother and each woman becomes a sister, when we honestly care for each other. Then Cambodians will help Jews, and Jews will help Africans, and Africans will help others. We will all become servants for each other's rights. . . . When we accept that we are part of a great human family—that every man and every woman has the nature of Buddha, Allah, and Christ—then we will sit, talk, make peace, and bring humankind to its fullest flowering.[43]

"And what is the one thing you would most like people to know about Cambodia?" I asked.

"The one thing I want people to know about Cambodia, I think, is about our desire for peace. And that a peaceful Cambodia will make a peaceful world."

"And what is the one thing that you most want people to know about you personally?"

He smiled. "What I want people to know about me is that I am," he paused and laughed, "a monk!"

"Just that you are a monk?" I questioned.

"Yes, just that," he replied, sipping his tea. A few moments later he added, "In Buddhism being a monk means that you are peaceful, that you have no enemy, and that you are fearless. That is the meaning of being a monk."

During my days I traveled around the city and beyond. I was particularly delighted to go to Siem Reap and to visit the ruins of Angkor. Angkor Wat is well known, but it is just one of several important sites within the larger Angkor complex. Angkor Wat was constructed as a homage to Vishnu, its massive structure symbolizing a mythological mountain. Angkor Thom, the second most grand temple in the area, was a large shrine based on Buddhism.

I knew that the ruins symbolized both the good and the bad forces in humankind. The sheer scale and the powerful architecture of the buildings inspired my imagination about the construction of cities that could reflect our artistic, spiritual proclivities. Yet I also know that the structures were built by conscripted labor, maintained by onerous taxes, and overburdened the local environment. If Cambodia can sustain peace, however, Angkor Wat can be used to bring in tourist dollars and to promote self-esteem, both of which are much needed if Cambodia is going to continue to rebuild itself.

It was so hot, even in the early mornings, that stepping no more than twenty feet from the car caused my shirt to become soaked with sweat. By the time I would reach the top of ancient stone stairways in the ruins, even my jeans would be wet with sweat. I couldn't imagine having built and maintained these magnificent stone temples in such heat. Neither could I imagine fighting in combat gear in such conditions. I could understand, as Maha Ghosananda said, that we can have compassion even for the Khmer Rouge, who have become worn out from the fighting. The life of a soldier, I reflected, must be dreadful, and the average soldier will receive comparatively little benefit from his fighting.

Back in the town I found a street café with decent food and cold drinks. I ended up going there nearly every day in the late afternoon. At around that time, four or five Westerners would arrive who worked for the demining operations. They played pool and drank beer and, I imagine, tried to forget about the stress of the day. I couldn't help but remember how Maha Ghosananda had said at one point that we can remove the land mines in the earth but still have no peace. "Land mines in the ground start from land mines in our mind," he had said. "We must uproot the land mines in our mind as well."

One evening I hired a motorcycle driver to take me to a nearby roadside restaurant. On the other side of a small bridge, along a quiet part of the bumpy road, a soldier jumped out and lifted his automatic rifle toward us. He motioned for us to pull over and shouted at us to get off the motorcycle. I wanted to tell my driver to get us the hell out of there, but I realized that there was no way we could have outrun the bullets should the soldier start shooting. It was best to obey his orders.

The soldier seemed agitated and several times thrust the barrel of his gun against my driver and also against my chest. He was clearly trying to make us respect his authority. He patted us down—to check for weapons, I presume—and then demanded that we give him some money as a "toll" for using the street that he was guarding against bandits and rebels. I gave him five dollars and my driver gave him a cigarette. What was odd to me, even at that time, was that I was neither afraid nor angry. I simply went along with the situation, surrendering to the fact that I would have to meet his demands and not doing anything to escalate the matter. The benefit was not only that nothing bad happened, but also that I was able to enjoy my meal and not lose any sleep that night.

Back in Phnom Penh, at dinner one evening a local Khmer man sat at a couch next to me and said hello. He had once lived in the United States but came back to try his hand at business in Phnom Penh. He had hoped to be a consultant for Western businesses trying to get into the Cambodian market, but between the economic slump in Asia and the continued fighting in Cambodia, there wasn't much of a market. He said that he had seen me in the Foreign Correspondents Club several times and asked what I was doing in Cambodia, especially since there was fighting recently in the capital. When I told him about my book, he simply said that Cambodia had a long way to go to rebuild what the Khmer Rouge had destroyed.

"Do you care who is in power?" I asked him.

"No, not really," he replied, "just as long as there is an end to the fighting and there is some stability. Without it, we can't hope to attract businesses, and we won't have much of a future. Hun Sen is acceptable, just as long as there is stability."

It took quite a lot of coaxing over the next few times that I ran into him, but he finally opened up to me one night and told me about his experience in 1975 when the Khmer Rouge seized power.

"We used to live in a house over there," he said, pointing to the east. "When the Khmer Rouge entered Phnom Penh they announced on loudspeakers that we had to leave our houses. They told us that they had to search every house for weapons and rebels, and then they would let us come back. We had no reason to doubt them, but we had no choice. So we left. We weren't allow to take anything with us. We just left everything we owned in the house."

"Where were you supposed to go?" I asked.

"They just told us to march along a road. When we reached somewhere, they would give us new orders to march somewhere else."

"Did they feed you or give you water?" I asked.

"No. We had to fend for ourselves. The road was full of people who died along the way. Some were shot for disobeying or for carrying personal possessions or something like that."

"Your whole family was together?" I questioned.

"Oh, no. We were split up. My mother and father and brothers and sisters were all split up. I was on my own."

I shook my head, imagining a boy of about nine or ten years old, in the chaos, split from his family. He went on to tell me a bit about the conditions under which he lived, which he found almost too disturbing to recount. After the Vietnamese toppled the Khmer Rouge, he made his way back to Phnom Penh. Finally, an international aid organization helped him reunite with the sole surviving member of his family, his older sister.

It is one thing to read about such stories in a book, but it really hits home when you look someone in the eyes and hear their tale of the Khmer Rouge. It was hard for me to sleep that night as my mind was disturbed by the unfairness and senselessness of it all.

A few days later I made my way to visit Maha Ghosananda again.

"I've spent a lot of time talking with people in Cambodia, and it seems that people still have a lot of sadness and a lot of anger. Many Cambodians have incredible anger toward the Vietnamese, and incredible anger toward the Khmer Rouge," I observed. "How important is forgiveness in peacemaking?"

He reminded me of something he had said during our last discussion. "There is an eternal law, and that law is: hatred can never cease by hatred; hatred can only cease by compassion, by loving-kindness. That is an eternal law of the universe."

"I understand this. I try to live by this principle. But how do you convince other people that it is important to overcome hatred—even hatred toward Pol Pot and the Khmer Rouge, for example? How can it be done?"

"If they have hatred, they harm themselves first," he replied. "It is like if you drink blood, then you will spoil your mouth. You will taste nothing but blood. So holding onto your anger harms you first. Then, if you are angry with Pol Pot, and you spit at him, he suffers also. You give your own suffering to other people."

"But do you have *compassion* for Pol Pot, after everything he has done?" I asked.

"Yes," he replied without hesitation. "If we are compassionate, then our mind becomes peaceful. This is the only way to have true peace in our mind. Then, when we have peace in our mind, our neighbor will also be peaceful. It is contagious. Everything is like a tape recorder. We speak here into this microphone, and it is recorded there on the tape. Each person has six tape recorders. One is the eye, the second is the ear, the third one is the nose, the fourth is the tongue, the fifth is the body, and the last one is the mind. Our whole personality records every moment. If we record peace, we play back peace."

For Maha Ghosananda, the potential for goodness is never extinguished, though in the wicked it must be replanted. The only method for replanting goodness is loving-kindness.

"I know we discussed this last time, but *how* do we get this message across to people, that they must give up their hatred and have compassion?" I asked.

"Just tell them!" he said plainly. "I will tell you, and you spread this truth to them!" he said, smiling. "It is really very simple. If they have hatred, they harm themselves first. Then they will harm their own family. And their own family will harm the community. And the community will harm the country. And the country will harm the world. Therefore, it spreads like a broadcasting station. You know when you throw a stone into the water, there are waves like this," he said, spreading his arms wider and wider. "Everything has waves. In the radio station, there are waves. In our mind also there are waves, mental waves. If we have good mental waves, then we broadcast them and they touch the heart of all the people, and then they feel happy."

"Are you confident that the stone of peace has gone into the water now? Is it making waves in Cambodia?" I asked.

"Oh, yes. Yes. It is making waves right now," he said with a big smile.

"So, you feel optimistic about peace in Cambodia?" I asked.

"Buddhism is neither optimistic nor pessimistic," he responded. "It is realistic. *Dharma* means truth. The truth is realistic. People are fighting because they still have hatred, they are against each other. But we tell them that everything is changing every moment. Breathing in changes into breathing out. Every moment is like that. Life will change into death. That is the first teaching of the Buddha—impermanence. Because of impermanence we suffer. We cannot stop things from changing. And we cannot control suffering because we are ultimately not permanent ourselves. We are therefore selfless. We have no permanent self. We are only a composite. Our own body is composed of elements: air element, water element, earth element, and also element of consciousness, element of space. Everything changes. Even hatred will change."

"And you are convinced that Cambodia, and indeed the world, will one day have peace?" I questioned.

"Yes. We try!" he said, laughing. "We try! You know, peace is like everything else. Like eating. You have to eat every day. Making peace must be done every day. It is like walking too. You have to make every step. If you forget a step, then you will fall down, you will fail."

"In 1979, when you went to Sakeo Camp, how did you know that you would not be killed?" I wondered.

"The Khmer Rouge also wanted peace," he replied. "They had suffered so much. They were fighting so much they could not even sleep. They had to hide themselves out of fear of being killed. So I knew that they were tired of fighting," he said, giggling.

"Every day I read in the papers that the king seems very depressed, very sad," I observed.

Maha Ghosananda laughed. "Yes, because he wants peace," he said.

"You seem to have such optimism and happiness. Even your face, your body, seems to shine with happiness. What advice would you give to the king and to others who feel very depressed about the lack of peace?" I asked.

"We always remind the king to be in the present. He always thinks about the future, he always regrets the past, then he suffers. If he stays in the present moment, then he will be happy. Life is in the present moment. Breathing in, present moment, breathing out, present moment. We cannot breathe in the past, we cannot breathe in the future. Only here and now we can breathe. We always say, take care of the present moment. The present moment is the mother of the future. Take care of the mother, then the mother will take care of the children."

"Your peace marches are aimed at education and participation, at direct action. Do you think that you've accomplished—that the whole organization has accomplished—good things with the peace marches?"

"Yes. If you want peace for your country and for the whole world, you must be peaceful yourself." In his words was a slightly concealed gem: whether the good action has a discernable accomplishment is not the most important point. Aligning oneself with goodness is all important, and it is already the highest accomplishment.

"And so the marches are like the waves of peace going out?" I asked.

"Yeah. You want good speech, good asking and good replying now, then you have to be peaceful yourself. Then I also become peaceful, relying on your peacefulness.

"We do not blame the people. The dharma of the Buddha is the truth of cause and condition. We always ask ourselves, what are the cause and condition of fighting? The cause and the condition of fighting each other are greediness, anger, and ignorance." He pointed to a Tibetan painting hanging on the wall depicting the Wheel of Life with its cycle of birth, death, rebirth. At the center of the wheel were the three poisons, depicted as three animals. "The pig is ignorance, always eating and sleeping. The cobra, the snake, that represents hatred. And the rooster represents lust, that is, greediness. These are the three conditions in our own mind which make us fight each other. If we have morality, concentration, and wisdom, then we will kill these negative conditions. Then we will have peace for ourselves, for our families, for our country, and for the whole world."

"Do you have a message for all the religions about how we can work together better?" I asked.

"Yes. If we want to work together better, we must have four feet to stand," he said, pointing to the table. "The first one is loving-kindness (*metta*). The second one is compassion (*karuna*). The third one is joy (*mundita*). The last one is equanimity (*upekkha*)."

"And this is something all religions can agree upon?" I asked.

"Yes. Those are the faces of God. The *visages de Dieu,* we say in French. We can all agree on these things."

"Living in peace seems to be narrowly defined by many people. Some say it simply means to stop fighting one another. Others say it also means taking care of our physical environment," I said.

"Yes. We are elements, inner element and outer element. This inner element and outer element depend on each other. The dharma of the Buddha is interdependent. We depend on each other."

"Protecting the forests and protecting the wild animals then also protects us. Is that what you mean?" I asked.

"Yes. If we protect the world, we protect ourselves. If we harm the world, we harm ourselves. We are in the world. We are in the boat. We are in the same boat. Therefore, we must take care of the boat."

"Anything else you would like to add? Anything you would like people to know?" I wondered.

"Yes. I always tell them to take care of themselves." He pointed to me and looked deeply into my eyes, smiling lovingly. "If I tell you to take care of yourself, then you will take care of the whole world. Now you broadcast this to the whole world, then they will listen to you and become peaceful."

The fact that the world needs to be taken care of is indisputable. As we shall see in the coming pages, we are facing an enormous environmental crisis that threatens our peace and well-being. Fortunately, there is hope, as evidenced by the next extraordinary peacemaker I encountered.

Seven

JANE GOODALL AND THE FIGHT FOR THE PLANET

In downtown San Francisco I used to see a billboard every day on my way to work, at lunch, and on coffee breaks. Despite having looked at it often, each time I found something new and interesting about it. It was a brilliant black-and-white photograph of a woman standing in profile, dressed in khaki shorts, in a jungle setting. Her long blond hair was pulled back in a ponytail, partially radiant from the sunlight that filtered through the vegetation. She stood motionless, her right arm tucked gently behind her back in a gesture of purposeful defenselessness, as if to say, "I will do you no harm." Her head was turned ever so slightly toward the camera. The tenderness of her gaze, however, was not meant for us. She was looking downward at a small creature at her feet. A chimpanzee, who only half faced her, was reaching up toward her with a long extended arm, extended hand, extended fingertips delicately lifting her shirttail, peering inquisitively at the strange garments.

The advertisement was for a computer company beckoning us to "think different." It was, of course, intended to highlight the fact that the woman pictured—Dr. Jane Goodall—became world renowned for bucking the norm and thinking differently.

Yet I also saw an unusual, alluring subtlety in the picture that instilled in me thoughts of peace and natural beauty. Jane Goodall's expression of softness and delight reminded me of Mary in

Leonardo da Vinci's *Madonna Litta* or in Raphael's *La Belle Jardinière*. There was, I sensed, a deep spirituality in her—a true union between her heart and the splendor of the natural world.

I realized during the writing of this book that I had yet to pay adequate attention to a topic that I hold in high importance: the connection between nature and peace. After all, it was in a beautiful natural setting that I conceived of this book in the first place. Our natural settings are our places of retreat, our refuge, our connection with something greater than ourselves, and when we lose them, we necessarily lose our sense of tranquility; we lose the places where we can shed our grief, regain our strength, and stimulate our imagination.

I also had explored with several of the peacemakers the topic of our natural human inclination toward violence. It dawned on me one day that there was one person who could address the environmental connection with peace and with human nature, and that person I had seen every day on that giant billboard in downtown San Francisco. I dispatched a message to the Jane Goodall Institute and heard back promptly that they would try to arrange a meeting with Dr. Goodall at the earliest possible opportunity.

The relationship between greed and violence is fairly well established in most people's minds. We know that beneath violence there always lies a strong dose of greed. When we greedily seek power, prestige, land, wealth, and goods of all sorts, we are eventually brought into competition with other people who are seeking the same. When we are greedily pursuing our self-interests or limited national interests, we are not being mindful of the consequences of our pursuits. Being mindful, we understand that only compromise can lead to harmony, and only compassion can preserve it.

I think greed is also at work in our treatment of the environment. How we treat our environment is an enormously important indicator of our commitment to fairness and the foundations of peace. It would be disingenuous to say that we can have peace in our hearts if we gleefully destroy natural settings and harm animals for our own comfort and enjoyment. It should never be thrilling, I believe, to cut down forests, dry up rivers, plow up prairies, or slaughter animals needlessly. Even when development makes some environmental degradation necessary, it should be done with great thought, care, and respect. In short, if we want to value peace, we must value life in all its abundant forms.

The concept of stewardship is quite important here. We have in fact taken on the role of stewards for most of nature. We have made weapons that can destroy the entire planet as we know it. We have the power to kill virtually all the animals. We can poison just about any land or waterway we wish. With this enormous power, we are necessarily forced to choose between right action and wrong, between sound decisions and ill-advised ones.

"The great dilemma of environmental reasoning," the eminent Harvard biologist Edward O. Wilson concludes, "stems from [the] conflict between short-term and long-term values."[1] Wilson's remark reminds me of something I learned during my youth while taking long walks in the forest with my grandmother, Winona. She taught me to appreciate nature and told me about my American Indian ancestors who lived in balance with their surroundings. The forests in which we walked once provided food and materials to the Iroquois, the ancient nation that so impressed George Washington and the founding fathers with their federation of tribes and system of governance. The Iroquois tribes managed to stop their traditional rivalries and bury their hatchets in a deep chasm in the earth. Then the messenger of the Chief of the Sky Spirits spoke to them: "I charge you never to disagree seriously among yourselves," he said. "If you do, you might cause the loss of any rights of your grandchildren, or reduce them to poverty and shame. Your skin must be seven hands thick to stand for what is right in your heart. Exercise great patience and goodwill toward each other in your deliberations. . . . Cultivate good feelings of friendship, love, and honor for each other always."[2]

What he meant by skin that is seven hands thick is that in any undertaking we should consider the effect of our action on those who will live seven generations from now. How will our treatment of the environment affect those people yet to come? What kind of planet will we leave for them?

Unfortunately, for centuries we have paid too little attention to the long-term effects of our actions. We have viewed nature and its resources as virtually limitless and indestructible, dumping count-less tons of toxic chemicals into our air and waterways, clear-cutting ancient forests, overusing grasslands until they are turned to deserts, wiping out entire species, and other such acts of severe degradation.

Even today, when we are reminded continually by scientists that our habits are destroying large parts of our environment, most soci-eties continue to act as if it will all sort itself out somehow—that Mother Nature will persevere and continue to host billions of peo-ple without major upheaval. This attitude threatens to cause widespread human and animal suffering through deprivation, dis-ease, and social instability. We already see these outcomes in many parts of the world.

So how bad is the environmental crisis really, and what does this have to do with the future of peace? These are important questions that we must consider. Some people have argued that the environ-mental crisis is overstated by scientists and activists. This may be partially true. Some few well-intended individuals may overstate the case, predicting nothing but gloom and the inevitable end of our species. The impulse to do so is certainly understandable. Our envi-ronmental problems at times seem insurmountable and downright discouraging. I sometimes have to put down what I'm reading and remind myself that forests do still exist and water still flows and my next breath probably won't be laden with so much pollution that it will be my last. There is indeed reason for hope, as we will discuss later. Nature is resilient, as resilient as the human spirit itself, and we can't give up on either.

Yet the crisis is real and it requires our immediate attention and action. The sky may not be falling, but it certainly is becoming destructively polluted and warm. As Edward O. Wilson puts it, "Earth's capacity to support our species is approaching the limit."[3] He points out that if everyone in the world consumed resources at the present U.S. levels with existing technology, it "would require four more planet Earths." To point out the obvious, we don't have four more planet Earths at our disposal. And even if we did, would it be wise to continue the trend of growth and consumption until we depleted those planets as well? Or instead is it time to make the changes necessary to protect the quality of life for current and future generations?

In 1997 Al Gore, then vice president, addressed the issue of the environment, appealing not to a moral duty to act more responsibly, but rather to pragmatic concerns. "Environmental problems such as global climate change, ozone depletion, ocean and air pollution, and resource degradation—compounded by an expanding world population—respect no border and threaten the health, prosperity, and jobs of all Americans," he said. "All the missiles and artillery in our arsenal," he continued, "will not be able to protect our people from rising sea levels, poisoned air, or foods laced with pesticides. Our efforts to promote democracy, free trade, and stability in the world will fall short unless people have a livable environment."[4]

Gore's message that one day the environmental crisis will affect Americans' health and wealth has largely fallen on deaf ears. The problem is that few people in the highly developed nations have suffered physically from the effects of environmental degradation. The issue is to them, therefore, chiefly theoretical. New York City recently entered a period of critical drought, but everyone expected that to end with more rainfall or by diverting water from elsewhere; and meanwhile toilets still flushed, dishwashers still ran, and people could always buy Evian at the corner store. In California there was a shortage of energy in the winter of 2001, forcing rolling blackouts for a few hours at a time. Many angry consumers complained that the government had done too little to build new power plants instead of addressing the more fundamental concern that we are using too much energy in the first place. Yet the wealth of the state made it rather painless (if incredibly costly) to purchase more power and bring new plants on-line, averting the crisis for the time being.

The situation is entirely different for the billions of people immediately dependent upon natural resources for their well-being. Two and a half billion people, for instance, must collect and burn wood, charcoal, grasses, or cow dung to cook their food and heat their homes. In fact, half the world's inhabitants are directly dependent on local natural resources to sustain their lives.

We can begin to understand our environmental problems by considering the availability and use of fresh water, the most rudimentary substance necessary for life. "Water may be the resource that defines the limits of sustainable development," the United Nations notes. "It has no substitute, and the balance between humanity's demands and the quantity available is already precarious."[5] Global population tripled over the last hundred years, but water use grew sevenfold during the same period.

While it is essential for humans to have water, only about 3 percent of all the water on Earth is fresh water, and only 0.5 percent of that amount is available to humans as ground or surface water. Yet most of us in highly developed countries enjoy baths and long showers; easily wash dishes, clothes, and cars; and repeatedly flush our toilets—all with drinkable water. More than 1.1 billion people do not have access to clean drinking water, and from 2 to 3 billion people have inadequate sanitation facilities.[6]

People living in thirty-one countries have limited or very scarce water at their disposal. Of China's 617 cities, for example, 300 face water shortages. In just a couple of years, it is predicted that 3 billion people in forty-eight countries will have inadequate water supplies; that figure rises to 45 percent of the global population (4.2 billion people) by the year 2050.[7]

While it is important for individuals to conserve water, most of our fresh water is going not to households but to fields and factories. Worldwide, 92 percent of freshwater consumption is for agriculture and industry. Agriculture globally comprises 69 percent of all freshwater consumption, while commerce and industry comprises 23 percent.[8] An increasing world population needs more food and more economic opportunities, both of which rely on freshwater supplies.

Many countries exacerbate water shortage, mismanaging their water use. It is especially troubling that these countries are drawing down and depleting local aquifers. In short, more water is drawn from the ground reserves than is replenished by natural processes. Ground reserves (called the "water tables") in China, Latin America, and Southeast Asia are declining at rapid rates. Under some of the major grain-producing areas in northern China, for example, the water table is falling at a rate of five feet per year. In India water tables are falling an average of three to ten feet per year.[9] It is important to note that whereas river water can be replenished in only twenty days, the average recycling time for groundwater is fourteen hundred years. "So when we pump out groundwater," researcher Payal Sampat notes, "we're effectively removing it from aquifers for generations to come. It may evaporate and return to the atmosphere quickly enough, but the resulting rainfall (most of which falls back into the oceans) may take centuries to recharge the aquifers once they've been depleted."[10]

Continued consumption will mean that aquifers will not be replenished and severe shortages may cause untold hardships, including the loss of vital food crops. The International Water Management Institute estimates that India's grain harvest, for instance, could be reduced by up to one-fourth as a result of aquifer depletion; meanwhile, the number of mouths to feed will continue to grow.

In developing countries nearly all of the sewage, and the majority of industrial waste, is dumped untreated into surface water, thereby contaminating the water supply. Of China's fifty thousand kilometers of major rivers, 80 percent are so polluted that they no longer support fish. In Russia, less than half the population has access to clean drinking water because of dumping of waste into water supplies. Industrial waste dumped into rivers and lakes is either inadequately treated or not treated at all. As a result, life expectancies for people living around the deltas of the Ob and Yenisey Rivers, for instance, have fallen by sixteen years since 1961 and are twenty-five years below the Russian average. In richer countries, we see contamination of surface water supplies from acid rain and from chemical fertilizer, manure, and pesticide runoff. Fortunately for those in the richer countries, the water can be filtered and treated, although at considerable expense.[11]

What is perhaps more alarming, however, is the contamination not of surface water, but of groundwater. Payal Sampat points out that only 1 percent of the water in the Mississippi River system exists in the river that flows into the Gulf of Mexico; the rest lies beneath the riverbed locked in the rock and sand. The same is true all over the world. Ninety-seven percent of all the planet's available fresh water is stored in aquifers. Unfortunately, studies around the world show that nitrate pollution in aquifers (nitrates are used to boost crop yields) is particularly severe in places where high population demands high food productivity.[12] In Beijing and other northern counties in China, nitrates were found to be five times higher than the World Health Organization standards, and in some places they were thirty times higher. In India, the Central Pollution Control Board surveyed twenty-two major industrial areas and found that groundwater in every one of them was undrinkable due to contaminants.

Lest we condemn the developing nations without appreciating the difficulties in promoting industry while at the same time maintaining clean water supplies, we should acknowledge that the United States also pollutes its groundwater supplies. Even in the environmentally conscious San Francisco Bay Area, the Environmental Protection Agency (EPA) noted that Silicon Valley had the highest concentration of federally mandated cleanup sites in the entire country: twenty-eight hazardous waste sites in a fifteen-mile radius, all of which were affecting Bay Area groundwater.[13]

It will surprise many people to learn that the majority of the United States' liquid hazardous waste—some 9 billion gallons of it—is pumped untreated deep into the ground. The EPA estimates there are 400,000 ground wells into which billions of tons of wastes (both hazardous and nonhazardous) are injected as a less costly method than treating the wastes. Though the hazardous wastes are injected below water supplies, and therefore declared safe by the EPA, some of these wastes in fact have been found in aquifers supplying water for parts of Florida, Texas, Ohio, and Oklahoma.[14] No one can say exactly what effect billions and billions of gallons of wastes deep in our earth will have in generations to come. This would suggest, to me, that we should bear the cost of treating the waste to make it as safe as possible.

It is also surprising, I think, to learn from the Environmental Protection Agency that "leaking underground tanks are a potentially large groundwater pollution problem. And no one is really sure how large the problem will be" because "it's been estimated that the locations of only *half* of all the underground storage tanks are known in the U.S." Nevertheless, the EPA knows of 705,000 underground storage tank systems (USTs) in the United States storing petroleum or hazardous substances that can harm the environment and human health if the tanks release their stored contents. From these USTs, over 418,000 hazardous releases were confirmed; 268,000 have been cleaned up, and 150,000 sites are remaining to be cleaned up. At least 18,000 of these leaks contaminated the groundwater. In Texas alone, 88 percent of the counties had leaky USTs that affected or may have affected every major and minor aquifer in the state.[15]

The point is, the world's water supply is a critical issue, and it threatens to get much more acute. We simply must change our habits if we are to protect our vital supplies of water. We see a similarly worrisome picture when it comes to soil. Most of us take soil for granted. Yet soil is an extremely thin layer, geologically speaking, of disintegrated rock material and decomposed vegetation. If the soil is fertile, it can support plant growth. In many places, though, the soil is of poor quality. That's why fertile soil is so precious and sought after. Even in areas with fertile soil, agriculture naturally depletes the soil of nutrients, which the plants use to grow, so fields must be fertilized to replenish their nutrients. (Unfortunately, fertilizer, as noted above, can run off from fields and contaminate water supplies.)

Soil erosion and degradation, often caused by mechanized farming techniques and destruction of forests, rob us of from five to seven million hectares of farmland each year. This can have a profound effect on a country-by-country basis. In the Sudan, for example, an estimated seventeen million hectares of arable land—almost half the country's potential arable land—has lost its topsoil. Worldwide, but mostly in the developing countries, land degradation endangers the livelihoods of at least one billion farmers and ranchers. Soil loss concomitant with population growth and the need for more food poses a serious problem that we must redress.[16]

Our forests are also in terrible decline. It is clear from many studies and satellite maps that forest destruction is a global phenomenon. Four-fifths of the Earth's original forests have been wiped out. Seventy-six countries assessed in one study have lost all of their frontier forest. There are no remaining frontier forests in the Middle East or the Mediterranean. Asia has lost 95 percent of its frontier forests, and those that remain are under threat. Except for the Congo Basin, Africa's frontier forests have largely been destroyed.[17]

Eleven countries, including Finland, Sweden, Vietnam, Guatemala, Nigeria, and Thailand, are on the verge of losing their frontier forest altogether. These countries have no more than 5 percent of their original forest as frontier, the entirety of which is threatened. The United States would be included in this list of countries "on the verge" if not for the expansive boreal forests of Alaska; the continental United States has little remaining frontier forest. Roughly 70 percent of the world's remaining frontier forests are located in just three countries: Canada, Brazil, and Russia. It so happens that these forests are under enormous risk due chiefly to logging, land conversion, and mining. In the Canadian province of British Columbia, for example, two-thirds of its coastal rain forest—"one of Earth's biologically richest temperate ecosystems"—has been severely degraded by logging and development.[18] The rest of the world's forests are fragmented and degraded. "Of the forests that do remain standing," the World Resources Institute reports, "the vast majority are no more than small or highly disturbed pieces of the fully functioning ecosystems they once were."[19]

Trees are felled at an alarming rate: *every minute* about twenty-six hectares of forest (the size of thirty-seven football fields) are lost. Even in the United States 1,000 acres a day are deforested. In the rain forests, two thousand trees are cut down *every minute*. Tropical forests are now disappearing worldwide at the rate of almost 42.5 million acres a year. Nearly another 60 million acres are seriously degraded.

The rate of destruction is alarming. In the ten-year period from 1980 through 1990, Jamaica lost 53 percent of its forests, Bangladesh lost 33 percent, Thailand lost 29 percent, the Dominican Republic 25 percent, and Mexico, Burma, and Tanzania each lost 12 percent. Worldwide, forest destruction during the 1980s took place at a rate 50 percent greater than in the 1970s. Though some believe the rate of destruction has slowed, deforestation is still by all accounts a severe problem. Between 1990 and 1995, 65.1 million hectares (160 million acres) of forests were lost in developing countries alone.[20]

Often in our past the felling of forests signaled progress. New farms and towns were created from the converted land, and timber allowed the rapid construction of houses, shops, and factories. Today we could theoretically switch from timber to other building materials. So why is deforestation such a concern? Because beyond their aesthetic value, forests are essential in the web of life. Almost all of the water that we need, according to the *Columbia Encyclopedia,* "ultimately feeds from forest rivers and lakes and from forest-derived water tables." In addition, forests absorb the carbon dioxide that we continually dump into the atmosphere, and they also provide an essential, irreplaceable supply of both oxygen and soil nutrients. Moreover, the earth's temperature and humidity are both destabilized by a loss of forests.

Still, many people downplay or ignore the effect of environmental degradation on our lives. They say that the Earth can provide, that it will adapt, that it will compensate for our actions. In contrast to this view, there is ample evidence that environmental degradation negatively affects hundreds of millions of people around the world. "In fact," UN secretary-general Kofi Annan notes, "the absence of a safe water supply contributes to an estimated 80 percent of disease and death in the developing world."[21]

A report by the United Nations Research Institute for Social Development provides a pithy summary of this and other health and welfare threats posed by environmental degradation:

> *Water pollution and water scarcity:* More than two million deaths and billions of illnesses a year are attributable to water pollution; water scarcity compounds these health problems. Productivity is affected by the costs of providing safe water, by constraints on economic activity caused by water shortages, and by the adverse effects of water pollution and shortages on other environmental resources (for instance, declining fisheries and aquifer depletion leading to irreversible compaction).
>
> *Air pollution:* Urban air pollution is responsible for 300,000 to 700,000 deaths annually and creates chronic health problems

for many more people; in addition, 400 million to 700 million people, primarily women and children in poor rural areas, are affected by smoky indoor air. Restrictions on vehicles and industrial activity during critical periods affect productivity, as does the effect of acid rain on forests and water bodies.

Solid and hazardous wastes: Diseases are spread by uncollected garbage and blocked drains; the health risks from hazardous wastes are typically more localized but often acute. Wastes affect productivity through the pollution of groundwater resources.

Soil degradation: Depleted soils increase the risks of malnutrition for farmers. Productivity losses on tropical soils are estimated to be in the range of 0.5–1.5 percent of GNP, while secondary productivity losses are due to siltation of reservoirs, transportation channels, and other hydrologic investments.

Deforestation: Death and disease can result from the localized flooding caused by deforestation. Loss of sustainable logging potential and of erosion prevention, watershed stability, and carbon sequestration provided by forests are among the productivity impacts of deforestation.

Loss of biodiversity: The extinction of plant and animal species will potentially affect the development of new drugs; it will reduce ecosystem adaptability and lead to the loss of genetic resources.

Atmospheric changes: Ozone depletion is responsible for perhaps 300,000 additional cases of skin cancer a year and 1.7 million cases of cataracts. Global warming may lead to a shift in vector-borne diseases and increase the risk of climatic natural disasters. Productivity impacts may include sea-rise damage to coastal investments, regional changes in agricultural productivity, and disruption of the marine food chain.[22]

Reports also show that people whose livelihoods depend on the environment cannot easily adjust to environmental degradation. According to the World Bank, "The roughly 2.8 billion poor and near-poor people in the world—those living on less than $2 a day—are disproportionately affected by these bad environmental conditions. They are particularly vulnerable to shocks from environmental change and natural catastrophes."[23] In the Brazilian Amazon region, for example, those people depending on the health of the environment for their livelihood were forced into low-paying mining and urban development when the environment was degraded. These jobs proved to be temporary, leaving no sustainable means for making a living.

As the UN report above points out, while we are depleting our freshwater supplies, our soil, and our forests, and polluting our air, we are destroying our planet's biodiversity. Globally, we have discovered and named only between 1.5 and 1.8 million species, although it is estimated there are anywhere from 3.6 million to 100 million species. "The truth is," says Edward O. Wilson, "that we have only begun to explore life on Earth." Our newfound interest in conservation, he concludes, "has generally come too little too late to save the most vulnerable of life forms."[24]

We can lay out all kinds of arguments for the protection of species. Some may contain cures for humankind's most deadly diseases, others may be useful in manufacturing, still others may show us incredible new ways of sustaining and improving our lives. It is quite possible that we have already eliminated plants that could have led to a cure for AIDS, cancer, heart disease, or a host of other afflictions. Many species have been destroyed before even being found, and we'll never get to study their potential benefits to us. We've been given millions of lottery tickets, and we're throwing them away before checking to see if they have the winning numbers.

So what effect does environmental degradation have on peace? The link between the two has received inadequate attention, in my opinion, although it was clearly noted in 1987 by the World Commission on Environment and Development, which said, "Environmental stress is both a cause and an effect of political tension and military conflict."[25]

The most obvious link between the environment and peace comes in the form of violent clashes between states for scarce and valuable resources, which have sometimes been called "resource wars." The one commodity over which nations are most likely to fight today is oil. The world's appetite for oil appears insatiable and is only likely to grow along with the world's population unless significant conservation measures and alternative energy sources are developed. Secretary of State Henry Kissinger admitted that during the oil shocks of 1973–74 the United States was prepared to go to war over threats to our oil supply. In 1979, during the next threat to our oil supply, President Carter declared that any hostile power that disrupted oil supplies in the Persian Gulf would be "repelled by any means necessary, including military force." This became known as the Carter Doctrine, and it was promptly invoked when Iraq invaded Kuwait in 1990, triggering a massive United States–led military response. Few people believe that the United States would have gone to war with Iraq if Kuwait had not contained such enormous oil deposits, which the United States did not want in the hands of the Iraqi regime. The Carter Doctrine is still very much in effect today; about a quarter of the U.S. military budget (or $75 billion per year) is spent on American forces either stationed in or prepared for deployment in the Persian Gulf.[26]

Professor Michael Klare argues convincingly that the oil-rich Caspian Sea area is a potential hot spot for conflict over oil. Azerbaijan, Iran, Kazakhstan, Russia, and Turkmenistan already have territorial disputes over areas where they want to drill for oil or to place pipelines to bring oil to market. Russia devotes a large portion of its defense budget to this area. Another potential hot spot is the South China Sea, with its undersea resources and the fragility of the peace among the nations surrounding the sea.[27]

Despite these dangers, there is currently no truly global agreement to share oil resources and prevent conflict over oil shortages. It would be a huge step in the right direction if such an agreement were developed now, before serious conflicts erupt. For instance, an international strategic reserve might be established, and in addition every nation might be guaranteed by a neutral administrator the right to acquire enough oil to meet critical needs. It is certainly true that the details of such an agreement would not be easy to hammer out, but it would certainly be less harrowing than responding to an international crisis.

Of course, it is not only oil that is a limited and valuable resource. Water, forests, and arable land are also commodities over which nations might fight. If nations will go to war over oil, asks former U.S. senator Paul Simon in an article he authored in the *New York Times,* "how much more intractable might wars be that are fought over water, an ever scarcer commodity for which there is no substitute?"[28] Shared water supplies in fact have already brought Israel, Jordan, and Syria into armed conflict on nine separate occasions, and water is considered by many experts one of the main issues over which a new Middle East conflict may erupt. Authors James A. Winnefeld and Mary E. Morris conclude that "lasting peace in the Middle East depends as much on developing and implementing a sound regional water management policy as it does on 'solving' the Palestinian problem and neutralizing the threat of radical political fundamentalism."[29] Ethiopia and Somalia engaged in armed conflict over water and oil resources; Iraq and Syria reportedly mobilized their armies several times over water rights; and South Africa moved troops into Angola to occupy and defend water resources.

Yet it is not interstate conflict but conflict within a country that environmental degradation and resource scarcity are most likely to cause. Researchers Anne H. Ehrlich, Peter Gleick, and Ken Conca undertook five detailed case studies of environmental change and violence in Gaza, Haiti, Pakistan, Rwanda, and South Africa. Environmental scarcity stemming mainly from the degradation and depletion of renewable resources, the increased demand for these resources, and their unequal distribution rarely contributes directly to interstate conflict, the studies showed. However, scarcities of renewable resources such as cropland, fresh water, and forests do produce civil violence and instability. "The intermediate social effects of environmental scarcity," the report concludes, "including constrained economic productivity, population movements, social segmentation, and weakening of states, can in turn cause ethnic conflicts, insurgencies, and *coups d'état.*"[30]

Professor Thomas F. Homer-Dixon concurs. Research indicates, he notes, that "scarcities of critical environmental resources—especially of cropland, freshwater, and forests—contribute to violence in many parts of the world," and that the conflicts generated are most often "chronic, diffuse, subnational violence—exactly the kind of violence that bedevils conventional military institutions."[31]

Scholar Mohamed Suliman points out that scarcity becomes a particularly critical contributor to conflict in situations already experiencing social or economic instability. Somalia, for example, is a homogenous country ethnically, religiously, and culturally. It is not fragmented as many societies are, such as Israel/Palestine or Northern Ireland. Yet as competition over scarce resources (chiefly land and water) grew, the contestants emphasized subethnic, clan differences and began a bitter battle. Suliman further points out that in the Horn of Africa, war, poverty, and environmental degradation form three legs of a triangle, and instability in any one of these areas can destabilize the entire system.[32] Examples of this also come from Senegal, Mali, Nigeria, Sudan, Ethiopia, and of course the horrendous brutality in Rwanda.

In Bangladesh as well we see that environmental degradation can destabilize a whole region. Large numbers of Bangladeshis have fled environmental degradation in their own land and relocated in neighboring areas of India. In West Bengal, the Bangladeshis living in horrific poverty have been easily incited to rioting and bloodshed. In Assam, the Assamese violently opposed the migrant Bangladeshis, and the situation "turned into a fury of human carnage."[33] We simply cannot afford to ignore the inequalities, the lack of resources, and the environmental degradation that exist all over the world. To do so puts the future of peace in peril.

Is the state of the global environment, then, a hopeless problem? Can we prevent future conflicts by coming together to protect our environment? To find answers to these questions, as well as questions about humankind's tendencies toward violent conflict, I turned to Dr. Jane Goodall, a leading peacemaker on the front lines in the battle to save the planet.

Goodall is an internationally renowned primatologist and the world's foremost authority on chimpanzees. Her pioneering and courageous endeavor to observe and understand chimpanzees—humankind's closest living relative—is legendary, as told in films, books, and documentaries and taught in classrooms all over the world. She has been called "the Einstein of behavioral sciences," "one of the ten most influential women ever," "a heroine," and "without question one of the most significant contributors to our knowledge of the world around us." The late famed Harvard evolutionary biologist Stephen Jay Gould said that "Jane Goodall's work with chimpanzees represents one of the Western world's greatest scientific achievements."[34]

She has also been called "the hopeful messenger" who "like the late Carl Sagan . . . or Stephen Hawking . . . is one of the few scientists who has been elevated to the status of sage."[35] It may be hard at first to see a scientist as a sage, but in nearly a dozen conversations with Goodall, I came to see how appropriately the label suits her. She does not seek information for its own sake but rather contemplates how that information should be used, how it might make the world a better place. And so she has become a philosopher and a messenger of peace as well as a renowned scientist. In April 2002 she was appointed by Secretary-General Kofi Annan as a United Nations Messenger of Peace.

While deeply ethical and vigilant in practicing what she preaches, Goodall has never set out to be, nor does she make any attempt to be seen as, a saint. She will enjoy her coffee in the morning and unwind with a small drink in the evening. She has her opinions, and she herself admits that at times she's too demanding. Yet people who admire her do so not only for her work, but for her kindness and generosity as well.

Goodall's legend was formed in Africa, in the Tanzanian forests of Gombe, yet her fascination with nature and love of animals can be traced to her early childhood. She grew up in England and tells audiences today that her faithful dog, Rusty, as well as a succession of cats and other creatures, taught her important lessons about the mutual affection between humans and other animals. She learned from observation too, staking out the chicken coop as a young girl to figure out how those big eggs could possibly come out of the hens. She also recalls how her mother was always supportive, even when Goodall took earthworms to bed with her or let snails loose all over her room. Her grandmother taught her the valuable lesson to live one day at a time, and her mother added that Goodall could be anything she wanted to be.

As a child Goodall had a crush on Tarzan and a jealousy toward his Jane. "I thought I would have made a better Jane than her," she tells audiences. Her dream of going to Africa came true when in 1956 a girlfriend of hers, Clo, asked Jane to visit a farm in Kenya that Clo's family had recently purchased. To raise the money for the trip, Goodall waited tables.

In 1957 in Africa Goodall was fortunate to encounter Louis Leakey, by then one of the most prominent scientists in the world. Goodall impressed Leakey with her knowledge of animals and her spirited manner. As it turned out, she was precisely the type of person Leakey had been waiting for to undertake an ambitious project. Leakey conjectured that we might learn more about our species's past if we studied our closest wild relative, the chimpanzees, with whom we share 99.98 percent of our genes. Of course, Leakey reasoned, such a study might take a decade or more to uncover meaningful results. Goodall, twenty-six years old at the time, eagerly accepted his offer to send her into the forests of Gombe, then a game reserve but now a national park. But several problems had to be solved before the project could begin. First, Leakey had to overcome the prejudice of the time among scientists who scoffed at the seriousness of the proposal and the idea of employing such an untrained, young woman. Leakey managed to find funding for six months. The second obstacle came from the Tanzanian government, which refused to allow a white woman to go unescorted into the bush.

Goodall's closest friend and companion, her mother, Vanne, solved the problem by agreeing to fly to Africa and help Goodall set up a small observation center at Gombe. When the two reached Gombe on July 16, 1960, standing on the pebble beach of Lake Tanganyika, surveying the rugged terrain, one of Goodall's first thoughts was, "How on earth will I manage to find the chimpanzees?"[36]

Find them she did, but that brought its own disappointments. In the first months the chimpanzees feared Goodall and ran off into the thick forests whenever they saw her. Overcoming threats by wild animals and surviving a horrendous bout with malaria without medication, Goodall patiently waited for each chimpanzee sighting and slowly began to understand generalities of chimpanzee society at Gombe. It was then that she did something unthinkable in scientific circles: she named the chimpanzees rather than give them impersonal numbers as convention dictated.

Vanne was a pillar of support. Goodall spent many nights camped out alone in the forest, staying as close to the chimpanzees as possible, while Vanne tended the main camp and set up a small clinic with rudimentary medicines. Her kindhearted work at the clinic eventually earned her both the affection of the local people and the honorific title of White Witchdoctor.

Vanne later returned to England, leaving Goodall to fend for herself with support from only two hired hands to cook meals and watch over the camp. With funding running out and no major findings to report, the project apparently was coming to an end. Yet Goodall made a breakthrough discovery that caused an enormous stir. Goodall observed one of the chimpanzees, David Greybeard, use a blade of grass to fish out termites from a mound. A few days later David Greybeard stripped the leaves off a twig and used it as he had the piece of grass. What Goodall had discovered had never been documented: another animal making and using a tool. When her discovery was reported to the outside world, a controversy raged over what it all meant, but during the dabate Goodall continued her work, with new funding from the National Geographic Society.

One of the most vivid events in her career took place nearly four years later. She slowly followed David Greybeard through the dense brush near a stream, where he finally sat, almost as if waiting for Goodall. "I looked into his large and lustrous eyes," she recalls, "set so wide apart; they seemed somehow to express his entire personality, his serene self-assurance, his inherent dignity." She picked up a palm nut that had been lying on the ground and extended it toward him in her open hand. He looked at her, reached for the nut, but then let it fall to the ground and took hold of her hand instead. He was acknowledging Goodall's gesture of kindness. "We had communicated in a language far more ancient than words," she writes, "a language we shared with our prehistoric ancestors, a language bridging two worlds."[37]

The next ten years brought many changes for Goodall. She received a doctoral degree from Cambridge, taught human biology at Stanford University, and endured an episode in which four of her students at Gombe were kidnapped; she married, had a son, divorced, and kept at her work at Gombe. Throughout, her increasing number of lecture tours convinced her that she had a calling to try to do everything she could on behalf of the animals in the wild.

Something that had long fascinated Goodall was the enormity of human cruelty to other humans. "How could people behave that way?" she asked herself. During the 1970s there was quite a bit of debate, as Goodall remembers, between those who held that human aggression was genetic, inherent in our nature, and those who regarded human infants as blank slates, shaped by the events of their lives. As she was thinking about these issues, Goodall and her team at Gombe made a shocking discovery.

Male chimpanzees were seen brutally attacking and mortally wounding a female from another community. During the attack the female's infant was attacked, killed, and partially eaten. Goodall and her team tried to see the incident as an isolated, unusual event. But then came another shock. A high-ranking female and her grown daughter killed and ate infants in their own community. There was no shortage of food to explain the cannibalism. The main chimpanzee community studied by Goodall also divided into two distinct groups. Eventually an all-out war against the breakaway community ensued, and in a series of brutal attacks the entire breakaway community was systematically annihilated.

Goodall deduced from the chimpanzees' behavior an innate human aggressiveness and tendency toward violence. "I had come to accept," she recounts, "that the dark and evil side of human nature was deeply rooted in our ancient past. We had strong predispositions to act aggressively in certain kinds of contexts; and they were the same contexts—jealousy, competition for food or sex or territory, fear, revenge, and so on—that triggered aggression in chimpanzees."[38] Yet Goodall also saw an important distinction between the two species: the chimpanzees could act brutally, but humans alone were capable of evil—of deliberately, systematically inflicting physical and mental pain on living creatures, in full knowledge of the effects of that pain. Torture and genocide, Goodall observed, were not characteristic of chimpanzee aggression. Humans alone have that distinct wickedness. Of course, whether we are genetically bound to carry out such wickedness is an important question, and one that I later put to Goodall in our conversations.

Much of Goodall's work these days is to promote human goodness. Her Roots & Shoots program has grown from a concept hatched on Goodall's front porch in Dar es Salaam in 1991 to a worldwide movement composed of more than three thousand groups in sixty-eight countries. Roots & Shoots is the Jane Goodall Institute's international environmental and humanitarian program for young people. The mission of the program is to foster respect and compassion for all living things, to promote understanding of all cultures and beliefs, and to inspire each individual to take action to improve the world. "Roots creep underground everywhere and make a firm foundation," Goodall explains. "Shoots seem weak, but to reach the light they can break open brick walls. Imagine that the brick walls are all the problems we have inflicted on the planet. Hundreds and thousands of roots and shoots can break through these walls."

Goodall's life represents a unique mixture of passion for action, adventure, and accomplishment, on the one hand, and good judgment based on patience, observation, and reflection, on the other. It is, Buddhists would say, the union of action and wisdom. In fact, Goodall's account of her time in the forests reminds me of Buddhist masters who in solitude develop mindfulness and deep insight, clearly perceiving all things in their true light:

> I lay there, part of the forest, and experienced again that magical enhancement of sound, that added richness of perception. I was keenly aware of secret movements in the trees. . . . It is all but impossible to describe the new awareness that comes when words are abandoned. . . . Words are a part of our rational selves, and to abandon them for a while is to give freer rein to our intuitive selves.[39]

Though Goodall is a Christian, she embraces the goodness in all religions and is well versed in diverse spiritual beliefs. She holds indigenous traditions in the highest regard and often praises them for their plain-speaking, unadulterated wisdom. Among her closest friends is an American Indian whom she describes as her "spiritual brother." Goodall also leaves open the possibility of intelligent extraterrestrial life and methods of interplanetary communication that we have yet to discover. In short, her mind is open; she well epitomizes the slogan "Think Different!"

I first met Dr. Goodall in San Francisco. She was kind enough to speak with me in her hotel room after she attended a meeting with Conservation International. Her executive assistant, Mary Lewis, greeted me with a warm smile and warned me that Dr. Goodall's room might be in "a bit of chaos." I saw when I entered that in fact the room was rather a jumble of papers.

"Hello," Dr. Goodall said slowly in her English accent.

"I think we should remove this cart," she said, pointing to the rollaway table with the remnants of the morning's breakfast. She peered under the cart to see how to lower the table's sides. "Could you perhaps figure this out, Scott?" she asked.

I managed to comply. "Terrific," she said, turning to take a seat in a wingback chair and motioning for me to sit in a similar chair facing hers. I had brought a small donation for the Jane Goodall Institute as well as some Tibetan incense and traditional protection amulets, which both Goodall and Lewis were delighted to receive.

"I recall in your latest book," I said, "that you wrote, 'The time I spent in the forest following and watching and simply being with the chimpanzees provided not only scientific data, but also gave me a peace that reached into the inner core of my being.' It strikes me that in our destruction of the environment, we are destroying peacefulness as well. We are destroying places of refuge, places where we can restore our inner peace. And on a societal level, environmental destruction leads to incredible social instability and even conflict. I think the connection is particularly apparent in Africa these days, is it not?"

"That is really true," she said. "But I must add that there is hope. The first jointly managed cross-border national park—the first in the world—just opened between South Africa and Namibia." She paused before adding slowly, "It is such a beautiful idea."

"I've heard that you travel virtually all the time—over three hundred days a year—and that you have not spent more than a few weeks in one place for the past ten years. I can only imagine the toll this takes on your body and mind. Don't your close friends ever tell you to slow down?" I asked.

"The most important message about slowing down comes from my mother," she said, "and now that she is in a better place [her mother died in 2000], the messages come very frequently. Yes, all my friends tell me I should slow down, but how can I? You know, everywhere I go my visit seems to start some new initiative—some *good* initiative. Like when I was in China for the second time, all I had done was visit a few schools and I got this summons from the vice minister of environment. I had to change the whole schedule just for a ten-minute appointment. I think he wanted to see who this old English lady was. The media kept following me, you see, and he couldn't understand it, I think.

"So we ended up meeting for one and a half hours, and he said, 'I would like you to introduce your institute's program into my schools.' I told him that doing so would mean setting up a little office in Beijing. He said, 'Yeah, do that.' I informed him how very difficult that would be, but he said it wouldn't be. So we set it up. It's the only one in Shanghai as well. And within less than a year something like fifty Chinese schools joined the institute's project."

"People don't think about China as a place where people care much about the environment. Do you find that conservation takes place there? Do the children care as much there as they do elsewhere?" I asked.

"Oh, they are beginning to," she said. "Absolutely. There is such a difference in only one year, and these little kids were telling me what they had done for the environment. You know, one little boy said to me that his friend had bought a bird and had this poor little bird in a cage. And he said to his friend, 'Do you think the bird likes being in there?' and they discussed this. Finally they let it go. Well, that was new thinking for them.

"There are a lot of people who say why bother to promote conservation and environmental awareness in a place like China because it's against their culture. Well, in England, we used to have public hanging as part of our culture, but we eventually stopped it. If you look all around the world, in the so-called civilized world, cultures have changed as understanding grows."

"Absolutely," I agreed. "I can't think of a country that hasn't had something negative in the past that has been changed when people demanded a change."

"Oh, what about in the present?" she added. "In England we still have fox hunting. And there's a huge secret ring of dog fighting and cock fighting. So we're not so wonderful. You know, I had a big press conference when I went to South Korea. I had an interpreter, and somehow something cropped up and I was reminded about the Koreans eating dogs. So I said to them, 'You know, there is a lot of bad press in the West because of your culture of eating dogs.' And this interpreter kind of went pale, and she said it is a very sensitive subject. I said okay, I know, just translate for me. I told them that the bad press is true because we have dogs as pets and we can't imagine eating them. But I also said that we eat pigs, and pigs are every bit as intelligent as dogs. I said, I actually love pigs. And I said, 'We eat the pigs; you eat the dogs. Quite honestly, it's not what we eat. I don't eat any of it, but you know people do. The important thing is how we treat them and how kindly we kill them.' And they all started talking about it among themselves. They were saying things like, 'We were nice to our pet dogs, but now I've seen dogs sold for food and they were treated very badly. Probably they shouldn't be treated like that.'"

"It is a huge moral dilemma," I said. "How do we decide which animals we can eat?"

"Yeah, well," she said, "anyway, I don't think we have any moral right to eat pigs and dogs! Pigs are wonderfully smart. They're a lot more intelligent than some dogs," she asserted. "Did you read about the potbellied pig who, for the first time in her whole life, broke down the hedge and sat in the road? Finally a car stopped and she got up and went back through the hole and the man followed and discovered that her owner had had a heart attack. And because of her actions they got the owner to hospital in time. Isn't that amazing?"

"That is amazing. Well, it's amazing only if we assume that animals don't have such intelligence and such feelings as compassion or devotion. Why is it that we don't want to acknowledge that animals have feelings and emotions? Is it because then we have to really worry about them and how we treat them?"

"That's right," she replied. "And yet it's not up to us. They have emotions whether we give them to them or not," she laughed.

I recalled that Goodall at Gombe had observed and written about the chimpanzees kissing, embracing, holding hands, patting one another on the back. "I gradually learned about the long-term affectionate and supportive bonds between family members and close friends," she noted. "I saw how they helped and cared for each other."[40]

"You were among the first in anthropology to really break with that tradition of ignoring animal emotions, weren't you?" I asked.

"Yeah. The first paper I wrote for *Nature,* I was writing about tool using among chimpanzees, and I talked about one of the chimps I named David. I shouldn't have given them names, according to tradition, but *Nature* let that pass. They seemed to have thought that was okay. But when I put in their gender, you know, for Flo *she* and for David *he,* they crossed all that out. *He* and *she* became *it.* And *who* became *which.* I was very angry and I crossed out the *it*s and the *which*es and put back the *he*s, *she*s, *who*s, and they finally left it like that."

"What was the reaction of your colleagues when you began to use names and genders for animals?" I asked.

"When I got to Cambridge, I was greeted with almost hostility."

"You were that upsetting to them?" I asked.

"Quite so, because I didn't have a B.A. and they wondered who was this little upstart and what was she doing. *National Geographic* was supporting me by then, and I had had an article published. So, I was really almost disliked. Anyway, I had nobody there that I could speak to because they were dissecting rats and deafening chickens and studying monkeys in cages, and they just didn't understand my compassion for these animals that they were treating badly."

"In Buddhism, we're told to believe that all sentient beings have the potential to be a Buddha. So they all have to be respected," I said. "But if you do respect animals, then you have to admit that animals have rights, as it were, and must be treated well if used in experiments and so forth."

"Well, that's what people are working on," she said. "Animal rights, a bill of rights for apes, for example. Peter Singer is working to admit the great apes into our circle of moral compassion."

"But this debate still rages, doesn't it, among scientists?" I asked.

"Oh yes. Absolutely!" she said.

"While only a handful of scientists believe that animals feel and have emotions," I noted, "most people who are not scientists can tell you that their dog or cat feels emotions, that animals in general have feelings of happiness or contentment, sadness or loneliness."

"Yeah, that's true. Except all the people who deal with animals in intensive farming," she said. "I mean, that's what's wrong with meat eating. The reason I stopped eating meat was because I found out about intensive farming and I was shocked. It's horrible. So what is that bit of meat you are eating? If the animal was treated badly, that meat is fear, pain, and death. I wonder how many hundreds of people have become vegetarians because of my writing? About twenty have written to me and told me they did. And others have told me in person. I don't know how many have, but it is a lot.

"But you see, when you don't think, you just sort of compartmentalize what you do. When you eat, you don't think about where it came from. Most people don't even want to know about intensive farming. I'm too sensitive, perhaps; when I see people eating beef or chickens and things I think of the slaughter, of the death. And yet, on the other hand, look at the Holocaust. Look at the ethnic cleansings, look at the torture that goes on. So we do it just as easily to ourselves as we do to animals. So it doesn't make sense to say how can we treat animals that way unless we also say, well, this is a characteristic of humans, that we are capable of extreme cruelty to other sentient beings, and that includes us."

"That is an important factor in cruelty, seeing the other as inferior to yourself. Don't you agree?" I asked.

"Yes, it is," she replied.

"That's what I have noticed all around the world. In Israel, for example, I was shocked how the Israeli Jews constantly say the Palestinians don't value life or, worse, that they are subhuman, that they are dogs."

"I know," she said, shaking her head. "Isn't it awful? Sometimes I wonder, 'Is there hope? Are we really progressing?' I mean, sections of the world are progressing definitely, big sections of the world, but not enough, not quickly enough."

"I wanted to ask you about that, because if you look at the statistics, the state of the world is getting worse and worse. One of the statistics that shocks me is that over half of the children in India are malnourished yet the government is building nuclear weapons."

"Yeah, I know. It's awful," she said. "And [in this country] look at the food that's thrown away! So much food is wasted! Wasted! And farmers dump food," she said with a huge sigh.

I wondered where she found hope in the midst of these negative images.

"Organizations like Conservation International are doing so much. What they have already accomplished is huge," she said. What they're doing on the very top level is making partnerships with big businesses and with very wealthy individuals, and working with villages and governments. They're getting huge amounts of money and convincing people to protect beautiful forests and not take them for timber. They are doing that on a big scale around the world, and it's a very, very good reason for hope.

"I just made this image this morning which I'm rather fond of," she continued. "Because of the institute's program and because of the way I am traveling and getting this going in different parts of the world and using the chimps as ambassadors, linking the human and the animal, it's as though I am trying to create, from the children, the angels who will keep the stars shining when all of us are gone. If we don't educate children, if we don't help them to understand, if we don't try and create some new values so that the mark of success in the future isn't how many cars we have, then we will have failed. You know, what is the proper measure of success? How many houses one has? How many assets? How much is in the bank? No, the mark of success will be just to do well enough to be able to choose a good and kind lifestyle. Take Buddhism, for example, or a lot of the Eastern cultures; the successful people aren't the people with lots of money, they're the people who are good human beings and lead good lives and help others.

"It is clear that we have to change, and that isn't impossible! It'll just take time. But, there truly is a change afloat, a feeling that is traveling. People are getting more and more and more fed up with this materialistic, greedy, selfish lifestyle, and they are searching for meaning. And that's why people come flocking to my lectures."

"Is that purely anecdotal," I asked, "or do you feel that there is evidence out there that people are changing their attitudes?"

"Oh, well, if you just look at attendance to my talks, that's an actual fact. Okay, we've been always well attended, but now it's over the top and we are breaking attendance records everywhere. People want hope. I was talking to somebody from the *Sunday Observer* last week and he wanted to do a big thing about the environment, and he said, 'But you know, the trouble is people don't read this anymore.' And I said, 'No, there is a reason why they don't. If you don't tell them what they as an individual can do about it, if you just tell them everything's going down the drain and we can't do anything about it, of course, they're not going to read it!'

"But I try and tell every single person in the audience that what they do does make a difference. You may feel as one in six billion that what you do or you don't do really can't matter. I have to fight this feeling sometimes myself. Sometimes I am inclined to leave the tap running, thinking it won't matter if I do. But I turn it off instead. I sometimes feel it really can't matter if the light is left on, but I turn it off. Of course if all the millions of educated people do that, even if they don't think it's going to make a difference, it in fact will make a difference."

I laughed. "You're right, and I'm glad you point out that you're right in there with the rest of us who have to fight the feeling that our individual actions won't matter. They do matter."

"All of us who are wealthy enough to make ethical choices in what we buy and what we don't buy should take the time to do the right thing," she said. "And it will make a huge difference because ours is a consumer-driven society."

"Do you find that the main problem is that the people just never stop to consider the importance of their choices?" I asked.

"Yes, well, honestly, people feel helpless. The nicest thing people say is, 'After I heard you talking, I felt that my own life had more value.' And people have come up to me a year later and said, 'You know, I did what you said and I feel so much better. My hope is being renewed.' And, Scott, that's why I can't slow down!" she said, laughing.

"In talking to you," I said, "I am noting some of the same qualities that some great masters have, teachers who lived in the forest for twenty-five years meditating in solitude. You have that same sort of peacefulness about you."

"I think it's born of necessity," she replied. "You know, I've been wrenched away from the peace of the forest that I love so much. So I must take the peacefulness of the forest with me. Otherwise I'd go mad. I'd get stressed and need your incense all the time!"

"Do you feel that you are doing what you came in to this world for?" I asked.

She pondered for a moment. "I would say, yes, I think I am now. It's interesting because every stage led to the next, you know. I couldn't do Roots & Shoots if I hadn't spent all that time with the chimps. I mean, they really do link the two—the humans and the rest of the animal kingdom."

"You've written in your book, *Reason for Hope,* that you believe we're running out of time to save nature. But I take it that you are optimistic or else you would just go back to the forest and leave us to our madness."

"I'm optimistic, but there are times when I feel, 'Oh, dear, do we have enough time?' But I know that we *can* make the change, and that gives you the optimism. I know it's possible. And you've really got to look at some of the amazing human beings around to know what we're capable of. And we were talking this morning about Africa, poor old war-torn, corrupt Africa, but look how Europe was in its past. It was totally torn apart by war and corrupt knights and corrupt kings and cruelty and torture."

"Well, didn't Europe pass that on to Africa?" I said wryly.

"They did. We . . . well, we destroyed Africa's culture totally. We totally destroyed it and gave them nothing in return. Just a whole lot of different religions which are very confusing," she said.

"Do you think much of the battle for peace, if you will, is really against human biology?"

"I am afraid," she said, "that we are hardwired to be aggressive. But I equally, strongly feel that we have the capability to overcome our aggression. Our evolution is thought of as going from the physical to the cultural to the moral to the spiritual. Yet the spiritual is there all the time. In the West we've pushed it out, and that's what we're trying to get back. And as we let that back in, it'll speed up the moral evolution as well, I think. I've really just thought about it this second, and I think it's correct!"

"I know in my heart that is correct," I said.

"That's what people are searching for. They're searching to reestablish a relationship with nature and the meaning in life. Organized religions have kind of gone out, in so many cases, and even people who go to church often don't really believe in it anymore."

"In Buddhism, there is a word, *dukkha*. It means suffering," I said. "But it has two elements: one element is that we want to escape things that make us unhappy, things that cause us pain. The other element is the suffering that comes from our longing to be aligned with something greater than we are right now. And it's that second element, I think, that is so important for us to recognize. Many people feel disconnected from something greater. Whether they find it in an organized religion or simply in walks through nature, it doesn't really matter. The important thing is if you don't strive to find it then life seems to lack meaning. What do you think about that?" I asked.

"I agree. Looking back on my own life, I think of all the amazing people who've supported me and my work. There is this fable that I like about the birds coming together and having a competition as to who can fly the highest. The eagle naturally soars high above the others and he thinks he's won. But then a little wren who has hidden in the eagle's feathers on his back emerges and flies highest of all. The point here being that if we think of our life as a series of attempts to get higher and higher toward the goal, then we all need an eagle, we can't cope by ourselves. We need something to lift us up. And to answer your question specifically, I think there is a real longing in people to reach up to this higher state of being."

"Have you noticed," I asked, "that children in the West have so many things, from video games to cell phones, and yet they have a lot of loneliness and sense of anxiety as well? Meanwhile, in villages that are supposed to be absolutely impoverished, in which the conditions are horrid by Western standards, the children are playing and laughing and having fun and being creative, and they have a sense of connection with everyone else."

"I know! And the sad thing is that we're going to take that away from them. We're going to take that away from them."

"We're going to tell them they need a video game to be happy," I said.

"Yes! Yes! It's awful. My two grandchildren are half Tanzanian. Obviously, most of their friends are Tanzanians, and there we live by the sea and they play for hours and hours and hours and they don't have anything except coconuts and sticks and some blades of grass and the dogs. And they play and they laugh. And then you look at our children. They are forgetting how to play."

"Well, we sort of anesthetize our children. Don't we? We sort of distract them, keep them quiet."

"We stick them in front of televisions, we give them all these mechanical toys. I have this little grandnephew, and his pile of presents for Christmas was huge; he's one and a half years old. I think of what they have in Africa, and first of all, I feel angry. He doesn't need all that stuff, and his parents know it. They say, well, actually he doesn't like any of this. He likes playing with a stick or a ball or the dog's bone or something like that," she said, laughing.

"Once children have grown up with the video games and the violent movies, how do we change their mind stream?"

"We are trying, through Roots & Shoots, to provide hands-on action," she said. "The most idiotic piece of this whole situation we're talking about was pointed out in a publication in England. They published the results of a study that showed that because children no longer grew up to be outdoors, their immune system was not getting the boost that it needed. In other words, they were getting weak and their immune system wasn't resistant anymore.[41] So, do you know what the solution was? That children should get injections of synthesized dirt."

"Dirt?" I questioned. "You're kidding!"

"I'm not! It is the kind of muck that children would ordinarily get into. Now, the excuse for not letting children play outside in the dirt is often that the dirt is now contaminated by pollutants. Now, that's tragic, but it's probably true. So what have we created? What have we created for our children? A world that is unsafe to let your child grow up in, to play outside because he might be molested or kidnapped or killed? And for an older child maybe, you know, maybe raped? And then, as you say, in parts of the developing world they actually have a childhood. They have fun, they laugh, but we think that they ought to be molded like us to want to acquire stuff!"

"Yes, it is such arrogance," I said.

"It's awful! But it's catching on. McDonald's is everywhere, you know."

"Regarding consumption, how is this going to work? Do people think it out? I know the Dalai Lama has said frequently that if we in the West are entitled to have two cars, then morally everyone in China has the same right to be happy, everyone in India has the same right to be happy and have two cars. But if the Chinese all have two cars and if Indians all have two cars, we'll exceed the Earth's capacity to supply fuel and to absorb pollution."

"Absolutely. That's why there are three underlying problems that have to be solved. You have to level off population growth. That has to happen everywhere! And it may be true that the Western family size is smaller than in other parts of the world, but the consumption is so much faster and greater. That's all got to change, and nobody should have more than two children anywhere, ever. And the second problem is, what I talked about before, how do you try and change the value systems, to prevent this terrible overconsumption, so that we, the affluent societies around the world, realize that we don't need all this stuff? We don't need all this stuff that we have! And then, perhaps, the hardest of all, how do we help the developing world not to yearn for our mistakes? They are all very tough problems to solve."

"Are the children our best hope?" I asked. "Do you see Roots & Shoots and similar approaches as the best hope?"

"Well, in the end, it's *my* best hope. There is so much room for the program to develop in so many ways. It could spread, and it has already gone from preschool to university. Now, we're in prisons and old people's homes. It is making people think."

"You wrote something that brought tears to my eyes, about the peace beyond understanding that comes from the forests. You said that you took your grief to the forest [especially after the death of her second husband]. It reminds me of two things, one of a master who said take your grief to the earth. You can bleed on the earth and it takes it without complaint. You can pee on the earth and it takes it. You can shit on the earth and it takes it. You can pour your sorrows into the earth and it takes it without complaint. But even more than that I'm reminded of my grandmother, who used to take me around the forests, in upstate New York. She would say to me as the sun would be shining through the trees, 'This is my church.'"

"Oh, absolutely," she said. "That's what my spirit brother says. He takes me out into the redwoods. He says, 'This is our cathedral.' And it's become mine as well."

"I can say that from such exposure to nature from such a young age, I appreciate every plant, everything my grandmother told me about. A plant is not just a plant. There's an interconnection between the plant and my ancestors, for example, for they used this or that plant to heal or to eat. So I can attest to the fact that such an appreciation for nature established in childhood remains strong through one's entire life."

"Yes. The sad thing is that if we continue to multiply, we all know, everybody peeing and shitting on the earth, as that master said, we'd be standing on a cesspit," she said, laughing.

"But we do already!" I retorted. "It goes somewhere. It is just out of our sight."

"Well, that's true. And you know what, I'm always curious about something and I can't get an answer. We're pumping out all this oil from the earth. And we're pulling out water from our lower water tables. What's that actually going to do? I mean, surely something has to happen. Water tables are dropping all the time. Do we really know what oil does down there? We don't, you see. I know there are people in Ecuador who say that we shouldn't drill for oil because oil is the blood of the earth. The oil is the blood of the earth and the earth needs it. You know, the indigenous people have such wisdom that one wonders why we don't listen."

"But, we're told," I responded, "that if we agree with ancient wisdom that we're extremists because after all we need the oil. But I think the point is, even if we need to eat meat or we need to take oil from the earth, we need to do so mindfully and respectfully."

"Well, we don't *need* to eat meat," she said. "We don't *need* to take as much oil if we make use of other forms of energy and stop being so wasteful."

"That's true," I said. "But my point is that we should be more respectful if and when we do take from nature."

"Yes," she replied, "that's true."

"There's a passage in your book where you've talked about someone approaching you, chastising you for saying we shouldn't use animals for research because a dog's heart or something saved her daughter's life. But your point was, that's fine, but we should respect the animal's sacrifice and look for other ways."

"That's right. I replied that my mother had a pig's valve in place of her heart and I felt tremendously grateful to the pig, and I, you know, was prepared to try and help with the initiatives that would mean we could do the same thing without using any pigs. 'Aren't you grateful to the dog that saved your daughter?' I asked. 'And, wouldn't you like to think about a time when they don't have to be tortured?' And she said, 'I never thought of it like that before.' You have to talk to people, not accuse them, not point fingers at them, not say you're a bad person because you do this. Sometimes the best way around that is to talk of a time when you did these things because you didn't know any better. Like when I loved my mother's fox fur and I was about, I don't know, four or five. I loved it! I had it around my neck, with its little ears and its paws. And I used to read with such jealousy about children who lay on bearskin rugs.

But then suddenly came the realization: it was killed to make this. I realized that it didn't just die. It was alive and it was killed."

"I've heard that wearing fur coats is becoming popular again," I noted.

"I know. I can't believe it! I can't believe it, especially in New York. Every other woman has a mink. It's awful!"

"So, having pointed out so much that is wrong in the world, we should talk more about hope. Where are the best signs of hope?" I asked.

"Well, for one, there is hope in all the advances that have been made in doing things in a better way, in reusing and recycling. It is just a question of actually making use of all the technology out there and having the people buy that technology so it becomes cheaper and more widely available. And then there's the resilience of nature, which is so amazing. Think of the California condor, for example," she said. "The population was virtually extinct. There were only about twelve left in the early 1980s, but now there are nearly sixty today. The twelve were captured and raised and their offspring released, and now they are making a comeback. Well, this is magic!"

"So, your hope comes mainly from the resilience of nature?" I asked.

"Yes, in the way that nature will once again make something beautiful even if we've destroyed it. We have great examples around Gombe where all the forest is gone, but if you leave it, and you prevent people from doing any more harm, you don't have to do anything more—it will come back. And if you help the people who used to cut the forest to lead better lives, then they don't need to cut it anymore. So we have helped them with tree nurseries and things like that. And within five years, starting with nothing but stumps, little forests emerge. I was sent a picture this morning of such a budding forest," she said, pulling the photograph out of a stack of papers and handing it to me.

"Oh, it's quite beautiful!" I exclaimed.

"This looks like a totally dead tree, totally burnt," she said, showing me another photograph. "And yet from somewhere inside," she said, pointing to the other photo, "this is the same tree which has grown from within. Isn't it beautiful?"

"Do you know," I asked, "that my Iroquois ancestors had something called the seven generations rule?"

"Oh, I know it," she said.

"You know it?"

"I love it," she said. "Everything you plan, you think back seven generations to see if your plan's right. And then you think seven generations ahead to work out what is needed. It's perfect."

"It's absolutely right, and I think that kind of ancient wisdom is needed in dealing with our current situation," I said.

"Yes, and then we get all these bad stories about the terrible Indians and their bloodthirstiness, and, you know, of course they weren't perfect. But in fact, they had all this marvelous wisdom."

"Yet time and again you see indigenous people will resist colonizers, over and over again. Even in the animal world that's true, isn't it?"

"Yes. That's true. I don't think we were born peaceful. I just don't agree. But we can *become* peaceful. We've developed a sophisticated intellect and language. We can talk about something, discuss it. We can develop our innate sense of morality. And then our spirituality—we can put it into words, formulate it. Then we can accept it and it can change us. . . . I can't express it very well."

"I think that's expressed very well," I said.

"Do you?" she asked.

"Yeah. I mean, for one thing, the practical implication is that we don't have to wait for a crisis and simply react to the crisis. We can actually plan ahead to avert a crisis or to figure out the best way to respond when it comes."

"Yes, that's right," she said, nodding.

"We communicate and think. We can think about seven generations from now. We can question what a place is going to be like without forests."

"And yet," she said, "I think, the people around Gombe sort of know they should not be cutting down all the trees. They're driven to it because their numbers have gone up and refugees have come in. And now, we just had some terrible flooding. There was very heavy rain and the watershed's gone along with the trees and there's nothing left. Nothing. And so, there was this horrible flooding, and half a village was washed into the lake, and about fourteen people were killed. So, they are saying, 'The spirits are angry with us, the spirits of our ancestors.' And so my people were trying to tell them, 'No, it's not that; it's because you cut the trees and now there is nothing there to absorb the water.' But, then again, why utterly destroy their belief? Add to it and tell them: 'the spirits of your ancestors are angry because you cut down the trees.'"

"What about AIDS in Africa? What needs to be said about AIDS in Africa?"

"Not just Africa. AIDS in China. AIDS growing in Asia. AIDS creeping everywhere. What needs to be said about it? Well somebody said to me this morning—quite horribly—that it looks as though AIDS is on the side of conservation; if people die, perhaps that will curb population and put less pressure on the environment. I said no, because it's actually exacerbating the poverty. As poverty spreads, the need to exploit the environment spreads even more. It is all a vicious cycle."

"AIDS also surely breeds cynicism," I said. "I mean, who could care about the felling of a forest or the killing of chimps when your entire village is being decimated by disease? And I heard that many of the new recruits entering the guerrilla armies are orphans, having lost their parents to AIDS. So it is terribly destabilizing on society, adds to poverty and further pressures the environment, and also contributes to war."

"Yeah, the orphans have nothing, so why not fight," she said. "And a lot of them are HIV infected anyway. So it doesn't matter, they're going to die. It's horrible. But the governments are beginning to face it. In Uganda, they say, AIDS has leveled off. The paper in Tanzania last time I was there said about one in three people is HIV infected in Botswana, and the heading was 'Botswana Faces Extinction,' and that is a shock. The headline is an overstatement, but it is true that AIDS is a horrendous problem."

"The connection between environmental destruction and war receives scant attention. Yet it doesn't seem that you can truly promote peace when you are destroying the environment. People will fight over resources," I offered.

"Yeah, they have to because they have nothing left to share," she answered.

"And that's a very ancient thing, isn't it? Even in the animal world, you must have observed chimps fighting over resources."

"Yeah, they do. They do. I mean, the structure of the environment [is threatened] because of the increased number of people under poverty and starvation and disease."

"And the antidote to all of this is what?" I asked.

"The antidote is a stabilization of population growth and decrease in poverty. We must improve people's lives, educate them, particularly the women, and improve their self-esteem so their family size drops. All around the world, it's been shown that as women become more educated family size drops. And somehow, somehow, somehow, stop spreading Western bad values. I don't know how we do that, unless we lead and give an example. And I don't see any signs of that. The Bush administration is making things even more difficult," she declared. "Did you read where Clinton signed the law about halting logging and building roads in the national forests, and Bush delayed it by two months? It doesn't sound like much, but think what you can do in two months! You can do a lot of damage.

"You know," she continued, "I've been in a forest that was sustainably logged for forty-five years. It was like going into a cathedral, and there were so many animal species there. When I was there a big tree got pulled out by horses, and the guy who has protected this forest this way, he's now eighty-five, is struggling to make it safe when he's gone. At the moment there are students, foresters from all over the world, coming to see how you can do it and let nature thrive. It is totally organically farmed, sustainable forestry that's provided stable jobs for families for forty-five years, and it's still beautiful."

"So, now we have examples," I said. "We have the know-how, mostly, to turn the tide."

"And people don't want to do that because they won't make as much money!" she said.

"So the remaining element, as I see it, is to have people just stop for a moment and listen to people like you," I said.

"This is why I'm running around the world!"

"You've been called the guru to the environment," I noted, teasing her a bit.

"Have I?" she replied.

"Yeah. Are you comfortable with that?" I asked.

"The way *guru* is used over here now, I'm not sure that I am," she said, laughing.

"A sage then?"

"A sage!" she exclaimed. "That sounds better! Well," she said smiling, "I was described the other day as the Gandhi for the animal kingdom."

"You know you've arrived if you've got Mahatma Gandhi attached to your name," I joked. "What's your highest priority these days?" I asked.

"I'm working on a youth program for the United Nations. But my highest priority is Roots & Shoots, with its hands-on activity, its message of the value of the individual, that everyone makes a difference. It provides the tools for change—art, knowledge and understanding, persistence and hard work, love and compassion. It's very nonviolent. You don't confront people, you sit and talk, and listen. It's about breaking down the artificial barriers we've created between the rich and the poor, between cultures, between religions, between ethnic groups, between countries, between old and young very often, and between humans and animals. It's about breaking away those barriers. If you imagine that I give you a seed and you take it to Tibet and you plant it, well, it will grow in Tibet only if it's nurtured by the Tibetan people. And when the fruits come, they'll be the Tibetans' fruits. I can take a seed and plant it in Congo and the same will be true. When all these fruits and leaves blossom out there they will be something we all made together. So we can talk about Roots & Shoots as planting the seeds for global peace."

"So, will Roots & Shoots be your legacy?" I asked.

"That will be the legacy," she replied with a smile.

Goodall invited me to meet her in Washington, D.C., where I could hear her lecture at a school, visit the Jane Goodall Institute in Silver Spring, Maryland, and accompany her on her rounds. I spent two days with her and Mary Lewis, watching as girls and women wept upon meeting her and powerful men were taken by her soft-spoken charm. In everything she did she seemed keenly aware of her fame, yet she maintained a gentle, sometimes even vulnerable, disposition.

I once asked her, "What is it like for you to be a celebrity?"

"I'm not a celebrity," she said. "I would hate to be a celebrity!" She paused and thought for a moment. "*Am* I a celebrity?" she asked.

Lewis, who had been busy taking care of some business, chimed in. "Oh, yes. I think so. I think you've become a celebrity, Jane."

Goodall shook her head slowly. "Well, *I* don't think I am."

A few minutes later she showed me how she makes coffee by filling a sock with grounds and pouring the hot water through.

One afternoon Goodall had a meeting with the board of the World Bank. She was nonchalant about such an important appointment. In the back of a taxi on the way to her meeting we talked some more.

"Jane," I asked, "what do you think the moral argument is for why people should care about the suffering of others?"

"Or why *do* they, perhaps, is underlying why *should* they. I find it always extraordinary that we *can* feel compassion for people far away who we have never seen and who we are never likely to see. What is it that triggers that kind of compassion? Sociobiologists might say that looking at suffering makes us unhappy, therefore in order to help us alleviate that feeling we might help others. But that still doesn't get to the point of why we care. Why would sending a hundred dollars to help alleviate the suffering of someone far away help you feel better? Well, perhaps by doing that we can be perceived by our family and friends as a good person. Yet still underlying that is the question, what is it in our nature that makes helping others appear to be a good thing? Why is that a part of our moral value system? And I think we can certainly see the roots of it in chimp behavior—where they do care for each other, they do show compassion, they do show true altruism. It seems from an evolutionary perspective, individuals form very close family bonds first. For a mother or older brother to be compassionate and caring to the infants, for example, it benefits the family—makes it stronger, more members survive. That is the heart of it, I think: that the mother-infant relationship of caring gradually gets extended from the family to the group. When a member of the group is altruistic toward another member who is suffering, it's beneficial to the group as a whole; it makes it stronger. So our altruism probably extended as our brains became more complex, and we eventually came to consider that anyone who looked like us, or even sort of like us, even in faraway places, was part of our family in a way."

"That is fascinating to me," I said. "In Buddhism, compassion is built on the idea that everyone at one time or another in the course of time has been related to one another. In this way we are all truly connected. Everyone has been my mother, and I have been mother to everyone. Recalling that everyone has been in our immediate family, we feel compassion for them."

"When you say, why *should* we feel compassion, do you mean that as a moral question?" she asked me.

"Yes, I think it is a moral question. It goes along with the question of why we don't do more to alleviate the suffering of others, either in our own community or in distant lands."

"Well, I think people get to this feeling of apathy and helplessness. They think, 'Okay, if I help the earthquake victims in India, what am I going to do about the poor women in Afghanistan? And if I help the poor women in Afghanistan, what am I going to do about the refugees in another country?' And so on."

"That's compassion fatigue," I noted.

"Yes. It's compassion fatigue. And I think it is the same fatigue that you can get when you approach the environment. If you look at the entire problem, the whole picture is so huge, so monstrous, that you just get the feeling that it is hopeless. So you have to bring it back to tackling the problems one tree at a time, one dog at a time, one person at a time. And if we all take just that small view, and enlarge it as we are doing something helpful, then we won't get that fatigue. If you do nothing, you'll feel meaningless. It is very important for some people to see the individual that they're helping, to see a picture of the child they're helping. It brings it onto a very personal level, which is a very helpful thing.

"You should do it as a human being," she continued, "because we have evolved to a state where we have and we know about our feelings of compassion, and therefore we should act on them. It makes us better human beings, it changes us from cruelty to compassion, and that is the only way to attain a meaningful spiritual level of awareness."

"I actually believe," I said, "that you can't have peace in your heart if you know that someone is suffering and you could do something to alleviate the suffering."

"You can't!" she replied. "You absolutely can't. But then you also have to survive without this compassion fatigue. You have to realize that you actually cannot help every suffering person. So that's why we have programs like Roots & Shoots spreading the message, where you share this burden and get more and more people to help. You cannot do it all yourself. If you just become fatigued, you cannot act with your full potential."

"Of course, some people use the one-can't-save-the-whole-world argument as an excuse to do nothing at all," I said. "You know, when you do something helpful for someone, when you see that you've changed someone's life, that gives you more energy to do something for another person. It builds, and you're able to do more and more. You want to help more and more. Don't you find that to be true in your own work?"

"Yes, it is true. Absolutely. My favorite story is when I was in Tanzania. I saw two little boys, ages about eight or nine, tease a sick puppy. The dogs around there are not treated well at all. They are not treated with care and respect, often tied up in the yards without water and so on. Anyway, the pup was with its mother and siblings, but it was sick and weak. One of the boys was teasing it, grabbing its tail and giggling in that way that boys do. He wasn't actually hurting it, but it wasn't nice at all. And I was there with a seventeen-year-old from the Roots & Shoots program, and I said, 'Come on, let's go and talk to the boys.' A European man was standing there, and he said, 'Oh, you can't do anything about it. That's how they are all over Africa.' I thought, no, this isn't all over Africa; it is here! We went over and I asked the boy, 'If you were sick and you were about three feet tall and someone as big as that tree over there was picking on you, would you like it?' And he said no. Then I asked him if he thought the puppy liked it, and he said no. So I asked, 'Then why are you doing it?' I talked to him. I said, 'You actually like your dog, don't you? Many boys your age are cruel to their dogs, but you like your dog.' He said he did. I told him about Roots & Shoots and asked the boys if they would like to help us. We gave them some material, and the two boys went off terribly excited, carrying the puppy gently.

"Apparently I told that story at a lecture, and two or three years later I was at an international schoolteachers' conference and a woman came rushing up to me. She said, 'Jane, I've been waiting to meet you. I was teaching at a school in Bombay, and I just thought I'd have to quit. There were all these stray, mangy dogs and I couldn't take it. They were everywhere, all over the streets.' She talked to a friend of hers who was a veterinarian and asked, 'What can I do?' And the veterinarian told her my story about the two little boys and the puppy. 'I suggest you start with one dog at a time,' he told her. And that convinced her to do something. She took one dog off the street, cleaned it up, spayed it, and found it a home. So she began helping. And she did that little by little, and eventually they got some money and opened a little shelter, and it has made quite a difference on the streets. I just love that story and how it came back to me. You just never know what little thing is going to ripple out like that." Jane looked out the window with a slight smile.

"You said something interesting in your lecture yesterday. You said that in chimp society the leaders don't obtain their position through aggressiveness."

"Well, not always, not necessarily," she replied. "When I say the leader I'm not talking about the top ranking, or the alpha. I'm talking about the one that others follow, and though it can be the alpha, it isn't always. Why is that? Because the most aggressive ones can turn around and thump you. You don't want to spend time with them. And if you're fearful, then you have to raise your own aggressiveness to protect yourself. But most of the time you just want to wander around in peace and eat. We found that one of our greatest chimp leaders was totally out of the dominance picture—he didn't care. I think something happened to him when he was an infant; he hurt his foot, I think. And he was also kind of dumb. He did silly things that made us all laugh. Anyway, he never got involved in fights. He always stayed out of it. When he got big he became the great leader of adolescent males. When large males come around, adolescents normally seek out their mothers, but instead they sought him out." Jane laughed. "I used to see him leading all these adolescent males around the forest. It was so lovely."

"One would think that the group would follow the alpha male only, the one with all the brute power," I noted.

"Oh, alpha males aren't really followed at all," she said. "Alpha male is a power thing, it isn't about leadership. Being an alpha male gives you access to females, access to food. But it doesn't make you a leader. Sometimes alpha males are leaders, but sometimes they travel alone. Anyway, leaders don't choose to lead; followers choose to follow, and that's what makes a leader. If you are a nice male, the females choose to be with you. They want to be with you. If you are kind to them and groom them, they want to stay with you. Although they can't do much about it sexually, because the dominant male won't allow it."

"You have said that you chose to leave Gombe because you wanted to save it. Are you saying that if there were no problems there today, you would still be there?"

She pondered for a moment. "If there were no problems in all the forests in Africa . . . I don't know if I would still be at Gombe. Maybe I would have found something else. I just feel that I'm following the path that's been laid out for me. The loss of the forests, the spread of the deserts, the poverty and the suffering—they're all tied up with world pollution, globalization, and the evil, greedy ways of the West. So it is hard for me to imagine that leaving the forest wouldn't have been necessary. I guess I can't answer your question," she said.

I laughed. "I think anyone who is involved in fighting poverty and suffering has a dream that one day they can retire from it all. That they are no longer necessary. The Dalai Lama thinks of being in seclusion."

"Well, I can only realistically dream of being somewhere I find really beautiful if all these other problems are gone, because as long as they're there I couldn't be happy in my dream. That's why I'm not at Gombe. So, until we have a perfect world, there's no point in my dreaming," she said, smiling.

"Do you feel most peaceful when you're at Gombe?" I asked.

"No," she replied instantly. "I can feel peaceful almost anywhere if I can get some bit of greenery, some trees, and get away from all this noise, noise, noise, noise. It doesn't have to be Gombe. I feel very peaceful in temples in Japan, in places like that, in cathedrals. I had the biggest compliment paid to me by my youngest 'brother.' He's Japanese. When he was doing his thesis in Kyoto and felt the need to get away from the pressures, he went to a small temple where no tourists ever went. He took me there and said to me after hearing my first lecture, 'Jane, you gave me the same feeling of peace that I have at that temple.'" She smiled.

"I've felt that sense of peace from you," I said. "You have an amazing gift."

She let out a small laugh. "Oh, well," she said, "it's not *me*."

On September 11, 2001, I was staying in Jane Goodall's room in London. I was stunned by the news of the terrorist attacks at the World Trade Center. Jane was in New York, only a few blocks away from what became known as Ground Zero. When I was finally able to speak with her, she was the voice of reason and comfort. She called because she knew I was stuck far away and would feel helpless and out of sorts. "Scott, I keep telling people to stop watching the news," she told me. "This horrendous thing should make us want to do more to make the world a better place. We have to stop obsessing on the negative. I keep telling people, get out into the air, do something positive, and live your life!"

Perhaps the most important example Goodall sets is precisely that: doing something positive and living in communion with the goodness of life. Her message of urgency to save the planet is a spiritual call. As long as there is hope, we must pursue it.

There is in fact reason for hope. We have some good news about the environment, not the least of which is that people today are increasingly aware of the problem, thanks in large part to the selfless and courageous acts of people like Jane Goodall.

EPILOGUE

*What lies behind us and what lies before us are small matters
compared to what lies within us.*

Ralph Waldo Emerson

The future of peace rests squarely in our hands. We cannot leave
it to others to create peace. We cannot wait for divine intervention or for the miraculous enlightenment of the world's leaders. We
have to do something ourselves—within our hearts and within our
communities—to resist anger and greed and violence and form
instead a culture that cherishes and protects peace. What we must
do at long last is take the promise of lasting peace seriously.

Nowhere is our potential for lasting peace acknowledged more
than in our great spiritual traditions. It is often said today that our
spiritual traditions have failed us; but the truth is that we have
failed them. We have failed to truly embrace the compassion of our
spiritual elders, and we have failed to fulfill our moral obligations to
one another. Hinduism says that we should "live well together" and
"render peaceful whatever is terrible." Confucianism instructs that
we should "seek harmony with our neighbors" and "cultivate the
personal life" in order to establish "peace throughout the world."
Buddhism tells us to "live happily, without hating even those who
hate you," to "constantly seek happiness without violence," and to
realize that "if your mind is peaceful, all things in your world will

be peaceful." Judaism informs us to "love thy neighbor" and to "depart from evil, and do good, seek peace, and pursue it." Christianity beckons us to "be kind to one another, compassionate, and forgiving," and to create "peace of mind and heart." Islam instructs us to "enter into peace," to "act justly," and to "compete with each other in good works."

Hundreds of other spiritual paths challenge us to do the same. What is quite clear is that our spiritual traditions, and our secular ethics as well, do not view peace as unattainable. We are not told to work for peace halfheartedly and disbelievingly. Instead, we are instructed to hold it in the highest regard, to believe in it, and to make it happen right here, right now.

Admittedly, at times lasting peace seems improbable. Hatred is a universal ailment, existing in every corner of the world. I was forcefully reminded of this fact just days before the September 11 attack on the World Trade Center. Flanked by heavily armed soldiers and policemen in riot gear, I looked deeply into the faces of the people shouting on either side of me. Their voices were sometimes drowned out by the sound of the military helicopter hovering overhead. How strange anger looks, I thought. How profoundly it contorts the face, the entire posture of the body, into ugliness. And the people who are shouting and clenching their fists in anger seem to have no idea that the first person harmed by animosity is the one who is enraged: the body that generates the energy of hostility absorbs it as well.

The protesters were taunting a group of women and their young girls who were on their way to school, calling them dirty little whores, bitches, and worse. The girls were terrified, crying and clutching at their mothers. The day before a pipe bomb had been thrown from the crowd. It exploded, sadly, injuring a policeman who was trying to maintain order, but thankfully doing no other harm. In the evening, Molotov cocktails burst into flames in the streets as rioters clashed with security forces.

I could have been anywhere in the world where old rivalries burst into violence. Yet I happened to be in Europe. I had traveled to Northern Ireland to talk with Máiread Corrigan Maguire, recipient of the 1976 Nobel Peace Prize, and John Hume, a recipient of the same award in 1998. I had already had the privilege of spending a few days and having many subsequent conversations with Betty Williams, corecipient of the 1976 Nobel Peace Prize. When I set out for Northern Ireland, the area had been out of the world headlines for months. On my way from the Belfast airport my cab driver said that the only nuisance during the summer had been the poor weather. Yet as we approached the center of town I saw a convoy of armored vehicles race past. "Oh, no!" my driver exclaimed. The quiet summer had been shattered.

Explanations of the conflict in Northern Ireland have been improperly simplified as a battle of religions, Protestants versus Catholics. In fact, this is an affront to the compassion propounded by both faiths. The conflict is essentially the same as hostilities else-where: groups form, emphasize, and rally around a common iden-tity and then alienate and vilify the other. Vilification slowly turns to dehumanization, whereby the other is seen as less than human, and then horrendous acts of inhumanity become not only possible but quite likely.

In all conflicts, if you strip away the appearances and assump-tions you can find the true causes of discord. In the case of Northern Ireland, the roots of disagreement stem not from a clash of religions but from subjugation and intolerance. "The people are divided by identity," John Hume told me during a discussion in Derry. "The Protestant people regard themselves as British and the Catholic people regard themselves as Irish. The roots of the quarrel go back three centuries to the time of the Reformation. Ireland was seen by the British as being linked to the Catholic powers of Europe—Spain, France, and so on. They were concerned about being sand-wiched in between the Catholic powers, so they decided to colonize Ireland. In the north they colonized the area with Protestants, and right from the very beginning they underscored the difference in identities of the colonists and the native Irish Catholics."

After centuries of harsh control, Ireland managed to gain free-dom from English rule. Yet in deference to the loyal Protestants in the north, the British decided to retain control of the six northern counties. And so Ireland was partitioned.

Unfortunately, the Protestant majority in the north suppressed Catholics and made their lives miserable, denying them all but a few civil rights. This was epitomized by life in Londonderry. Catholics were primarily confined to an area called the Bogside, a horrendously impoverished, overcrowded ghetto of despair. After decades of injustice, some Catholics, like John Hume, campaigned tirelessly for civil rights through peaceful protests and other nonviolent means, while others, like the Irish Republican Army (IRA), took up arms and waged war. Protestants reacted to the Catholic demands for equality by digging in their heels. They feared that granting civil rights to the Catholics would erode the Protestants' dominance and lead to the eventual reunification with the Republic of Ireland. The IRA killed nearly two thousand people and hurt many more over the last quarter century in its battle with Britain and its Northern Irish partners. As nearly always happens in war, both sides committed terrible acts. The animosity between the Catholics and the Protestants became so bad that simply venturing into the other's neighborhood was an unbearable offense likely to result in a severe beating or even murder.

As we have seen throughout this book, there are always good people who emerge from bad situations. Maguire and Williams were, in their own estimation, unremarkable people who were worn down by the constant animosity around them. If anyone thinks they can do little to affect peace, justice, and human rights, then Maguire and Williams prove otherwise. One day in August 1976, while going about her life, Williams witnessed a terrible scene. A jeep carrying an IRA gunman was fleeing the police at high speed. The police fired their weapons, killing the driver and sending the jeep out of control. It struck down Anne Maguire, who was bringing her kids home from school. Her sons Andrew, six weeks old, and John, two, and her daughter Joanna, eight, were killed.

Sickened by the event and angered at the violence that destroyed so many lives on a daily basis, Williams rallied women from various neighborhoods to take to the streets in a peace march. Máiread Maguire, aunt of the victims, joined Williams, and for the first time the Protestants and Catholics walked side by side, united in the goal of peace. It was a huge step in a long process, but the idea of futility never dissuaded Williams, Maguire, or the people who united with them.

Williams never chose to become a leader; she simply could not stand by and do nothing. She refused to remain part of the problem. "If we simply wait and expect the answers from the top," she said to me, shaking her head, "we're never going to get them. To create a dignified, compassionate, and just world, we've got to start at the bottom. We've got to show our children true dignity and compassion and justice. And that is something each of us must do for ourselves."

Both women bristle at the misappropriation of religion to explain and perpetuate conflict. To do so is tantamount to Jesus saying, "I told you not to harm others, but since you've done everything you can to foster peace and justice in the world, go ahead and kill your enemy." Of course, no one can say with sincerity that we have done everything possible to set aside greed, feelings of superiority and entitlement, malice, and bias and instead have pursued a course of true and lasting peace. Yet still we evoke our religions to justify our violent acts. Maguire passionately denounces this tendency to declare that our violent actions can be deemed "just wars." "The just war is a lie," she said to me. "Using violence is a lie! It is not the Christian way. It is not the way showed to us by Jesus!"

Nonviolence, of course, does not mean that we shouldn't take action in the world. Nonviolence is not passivity; it is not inaction. Nonviolence denounces apathy. In fact, apathy is one of the greatest threats to peace. In the early to mid-1990s, the Hutus launched a genocide against the Tutsis in Rwanda. "No system of genocide ever devised has been more efficient: the daily kill rate was five times that of the Nazi death camps," notes journalist Scott Peterson. "The daily death rate averaged well more than 11,500 for two months, with surges as high as 45,000. During this peak, one murder was committed every 2 seconds of every minute, of every hour, for days: an affliction befitting the Apocalypse. Transfixed and aghast, the rest of the world watched, fiddled, then hid its eyes and did nothing."[1]

Journalist Ed Vulliamy makes a similar observation in his book *Seasons in Hell,* which includes his eyewitness accounts of the war in Bosnia that began in 1992: "It seemed incredible that the world could watch, read and hear about what was happening to the victims of this war, and yet do nothing—and worse."[2]

Peterson's and Vulliamy's observations are reminiscent of the words of historian Ian Kershaw, who said, "The road to Auschwitz was built by hate, but paved with indifference."[3] Despite our international declarations of respect for human life, we see indifference time and again, and especially poignantly in genocides such as those in Cambodia, Rwanda, northern Iraq, and Bosnia. We see the same indifference far too often in the elevation of international trade and power politics above human rights in China, Burma, Israel, and a host of other nations.

It is very difficult to reconcile such inaction with our professed morals, whether they be our secular sense of ethics or our spiritual beliefs. Inaction in the face of brutality and misery is, in my opinion, simply wrong, and we know it. If we somehow have found a justification for inaction while others languish in pain, we must be willing to accept what writer Norman Geras has called "the contract of mutual indifference."[4] This means that the same thoughts and feelings which keep you from helping others will be at work keeping others from helping you. I won't care for you, and you won't care for me. This certainly makes the world a much colder place, the ultimate realm of pessimism, knowing that no one will come to your aid when you need it. I don't want to live in such a world, and I refuse to accept that I must.

Either we accept mutual indifference, or we accept a moral duty to help others, no matter where they reside or how we are related to them. It may be an accident of birth that we enjoy relative peace and freedom, but one day, however inconceivable it may seem at the moment, any one of us can find ourselves in need. Helpless and suffering, we would want someone to rescue us. In such a situation, we would all surely become advocates for global responsibility.

Of course, people will not work for peace if they continue to believe in the futility of their actions. We first have to overcome the notion that violence is inevitable because of human nature. If people believe that violence is inevitable, and that history bears this out, then they will justify their inaction as being a prudent—even justified—conservation of their time and energy.

We should not forget, however, that whatever tendencies we have toward violence, we also have a profound tendency toward compassion. This compassion is the antidote of what some would call "social Darwinism," especially when it is espoused to justify the actions of the strong against the weak. It is simply human nature, the argument goes, that the strong will exploit the weak; it is simply a natural process of the survival of the fittest. Fascist regimes as well as republics extend this notion to politics, believing that a nation-state must either rule others or be ruled by others. This leaves little room for a truly peaceful nation within the world order.

Charles Darwin, the brilliant English naturalist who fathered the theory of organic evolution that we call Darwinism, would be horrified to hear his name attached to the notion that "survival of the fittest" necessitates self-serving acts, even war. "As man advances in civilization," Darwin wrote, "and small tribes are united into larger communities, the simplest reason would tell each individual that he ought to extend his social instinct and sympathies to all the members of the same nation, though personally unknown to him. This point being once reached, there is only an artificial barrier to prevent his sympathies extending to the men of all nations and races."[5]

Darwin's argument recognizes the goodness of humankind, our impulses toward altruism, and the capabilities of our reasoning, and at the same time serves as a profound call for secular ethics that place compassionate action above the limited interests of nation-states.

I think it is fair to say that most of us focus our attention today on limited interests. We are overly concerned with our narrow spheres and too inattentive to the needs of others. Our news coverage tends to solidify this shortsightedness by concentrating almost exclusively on negative events that continually reaffirm the cruelty of humankind. Sadly, we believe that these negative events portend a rather discouraging future: more hatred, more aggression, more violence, more wars. It all begins to sound inevitable, no matter what we do or fail to do. But we should not let the reports make us feel either helpless or hopeless. It would be far better if we read or listen to news reports thinking, "This we can change! It is time to do something to make this better!"

I hope that what stands out most in this book are not the horrors, the missed opportunities, and the broken promises, but rather the enormous reserve of goodness that lies in the hearts and minds of people all over the world. Perhaps as individuals you and I will never achieve what the great peacemakers in this book have achieved. Yet we can do something, however minute it appears. All of these small acts, these small achievements, can eventually tip the balance and create a new culture of lasting peace.

The leaders profiled in this book show us how to live harmoniously with one another; they demonstrate the best qualities that reside in all of us. The productive forces of humankind, our desire to elevate ourselves through conscious endeavor, our recognition of the brimming possibilities within us—these things are intimately tied to our sense of compassion. Because of our innate compassion, we can never truly be happy and enjoy our lives when we know that we could help alleviate suffering but choose not to instead. No matter how much we try to turn away from suffering, when we know our fellow beings are in pain, it affects our conscience. In our inaction, we will not be at ease, and we certainly will not have a sense of inner serenity or fulfillment. Only by aligning with and expressing our innate compassion through helpful actions can we feel the sense of inner peace and satisfaction that we so fundamentally desire.

I write these final lines sitting in Peace Park in Hiroshima. There are perhaps equal but no greater symbols of our cruelty to one another than Hiroshima. In order to speed the end of war, and to demonstrate its power and extend its influence, the United States dropped an atomic weapon on this city. In an instant, temples, schools, grocery stores, clinics, libraries, pet shops, and restaurants were incinerated in a firestorm that reached several million degrees centigrade. The monks and schoolchildren, clerks and doctors and librarians, cooks and waitresses were incinerated too. The bombing killed 140,000 people, some right away, and some slowly. Most died gruesome and painful deaths, in great despair.

This bomb was followed by another one at Nagasaki. The necessity and the morality of the dropping of the atomic bombs on Hiroshima and Nagasaki are still debated among historians. After all, isn't the targeting of civilian populations to break the will of a nation precisely what we call terrorism? For philosophers and the spiritually minded, the issue is rather more clear: would God or Jesus or Muhammad or Krishna or Buddha or Guru Nanak or the Chief of the Great Sky ever support our dropping an atomic weapon on civilians in the name of expediency, power, or retribution?

A few days before my visit to Hiroshima, the United States and Russia announced an agreement to slash their nuclear arsenals by two-thirds, although many of the weapons will simply be stored instead of destroyed. The agreement is a step in the right direction—a direction that must culminate in the complete abolition of these horrendous weapons. That goal today seems far-fetched—as far-fetched as lasting peace itself. Yet that is precisely the goal that we should set and work tirelessly to achieve.

At the spot that was the epicenter of the atomic blast, where once everything was ashen and stark, red and yellow roses now sway gently in the afternoon breeze. In the river that was once filled with blackened corpses, children now play in brightly colored outfits. Yes, we have hurt each other far too many times, but hope and beauty remain, and so too does the promise of lasting peace.

On bended knee, in the sunshine of late spring, on this spot of former despair, and filled with hopefulness about the future, I slowly utter the words of *metta sutta,* an ancient Buddhist invocation of kindness.

> *In gladness and in safety*
> *May all beings be at ease.*
> *Whatever living beings there may be,*
> *Whether they are weak or strong, omitting none,*
> *The great or the mighty, medium, short or small,*
> *The seen and the unseen,*
> *Those living near and far away,*
> *Those born and to-be-born,*
> *May all beings be at ease!*

Peace, of course, cannot be achieved in a single prayer, but it can be built; and a multitude of prayers would be a very good place to start.

NOTES

INTRODUCTION

1. Albert Einstein, *Ideas and Opinions,* ed. Carl Seelig, trans. Sonja Bargman (New York: Wings Books, 1998), 131.

2. Thomas Merton, ed., *Gandhi on Non-violence: Selected Texts from Mohandas K. Gandhi's Non-violence in Peace and War* (New York: New Directions Publishing, 1965), 64.

CHAPTER ONE

1. The military government of Burma renamed the country Myanmar, but the rightful, democratically elected leaders of Burma do not recognize the military's right to do so without the approval of the people.

2. Sucheng Chan, ed., *Hmong Means Free: Life in Laos and America* (Philadelphia: Temple University Press, 1994).

3. Quoted by *Dateline NBC,* August 13, 2000; taken from Aung San Suu Kyi, *Freedom from Fear: And Other Writings,* ed. Michael Aris (New York: Viking, 1991).

4. According to the U.S. State Department, 280 of 480 members of the parliament-elect have been disqualified, jailed, or forced to resign under pressure, or have gone into exile or died. A total of 43 successful candidates from 1990 languish in prison.

5. U.S. Department of State, *Burma Country Report on Human Rights Practices for 1998,* released by the Bureau of Democracy, Human Rights, and Labor, February 23, 2001.

6. Amnesty International, "Report 2001," available at www.web.amnesty.org/web/ar2001.nsf/webascountries/MYANMAR?Open Document.

7. Suu Kyi's letters were published in Japan and received the prestigious Japanese Newspaper Association's Award in 1996.

8. Letters from Burma, chap. 51.

9. Upon independence in January 1948, Burma fell into immediate chaos. Long-suppressed ethnic tension erupted into armed conflict. Of the many insurgencies in

the country today, the battle between the Karen National Union and the govern-ment-supported Democratic Karen Buddhist Organization is one of the largest.

CHAPTER TWO

1. *Time* (Asia), August 23, 30, 1999.

2. The Norwegian Nobel Committee, Nobel Peace Prize, 1989 press release; available at www.nobel.se/peace/laureates/1989/press.html.

3. The Dalai Lama, *Ethics for the New Millennium* (New York: Riverhead Books, 1999), 202.

4. Dalai Lama, *Ethics,* 203.

5. Dalai Lama, *Ethics,* 216–17.

6. *Newsweek,* October 13, 1997, 18–19.

7. U.S. Department of State, Bureau of Democracy, Human Rights, and Labor, Country Reports on Human Rights Practices—2001, "China," released March 4, 2002, available at www.state.gov/g/drl/rls/hrrpt/2001/eap/8289.htm.

8. United Kingdom Foreign and Commonwealth Office, "Annual Human Rights Report 2001," presented to Parliament by command of Her Majesty, September 2001, available at www.hrpd.fco.gov.uk/reports.asp.

9. Human Rights Watch, *World Report 2001,* "China and Tibet," available at www.hrw.org/wr2k1/asia/china.html#tibet.

10. *Asiaweek,* May 10, 1996.

11. Dalai Lama, "Exile," *Time,* October 4, 1999.

12. His Holiness the Dalai Lama, *Freedom in Exile* (New York: HarperCollins, 1990), xiii.

13. CNN, www.cnn.com/specials/1999/china.50/inside.china/profiles/dalai.lama.

14. Dalai Lama, *Ethics,* 3–4.

15. Dalai Lama, *Freedom in Exile,* 8.

16. Michael Ferris Goodman, *The Last Dalai Lama* (Boston: Shambhala, 1986), 41.

17. John F. Avedon, *In Exile from the Land of Snows: The Dalai Lama and Tibet Since the Chinese Conquest* (New York: Harper & Row, 1984), 41.

18. Dalai Lama, *Freedom in Exile,* 53.

19. Quoted in Avedon, *In Exile,* 40.

20. Quoted in Goodman, *Last Dalai Lama,* 220.

21. A Chinese document captured by Tibetan freedom fighters in the 1960s stated that between March 1959 and September 1960, eighty-seven thousand deaths through military action were recorded. These statistics did not include deaths caused by suicide, torture, or starvation. See Dalai Lama, *Freedom in Exile*, 148.

22. Dalai Lama, *Freedom in Exile*, 152.

23. Dalai Lama, *Ethics,* 8.

24. Dalai Lama, *Ethics,* 2.

25. Quoted in *Shambhala Sun,* November 1995, 20; *Mother Jones,* November/December 1997, 30.

26. Quoted in *Shambhala Sun,* November 1995, 22.

27. His Holiness the Dalai Lama and Howard C. Cutler, *The Art of Happiness: A Handbook for Living* (New York: Riverhead Books, 1998), 306–7.

28. Quoted in *Shambhala Sun,* November 1995, 22.

29. Quoted in *Newsweek,* March 27, 2000.

30. Epictetus, quoted in Sharon Lebell, *The Art of Living: The Classic Manual on Virtue, Happiness, and Effectiveness* (San Francisco: HarperSanFrancisco, 1995), 60.

CHAPTER THREE

1. Official statement by the Ministry of Foreign Affairs, available at www.israel.org, under "FAQs."

2. Jews for Justice, "The Origin of the Palestinian-Israeli Conflict," 2nd ed., www.mediareviewnet.com/JewsForJustice.htm.

3. Benny Morris, *Righteous Victims* (New York: Vintage, 2001), 661.

4. Sami Hadawi, *Bitter Harvest* (New York: Olive Branch Press, 1991), 9.

5. Mark Tessler, *A History of the Israeli-Palestinian Conflict* (Bloomington: Indiana University Press, 1994), 1.

6. Avi Shlaim, *The Iron Wall: Israel and the Arab World* (New York: W. W. Norton, 2001), 4.

7. Shlaim, *The Iron Wall*, 4.

8. Quoted in Edward W. Said, *The Question of Palestine* (New York: Vintage, 1992), 28.

9. Morris, *Righteous Victims,* 133–35.

10. Quoted in Colin Chapman, *Whose Promised Land? The Continuing Crisis Over Israel and Palestine* (Oxford: A Lion Book, 2002), 211.

11. Asher Ginsberg, quoted in Gary Smith, *Zionism, the Dream and the Reality* (New York: Harper & Row, 1974), 31.

12. Ginsberg, quoted in Smith, *Zionism,* 31.

13. Yitzhak Epstein at the 1905 Zionist Congress, quoted in Chapman, *Whose Promised Land?,* 41.

14. Morris, *Righteous Victims,* 47.

15. Albert Einstein, *Out of My Later Years* (New York: Philosophical Library, 1950), 262ff.

16. Lord Balfour, quoted by Samih K. Farsoun with Christina Zacharia, *The Question of Palestine and the Palestinians* (Boulder: Westview Press, 1997), 10.

17. Chapman, *Whose Promised Land?,* 70.

18. Tom Segev, trans. Haim Watzman, *One Palestine Complete: Jews and Arabs Under the British Mandate* (New York: Metropolitan Books, 2000).

19. Farsoun and Zacharia, *Question of Palestine,* 75.

20. Mahatma Gandhi, quoted at www. palestinechronicle.com/article.php?story=2001905074343361.

21. Quoted in Farsoun and Zacharia, *Question of Palestine,* 70.

22. Morris, *Righteous Victims,* 45.

23. David Hirst, *The Gun and the Olive Branch: The Roots of Violence in the Middle East* (London: Futura, 1978),131-32.

24. Truman's memoirs and comments to the Arab ambassadors quoted in Chapman, *Whose Promised Land?*, 72.

25. Farsoun and Zacharia, *Question of Palestine*, 111.

26. Majid Al-Haj, *Education, Empowerment, and Control: The Case of the Arabs in Israel* (Albany: State University of New York Press, 1995), 15.

27. Shlaim, *Iron Wall*, 34.

28. Shlaim, *Iron Wall*, 35.

29. Shlaim, *Iron Wall*, 35–36.

30. Shlaim, *Iron Wall*, 3.

31. Quoted in Hadawi, *Bitter Harvest*, 85.

32. Quoted in Chapman, *Whose Promised Land?*, 78.

33. Quoted in Hadawi, *Bitter Harvest*, 90.

34. Benny Morris, *The Birth of the Palestinian Refugee Problem, 1947–1949* (Cambridge: Cambridge University Press, 1987), 292–93.

35. David Ben-Gurion, *The History of the Hagarah,* World Zionist Organization, 1954, quoted in Chapman, *Whose Promised Land?*, 61.

36. Morris, *Righteous Victims,* 179.

37. Nathan Chofshi, *Jewish Newsletter,* February 9, 1959; also quoted by Erskine Childers in "The Other Exodus," *The Spectators,* May 12, 1961.

38. Quoted by Nahum Goldmann in *The Jewish Paradox* (New York: Grosset & Dunlap, 1978), 99–100.

39. Quoted in Said, *The Question,* 14.

40. Quoted in Chapman, *Whose Promised Land?*, 81.

41. Uzi Landau, "Is There Still a National Camp?" (address given at the Middle East Forum, New York, June 28, 2000), available at www.meforum.org/wires/landau.shtml.

42. Amir Cheshin, Bill Hutman, and Avi Melamed, *Separate and Unequal: The Inside Story of Israeli Rule in East Jerusalem* (Cambridge, MA: Harvard University Press, 1999).

43. Cheshin, Hutman, and Melamed, *Separate and Unequal,* 46–47.

44. Cheshin, Hutman, and Melamed, *Separate and Unequal,* 10.

45. Cheshin, Hutman, and Melamed, *Separate and Unequal,* Epilogue.

46. Said, *The Question*, xxi.

47. Hanan Ashrawi, *This Side of Peace* (New York: Touchstone Books, 1996), 29–30.

48. Ashrawi, *This Side of Peace,* 302.

49. Quoted in Chapman, *Whose Promised Land?*, 206.

50. Its activities are published at www.gush-shalom.org.

51. Quoted in Chapman, *Whose Promised Land?*, 207.

52. *The Economist,* February 2, 2002.

53. *The Economist,* April 6, 2002, 11.

54. *The Economist,* June 29, 2002, 11.

CHAPTER FOUR

1. Edward Said, "Culture and Imperialism" (speech given at York University, Toronto, Ontario, February 10, 1993).

2. *Illustration,* November 1931, n.p. Quoted in Arthur Chandler, *World's Fair Magazine* 3, no. 4, 1988, available at www.charon.sfsu.edu/PARISEXPOSITIONS/ 1931 EXPO.html.

3. Frantz Fanon, *The Wretched of the Earth* (New York: Grove Press, 1963), 42, 41.

4. Vietnamese nationalist Phan Chau Trinh in a 1907 letter to the French governor-general, quoted in Truong Buu Lam, *Colonialism Experienced: Vietnamese Writings on Colonialism, 1900–1931* (Ann Arbor: University of Michigan Press, 2000), 126.

5. Quoted in Lam, *Colonialism Experienced,* 85–86.

6. George C. Herring, *America's Longest War: The United States and Vietnam, 1950–1975,* 2nd ed. (New York: Alfred A. Knopf, 1986), 7–8.

7. Ho Chi Minh, *Selected Writings* (Hanoi: Foreign Languages Publishing House, 1977), 535–36, available at www.fordham.edu/halsall/mod/1945vietnam.html.

8. Herring, *America's Longest War,* 10.

9. Stanley Karnow, *Vietnam: A History* (New York: Penguin Books, 1997), 190.

10. Herring, *America's Longest War,* 39, 15.

11. According to Herring, $2.6 billion in military aid between 1950 and 1954; *America's Longest War,* 42.

12. Quoted in Herring, *America's Longest War,* 39.

13. Neil Sheehan, *A Bright Shining Lie: John Paul Vann and America in Vietnam* (New York: Vintage, 1989), 131.

14. Louise Brown, *War and Aftermath in Vietnam* (New York: Routledge, 1991), 236.

15. Donovan Webster, *Aftermath: The Remnants of War* (New York: Vintage, 1998), 166.

16. Stanley Karnow, *Vietnam: A History* (New York: Penguin, 1997), 551.

17. Herring, *America's Longest War,* 151.

18. David Reynolds, *One World Divisible: A Global History Since 1945* (New York: W. W. Norton, 2000), 325.

19. Nixon, quoted in the *New York Times,* June 30, 1974; statistics on air strikes from Herring, *America's Longest War,* 253.

20. Karnow, *Vietnam: A History,* 20–21.

21. U.S. Department of State, Bureau of Democracy, Human Rights, and Labor, *Annual Report on International Religious Freedom: Vietnam* (Washington, DC: Government Printing Office, 2001).

22. Human Rights Watch, *World Report 2002,* "Vietnam," available at www.hrw-org/wr2k2/asia11.html.

CHAPTER FIVE

1. Albert Einstein, *Ideas and Opinions*, 128–29.

2. Einstein, *Ideas and Opinions,* 130.

3. Lars Schoultz, *Beneath the United States: A History of U.S. Policy Toward Latin America* (Cambridge, MA: Harvard University Press, 1998), xxi.

4. John Charles Chasteen, *Born in Blood and Fire: A Concise History of Latin America* (New York: W. W. Norton, 2000).

5. Theodore Roosevelt, quoted in Schoultz, *Beneath the United States,* 78.

6. Theodore Roosevelt, "Expansion and Peace," *Independent,* December 21, 1899; reprinted in Theodore Roosevelt, *The Strenuous Life: Essays and Addresses* (New York: Century, 1900), available at www.bartleby.com.

7. Peter H. Smith, *Talons of the Eagle: Dynamics of U.S.–Latin American Relations* (New York : Oxford University Press, 1996), 50.

8. Schoultz, *Beneath the United States,* xxi.

9. Schoultz, *Beneath the United States,* 373–74.

10. Chasteen, *Born in Blood and Fire*, 186.

11. Chasteen, *Born in Blood and Fire,* 256.

12. Nick Cullather, *Secret History: The CIA's Classified Account of Its Operations in Guatemala, 1952–1954* (Stanford: Stanford University Press, 1999), 22.

13. Stephen Schlesinger and Stephen Kinzer, *Bitter Fruit: The Story of the American Coup in Guatemala* (Cambridge, MA: Harvard University Press, 1999).

14. Schlesinger and Kinzer, *Bitter Fruit,* 129.

15. Piero Gleijeses, Afterword to Cullather, *Secret History,* xxviii. Gleijeses is professor of American foreign policy and Latin American Studies at Johns Hopkins University.

16. Chasteen, *Born in Blood and Fire,* 257.

17. Quoted in U.S. Department of State, "President Reagan: U.S. Interests in Central America," *Current Policy,* no. 576 (May 9, 1984): 1–5.

18. William M. LeoGrande, *Our Own Backyard: The United States in Central America, 1977–1992* (Chapel Hill: University of North Carolina Press, 1998), 10.

19. Quoted in School of the Americas Watch, "What Is the SOA?," available at www.soaw.org/new/type.php?type=8.

20. School of the Americas Watch, "What Is the SOA?," available at www.soaw.org/new/type.php?type=8.

21. Office of Congressman Kennedy, Press Release, September 27, 1996.

22. Office of U.S. Representative Jim McGovern, "U.S. Rep. Jim McGovern Applauds House Vote to Shut Down the School of the Americas," Press Release, July 30, 1999.

23. LeoGrande, *Our Own Backyard,* 258.

24. Gleijeses, Afterword to Cullather, *Secret History,* xxxi.

25. Mark Danner, *The Massacre at El Mozote: A Parable of the Cold War* (New York: Vintage, 1994).

26. Danner, *Massacre,* 159.

27. Danner, *Massacre,* 25–26.

28. Danner, *Massacre,* 160.

29. Christian Smith, *Resisting Reagan: The U.S. Central America Peace Movement* (Chicago: University of Chicago Press, 1996), 86.

30. OAS Inter-American Commission on Human Rights, "Report on the Situation of Human Rights in Nicaragua," OEA, ser. L.V.II.45, doc. 18, rev. 1 (November 17, 1978).

31. OAS Inter-American Commission on Human Rights, "Report on the Situation of Human Rights in Nicaragua," OEA, ser. L.V.II.53, doc. 25 (June 30, 1981).

32. LeoGrande, *Our Own Backyard,* 104.

33. LeoGrande, *Our Own Backyard,* 502.

34. LeoGrande, *Our Own Backyard,* 506.

35. LeoGrande, *Our Own Backyard,* 507.

36. LeoGrande, *Our Own Backyard,* 507.

32. LeoGrande, *Our Own Backyard,* 510.

CHAPTER SIX

1. Kimmo Kiljunen, ed., *Kampuchea, Decade of the Genocide: Report of a Finnish Inquiry Commission* (London: Zed, 1984), 19.

2. You may look at some of the pictures that have been collected on the Internet by Yale University's Cambodia Genocide Program at www.yale.edu/cgp. In the search field, look up "youth" and see the young, precious faces standing before they were murdered.

3. David P. Chandler, *Voices from S-21: Terror and History in Pol Pot's Secret Prison* (Berkeley and Los Angeles: University of California Press, 1999), 130; "Report of the People's Revolutionary Tribunal Held in Phnom Penh for the Trial of the Genocide Crime of the Pol Pot–Ieng Sary Clique" (August 1979), 4, available through Yale University's Cambodia Genocide Program, www.yale.edu/cgp.

4. See David P. Chandler, *A History of Cambodia,* 2nd ed. (Boulder: Westview, 1996), 9.

5. So named because the Chinese chronicled a Kingdom of Funan in the southeast part of this region.

6. Chandler, *History of Cambodia,* 126.

7. Chandler, *History of Cambodia,* 153.

8. David M. Ayres, *Anatomy of a Crisis: Education, Development, and the State in Cambodia, 1953–1998* (Honolulu: University of Hawaii Press, 2000), 22.

9. Henry Kamm, *Cambodia: Report from a Stricken Land* (New York: Arcade, 1998), 26–27.

10. For a fascinating discussion of the decision-making process that led the Japanese to retain French administration while permitting the independence of the three countries in Indochina, see Masaya Shiraishi and Motoo Furuta, "Two

Features of Japan's Indochina Policy During the Pacific War," in *Indochina in the 1940s and 1950s,* ed. Takashi Shiraishi and Motoo Furuta (Ithaca: Southeast Asia Program, Cornell University Press, 1992). In sum, the Japanese decisions were haphazard and based on the false assumptions that a U.S. invasion was imminent and that granting immediate independence would keep the Soviet Union from entering the war against Japan.

11. Kamm, *Cambodia,* 29.

12. Chandler, *History of Cambodia,* 200.

13. A. J. Langguth, *Our Vietnam: The War 1954–1975* (New York: Simon & Schuster, 2000), 559.

14. Ben Kiernan, *The Pol Pot Regime: Race, Power, and Genocide in Cambodia Under the Khmer Rouge, 1975–79* (New Haven: Yale University Press, 1996), 18.

15. Kiernan, *Pol Pot Regime,* 20.

16. Kiljunen, ed., *Kampuchea,* 7.

17. Quoted in Langguth, *Our Vietnam,* 563–64.

18. President Richard Nixon, television address, April 30, 1970, available at www.vietnam.vassar.edu/doc15.html.

19. Herring, *America's Longest War*, 237; Kamm, *Cambodia,* 101.

20. Chandler, *History of Cambodia,* 206.

21. Langguth, *Our Vietnam,* 262; Chandler, *History of Cambodia,* 207.

22. Stephen Heder, quoted in *Facts on File* 33 (1973): 700E1, 601C3; Jonathan Ladd, quoted in Kamm, *Cambodia,* 104.

23. Jonathan Glover, *Humanity: A Moral History of the Twentieth Century* (London: Jonathan Cape, 1999), 301.

24. Kiernan, *Pol Pot Regime,* 25; "Cambodian Women in the Revolutionary War for the People's National Liberation (1973)," Khmer Rouge Wartime Propaganda on Women, Yale University Cambodia Genocide Project, www.yale.edu/cgp.

25. John Pilger, "Friends of Pol Pot," *Nation,* May 1, 1998.

26. Bruce Palling's interview with Chhit Do, quoted by Kiernan, *Pol Pot Regime,* 23.

27. Quoted by William Shawcross, *Sideshow: Kissinger, Nixon, and the Destruction of Cambodia* (New York: Simon & Schuster, 1979), 391.

28. Kamm, *Cambodia,* 119.

29. Teeda Butt Mam, in *Children of Cambodia's Killing Fields: Memoirs by Survivors,* ed. Kim DePaul, comp. Dith Pran (New Haven: Yale University Press, 1997), 11–12.

30. Teeda Butt Mam, in *Children of Cambodia's Killing Fields,* 11–12.

31. Savuth Penn, in *Children of Cambodia's Killing Fields,* 44.

32. Kiljunen, ed., *Kampuchea,* 17.

33. Glover, *Humanity,* 307.

34. Ranachith (Ronnie) Yimsut, "The Tonle Lap Lake Massacre," Digital Archive of Cambodian Holocaust Survivors, available at www.cybercambodia.com/dachs/stories/ronnie.html.

35. Kiernan, *Pol Pot Regime,* 387–89.

36. Kamm, *Cambodia,* 151.

37. Maha Ghosananda, *Step by Step,* ed. Jane Sharada Mahoney and Philip Edmonds (Berkeley: Parallax Press, 1992), 69.

38. Ghosananda, *Step by Step,* 69.

39. Ghosananda, *Step by Step,* 17–18.

40. Ghosananda, *Step by Step,* 40.

41. Ajaan Lee Dhammadharo, "Food for Thought: Eighteen Talks on the Training of the Heart," trans. from Thai by Thanissaro Bhikkhu, 1995, available at www.accesstoinsight.org/lib/thai/lee/foodthought.html.

42. Ghosananda, *Step by Step,* 53.

43. Ghosananda, *Step by Step,* 70.

CHAPTER SEVEN

1. Edward O. Wilson, *The Future of Life* (New York: Alfred A. Knopf, 2002), 41.

2. Quoted from www.indians.org/welker/hiawatha.htm.

3. Wilson, *Future of Life,* 3.

4. Gore's remarks available at www.pnl.gov/ces/earth/gore.htm.

5. U.N. Population Fund, "State of the World Population 2001," chap. 2, available at www.unfpa.org/swp/2001/english/ch02.html.

6. U.N. Population Fund, "State of the World Population 2001."

7. U.N. Population Fund, "State of the World Population 2001."

8. Stephen Libiszewski, "International Conflicts over Freshwater Resources," in *Ecology, Politics, and Violent Conflict,* ed. Mohamed Suliman (London: Zed, 1999), 115.

9. National Intelligence Council, *Global Trends 2015,* www.cia.gov/nic/pubs/index.htm.

10. Payal Sampat, "Groundwater Shock: The Polluting of the World's Major Freshwater Stores," *World Watch Magazine,* January/February 2000, 10.

11. On industrial waste worldwide, see U.N. Population Fund, "State of the World Population 2001," chap. 1, p. 5. On fresh water in Russia, see Marcus Noland, "Russia's Physical and Social Infrastructure: Implications for Future Development" (paper presented at a seminar sponsored by the National Intelligence Council and the Bureau of Intelligence and Research of the U.S. Department of State, Washington, DC, December 2000), available at www.cia.gov/nic/pubs/conference_reports/russia%27s_infrastructure.html; also see Joop de Schutter, "Russia" (paper presented at the Second World Water Forum, the Hague, Netherlands, March 17, 2000), available at www.worldwaterforum.net/Dossiers/docs/russia_session.pdf. According to Schutter, only about 33 percent of the industrial waste water is treated adequately in Russia, for instance, and about 20 percent is not treated at all. On life expectancies in the Ob and Yenisey River deltas, see Michael Schwellen, *Die Zeit,* November 17, 1994. For surface water

contamination in richer countries, see U.N. Population Fund, "State of the World Population 2001," chap. 1, p. 5.

12. Sampat, "Groundwater Shock," 10, 15.

13. U.S. Environmental Protection Agency, "Clean Land: Removing Waste and Reclaiming the Land," *1999 Annual Report, Pacific Southwest,* available at www.epa.gov/region09/annualreport/99/land.html.

14. U.S. Environmental Protection Agency, "Underground Injection Controls: How to Find Safe Storage Space," available at www.epa.gov/region6/6xa/uic_safe.htm; on the wastes appearing in groundwater, see Payal Sampat, "Groundwater Shock," 19.

15. On leaking USTs, see U.S. Environmental Protection Agency, "Groundwater Information," available at www.epa.gov/region4/water/drinkingwater/groundwater.htm. On numbers of USTs, see U.S. Environmental Protection Agency Office of Underground Storage Tanks, available at www.epa.gov/swerust1. On groundwater contamination from USTs, see Payal Sampat, "Groundwater Shock," 16.

16. On the Sudan, see *Ecology, Politics, and Violent Conflict,* 17; on land degradation worldwide, see U.N. Population Fund, "World Polupation Report," 16.

17. D. G. Bryant, *The Last Frontier Forests: Ecosystems and Economies on the Edge* (Washington, DC: World Resources Institute, Forest Frontiers Initiative, 1997).

18. World Resources Program, "Fragmenting Forests: The Loss of Large Frontier Forests," *World Resources 1998–99* (Washington, DC: World Resources Institute, 1998); Bryant, *The Last Frontier Forests.*

19. Bryant, *Last Frontier Forests.*

20. Food and Agricultural Association of the United Nations, available at www.fao.org/docrep/w6251E/w6251eOc.htm..

21. Kofi Annan, Message of World Water Day, March 22, 2001, available at www.worldwaterday.org/2001/news/msgun.html.

22. United Nations Research Institute for Social Development, "Environmental Degradation and Social Integration," Briefing Paper No. 3, World Summit for Social Development, November 1994, available at www.unrisd.org/engindex/publ/list/bp/bp3/bp3–01/htm#TopOfPage.

23. World Bank Group, "World Development Indicators 2001," Environment, available at www.worldbank.org/data/wdi2001/environment.html.

24. Wilson, *Future of Life,* 14, 99.

25. World Commission on Environment and Development, *Our Common Future* (Oxford: Oxford University Press, 1987), 290.

26. Michael T. Klare, *Resource Wars: The New Landscape of Global Conflict* (New York: Metropolitan Books, 2001), 33, 222.

27. Klare, *Resource Wars,* 109.

28. "In an Empty Cup, a Threat to World Peace," *New York Times,* August 14, 2001.

29. James A. Winnefeld and Mary E. Morris, *Where Environmental Concerns and Security Strategies Meet: Green Conflict in Asia and the Middle East* (Santa Monica: RAND, 1994), xiii.

30. Anne H. Ehrlich, Peter Gleick, and Ken Conca, "Resources and Environmental Degradation as Sources of Conflict" (50th Pugwash Conference on Science and World Affairs, Cambridge, U.K., August 2000), available at www.pugwash.org/reports/pac/pac256/WG5draft.htm.

31. Thomas F. Homer-Dixon, *Environment, Scarcity, and Violence* (Princeton: Princeton University Press, 1999), 12–13.

32. Suliman, ed., *Ecology, Politics, and Violent COnflicts,* 32–35.

33. Narottam Gaan, *Environmental Degradation and Inter-State Conflict: India vs. Bangladesh* (Denver: International Academic Publishers, 1998), 109, 111.

34. Quoted from, respectively, *Los Angeles Times,* Pulitzer Prize–winning playwright Wendy Wasserstein, the *Christian Science Monitor, Encyclopedia Britannica.*

35. Susan McCarthy, "Jane Goodall: The Hopeful Messenger," Salon.com, available at www.salon.com/people/feature/1999/10/27/reason.

36. Jane Goodall, with Phillip Berman, *Reason for Hope: A Spiritual Journey* (New York: Warner, 1999), 60.

37. Goodall, *Reason for Hope,* 80–81.

38. Goodall, *Reason for Hope,* 134.

39. Goodall, *Reason for Hope,* 79.

40. Goodall, *Reason for Hope,* 76.

41. Dr. Goodall is referring to the "hygiene hypothesis," which contends when the immune system lacks practice fighting bacteria and viruses, perhaps from an overly sanitary lifestyle, the system can overreact to harmless substances such as pollen.

EPILOGUE

1. Scott Peterson, *Me Against My Brother* (New York: Routledge, 2000), 252–53.

2. *Seasons in Hell: Understanding Bosnia's War* (New York: St. Martin's Press, 1994), ix–x.

3. Available at www.igc/ddickerson/holocaust/html.

4. Norman Geras, *The Contract of Mutual Indifference: Political Philosophy After the Holocaust* (London: Verso, 1998).

5. Charles Darwin, *The Descent of Man, 1871,* Ch. 4, "Comparison of the Mental Powers of Man and Lower Animals," available at www.literature.org/authors/darwin-charles/the-descent-of-man/chapter-04.html.

ACKNOWLEDGMENTS

I wish to thank all the people interviewed in this book, as well as their hardworking assistants who made all the meetings possible. My deepest gratitude for the help and encouragement provided by Joseph Aldridge, Linda Allen, Niel Armstrong, Josh Baran, Marilyn Barker, Natasha Batianoff, Michelle Bernard, John Carmichael, Tenzing Choepel, Sangeeta Chowdhry, Wilson Condon, Dennis Conkin, Marshall and Ester Corey, Clifton Cortez, H. Raphael Cushnir, Sherry Darville, Mark Drooks, Robin Edwards, Penelope Faulkner, Peggy Foote, Tenzin Geyche, Marc and Karen Gifford, Scott Glascock, Michael Greenberg, Bettyrae Hanner, Justin Hecht, Linda Heller, Len Hilgermann, Philip Ho, Poshun Huang, P. Michael and Sherry Hunt, Rhonda Jones, Helena Kearney, Seong Cheol Kim, Christopher King, Wayne Knight, Gail Knudson, Arnie Kotler, Mihail Lari, Mary Lewis, Valerie Lewis, Jane Mahoney, Rana Malki, Elizabeth Marro, Roberta McCutcheon, Jim McDade, Evelyn P. Meyer, Tamiko Moore, Charol Morikawa, Thubten Ngodup, Steve Nguyen, Mathew Pauley, Steve Peskind, Tenzin Rabgyal, Patricia Rivas, Ed Saucedo, Terry Shaller, Mr. and Mrs. Joghindar Singh, Priscilla Stuckey, Tsering Tashi, Helen Tworkov, Visit Vichaivutikoun, Deanna Vosper, Gideon Weil, Skip Whitney, Denise Wike, Jeff and Nancy Williamson, Alison Wright, and Lisa Zuniga.

INDEX